Hegel's Political Aesthetics

Also Available from Bloomsbury

Political Aesthetics: Addison and Shaftesbury on Taste, Morals and Society,
Karl Axelsson
The New Aesthetics of Deculturation: Neoliberalism, Fundamentalism, and Kitsch,
Thorsten Botz-Bornstein
Hegel on Possibility: Dialectics, Contradiction, and Modality, Nahum Brown
From Marx to Hegel and Back: Capitalism, Critique, and Utopia, ed. Victoria Feld and
Hannes Kuch
The German Idealism Reader, ed. Marina F. Bykova

Hegel's Political Aesthetics

Art in Modern Society

Edited and with an Introduction
by
Stefan Bird-Pollan and Vladimir Marchenkov

BLOOMSBURY ACADEMIC
LONDON • NEW YORK • OXFORD • NEW DELHI • SYDNEY

BLOOMSBURY ACADEMIC
Bloomsbury Publishing Plc
50 Bedford Square, London, WC1B 3DP, UK
1385 Broadway, New York, NY 10018, USA
29 Earlsfort Terrace, Dublin 2, Ireland

BLOOMSBURY, BLOOMSBURY ACADEMIC and the Diana logo are trademarks of
Bloomsbury Publishing Plc

First published in Great Britain 2020
This paperback edition published in 2021

Copyright © Stefan Bird-Pollan, Vladimir Marchenkov and Contributors, 2020

Stefan Bird-Pollan and Vladimir Marchenkov have asserted their right under the Copyright,
Designs and Patents Act, 1988, to be identified as Editors of this work.

Cover design by Charlotte Daniels
Cover image: Oil on canvas by Vassily Kandinsky (1914)

All rights reserved. No part of this publication may be reproduced or transmitted
in any form or by any means, electronic or mechanical, including photocopying,
recording, or any information storage or retrieval system, without prior
permission in writing from the publishers.

Bloomsbury Publishing Plc does not have any control over, or responsibility for, any
third-party websites referred to or in this book. All internet addresses given in this
book were correct at the time of going to press. The author and publisher regret any
inconvenience caused if addresses have changed or sites have ceased to exist,
but can accept no responsibility for any such changes.

A catalogue record for this book is available from the British Library.

A catalog record for this book is available from the Library of Congress.

ISBN: HB: 978-1-3501-2269-7
PB: 978-1-3502-7917-9
ePDF: 978-1-3501-2270-3
eBook: 978-1-3501-2271-0

Typeset by Deanta Global Publishing Services, Chennai, India

To find out more about our authors and books, visit www.bloomsbury.com and
sign up for our newsletters.

Contents

List of figures   vi

Introduction   1

Part I Art's Contribution to Modern Ethical Life

1. Hegel on Aesthetic Reconciliation *Mark Alznauer*   11
2. Hegel on the Aesthetic Basis of State Sovereignty *David Ciavatta*   31
3. *Bildung* and the Novel in Hegel's Lectures on Aesthetics *Timothy L. Brownlee*   52
4. On Art, Religion, and Recognitive Communities *Philip T. Grier*   72

Part II Art's Persistence and Authority

5. Hegel on Romantic Art and Modernity *John Russon*   95
6. *A View from an Apartment*: Hegel on Home and Homelessness in Romantic Art *Shannon Hoff*   119
7. Hegel's Symbol and Symbolic Art: Revisiting Ambiguity? *Olga Lyanda-Geller*   140
8. Hegel, Danto, Cavell, and the End of Art *Stefan Bird-Pollan*   158

Part III Thinking beyond Hegel's Views on Art and Society

9. Greek Tragedy and Self-Authorship in Hegel's *Phenomenology of Spirit* *Eliza Starbuck Little*   179
10. Rethinking Hegel's Modern Conception of Art *Georg W. Bertram*   196
11. Hegel contra Moralism: Hegel's Aesthetics as an Argument against the Moralist Approach to Art *Vladimir Marchenkov*   212

Index   233

Figures

1 Stefano da Verona. *The Crucifixion* (ca. 1400). Tempera on wood, gold ground, 33 ⅞ × 20 ⅝ in. The Metropolitan Museum of Art, New York ... 106
2 Pieter Bruegel the Elder. *The Harvesters* (1565). Oil on wood, 46 ⅞ × 63 ¾. The Metropolitan Museum of Art, New York ... 109
3 Frans Hals. *Merrymakers at Shrovetide* (ca. 1616–17). Oil on canvas, 51 ¾ × 39 ¼ in. Metropolitan Museum of Art, New York ... 110
4 Jan Steen. *The Dissolute Household* (ca. 1663–64). Oil on canvas, 42 ½ × 35 ½ in. The Metropolitan Museum of Art, New York ... 112
5 Jeff Wall, *A View from an Apartment*, 2004–05, transparency in lightbox, 167 × 244 cm ... 129

Introduction

For the past several centuries, the history of Western ideas about art has unfolded under the dual aegis of two unequal and mutually opposed currents. The first and older one, going back to Plato and even further into the mythological strata of ancient Mediterranean cultures, can be called the *moralist* view. It consists in setting moral concerns over and above all others in judgments about art. The second and newer one, distinctly modern, can be described as *aesthetic*. Unlike moralism, it treats artistic expression not only as having its own intrinsic value but also as entirely independent and separate from morality. The aesthetic sensibility as such is not something specifically modern or Western; it can be found in pre- and nonmodern cultures as well.[1] What distinguishes the aesthetic sensibility in the modern period is that, rather than being a marginal element, it moves closer to, and sometimes right into, the center of cultural interests and concerns. In pre- and nonmodern settings, aesthetic sensibility manifests itself most clearly in the creation of and admiration for the culturally marginal objects that arouse aesthetic pleasure, but it can also be present in the valuation of works and practices in the center of cultural life. And yet, despite this seemingly central position, it remains marginal. Attic tragedy, for example, was a truly substantive aesthetic phenomenon, but in the eyes of the ancient Greek society it was first and foremost a civic-religious ritual whose aesthetic component, while distinctly present, was secondary at best. Generally speaking, premodern European cultures, both ancient and medieval, thought of what today is called their "art" chiefly in moralist terms, and the aesthetic view proper was gradually taking shape in moralism's shadow during the Renaissance and the Baroque—until it finally matured and emerged as a challenge to moralism at the end of the Enlightenment. In Alexander Baumgarten's *Aesthetica*, this aesthetic view received its initial open philosophical recognition, and half a century later Immanuel Kant's *Critique of the Power of Judgment* gave it the authoritative form in which it is recognized to this day. Kant's notion of the aesthetic remains complicated. While the *Critique of Judgment* emphasizes the notion of reflective judgment already adumbrated in the *Critique of Pure Reason* as central to all theoretical judgment, in particular judgments of taste and judgments of teleology, Kant also insists that philosophy must be fundamentally understood as in the service of practical reason. Judgments employing reflective judgments, while they underlie their determinative counterparts, cannot themselves yield cognition.

Kant's elaboration of the aesthetic perspective, often considered the pillar and exemplum of formalism and aesthetic autonomy by later commentators, was thus haunted by the older moralism. This was the case, incidentally, for the Enlightenment as a whole, and in this regard Kant did not part ways with Jean-Jacques Rousseau or Denis Diderot. When we speak of Baumgarten's *Aesthetica* and Kant's *Critique of the*

Power of Judgment as turning points in the history of Western ideas about art, we should therefore never lose sight of the fact that, for their contemporaries Voltaire, Rousseau, and Diderot, art was an instrument of moral instruction, social critique, and, generally, moral betterment of humanity. And when enlightened thought in the person of Diderot confronted the phenomenon of a thoroughly aestheticized consciousness, a mind that went all the way down the path opened by the abstract intellect of the *philosophes*, this phenomenon assumed the disconcerting—not to say scandalous—shape of "Rameau's nephew": utterly uprooted and rudderless, even as he was endowed with keen understanding and a refined aesthetic sensibility.[2] In other words, the Enlightenment perched art on the horns of the ethic-aesthetic dilemma, and art has not been able to extricate itself from this uncomfortable position ever since.[3]

It may seem that the romantics liberated art from the hegemony of moralism, but they merely imitated the gestures of the enlightened moralist by inverting them: romanticism elevated art over and above everything else—morality, religion, and philosophy—which resulted in an alternative but hardly more sensible standpoint. Still, as a result, the philosophical debate about art from the early nineteenth century on finally acquired two fully distinct poles, moralism and aestheticism, whose problematic mutual conjunction, in fact, had always constituted the driving engine of the history of the arts but until that moment had remained largely hidden. Hegel's philosophy of art can be seen as a response to this intense dialectic and a heroic attempt to move beyond both the moralism of the Enlightenment and the romantic exaggeration of art's role. He sought to find a place for art in his overall system, a place that would at once reflect art's unique role in human affairs and link it to other human pursuits—above all, the pursuit of knowledge and truth. In this quest he created a body of thought that looms large over the subsequent history of aesthetic debates to this day, but it would be an overstatement, to say the least, to claim that his achievement brought about anything remotely resembling a consensus. Quite the contrary, the history of aesthetics from the second third of the nineteenth century to our time is a theater of war where various permutations of the two basic attitudes battle with one other. Their interactions do not boil down, of course, to mere conflict; sometimes they fuse to produce partial and temporary syntheses. But the story of these interactions has not unfolded along a Hegelian trajectory; it has not resulted in a dialectical reconciliation of opposites and remains to this day at the level of the abstract understanding, in a permanent crisis. The pendulum of theoretical attitudes toward art in mature and late modernity swings from one side to the other, now to formalist aestheticism, now to didactic moralism (to say nothing of flagrant ideologism). Hegel liked to quote Horace's dictum: *Et prodesse et delectare volunt poetae* (The poets wish at once to instruct and to delight), but *prodesse* and *delectare*, to be useful and to delight, are forever at odds in the modern artist's work.

The essays collected in this book examine precisely this discomfort, by peering into the aesthetic-ethical conundrum in Hegel's thought. The book does not deliver a unified argument because the authors' perspectives are too diverse, and the editors set themselves no such goal. What brings the authors together is rather their overlapping interests in similar questions and problematic areas in Hegel's philosophy of art, the chief among them being, as we just pointed out, the conjunction of the aesthetic understanding of art, on the one hand, and the moral, social, or political implications of Hegel's position, on the other. Many of the chapters display also a *critical* engagement with Hegel, questioning his opinions and procedures, highlighting unresolved dilemmas, pointing up unfinished and incomplete projects, exposing internal contradictions and inconsistencies, and ways of carrying Hegel's arguments further than Hegel himself did. The only thing on which the authors seem to agree is that Hegel's philosophy of art remains relevant, stimulating, and, in fact, vital to our own attempts to come to terms with art as an indispensable part of being human.

Synopsis

The book is divided into three parts, each comprising chapters that are loosely connected by a common theme. What follows is a brief survey of their contents.

The first part, "Art's Contribution to Modern Ethical Life," contains analyses of Hegel's views on such things as art's effects on the ethical life of the human community and on sociopolitical institutions. It closes with a probing look at how religion and art are intertwined in Hegel's thought. One of the fault lines in the interpretation of Hegel's project in his aesthetics, Mark Alznauer argues in "Hegel on Aesthetic Reconciliation," is whether one believes that artworks are capable of reconciling us to social reality as Hegel seems to suggest. Left-Hegelian critics like Robert Pippin and Raymond Geuss take this project to be ideological in the sense that it presents art as capable of a theodicy. Alznauer argues that the criticism misses the mark because these critics do not sufficiently distinguish between social and aesthetic reconciliation. In order to clarify Hegel's conception of aesthetic reconciliation, Alznauer proposes replacing the ambitious theses attributed to him with more limited and defensible ones. Accordingly, Alznauer proposes to read Hegel's project of reconciliation not as a social or political reconciliation but as a more finite aesthetic reconciliation. The second left-Hegelian thesis is that Hegel must choose between claiming that art reveals metaphysical truth and that it reveals deepest insights of a people. But, Alznauer argues, the latter horn of the dilemma can be embraced if we understand the question of a people's deepest held insights as what a people can affirm, hence to what it can reconcile itself. The third thesis Alznauer seeks to call into question is the idea that art is supposed to dispose us to appreciate the sociopolitical structure of the state. On textual grounds, Alznauer argues that no such claim is to be found in Hegel. Rather, what the artwork offers us, in Hegel's view, is an opportunity to contemplate the contradictions of modern life without denying them. Aesthetic reconciliation, Alznauer concludes, is the idea that we are capable of overcoming our dependence on the finite world for our ultimate satisfaction.

In "Hegel on the Aesthetic Basis of State Sovereignty," David Ciavatta sets himself the goal of understanding the extent to which the aesthetic may have a role to play in our understanding of the state. While it is typically noted that modern ethical life is more fully rationalized than Greek ethical life, and so no longer seems to need the intuitive unity present in Greek life, Ciavatta proposes that modern ethical life still requires a certain relation to particularity, which is offered by aesthetic reflection.

Noting that modern ethical life is prosaic in the sense that the rationality of the state typically appears only as a background condition, Ciavatta turns to instances in which the state needs to be affirmed as such in order to understand whether there might yet be a role for the aesthetic in modern life. The rational character of the constitution that must nevertheless also be positive and historically owned or authorized by the people offers an instance in which universality can be supplemented by reflection on the particular. Here it is for Hegel the stateless hero, Odysseus or Antigone, who becomes the model for the rational instantiation of the state as both universal and particular. The extraordinary condition of the founding of a state has a parallel, Ciavatta argues, in the condition of war in which the individual is forced to make explicit her allegiance to the state, hence to affirm her background assumptions about what the rationality of the state means to her. The condition of war then, Ciavatta shows, reveals an equally fruitful subject for aesthetic treatment and can further our understanding of the rationality of the state, making it appear a little less prosaic.

It is the prose of life that the modern novel helps to dispel, according to Tim Brownlee's analysis of Hegel's treatment of this literary genre. In his chapter on "*Bildung* and the Novel in Hegel's Lectures on Aesthetics," Brownlee gives a close level-headed account of this treatment, focusing on Hegel's identification of the novel as a species of epic, on the one hand, and his far more perceptive commentary on individual specimens of the genre, on the other. To cling to the former aspect of Hegel's thinking, Brownlee argues, does not take us very far: Hegel himself frequently spoke of the ways the novel *fails* to be an epic. Instead, Brownlee proposes, we should mine Hegel's readings of such novels as Cervantes's *Don Quixote* and especially Goethe's *Wilhelm Meisters Lehrjahre* for ways in which the novel contributes to *Bildung*, the formation of culture, which, as Brownlee notes, is a critical aspect in the formation of civil society. Both *Bildung* and the rise of civil society in Hegel's philosophy center on the "individual overcoming a separation from others" and attaining a more universal grasp of his or her relation to human community. Brownlee then takes his argument further by observing that, a great achievement though it is, civil society still remains a limited condition for spirit and the prose of modern institutions is only a symptom of this purely formal freedom; spirit must learn to look beyond it. Like art in general, the novel, Brownlee argues, holds the potential to teach us just that: not mere reconciliation to the Philistine (Habermas would say bourgeois) circumstances of modern life but an ascent to another level of comprehending what our freedom is.

Philip T. Grier's chapter, "On Art, Religion, and Recognitive Communities," expounds Hegel's aesthetics by parallel readings of the *Lectures on the Philosophy of Religion* and *Lectures on Fine Art* in the belief that Hegel's understanding of art and of its historical trajectory can be best illuminated through its function in religion. The rise of art, Grier observes, is inextricably linked in Hegel's philosophy to the emergence of spirit from nature and as such is also part of the process through which spirit evolves from immediate (natural) to universal (social) singularity. The result of this emergence that is central to Grier's analysis is "mutually recognitive community," which, in the familiar sequence of art seeking the ideal of beauty (symbolic phase), attaining it (classical phase), and then transcending it (romantic phase), first takes shape in the Greek polis, signifying at once the emergence of genuine art. The unity of ethical life, the state, and religion constitutes, Grier observes, the fertile soil for art where, in Hegel's words, it depicts "the divine, the highest demands of spirit." But this perfect balance between religion and art is upset with the transition to romantic art—a transition that is driven by the evolution of religion itself from the still too finite Greek notion of divinity to the Christian absolute. Romantic art strives to depict this new divinity in Catholicism but ultimately fails, for the finite cannot truly accommodate the infinite. Grier finds that, in Hegel's account, the rise of the Protestant Reformation with its belief that God cannot be represented in sensuous imagery spells spirit's arrival at the "terminus of art in its highest vocation." From now on art increasingly detaches itself from religion, that is to say, from serving "the highest demands of spirit," and becomes immersed in the finite, the trivial, and the purely subjective. In a word, art becomes modern. The *Humanus* takes the place of divinity in it and Hegel, while acknowledging the ability of great artists to rise above the mundane and the finite, nonetheless grows less and less optimistic about modern art's capacity to fulfill its true function. Having noted similar pessimism in post-Hegelian thinkers, from Friedrich Nietzsche to Richard Eldridge, Grier returns to the notion of mutually recognitive communities: without them, the function of art, upheld by Hegel in his aesthetics and philosophy of religion, is in peril.

The second part of the book, "Art's Persistence and Authority," deals with various aspects of Hegel's philosophy of art that show art's continuing relevance across historical eras. John Russon takes as the starting point of his contribution, "Hegel on Romantic art and Modernity," the thesis that art and philosophy gradually emerge out of religious life, with philosophy initially understood as devotion and art understood as a form of religion. He sets himself the task of exploring what the Christian religion is for Hegel such that art can emerge from it in a secular world. To grasp this point we must, Russon contends, understand the Absolute as the total of the reality we experience and understand the different versions of the absolute—art, religion, and philosophy—as gradually separating themselves out from it. It is only in romantic art that art properly distinguishes itself from religion. This separation, however, is not a disconnection but rather, as Russon puts it, the exhortation to *do* something, namely to overcome the division within the Absolute that has arisen historically. Art seeks to overcome alienation by portraying us as rational *individuals* with the authority to interpret the division that has arisen in the Absolute. Art does this by portraying the finite making its own reality into the affirmation of the Absolute. Russon shows this through a reading of the paintings of several Dutch masters.

Shannon Hoff's reflections on romantic art in "A View from an Apartment: Hegel and Homelessness in Romantic Art" arise from a concern to understand the different ways of being at home in the domains of objective and Absolute Spirit. Being at home in objective spirit, she proposes, has to do with making specific locations one's own in a more or less exclusionary way (think property, legal rights); being at home in Absolute Spirit, by contrast, consists in acknowledging the inadequacy of the ways we are at home in objective spirit and therefore requires a further form of reflection. Romantic art, Hoff argues, recognizes that the mode of life objective spirit seeks, and fails, to reconcile us to is itself to be sought through the reflections of Absolute Spirit, in the *here* of objective spirit. Romantic art thus represents a two-sided vision in which finite specificity is given place alongside infinite subjective inwardness. Hoff deepens this point by reflecting on Jeff Wall's photograph "A View from an Apartment" (2004–05), which she analyzes in terms of the photograph's power to get us to pay attention to the ordinary.

In the chapter on "Hegel's Symbol and Symbolic Art: Revisiting Ambiguity," Lyanda-Geller delves into Hegel's treatment of the symbol, mostly as this concept functions in Hegel's account of the symbolic phase of art, but also in its broader significance in his aesthetics. She argues that Hegel has all the building blocks for a full-blown theory of the symbol but chooses not to pursue it; this work was taken up by post-Hegelian theorists. The key aspects that Hegel recognizes in the symbol, Lyanda-Geller notes, are the simultaneous identity of inner content and external form—along with an impassable gap between them. It is this gap, she finds, that constitutes for Hegel the chief limitation of the symbol: the ambiguity at its heart that Hegel regards as an obstruction to rational thought. On the one hand, the symbolic principle permeates all phases of art in Hegel's account but, on the other hand, it remains a limited form of expression, continually calling for its own transcendence. Lyanda-Geller believes that Hegel does not sufficiently appreciate the role of what she calls *homo admirans*, the wondering human subject, as a productive agent of cognitive engagement with the world. Some later philosophers, such as Ludwig Wittgenstein, also fall into this category, typical of the modern attitude toward wonder in general. A contrasting theory of the symbol was developed by the Russian philosopher Aleksei Losev, who incorporated an analysis of the miracle into his philosophy of myth, language, and symbolism. Rather than an obstruction to thought waiting to be cleared, Lyanda-Geller explains, Losev understands the "apophatic" moment in miracles, myths, and symbols as the source of their polysemy and ceaseless generation of meanings, that is to say, as productive rather than obstructive. The chapter closes with a comparison between Hegel's and Losev's respective treatments of the Prometheus myth, illustrating the deepening of philosophical interest in the symbol in post-Hegelian thought.

One of the lasting and most stimulating ideas bequeathed by Hegel to later aestheticians has been his famous—or infamous—"end of art" thesis, which is the theme of Stefan Bird-Pollan's contribution "Hegel, Danto, Cavell and the End of Art." Bird-Pollan begins from what he identifies as an ambiguity in Hegel's treatment of the relation between objective and Absolute Spirit: either the end-of-art thesis can be taken to reflect a historical trajectory in which art is at an end because it factually or historically no longer plays a central role in modern ethical life, or the thesis can be taken as reflecting a systematic inadequacy of the mode in which art functions, namely, that of intuition (*Anschauung*), which is no longer adequate to the higher rational status of the reflections on ethical life as expressed in philosophy. The former thesis, termed the supplementary interpretation, claims that we have simply moved on from the way the Greeks conceptualized the relation between art, religion, and philosophy and that art can play only a supplementary or reconciling role. Arthur Danto is interpreted as a transitional figure between the two sides. The dialectical interpretation, by contrast, casts doubt on the idea that philosophy really has extricated itself from intuition in the way Hegel seems to propose. This interpretation, defended by T. W. Adorno as well as contemporary writers like Gregg Horowitz and T. J. Clark, claims that art is needed to reveal the ways in which philosophy seeks to colonize the social world without attending adequately to the particular which art allows us to see. Finally, Bird-Pollan argues that we should think of Stanley Cavell's writings on film as proposing to understand the "golden age" of Hollywood cinema *as philosophy* in the sense that, *pace* Cavell, film did constitute the primary forum for the discussion of social issues surrounding the emancipation of women in such a way as to combine the rational discourse of objective spirit with the aesthetic dimension's attention to particularity.

Virtually all of the chapters in the book, whatever part they are grouped in, point to ways in which contemporary philosophical aesthetics can build on Hegel's ideas in order to move beyond Hegel and to respond to contemporary challenges. The third part of the volume, "Thinking beyond Hegel's Views on Art and Society," is thus linked by many threads to the other two parts, but the chapters that are gathered in it manifest a relatively concentrated effort to take Hegel into the current moment.

In her chapter on "Greek Tragedy and Self-Authorship in Hegel's *Phenomenology of Spirit*," Eliza Little examines the role of tragedy in the *Phenomenology of Spirit* as part of Hegel's systematic epistemology. She argues that tragedy, for Hegel, is a way of Spirit's "coming to know" itself—Spirit, which she understands, in a felicitous phrase, as "collective human mindedness." As an early form of Spirit's self-knowledge in the *Phenomenology* (actually, the first such form, according to Little), tragedy is marked by the discrepancy between the truth that it is supposed to communicate and the form that this truth assumes in it. This discrepancy, Little observes, is crucial to Hegel's entire project in the *Phenomenology* that describes the process by which it is ultimately overcome, and Spirit attains the perspective of absolute knowing, that is to say, the philosophical concept. Little approaches tragedy as a model *in ovo*, as it were, of the overall epistemological process described in the book. In particular, self-recollection and self-recognition that constitute the dynamic of Spirit's ascent, she argues, are the cognitive powers that shape the tragic collision in Attic drama as well. Here Little brings to bear Christoph Menke's notion of the author and the protagonist swapping places in Sophocles's *Oedipus Tyrannus*, which, she proposes, "thematizes [tragedy] as an art form." This is important because, as Menke proposes, aesthetic judgment levels itself not only at objects but also at judgment as such; it is a form of judgment that thematizes judgment, and, hence, is a critique. In sum, tragedy involves "multiple registers of self-reflexivity," and this makes it a step in reconciling the author and the actor, the knower and the agent, destined to be completed in Absolute Knowledge. Little closes by a rather expansive claim on behalf of tragedy: it is not merely one among art forms, but *the* art form in which the self-knowledge of Spirit realizes itself.

Georg Bertram's chapter, "Rethinking Hegel's Modern Conception of Art," steps squarely into the debate about Hegel's end-of-art thesis by claiming that the thesis should be rejected. He argues that it is not Greek but romantic art that should be considered the highest form of art for Hegel. This is because romantic art must be seen as the sublation of the two previous forms, symbolic and classical art. Bertram substantiates this thesis by arguing that the significance of art is to be sought in its function of social stabilization. As social structures fail, so does the art that goes with them. The end-of-art thesis thus means that art has lost its self-evident social foundations and no longer stands on its own. Since artworks now stand on their own, they must address themselves to a plurality of artworks within the context of which they must situate themselves. And this plurality makes it possible once again for artworks to address themselves to human practices in an ongoing way.

Vladimir Marchenkov's point of departure in "Hegel contra Moralism: Hegel's Aesthetics as an Argument against the Moralist Approach to Art" is the diagnosis of the current state of affairs in aesthetics as the triumph of moralism. This triumph, he maintains, signifies the hegemony of the will to power over reason in modern culture. Hegel is then approached as a possible, if somewhat problematic, ally in resisting the moralistic approaches to art. On the one hand, Hegel's view of art is antimoralist in the sense that Hegel forcefully denies that art's chief and proper function is moral in nature. Art, he insists, fulfills its own, unique role in culture: to manifest the truth in sensible imagery. Such an attitude seems to elevate art above and beyond the domain of objective spirit. But, on the other hand, when art is superseded by religion, the latter brings back with it the moral concerns of human community. In fact, these concerns, according to Hegel, constitute the true substance of religious life. We thus find ourselves back in the domain of objective spirit or, to use Kant's language, practical reason—which art seemed to have extricated us from as it made the transition from objective to Absolute Spirit. Marchenkov links this inconsistency to the conflation of myth and poetry, ritual and theater, and, ultimately, religion and art in Hegel's aesthetics. The distinction between religion and art, he further argues, should be drawn, not along the axis of the finite and the infinite, the sensible and the intelligible, but along the axis of the serious and the ludic. Hegel's philosophy of art can be made consistent, Marchenkov proposes, by the incorporation of a ludic approach to art, which will cause a rearrangement in the dynamics of Absolute Spirit. Namely, religion rather than art needs to be understood, according to this proposal, as the zone of transition from practical concerns, from the world of morality, to cultural concerns, to the world of religion, art, and philosophy. The resulting dialectic of Absolute Spirit, Marchenkov concludes, is an argument in favor of reason as the pinnacle of human faculties, as opposed to the will to power that is currently upheld as their crowning glory.

Notes

1 "Nonmodern cultures" refers to those that continued and, in some cases, continue today to coexist with the (Western) modern culture. "Premodern" refers to those cultures, such as that of medieval Europe, that have been succeeded by modern culture, a process that has occurred at various times in the past and in some cases is still occurring today.
2 Denis Diderot's dialogue *Le Neveu de Rameau*, apparently written before 1773 and first published in Goethe's German translation in 1805, is a text whose interpretation has proved to be as elusive as its publication history has been tangled. See Leonard Tancock's "Introduction to *Rameau's Nephew*," in Diderot, *Rameau's Nephew and D'Alembert's Dream*, ed. and trans. Leonard Tancock (London: Penguin Books, 1966), 19–31.
3 Incidentally, other periods of enlightenment, such as the classical Greek one, produced similar dynamics in the cultural situation of art. Plato's diatribes against popular entertainment, dramatic performance, and poetry negatively reveal the extent to which the aesthetic attitude asserted itself in Greek culture.

Part I

Art's Contribution to Modern Ethical Life

1

Hegel on Aesthetic Reconciliation

Mark Alznauer

Introduction

In his lectures on fine art, Hegel claims that art's "final end" (*Endzweck*) is to reconcile certain deep contradictions in human life, contradictions that stem from the opposition between mind and nature.¹ Art does this, he says, by unveiling or displaying the idea (*die Idee*) in the "form of sensuous artistic configuration." It follows that artworks, art forms, and artistic genres are good *qua art* only to the degree that they afford us experiences of this kind of reconciliation (*Versöhnung*). Naturally, Hegel concedes that works of art can also be assessed in light of other ends—we can ask whether they are entertaining, instructive, morally edifying, and so forth—but he claims that these other forms of assessment instrumentalize the artwork; they put the artwork in the service of ends drawn from outside the sphere of art, ends not determined by its very concept or nature. Hegel's claim is that reconciliation is the only end or aim of art that is autonomous in the sense of being directly derivable from its own concept.

Although there are certainly some distinctively Hegelian commitments involved in putting the point in just this way, the general idea that art's highest vocation is to somehow reconcile mind and nature was quite common during the period in which he lived. In Hegel's own brief recapitulation of the history of aesthetics, Friedrich Schiller is credited with being the first to clearly recognize the reconciliatory vocation of art. But Hegel acknowledges that similar claims about art were advanced by several of his own contemporaries, including Friedrich Wilhelm Joseph von Schelling and some of the most prominent of the German romantics (he explicitly mentions the Schlegel brothers, Karl Solger, and Ludwig Tieck, but Novalis and Hölderlin would, by most reckonings, also belong in this group).

It should also be noted that this way of thinking about art was not unique to the German context. If we cast our gaze further afield, we see a strikingly similar emphasis on the reconciliatory function of art emerging at around the same time among the most prominent figures in the English romantic tradition: like Samuel T. Coleridge, William Wordsworth, and Percy B. Shelley. Though some of these figures were directly influenced by German currents of thought—Coleridge, most notably—others seemed to have been drawn to this way of thinking about art on their own. As M. H. Abrams remarks, the notion that art could preside over a kind of wedding between nature and mind was a "prominent period-metaphor" among poets and philosophers of the time.[2] The general thought that seems to have been shared by all these romantics and idealists was, to put it in Abrams' own terms, that art's highest task is to overcome certain experiences of human alienation and that it accomplishes this by yielding a new vision of the world, one that shows the ultimate falsity of the opposition between mind and world. I will henceforth refer to this as the reconciliatory theory of art.

In the following, I will revisit Hegel's own version of the reconciliatory theory of art, attempting to articulate its basic structure and justification. I should note that although I will not be speaking in any great detail about other versions of the theory, my intention is to focus on those features of Hegel's account that I think have significant overlap with other defenses of the reconciliatory theory of art, while bracketing treatment of the more notorious and original claims Hegel makes about the "end of art" and about the ultimate superiority of philosophy to art. For commentators like Manfred Frank, once these more distinctive aspects of Hegel's philosophy of art are brought into the picture, any commonality between Hegel and the other figures in the romantic-idealist tradition starts to look comparatively insignificant; and to some degree Hegel himself saw things this way.[3] But the usual emphasis on points of difference has led to a failure to understand the common project that Hegel shared with the romantics (Schelling included), a project that has been rightly characterized as an attempt to sacralize art, to view it in terms of a function more commonly associated with religion.[4] So although Hegel's differences from the romantics are certainly real and important, my more restricted goal here is to show that Hegel offers a particularly powerful defense of a thesis that they share, which is that art has the vocation of reconciling mind (or spirit) and nature and that his defense of this shared view does not depend in any straightforward or obvious way on his more distinctive and controversial claims about the systematic subordination of art to philosophy.

In developing my interpretation of Hegel's theory of aesthetic reconciliation, I will be placing myself in dialogue with a prominent "left-Hegelian" line of criticism of Hegel, one that has convinced many that Hegel's emphasis on reconciliation is the least salvageable and most unfortunate aspect of his philosophy of art. The critics I have in mind follow Hegel in thinking that it is important to understand the artwork as addressing certain contradictions in modern life, and as revealing those contradictions to us through artistic objects or representations—indeed, it is this sensitivity to historical reality that is thought to make Hegel's theory superior to its romantic alternatives. But they reject the further thought that by doing so, art can or should reconcile us to life. For these critics, Hegel's insistence on the supposedly reconciliatory function of art founders on a fundamental problem, which is that the contradictions that art reveals as present in modern life have never been overcome and indeed show no prospect of dissolving in the near future. It follows from this that any artwork that leads us to affirm the reality we live in is ideological in the pejorative or critical sense. It encourages us to reconcile ourselves to something we *ought not* be reconciled to: a world that, despite Hegel's protestations to the contrary, is in fact pervasively irrational or unsatisfactory to reason.

I will be arguing that this common "left-Hegelian" line of criticism rests on a fundamental misunderstanding of the nature of aesthetic reconciliation in

Hegel's thought, one that wrongly treats aesthetic reconciliation as a facet of social reconciliation. On the alternative reading I will defend, art reconciles the contradictions we experience in life, not by effecting some change in our political or social world, or even by attempting to show us the ultimate rationality of our world, rather, it reconciles spirit and nature only in the sense that it provides us with access to a distinct mode of human activity in which the individual overcomes the subject-object opposition and the forms of suffering that are endemic to it.[5] The truth that art reveals is not a potentially dubious claim about the rationality of the modern political and social institutions, but a truth about human subjectivity or agency; and art reveals this truth about spirit not by representing it propositionally, or by making this truth its hidden or overt theme, but merely by being organized in such a way that it can only be properly experienced in this higher mode of activity.

In understanding art in this manner, Hegel proves himself to share the romantic-idealist tendency to invest ultimate human reconciliation not in religious eschatology, or in the achievement of any utopian political or social condition, but in the powers inherent in human consciousness as they manifest themselves in the contemplation of works of fine art (a commonality unaffected, or so I am arguing, by Hegel's un-romantic claim that still higher forms of reconciliation are possible). But he offers us a defense of this recognizably romantic position that is unique in two important ways. First, it is supported with a systematic account of the various different standpoints that spirit or mind can adopt toward nature, one that can articulate exactly what it means for art to transcend the oppositions characteristic of ordinary life without lapsing into mystificatory discourse or evocations of the unsayable. Second, his account consciously situates itself within a sophisticated historical narrative of changing conceptions of aesthetic transcendence, one that goes beyond the sketchy contrasts between the classical and the romantic, which are typical of romantic treatments of the history of art.

The "Left-Hegelian" Critique

In order to see why Hegel's emphasis on the reconciliatory vocation of art has come to be viewed as such a liability, it is helpful turn to an important and influential essay by Raymond Geuss entitled "Art and Theodicy."[6] On Geuss's interpretation of Hegel, the final end of art—its "inherent teleological goal"—is to provide us with a theodicy, a way of reconciling spirit or humanity to the negative aspects of existence. But Geuss makes three assumptions about how this works that lead to a clear problem for Hegel. The first assumption is that the negative aspects of existence that art addresses are primarily *contingent failings* in the social world, aspects of the social world that might appear to frustrate important aims we have, aims that could, in principle, be satisfied under better conditions.[7] The second is that art addresses our concern with these negative aspects of existence by unveiling certain truths *about us and about our society*: it gives us both an "awareness of what our deepest interests are" and some assurance that, despite the apparent obstacles we face, these interests can be "realized in the world as [we] find it."[8] The third assumption Geuss makes concerns the specific subjective reaction that this content is meant to provoke in us. By showing us that the world we live in is, in fact, congenial to our deepest interests, Geuss thinks, art is supposed to allow us to see that "life as we know it in our world is inherently worth living," thus generating in us "an *affectively positive optimism*" (my italics).[9]

If we take these three interpretive assumptions for granted, then Geuss is surely right that the most important condition for the success of Hegel's aesthetic theodicy is that it must "actually be the case that the world we live in is basically rational, comprehensible in principle, and 'commensurate' to us in the sense that it is amenable to allowing us to realize our deepest human interests and aspirations."[10] But admitting this makes Hegel's theory vulnerable to a rather devastating objection. For if the modern world turns out to be less rational than Hegel believed, as seems likely, then, on Hegel's own grounds, any art that aimed at reconciliation would be problematically ideological, offering us false reconciliation with the world. Geuss places this concern with false reconciliation in the mouth of one of Hegel's most trenchant critics, Theodor Adorno. He says that if we concede for the sake of argument Adorno's claim that the world is evil, then "any form of art … that contributed to trying to 'reconcile' people to this world or that caused them to affirm it would be not just mistaken, but defective in the most fundamental way possible."[11]

Although Adorno's worry that the modern world is pervasively evil is more controversial, his basic claim that the persistence of contradictions and irrationalities in modern life undermines Hegel's contentions about the reconciliatory aim of art has been adopted quite widely among contemporary interpreters of Hegel's aesthetics. For example, Robert Pippin has recently argued that the "blind spot" or "cardinal error" of Hegel's philosophy is clearly his "failure to appreciate the dissatisfactions that this 'prosaic' world (as he often called it) would generate, or his failure to appreciate that there might be a basic form of disunity or alienation that his project could not account for, for which there was no 'sublation' or overcoming yet on the horizon."[12] Pippin goes on to argue that, if art is still tasked with telling us the truth about our place in the world, and that world is characterized by endemic dissatisfactions, then art's task cannot be to reconcile us to the world we live in, but something closer to the opposite: its task must be to reveal the unreconciled contradictions and difficulties of modern life, difficulties that might prove impossible to ever wholly overcome. Similar attempts to retain Hegel's idea that art plays some role in *Zeitdiagnosis* (the "truth" function of art) while excising any expectation that this should lead to reconciliation (the theodicy bit) can be seen in the work by Christoph Menke, who attempts to preserve Hegel's theory of tragedy without its reconciliationist frame; by Gregg Horowitz, who thinks the only reconciliation offered by art or philosophy is knowledge of the insurmountable conflicts and contradictions of modernity; and by Jay Bernstein who wants to salvage Hegelian dialectics from Hegelian dogmas of completeness. In the following, I will be referring to this general strategy as the "left-Hegelian" line of criticism.[13]

I am going to challenge the "left-Hegelian" line of criticism by raising questions about each of the three interpretive assumptions that I identified in Geuss's articulation of the view, assumptions that are more or less present in these other accounts. I will argue that Geuss has misunderstood the kind of contradictions that art is supposed to reconcile, he has misconstrued the nature of the truth that art is supposed to reveal, and he has mischaracterized the experience of reconciliation that art is supposed to provide. By replacing each of the planks of Geuss's argument with more textually defensible ones, I will be assembling an alternative framework for approaching Hegel's theory of aesthetic reconciliation, one that does not make such reconciliation contingent on a demonstration of the fundamental goodness or rationality of the modern world.

The Opposition of Spirit and Nature

The first issue I want to address concerns the nature of the oppositions or contradictions that Hegel says art is supposed to set forth as reconciled. The departure point for several recent treatments of this theme in Hegel is a passage in the Introduction to the *Lectures on Fine Art* where Hegel identifies the contradictions characteristic of modern life in the following, provocative way:

> Spiritual culture, the modern intellect, produces this opposition in man which makes him an amphibious animal, because he now has to live in two worlds which contradict one another. . . . For on the one side, we see man imprisoned in the common world of reality and earthly temporality, borne down by need and poverty, hard pressed by nature, enmeshed in matter, sensuous ends and their enjoyment, mastered and carried away by natural impulses and passions. On the other side, he lifts himself up to eternal ideas, to a realm of thought and freedom, gives to himself, as will, universal laws and prescriptions, strips the world of its enlivened and flowering reality and dissolves it into abstractions, since the spirit now upholds its right and dignity only by mishandling nature and denying its right, and so retaliates on nature the distress and violence which it has suffered from it itself.[14]

This passage on the "amphibious" nature of the modern mind has suggested several things to readers. It has suggested that the central problem art must address is not a perennial one, like the metaphysical problem of understanding how mind and matter interact, but a specifically social or cultural difficulty of achieving satisfaction in life.[15] It has also suggested that Hegel thinks the source of this problem is our own modern self-understanding, which "produces this opposition" by adopting a basically Kantian dualism between nature and moral freedom, thus leaving us in a hopelessly contradictory, self-alienated state.[16]

This way of reading the amphibian passage makes it easy to infer a certain picture about how Hegel himself might have thought that art or philosophy might overcome these divisions. It suggests that, if we were able to give up the roughly Kantian conception of the incompatibility of freedom and nature, and move to a more harmonious or dialectical conception of the relationship between nature and freedom, we would be able to see that the oppositions or contradictions that we experience as modern individuals have *already* been resolved. This would show that our experience of these contradictions in modern life was due to conceptualizing our practical lives in the wrong (that is, the Kantian) way, and was not due to anything objectively unsatisfactory in modern life itself. But if that's what Hegel is up to, then it is easy to see the force of the "left-Hegelian" critique, for it seems prima facie unlikely that whatever concrete historical dissatisfactions we experience as moral and political beings in modernity are philosophically induced illusions: simply a product of some theoretical mistake that can be dissolved merely by means of reconceiving the relation between nature and spirit. Hence the aptness of Bernstein's verdict that Hegel's response to the amphibian problem "combines philosophic insight with historical disingenuousness"; it is insightful insofar as it corrects these Kantian mistakes, but disingenuous insofar as it pretends this will remove the practical dissatisfactions that afflict modern life.

But Hegel provides a more detailed account of the relation of art to the oppositions of the finite world at the beginning of the first part of the lectures proper, and this account gives us a very different picture both of the nature of these oppositions and of what it might mean for art (or for philosophy) to overcome them.[17] These later passages in the lectures involve the same emphasis on the amphibian problem: on the opposition or contradiction between the worlds of nature and spirit. But in these passages, Hegel is explicit that the opposition or contradiction he has in mind is located at a much deeper, more metaphysical level than the amphibian passage might seem to suggest: it is not a local or contingent feature of the relation of spirit to the world, one that could be overcome in better circumstances, but an ontological feature of all finite modes of spiritual activity, one that certainly takes on different forms at different times but which is constitutive of the activities in question.[18]

The problem with finite spiritual activity, for Hegel, is that it necessarily and invariably posits nature as outside of itself and as opposed to itself. Hegel's point can be illustrated with examples of finite activity drawn from his own philosophy of psychology. In thinking about a stone on the path in front of me, I presuppose the stone as independent of my thinking, as something outside of me that my thinking is answerable to. Similarly, in any voluntary action, like putting out a fire, I presuppose that there is a fire out there that I can change or modify in some way, something both external to my will and through which I can manifest my will in the world. In both of these cases, the specific spiritual activity in question (thinking, acting) would be literally unintelligible or impossible without this basic opposition to external nature being present. The opposition between spirit and nature that is characteristic of finite spiritual activity is thus not a consequence of a defective conception, nor is it due to some widespread social pathology, but is an intrinsic feature of such activity, part of its very ontological structure.[19]

Understanding the opposition between spirit and nature in this way puts some severe constraints on what it might mean to fully overcome it. It clearly cannot mean that our task is to somehow reform our ordinary thinking or willing so that spirit and nature do not come into opposition—that is simply inconceivable. Nor is the task to coordinate nature and spirit so that the opposition does not lead to problems—problems of knowing the world or of achieving our ends in it. Although such coordination is important for Hegel, he suggests that managing the contradictions in this way can only give us "relative satisfaction," for such coordination would not resolve the underlying opposition at all, which stems from the unchangeable fact that even when these activities are fully successful on their own terms they require spirit to engage with something outside of itself, something that has the power to constrain and limit its activity. To genuinely and satisfactorily overcome this opposition, Hegel says, we must seek satisfaction elsewhere, in a spiritual activity of *another kind*, one that is *not* constitutively opposed to nature.[20] The discovery of "nonfinite" or "absolute" forms of spiritual activity "overcomes" the opposition between spirit and nature not by denying that these oppositions are ineradicably present in the domain of the finite (what he also calls the ordinary or prosaic world) but by showing that human subjects are capable of operating independently of these constraints, though only insofar as they participate in some different and higher domain.

For our purposes, it is important to note that Hegel thinks *all* practical life falls within the lower domain of finite spirit, not just psychological phenomena like ordinary thinking and willing. Even the life of the state, which Hegel considers the fullest expression of freedom that is possible in the external world, offers us only a one-sided and insufficient form of human satisfaction. And it is clear from Hegel's treatment of this issue that our deepest dissatisfactions with the state cannot be traced to any merely contingent defects in our actual social and political world. They have to do with the very nature of the state: in particular, its "finite mode of existence."[21] The claim Hegel is making in these passages is that the deepest or ultimate source of our dissatisfaction in everyday life is not a worry that our rights and obligations as ethical and political beings are insufficiently realized, which of course they always are, but that these rights and obligations are themselves insufficient; they do not and cannot provide us with a full or complete experience of freedom or self-determination. This means that even if our rights and obligations were perfectly realized in our own social and political world, and even if we knew this fact with whatever certainty it admits of being known, we would still not be truly satisfied or reconciled. This is because the fundamental opposition between spirit and nature simply cannot be overcome at the level of social and political existence. For full satisfaction, we must leave the finite behind and enter into the "region of absolute, not finite, truth."[22] At first blush, this invocation of a higher world or region might sound baldly and unacceptably theological, an escape to Valhalla, but these passages clearly indicate that the higher world is not supposed to be a transcendent realm located in some alternative plane of existence, but a region that is opened up to us precisely when we take the standpoint on the world that art demands of us—when we view the artwork noninstrumentally, as independent of our finite ends.[23]

This shows that the first plank in the "left-Hegelian" critique of the project of aesthetic reconciliation mistakes both the nature of the problem art is supposed to address and art's manner of addressing this problem. The opposition or contradiction that art is to "reveal as reconciled" is not an experience of political or social alienation, but a dissatisfaction with finite spiritual existence as such. Insofar as that is so, there is no reason to think Hegel is under the erroneous impression that art must soft pedal the social or political problems that beset modern life, problems such as poverty, injustice, and so forth, proclaiming that these problems are not really there, or that they are simply a product of our having adopted an excessively dichotomous picture of the social world. Art reconciles us to the contradictions and oppositions between spirit and nature by affording us an experience of a human activity that is free of such contradictions and oppositions.

Truth in Art

The second plank in the "left-Hegelian" line of criticism concerns the nature of Hegel's aesthetic cognitivism. Hegel is explicit that art reconciles the opposition between spirit and nature by unveiling the "truth" or the "idea" in the form of sensuous artistic configuration, and this seems to imply that art has some cognitive, truth-evaluable content that is the most important source of its value to human life. On some traditional interpretations of Hegel, the truth that art expresses is some kind of profound metaphysical insight; Paul Guyer, for example, suggests it is the claim that "everything significant about reality is a product of thought."[24] Guyer rightly notes that this is not a particularly appealing position to anyone not already committed to idealist metaphysics. Indeed, one recent critic has claimed that this commitment yields "no theory of art that is remotely plausible by contemporary standards" insofar as the realm of art "includes many superb works that do not reveal transcendent truths—or any truths at all."[25]

One of the primary attractions of the "left-Hegelian" reading is that it offers us an interpretation of Hegel's aesthetic cognitivism that is not wedded to the idea that all artworks express the same metaphysical insight. According to the second plank of the "left-Hegelian" interpretation, the content art expresses is not some obscure metaphysical insight, but rather a presentation of a given historical people's deepest interests or values along with some assurance of their realizability in this world. This interpretation certainly provides Hegel with a more plausible and flexible form of aesthetic cognitivism than the traditional interpretation, for although it is far from clear how all art could be trying to express the same philosophical dictum, it has seemed quite promising to view art as a kind of self-reflection of ethical life. It is also very well-grounded textually, since Hegel repeatedly insists that art brings to consciousness the "highest needs of spirit" and that it "makes spirit aware of its interests"—passages that encourage us to view art as an expression of the needs and interests of historically concrete peoples.[26]

But reading Hegel's aesthetic cognitivism in the "left-Hegelian" manner also makes his position vulnerable to the concerns we have previously identified about ideology. If the truths artworks express concern our interests and their realizability in the social world we find ourselves in, then the truth of the artwork is beholden to something outside of the artwork: it is a matter of whether the picture the artwork provides us of ourselves and our world accurately reflects the reality of our particular historical circumstances.[27] If it turns out that our social world is *not* in fact one in which we can realize our interests, then any artwork that attempts to reconcile us to that world by depicting it as rational would be false in the very straightforward sense of failing to correspond to the facts of the matter.[28] In such circumstances, art is caught up in a double-bind: insofar as it is true, it cannot reconcile; and insofar as it reconciles, it cannot be true. The "left-Hegelian" response to this dilemma is unambiguous: we should keep the claim that art must reveal the truth about our ethical world (i.e., that it is beset by contradictions) but jettison the claim that art should reconcile us to that world.

To determine whether Hegel is really vulnerable to these criticisms, we will need to get clearer on what Hegel means when he speaks of truth in the sphere of the fine arts. This is an enormously complex issue, but I will make two points that, even if not fully dispositive, should point us in the right direction. The first point I want to make is a restricted and negative one, namely, that, although Hegel frequently insists that art should reveal the deepest interests of spirit, there is not a single place in the entirety of the *Lectures on Fine Art* where Hegel criticizes a work of art as untrue (*unwahr*) on the grounds that it fails to accurately depict the realizability of these interests in the social world from which the artwork is drawn. This, I think, is a puzzling omission if one is committed to the idea that art reconciles us to reality precisely by showing us that reality is a home, a place where our interests can be realized. The second point I want to make is more positive: when Hegel does criticize a work of art as "untrue," it is not because it fails to correspond to some reality outside of itself (a correspondence he terms "correctness" not "truth"), but because it fails to embody a conception of the aesthetic ideal that is capable of affording aesthetic reconciliation. This can be seen with particular clarity in Hegel's remarks about the comparative merits of the three art forms or styles that he distinguishes in his history of aesthetics: symbolic, classical, and romantic.

For Hegel, symbolic art is untrue (*unwahr*) not because it fails to adequately represent the world in which it was made, but because, although its ideal affords a kind of transcendence of the finite world, it offers no real reconciliation with it. In experiencing a symbolic work of art, Hegel says, we participate in a kind of striving for the achievement of a standpoint in which the natural and phenomenal world will simply fall away, being abstractly negated. But since such transcendence is conceived in entirely negative terms, it cannot be adequately embodied in the work of art. Classical art is superior to symbolic art, truer, not because it is better at depicting its own social conditions (those of the Greek or Roman world), but because it has a different aesthetic ideal, one that makes a positive reconciliation between spirit and nature possible for the first time. In classical art, nature is no longer merely negated in the attempt to achieve some sublimely independent standpoint; instead, it is transfigured into an object of beauty, one that provides the observer with an experience of things being exactly as they should be, a "happy harmony" between spirit and nature.[29]

But this classical form of reconciliation proves inadequate or incomplete precisely because it is restricted to reconciling us to that small fraction of natural and human existence that can be made beautiful. Christian or romantic art proves to be the "truest" form of art precisely because it allows a "higher freedom and reconciliation" to come into view in the artwork, one that does not shrink from the negative aspects of human existence—death, suffering, and agony—but is able to find affirmative meaning even in these.[30] In the experience of a romantic artwork, we are shown to be capable of achieving "a spiritual inwardness, a joy in submission, a bliss in grief and rapture in suffering, even a delight in agony."[31] The romantic art form can be said to afford a higher or more complete form of reconciliation precisely because it allows us to affirm the full scope of natural and human existence (including its negative elements), but it is important to note that this is an affirmation that is said to take place entirely *within* the inwardness of the heart and *not* in the external world. This inward affirmation or inner bliss is so complete and self-sufficient that it ends up being entirely "indifferent to the way the immediate world is configurated."[32]

So throughout the aesthetics, the question of the truth of an artwork or art form is treated as identical to the question of whether such a work or style offers us a kind of internal reconciliation with the negative aspects of existence. An artistic ideal is truer to the degree that it has a greater capacity to reconcile spirit to nature. We can now say exactly what is wrong with the second plank in the "left-Hegelian" interpretation. According to that interpretation, the truth-evaluable content of the artwork is a message about the realizability of our interests or value in the world, and this message is true to the degree that it correctly represents the world we live in. But for Hegel, any talk about external correspondence relations, relations between the content of the artwork and the world, moves in the realm of correctness, not truth. The truth-evaluable content of the artwork is the ideal it embodies, and this ideal is true precisely to the degree that it makes specifically aesthetic reconciliation possible. This has the striking consequence that, if we are to stay within Hegelian terminological universe, it is conceptually impossible for there to be an artwork that could fully reconcile and yet not be true. Truth in art is nothing other than the capacity to reconcile through sensuous representations. From this point of view, any concern that art correctly represents the world is extraneous to art as such (or said more carefully, it is only relevant when such correct representation contributes to the internal end of art).[33]

This reconceptualization of the terms of the debate might seem to answer the "left-Hegelian" line of criticism a little too well, refusing to allow what is clearly a legitimate concern with false reconciliation to even be formulated. But the point of inter-defining truth and reconciliation in the Hegelian manner is not to deny that an artwork might represent the world to be more orderly or rational than it in fact is and that recognizing this defect in the artwork might vitiate the satisfaction the work affords us. Surely, when that happens it is a defect. The point is to direct us to a different notion of reconciliation as more central and appropriate to fine art, one that does not saddle art with the task of representing the world as a place where things usually work out for the best. For Hegel, when we seek reconciliation in a Pietà, or in *King Lear*, or in a Flemish still-life, we are not hoping to be convinced that the world we live in is a little friendlier to our aims than we previously thought; we are seeking an experience of reconciliation, which shows us that we can accept or even affirm our lives despite the fact that the world includes things such as the agony of death, the ingratitude of children, and the prosaic everydayness of bourgeois life. To use a Nietzschean phrase, we are seeking an intrinsically aesthetic justification of life—a way of seeing the contradictions that afflict us as finite beings, but from a higher standpoint, one from which they no longer represent a threat to our freedom.[34] The truth art reveals is nothing other than the fact that spirit is capable of rising to a standpoint where spirit is not threatened by these finite concerns—this is what Hegel means by speaking of art as a revelation of "highest truth of spirit."

The Experience of Reconciliation

The last issue I want to address concerns the subjective aspect of aesthetic reconciliation: What specific affirmative attitude or feeling is successful art supposed to generate in us? The defining characteristic of the "left-Hegelian" interpretation I have been contending with is the belief that aesthetic reconciliation is to be understood as a subordinate aspect of social reconciliation, part of Hegel's attempt to reconcile individuals to the modern social world by showing it to be worthy of affirmation. Art contributes to this kind of reconciliation, upon this view, by showing us that there are no insuperable obstacles to the realization of our true interests or needs. This suggests that the attitude or feeling art is supposed to generate in us is some kind of positive attitude toward the modern social world. On Geuss's particular version of this reading, successful art is supposed to generate an "affectively positive optimism" in us, an attitude of hopefulness or confidence about our world.[35] This is the third and final assumption of the "left-Hegelian" reading I am contesting.

If we turn to the body of Hegel's lectures on fine art, we find little to no sign that art is supposed to make us feel optimistic or confident about our chances for realizing our interests in the world we live in.[36] Instead, in speaking of the attitude successful art engenders in its audience, Hegel typically uses a set of terms clearly borrowed from the sphere of religious experience. In these contexts, he speaks of feelings like joy (*Freudigkeit*), rapture (*Wonne*), and most importantly, bliss or blessedness (*Seligkeit*).[37] Indeed, he goes so far as to say that the single most important characteristic of the ideal work of art is a "serene peace and bliss" or "self-enjoyment in its own achievedness and satisfaction";[38] and that the "positive aspect of reconciliation," and the "greatest spiritual depth that the artist can provide" is the "spiritual elevation of the mind to its blessedness [*Seligkeit*]."[39]

It would be easy to hear Hegel's references to *Seligkeit*, a term that is also quite prominent in much of the romantic poetry of the period, as merely rhetorical. This would be to view bliss as differing only in degree from ordinary affirmative attitudes such as happiness or optimism, to view it as abundant or unqualified happiness. But throughout his writings, Hegel in fact marks a qualitative distinction between bliss (*Seligkeit*) and mere happiness (*Glückseligkeit*).[40] His earliest discussion of this distinction is in his 1802 essay on *Faith and Knowledge*, where he distinguishes between a vulgar eudaimonism, which views happiness from the point of view of the empirical subject's relation to ordinary life, and a properly philosophic conception of the matter, which views happiness as "blissful enjoyment of eternal intuition."[41] A similar contrast is drawn in the *Philosophic Propaedeutic* (1808–11), which states that whereas happiness involves the idea of good fortune (*Glück*), bliss or blessedness is not conditional on good fortune.[42] The most important passage for our purposes, though, is in his *Aesthetics*, where he marks the distinction this way:

> Good fortune and happiness still involve an accidental and natural correspondence between the individual and his external circumstances; but in bliss the good fortune still attendant on a man's existence as he is in nature falls away and the whole thing is transferred into the inner life of the spirit. Bliss is an acquired satisfaction and justified only on that account; it is a serenity in victory, the soul's feeling when it has expunged from itself everything sensuous and finite and therefore has cast aside the care that always lies in wait for us. The soul is blissful when, after experiencing conflict and agony, it has triumphed over its sufferings.[43]

There are two important things we can learn about bliss from this passage. The first is that bliss involves a kind of inner complexity; we are not talking about an unqualifiedly positive feeling, but a feeling that requires the presence of its opposite. Throughout the lectures on art, Hegel often emphasizes this paradoxical feature of bliss, that it incorporates negativity as a necessary moment; he speaks of the "bliss in grief,"[44] the "unhappy bliss in misfortune,"[45] and even the "bliss of torment."[46] Happiness, of course, is like this too: we are often happy with an outcome partly because we were worried that it wouldn't come to pass. To the degree that this is so, happiness too depends on the feeling of overcoming negativity.

But there is an important difference between the way bliss incorporates this negative moment and the way happiness does, and that is the second thing worth noticing about this passage. When an individual is happy, this is because external circumstances have been found to correspond to her interests or desires. Without this correspondence, happiness vanishes. Happiness is in this respect conditional on external reality being one way rather than another. Bliss, however, does not require any "correspondence between the individual and his external circumstances" and this indifference to the specific makeup of the external world is its defining feature. Hegel provides an illustration of this state of mind in his discussion of Aristophanic comedy, when he describes the "confidence felt by someone raised altogether above his own inner contradiction and not bitter or miserable in it at all; this is the bliss and ease of a man who, being sure of himself, *can bear the frustration of his aims and achievements*."[47] If to be happy is to have things work out the way you wanted them to, to be blissful is to achieve a state of mind where you do not need things to work out one way or the other. The overcoming of negativity that is characteristic of bliss, then, is not the limited and temporary satisfaction that comes from overcoming some particular obstacle to one's aims and achievements; it is an overcoming of one's very dependence on the external world for one's self-enjoyment.

The distinction Hegel marks in these passages between *Glückseligkeit* and *Seligkeit* is clearly indebted to a long history of thought on the relation between happiness and fortune in European philosophy. Aristotle, for example, appears to distinguish between *eudaimonia* and *makarios*, reserving the latter term to characterize the happiness of the gods, who possess a blessedness that is immune to misfortune.[48] And in Christian philosophy and theology, a similar distinction is often marked between *felicitas* and *beatitudo*; *felicitas* is associated with earthly happiness and beatitude is associated with that more complete happiness which awaits the believer in the afterlife. Hegel redeploys this traditional distinction, however, not to differentiate between the satisfaction available to humans and that available to the gods, or to distinguish between satisfaction available in this world from that which will be made available to us in the next, but to distinguish between two fully human forms of satisfaction that are both available in this life.

For Hegel, these two forms of satisfaction correspond to two different standpoints human individuals can take toward the world, two different ways spirit can relate itself to nature.[49] Happiness (*Glückseligkeit*) corresponds to the standpoint of "finite spirit," a standpoint characterized by the opposition between human subjectivity and the natural and social world. From within this standpoint, the only satisfaction that is available to us is relative and temporary: it comes from making the external world correspond to our desires, needs, or values in some particular instance. Bliss (*Seligkeit*), on the other hand, corresponds to the standpoint of "infinite spirit," a human self-conception that has transcended the fundamental opposition between spirit and nature. It requires not the overcoming of the recalcitrance of the external world, but the overcoming of a conception of ourselves as essentially finite beings, as dependent for our ultimate satisfaction on the cooperation of the external world. Bliss is characteristic of aesthetic experience for Hegel because he thinks to appreciate something as art requires viewing it as valuable for its own sake and independently of any of our finite ends, and to adopt this standpoint on a work of art just is to transcend a conception of ourselves as finite beings. This is a feature, Hegel thinks, that artistic activity shares with religious and philosophic activity, it is what makes them all forms of Absolute Spirit.

It might seem that any emphasis on bliss as characteristic of human encounters with art requires positing an implausibly ahistorical conception of aesthetic experience, one incapable of doing justice to the radical changes in the way people have experienced art over the course of history. But although Hegel thinks of bliss as the characteristic effect aimed at by all art, it is central to his ambitions to show that bliss takes on a different character at different times and that the forms it takes at any place and time are responsive to the historical context in which the artwork exists, particularly the religious beliefs of the time.

To simplify a much more complicated story, we can single out at least three different species of aesthetic bliss, each corresponding to a different historical art form. In the symbolic art form, bliss is experienced as a mystical union with the divine, a union in which all particulars are happily sacrificed "by the subject who thereby acquires the supreme enlargement of consciousness as well as, through entire liberation from the finite, the bliss of absorption into everything that is best and most splendid."[50] Hegel argues that the classical art form improves upon the symbolic one because the contemplation of classical art no longer requires complete absorption in the divine, with its attendant annihilation of the subject. This gives rise to a different experience of bliss or blessedness; in classical or Greek art, the audience is invited to participate in a divine perspective that shares the human form but lacks any "seriousness in distress, in anger, in the interests involved with finite spheres and aims," thus allowing us to experience, he says, the "smiling bliss of the Olympian gods, their unimpaired equanimity which comes home in men and can put up with anything."[51] The defect of the classical art form, in turn, is that, although it allows for partial reconciliation with life (unlike symbolic art), this reconciliation is limited to what is beautiful in life. Only romantic or Christian art is capable of also reconciling us to even the negative aspects of existence—to death, grief, misfortune—thus offering a "freedom and blessedness unknown to the Greeks."[52] Hegel characterizes this third form of bliss, romantic bliss, as "a harmony proceeding only from infinite grief, from surrender, sacrifice, and the death of what is finite, sensuous, and subjective."[53] The kind of bliss art gives rise to is thus capable of significant historical variation: from the bliss of absorption (*die Seligkeit des Aufgehens*), through the smiling bliss of the Olympian gods (*die lachende Seligkeit der olympischen Götter*), to the unhappy bliss in misfortune (*eine unglückselige Seligkeit im Unglück*) characteristic of post-Christian art.

Even this extraordinarily selective synopsis of Hegel's history of art shows that there could be no greater misunderstanding of his theory of art than to think that it aims at making us optimistic about contingent facts in the social and political world. Optimism plays no role at *any* stage of Hegel's story—not even in the Greek case where it might be thought most at home. Indeed, for Hegel, optimism and happiness are intrinsically *inaesthetic* attitudes, attitudes that are categorically inappropriate in the context of aesthetics, since they posit a contingent relationship between the ends of spirit and their realization. The distinctive attitude that fine art generates, on Hegel's account, is a bliss or joy that lifts us *above* the suffering, tragedy, and misfortune that are, even for Hegel, a necessary and ineliminable feature of prosaic life. Art affords us this experience of transcendence by showing us that we are capable of viewing the contradictions of the finite world as ultimately illusory (in the symbolic stage), as ultimately unserious (in the classical stage), or as ultimately overcome in the inwardness of the heart (in the romantic stage). For Hegel, romantic art is superior to its antecedents not because such art has the good fortune to exist in a social and political world that is fully rational, one worthy of being reconciled to, but rather because it is capable of generating an experience of *Seligkeit* even in depictions of the worst forms of human suffering or misfortune, hence the emblematic nature of Christ on the cross or Lear on the heath as subjects of romantic art. Romantic art is the deepest form of art because it is most capable of reconciling us to both the good and the evil in life.

Aesthetic Reconciliation

What I've been attempting in the foregoing discussion is a reconstruction of the core elements of Hegel's version of the reconciliatory theory of art. My foil was a common, "left-Hegelian" interpretation and critique of Hegel that we can now see was flawed by a failure to adequately distinguish between social and aesthetic reconciliation. I want to conclude, and consolidate our gains, by clearly delineating the differences between these two forms of reconciliation as they appear in Hegel's philosophy.

Michael Hardimon has done the most to identify the precise kind of reconciliation that is the main goal of Hegel's political and social philosophy.[54] I will term it social reconciliation because it involves becoming reconciled to one's own social world. Hardimon has argued that the attitude of social reconciliation must not be confused with mere resignation (which involves accepting existing evils without evaluation) or unqualified affirmation (which would presume that a world is only worthy of affirmation if it has no defects) but is something that involves a balance of these.[55] It is a realistic affirmative attitude whose inner complexity is warranted by the fact that, although there are still defects and conflicts in the modern world, and so no guarantee against personal misfortune or unhappiness, these defects are necessary or somehow compensated for by the overall rationality of the system.

For example, Hegel takes poverty to be an obvious evil of modern societies, indeed one that arguably makes it impossible for the poor themselves to attain reconciliation.[56] But he attempts to reconcile the rest of us to modern society, by showing that poverty is a necessary evil. Although we should strive to eliminate poverty as much as we can, he thinks it is systematically generated by that form of civil society which is a necessary component of a fully rational state. Obviously, this sort of reconciliation depends on the truth of the necessity of poverty that the theory advances. If poverty is *not* a necessary evil of the current system, or if there is a more rational way to organize society that does not give rise to poverty, then Hegel's social philosophy is open to the charge of being ideological, of encouraging reconciliation to a social world that we should instead be attempting to reform or abolish. This complaint, of course, is the heart of the traditional "left-Hegelian" critique of Hegel's social philosophy.

Aesthetic reconciliation, however, does not have the same structure as social reconciliation, and so it does not have the same vulnerabilities. Art does not address the contradictions or oppositions of modern life by denying they exist or by offering some account of their systematic necessity. If Hegel is right, the contemplation of the work of art as an end in itself offers us an experience of the transcendence of such contradictions and oppositions in a separate sphere of activity. Aesthetic reconciliation, then, is an affirmative attitude toward life in general warranted by the truth that we are capable of overcoming our dependence on the finite world for our ultimate satisfaction. Since art shares this "truth" with religion, it is perhaps unsurprising that, in Hegel's treatment, in a given society art is much more closely related to that society's religion, its conceptions of the relation of the divine to the human, than to its political or social structure. The apolitical, quasi-religious nature of aesthetic reconciliation is vividly on display in a passage where Hegel considers the possibility of a moral objection to art on the grounds that the wealth devoted to it would be better spent on alleviating human suffering. He responds to this objection by saying:

> However many moral and touching emotions may be excited in this connection, this is possible only by calling to mind again the distress and poverty which art precisely demands shall be set aside, so that it can but redound to the fame and supreme honour of every people to devote its treasures to a sphere which, within reality itself, rises luxuriously above all the distress of reality.[57]

So although social reconciliation depends on justifying poverty as a necessary evil of modern society, aesthetic reconciliation requires that our concern with poverty be set aside or simply put out of mind.

Needless to say, this view of art's ultimate justification as "a sphere that rises luxuriously above all the distress of reality" raises many problems of its own: the worry, for example, that it encourages a retreat into an illusory world that has the function of reinforcing existing social contradictions.[58] I do not have space to offer much of a reconciliatory theory of art against these common criticisms here. But I want to say that these are the right worries to have about Hegel's theory, not that art reconciles us to the social world by misrepresenting it as good but that it reconciles us to life by affording us a form of satisfaction that does not require the world to be good at all. This is what Nietzsche rightly called Hegel's "grandiose project"—which was not a project that "sanctioned the rationality of whoever happened to be ruling," as it has often been misinterpreted but an attempt to show us that "evil, error, and suffering" offer no argument against the full affirmation of life.[59]

Notes

1. The quotations in this paragraph are drawn from Hegel, *Hegel's Aesthetics* I:54–55; references to the German edition are to *Ästhetik* I:63–64.
2. Abrams, *Natural Supernaturalism: Tradition and Revolution in Romantic Literature* (New York: Norton & Company, Inc., 1971), 31. For an influential criticism of Abrams's "idealistic" interpretation of romanticism, see Paul de Man's "The Rhetoric of Temporality," in *Interpretation: Theory and Practice*, ed. Charles S. Singleton (Baltimore: Johns Hopkins University Press, 1969), 173–209.
3. See, for example, Manfred Frank's "On the Unknowability of the Absolute: Historical Background and Romantic Reactions," in *The Philosophical Foundations of Early German Romanticism*, trans. Elizabeth Millán-Zaibert (Albany: SUNY, 2008), 40–55.
4. See Schaeffer, *Art of the Modern Age: Philosophy of Art from Kant to Heidegger*, trans. Steven Rendall (Princeton: Princeton University Press, 2000), 135ff. A more sympathetic account is provided in Sebastian Gardner's "The Romantic-Metaphysical Theory of Art," in *European Journal of Philosophy* 10, no. 3 (2002): 275–301. Both Schaeffer and Gardner treat the commonality between Hegel and the romantics primarily in terms of a commitment to art as "ontologically revelatory," a commitment they share with a wide range of other thinkers in the German speculative tradition (like Schopenhauer, Adorno, Heidegger, etc.). In this chapter, I am interested in emphasizing a deeper commonality, one that they do not share with these later figures in the speculative tradition, namely, the claim that by revealing the truth art reconciles spirit and nature.
5. A similar emphasis on the role of experience in Hegel's philosophy of art can be found in Stephen Houlgate's *Freedom, Truth, and History: An Introduction to Hegel's Philosophy* (London: Routledge, 1991), esp. 137ff.
6. Geuss, "Art and Theodicy," in *Morality, Culture, and History* (Cambridge: Cambridge University Press, 1999), 78–115. All the references in the following two paragraphs are to this essay.
7. Ibid., 111 f. 5.
8. Ibid., 88. Geuss emphasizes that it is a complicated matter identifying exactly *how* art conveys these truths, since the "truths" art unveils are clearly not something that could be restated discursively, in a series of propositions.
9. Ibid., 89.
10. Ibid., 81.
11. Ibid., 99.
12. Pippin, *After the Beautiful: Hegel and Pictorial Modernism* (Chicago: The University of Chicago, 2014), 46.
13. Some examples of this strategy can be found in the following: Christoph Menke, *Die Tragödie im Sittlichen: Gerechtigkeit und Freiheit nach Hegel* (Frankfurt am Main: Suhrkamp, 1996); Gregg Horowitz, *Sustaining Loss: Art and Mournful Life* (Stanford: Stanford University Press, 2002); J. M. Bernstein, "Our Amphibian Problem: Nature in History in Adorno's Hegelian Critique of Hegel," in *Hegel on Philosophy in History*, ed. James Kreines and Rachel Zuckert (Cambridge: Cambridge University Press, 2017), 193–212.
14. *Hegel's Aesthetics* I:54; *Ästhetik* I:63.
15. This is emphasized in Pippin, *After the Beautiful*, 46.
16. This is suggested by Bernstein, "Our Amphibian Problem," 193–212.

17 Hegel, *Hegel's Aesthetics* I:112–13; *Ästhetik* I:119.
18 Even in the "amphibian" passage, Hegel emphasizes that these oppositions are *not* unique to modern culture, but "in numerous forms they have always preoccupied and troubled the human consciousness" (Hegel, *Hegel's Aesthetics* I:54; *Ästhetik* I:63). For a similar account of this passage, which came to my attention after I had written this, see Knappik, "'Gegenwärtige prosaische Zustände': Hegels melancholische Ästhetik und Schillers politische Eschatologie," in *Objektiver und absoluter Geist nach Hegel*, ed. Thomas Oehl and Arthur Kok (Leiden and Boston: Brill, 2018).
19 If we thought spirit was itself limited to activities of this sort, then we would indeed have a defective conception *of spirit*. But the claim that spirit is not finite, which is of course central to Hegel's project, has nothing to do with any denial of the essential finitude of ordinary thinking and willing. Indeed, Hegel everywhere emphasizes that his own conception of infinitude includes the finite; he is explicit that spirit is thus capable of *both* finite *and* infinite forms of activity. See esp. Hegel, *Philosophy of Mind*, trans. A. V. Miller and and William Wallace (Oxford: Oxford University Press, 1971), §386 Z.
20 See McCumber, *Poetic Interaction: Language, Freedom, Reason* (Chicago: University of Chicago Press, 1989), 92; and Terry Pinkard, *Hegel's Naturalism: Mind, Nature, and the Final Ends of Life* (Oxford: Oxford University Press, 2012), 175.
21 Hegel, *Hegel's Aesthetics* I:99; *Ästhetik* I:107.
22 Ibid.
23 One of Jean-Marie Schaeffer's chief complaints against the speculative theory of art is that it presupposes something that only makes sense within a theological worldview: that "beyond our world exists another truer world and that we are capable of acceding to this world by transcending our intramundane nature." Schaeffer, *Art of the Modern Age*, 92.
24 Guyer, "Aesthetics," in *The Oxford Handbook of German Philosophy in the Nineteenth Century*, ed. Michael Forster and Kristen Gjesdal (Oxford: Oxford University Press, 2015), 504.
25 Lopes, *Beyond Art* (Oxford: Oxford University Press, 2014), 35.
26 Hegel, *Hegel's Aesthetics* I:7; *Ästhetik* I:19.
27 Readers have attempted to integrate this sort of claim into Hegel's aesthetics in various ways. For example, Benjamin Rutter has characterized Hegel's theory of aesthetic truth as one that places an "epistemic constraint on artistic value"; in particular, it implies that an artwork must offer us a tenable picture of human life in order to succeed as art, though this is only a necessary, not a sufficient, condition. See Rutter, *Hegel and the Modern Arts* (Cambridge: Cambridge University Press, 2010), 18–19. Stephen Bungay's account of truth is more complex, admitting of two importantly different senses of truth in Hegel, but it also ends up separating the question of truth (does the artwork correctly depict the seriously held beliefs of a society?) from the distinct question of aesthetic merit. See Bungay, *Beauty and Truth: A Study in Hegel's Aesthetics* (Oxford: Oxford University Press, 1984).
28 Geuss, "Art and Theodicy," 111, f. 11.
29 *Hegel's Aesthetics* I:437; *Ästhetik* I:423.
30 *Hegel's Aesthetics* I:508; *Ästhetik* I:489.
31 *Hegel's Aesthetics* I:158; *Ästhetik* I:160.
32 *Hegel's Aesthetics* I:527; *Ästhetik* I:508.
33 In fact, Hegel is ambivalent about the need for historical correctness in art. See, for example, his interesting discussion of anachronism in art: *Hegel's Aesthetics* I:277ff.; *Ästhetik* I:271ff.

34 Friedrich Nietzsche, *The Birth of Tragedy and Other Writings*, trans. R. Speirs (Cambridge: Cambridge University Press, 1999), 33. For both Hegel and the early Nietzsche, art provides us with the satisfaction of viewing human affairs, not from the point of view of the finite individual but from a putatively divine or nonfinite perspective—the point of view, as Nietzsche puts it, of the "original artist of the world." Nietzsche differs from Hegel in thinking that this standpoint is "entirely illusory" rather than the supreme truth of spirit or human subjectivity. For a thorough discussion of what he calls Nietzsche's "epistemically neutral conception of justification," see Daniel Came, "The Aesthetic Justification of Existence," in *The Blackwell Companion to Nietzsche*, ed. Keith Ansell-Pearson (Oxford: Blackwell, 2005), 41–56. This connection between Hegel and the early Nietzsche—namely, their shared commitment to the idea of an aesthetic theodicy—is also helpfully discussed by William Desmond in *Art and the Absolute*, 150ff.

35 Geuss, "Art and Theodicy," 89.

36 The word *Optimismus*, for example, does not appear in the lectures on fine art. When Hegel uses the word in other locations, like in his unpublished lectures on the history of philosophy, he has Leibniz's metaphysical version of optimism in mind.

37 That aesthetic experience is essentially characterized by the feeling of bliss is also emphasized by Julia Peters in *Hegel on Beauty* (New York: Routledge, 2015), 64–66, though she associates it more closely with beauty and thus with the classical art form than I will here.

38 *Hegel's Aesthetics* I:157; *Ästhetik* I:159.

39 *Hegel's Aesthetics* II:831; *Ästhetik* II:206.

40 For a helpful general account of the contrast between *Glückseligkeit* and *Seligkeit* in German Idealism, see Massimo Mori, "Glück und Autonomie. Die deutsche Debatte über den Eudämonismus zwischen Aufklärung und Idealismus," *Studia Leibnitiana*, Bd. 25, H. 1 (1993): 38–42.

41 Hegel, *Faith and Knowledge*, trans. W. Cerf (Albany: SUNY Press, 1977), 59–60.

42 Hegel, *The Philosophical Propaedeutic*, trans. M. George and A. Vincent (Oxford: Blackwell, 1986).

43 *Hegel's Aesthetics* II:816; *Ästhetik* II:192.

44 Hegel, *Hegel's Aesthetics* I:158; *Ästhetik* I:160.

45 Hegel, *Hegel's Aesthetics* II:1232; *Ästhetik* II:581.

46 Hegel, *Hegel's Aesthetics* I:546; *Ästhetik* I:525. The actual phrase here is "die Seligkeit der Marter." All of these passages concern the romantic art form, which, as we will see, is characterized precisely by its capacity to maximize this internal dissonance.

47 *Hegel's Aesthetics* II:1200; *Ästhetik* II:553.

48 See, for example, *Eudemian Ethics* 1215a7-11. In the *Nicomachean Ethics*, the terms appear to be used synonymously. Whether there is any real distinction between these in Aristotle, or whether this distinction only emerged afterward, is controversial. See the helpful discussion in Frits Gåvertson, "Eudaimonism: A Brief Conceptual History," http://www.fil.lu.se/media/utbildning/dokument/kurser/FPRK01/20131/Eud aimonism_abrief_conceptual_history.pdf.

49 See Hegel, *Philosophy of Mind*, §384–86, and *Encyclopedia of the Philosophical Sciences in Basic Outline, Part I: Science of Logic*, trans. K. Brinkmann and D. Dahlstrom (Cambridge: Cambridge University Press, 2010), §212 A.

50 *Hegel's Aesthetics* I:371; *Ästhetik* I:361.

51 *Hegel's Aesthetics* II:1222; *Ästhetik* II:572.

52 *Hegel's Aesthetics* I:508; *Ästhetik* I:489.

53 *Hegel's Aesthetics* I:537; *Ästhetik* I:517.
54 Hardimon, *Hegel's Social Philosophy: The Project of Reconciliation* (Cambridge: Cambridge University Press, 1994). Hardimon himself clearly acknowledges that social reconciliation is only one part of Hegel's larger project of reconciliation.
55 Hardimon, *Hegel's Social Philosophy*, 91–92.
56 Ibid., 246.
57 *Hegel's Aesthetics* I:258; *Ästhetik* I:254.
58 This is another variant of the worry that art is ideological, though here the concern is not with certain epistemic features of the artwork, that is, the ways it might misrepresent the world, but rather with the way art might function to stabilize forms of domination or exploitation. For a classical statement of this worry, see Herbert Marcuse's "The Affirmative Character of Culture," in *Negations: Essays in Critical Theory*, trans. Jeremy J. Shapiro (London: MayFlyBooks, 2009).
59 Nietzsche, *The Will to Power*, trans. Walter Kaufmann and R. J. Hollingdale (New York: Vintage, 1967), §416.

Bibliography

Abrams, M. H. *Natural Supernaturalism: Tradition and Revolution in Romantic Literature*. New York: Norton, 1971.
Aristotle, *The Eudemian Ethics (Oxford World's Classics)*. Oxford: Oxford University Press, 2011.
Bernstein, J. M. "Our Amphibian Problem: Nature in History in Adorno's Hegelian Critique of Hegel." In *Hegel on Philosophy in History*, edited by James Kreines and Rachel Zuckert, 193–212. Cambridge: Cambridge University Press, 2017.
Bungay, Stephen. *Beauty and Truth: A Study in Hegel's Aesthetics*. Oxford: Oxford University Press, 1984.
Came, Daniel. "The Aesthetic Justification of Existence." In *The Blackwell Companion to Nietzsche*, edited by Keith Ansell-Pearson, 41–56. Oxford: Blackwell, 2005.
De Man, Paul. "The Rhetoric of Temporality." In *Interpretation: Theory and Practice*, edited by Charles S. Singleton, 173–209. Baltimore: Johns Hopkins University Press, 1969.
Desmond, William. *Art and the Absolute*. Albany: SUNY, 1986.
Frank, Manfred. "On the Unknowability of the Absolute." In *The Philosophical Foundations of Early German Romanticism*, translated by Elizabeth Millán-Zaibert, 35–76. Albany: SUNY, 2008.
Gardner, Sebastian. "The Romantic-Metaphysical Theory of Art." *European Journal of Philosophy* 10, no. 3 (2002): 275–301.
Gåvertson, Frits. "Eudaimonism: A Brief Conceptual History." Available online at: http://www.fil.lu.se/media/utbildning/dokument/kurser/FPRK01/20131/Eudaimonism_abrief_conceptual_history.pdf.
Geuss, Raymond. "Art and Theodicy." In *Morality, Culture, and History*, 78–115. Cambridge: Cambridge University Press, 1999.
Geuss, Raymond. *Outside Ethics*. Princeton: Princeton University Press, 2009.
Guyer, Paul. "Aesthetics." In *The Oxford Handbook of German Philosophy in the Nineteenth Century*, edited by Michael Forster and Kristin Gjesdal. Oxford: Oxford University Press, 2015. https://www.oxfordhandbooks.com/view/10.1093/oxfordhb/9780199696543.001.0001/oxfordhb-9780199696543-e-25?print=pdf.

Hardimon, Michael. *Hegel's Social Philosophy: The Project of Reconciliation*. Cambridge: Cambridge University Press, 1994.
Hegel, G. W. F. *Ästhetik*, Vol. 1. Berlin: Aufbau-Verlag, 1965.
Hegel, G. W. F. *Elements of the Philosophy of Right*, translated by H. B. Nisbet. Cambridge: Cambridge University Press, 1991.
Hegel, G. W. F. *Encyclopedia of the Philosophical Sciences in Basic Outline, Part I: Science of Logic*, translated by K. Brinkmann and D. Dahlstrom. Cambridge: Cambridge University Press, 2010.
Hegel, G. W. F. *Faith and Knowledge*, translated by W. Cerf. Albany: SUNY Press, 1977.
Hegel, G. W. F. *Hegel's Aesthetics: Lectures on Fine Art: Volume I*, translated by T. M. Knox. Cambridge: Cambridge University Press, 1975.
Hegel, G. W. F. *Lectures on the History of Philosophy 1825–6, Volume I: Introduction and Oriental Philosophy*, translated by R. F. Brown and M. Stewart. Oxford: Oxford University Press, 2009.
Hegel, G. W. F. *Lectures on the Philosophy of World History: Introduction*, translated by H. B. Nisbet. Cambridge: Cambridge University Press, 1975.
Hegel, G. W. F. *The Philosophical Propaedeutic*, translated by M. George and A. Vincent. Oxford: Blackwell, 1986.
Hegel, G. W. F. *Philosophy of Mind*, translated by A. V. Miller. Oxford: Oxford University Press, 1971.
Horowitz, Gregory. *Sustaining Loss: Art and Mournful Life*. Stanford: Stanford University Press, 2002.
Houlgate, Stephen. *Freedom, Truth, and History: An Introduction to Hegel's Philosophy*. London: Routledge, 1991.
Knappik, Franz. "'Gegenwärtige prosaische Zustände': Hegels melancholische Ästhetik und Schillers politische Eschatologie." In *Objektiver und absoluter Geist nach Hegel*, edited by Thomas Oehl and Arthur Kok, 504–26. Leiden and Boston: Brill, 2018.
Lopes, Dominic McIver. *Beyond Art*. Oxford: Oxford University Press, 2014.
Marcuse, Herbert. "The Affirmative Character of Culture." In *Negations: Essays in Critical Theory*, translated by Jeremy J. Shapiro. London: MayFlyBooks, 2009.
McCumber, John. *Poetic Interaction: Language, Freedom, Reason*. Chicago: University of Chicago, 1989.
Menke, Christoph. *Die Tragödie im Sittlichen: Gerechtigkeit und Freiheit nach Hegel*. Frankfurt am Main: Suhrkamp, 1996.
Mori, Massimo. "Glück und Autonomie. Die deutsche Debatte über den Eudämonismus zwischen Aufklärung und Idealismus." *Studia Leibnitiana*, Bd. 25, H. 1 (1993): 27–42.
Nietzsche, Friedrich. *The Birth of Tragedy and Other Writings*, translated by R. Speirs. Cambridge: Cambridge University Press, 1999.
Nietzsche, Friedrich. *The Will to Power*, translated by Walter Kaufmann and R. J. Hollingdale. New York: Vintage, 1967.
Peters, Julia. *Hegel on Beauty*. New York: Routledge, 2015.
Pinkard, Terry. *Hegel's Naturalism: Mind, Nature, and the Final Ends of Life*. Oxford: Oxford University Press, 2012.
Pippin, Robert. *After the Beautiful: Hegel and Pictorial Modernism*. Chicago: The University of Chicago, 2014.
Rutter, Benjamin. *Hegel and the Modern Arts*. Cambridge: Cambridge University Press, 2010.
Schaeffer, Jean-Marie. *Art of the Modern Age: Philosophy of Art from Kant to Heidegger*, translated by Steven Rendall. Princeton: Princeton University Press, 2000.

2

Hegel on the Aesthetic Basis of State Sovereignty

David Ciavatta

The particular question I will be addressing in this chapter is whether an appreciation of beauty has any essential role to play in Hegel's conception of the modern state and in the establishment of its sovereignty. Generally speaking, Hegel conceives of the beauty of art as playing a much less crucial role in modern life than it did in the ancient world.[1] In his account of ancient Greece and its "religion of art," Hegel argues that the intuition of beauty was itself the most fundamental and authoritative form in which the highest spiritual truths were revealed: it is precisely insofar as the divine manifested itself as *beautiful*—for instance, in the form of beautiful statues, temples, and in poetry—that the gods first came to life for the Greeks, and thereby came to inform their overall self-conception and their conception of the world as a whole.[2] Hegel thus comes to regard the intuition of beauty as the very foundation of all other aspects of Greek life, including its ethical life and politics.[3]

But with the demise of the ancient world, and in particular with the rise of Christianity, the ultimate form in which the highest spiritual truth is disclosed goes through a significant transformation according to Hegel: rather than being rooted primarily in intuition [*Anschauung*]—in an experience that takes the form of sensuous encounters with certain privileged external objects, particularly artworks, in their immediacy—there is now a turn inward, toward the interiority of the subject itself as the fundamental locus for the disclosure of ultimate truths.[4] Thus, for instance, the Christian ascetic can claim to attain a purer relation to the divine precisely by renouncing worldly things so as to be able to focus more intensely on the inherently inward and personal struggle to attain genuine faith: the divine, here, reveals itself above all in and through the inward, soul-searching of the heart, rather than to the senses.[5] For Hegel, the spirit of Christianity and, ultimately, the spirit of modernity as a whole are premised upon the recognition of the sovereignty of self-reflective subjectivity and the infinite freedom of the inner realm, and this renders beauty's rootedness in sensuous nature, and in the intrinsic significance of outward-directed intuition, inessential or merely supplementary.[6] Whereas the beauty of Greek art was an original and irreducible source of divine truth in its own right, the beauty of *modern* art—what Hegel calls romantic art—can at best offer a confirmation or elaboration of a truth brought into play independently of it by the historical development and religious teachings of Christianity and the secular spirit of modernity that grew out of it.[7] And, generally speaking, the sensuous, intuitive domain of modern art serves at best to draw attention away from itself as such, away from its own outward forms of beauty, and instead toward the primacy of the inner realm and its *inner beauty*[8]—toward a realm that is defined, in part, in terms of an opposition to, or at least a withdrawal and independence from, any and all specific outward forms.

To the extent that the politics of the modern world, as Hegel conceives of it, is itself essentially structured in terms of a recognition of the primacy and infinite freedom of subjectivity's internal self-relation, then, it would seem that art and its beauty could have at best an inessential, supplementary role to play in the political realm as well.[9] Ultimately, the state's sovereign law, its fundamental universality, is located in the element of self-conscious thought and rationality.[10] This means that its authority is something we all have direct access to from within ourselves as self-conscious, rational beings, rather than having to have its authority made manifest to us as such in an outward, immediate form that is adequate to it. That is, beauty in its ideal form, understood in terms of a meaning or truth that finds its proper and sufficient expression in an immediate, intuitable form, becomes inessential to the modern state and to political self-consciousness.

However, the modern state and its sovereignty are not *just* ideal, internal, and universal in nature. The state is also, necessarily and by its own internal logic, a finite, concrete individual that, as such, is necessarily embroiled in the contingent events of history and has to affirm and demonstrate its sovereignty precisely in and through essentially finite events and decisions. That is, *the state must appear*, must have an *outward* side,[11] and so, it seems, cannot be *wholly* independent of the sphere of sensuous intuition. As we will see, Hegel argues that it is in the state's encounters with other states in times of war, and notably in the momentous decisions and events that arise in such crisis moments, that the concrete individuality of its sovereignty makes itself most pronounced to the consciousness of its citizens: for, in such extraordinary, crisis moments what becomes immediately present to all citizens as overriding their own particularity and its serial, atomized reality, is precisely their collective unity as such in its concrete, historical destiny. Hegel even goes so far as to suggest that the state occasionally *needs* such moments of crisis in order to reaffirm its sovereignty in the lives of its citizens. This would seem to imply that there is something inherently *disillusioning* about everyday, prosaic life within the state, something that in effect *conceals* and thus works to undermine the absolute, essentially self-conscious character of its sovereignty. So, though wars are typically occasioned by contingent, external events, Hegel notoriously suggests that the very logic of the state makes them necessary:[12] for, by punctuating the flow of everyday life with such moments of crisis, the state makes the distinctive, overriding power of its universality vividly and immediately manifest to citizens who otherwise tend to get lost in relative, prosaic, and partisan concerns of the everyday.

I will be exploring the possibility that it is precisely here, in relation to such extraordinary moments of concrete self-manifestation on the part of state sovereignty, that we enter a terrain in which aesthetic intuition and the beautiful may have a decisive political role to play in the modern state after all. What is vividly and concretely apparent in moments of state crisis is precisely the unity of the state's universality with its concrete, historical individuality, the compelling sense that what is happening here and now, in the drama of the concrete, finite event that we as a collective are involved in, directly concerns nothing other than the fate of the universal as such, the fate of that collective itself, which alone makes possible the lives and freedoms to which we have become accustomed. These momentous events are not merely one instantiation among others of the state's universal sovereignty—merely prosaic instantiations of its existing, stable laws, for instance—but are distinguished precisely by their extraordinariness and all-or-nothing character, and by the fact that what is fundamentally in question in them is the very sovereignty and efficacy of law itself. As I will argue, for Hegel, beauty is concerned precisely with such intense and vivid unities of universality and individuality, and precisely with the sorts of decisive, dramatic, and extra-legal moments in which alone law comes to establish its sovereignty. It is worth exploring, then, whether such a heightened and privileged manifestation of the state's sovereignty requires special appeal to a direct, concrete, and sensuously mediated intuition of its universality, and so to the sort of phenomena at the heart of beauty, rather than merely to the distinctively inward, rational core of sovereign authority.

I begin with an exploration of Hegel's account of the inherently finite and prosaic character of practical life *within* the modern state, and the implication that life within such a state affords only very meager opportunities for the concrete intuition of beauty. It is against this backdrop that we can appreciate Hegel's account of why it is that artworks often turn to the stateless individual hero—what Hegel calls "beautiful individuality"—for their subject matter. Hegel argues essentially that there is a much greater poetic potential, and so a much greater opportunity for the intuition of beauty, in an encounter with a heroic life freed from the prosaic limitations of the laws and institutions of a developed state.[13] I then compare the specific, stateless conditions of the beautiful appearance of such heroic action with the sort of extraordinary, crisis moments brought on by the modern state's internal need to reaffirm its sovereignty. Such crises are likewise premised upon entering into a terrain beyond the scope of prosaic life, a dramatic terrain in which sovereignty itself hangs in the balance, and in this respect the prosaic ways of seeing essential to state life are themselves fundamentally disrupted: what is required, in effect, is a way of seeing that is capable of appreciating the heightened, all-or-nothing stakes of an extraordinary moment of action and, I suggest, this way of seeing is essentially the same as what is appealed to in Hegel's account of our aesthetic appreciation of artistically rendered heroic action.

The Prosaic Character of Modern Life

In the context of his *Aesthetics*, Hegel goes to some length to argue that there is little in our actual lives as members of the modern state that is itself capable of manifesting beauty: there may still be beautiful artworks, but there is no broader sense in which *life itself* manifests beauty, as it arguably did in the Greek world according to Hegel's account, and there seems to be no sense in which our relation to the state and its sovereignty (and indeed our relation to practical life generally) is essentially dependent upon, or informed by, an aesthetic intuition of beauty. However, even if Hegel is right in his broader, historical judgment that beauty has ceased to be the most essential form in which ultimate truths about ourselves and the world are disclosed to us, this does not imply that we moderns somehow became wholly indifferent to beauty. That is, we still have a fundamental interest in and openness to being gripped by beautiful phenomena, and presumably the *lack* of any such phenomena would be an impoverishment of our lives. And, since we cannot but engage in an ongoing intuition of the external world in its individuality and concrete immediacy, it seems that we cannot but be alive to the issue of whether the various individuals and concrete situations we intuit are beautiful or not, the issue of whether or not the world around us, as well as our own concrete actions in this world, are capable of manifesting in themselves, *in their immediate, intuitable form*, the higher truth of who we are as spiritual agents. And so if modern social life itself is indeed essentially *prosaic* in character, and so lacks any prospect of manifesting beauty in itself, this would seem to be a deficiency.

Indeed, Hegel argues that beauty is, among other things, something that makes manifest to us the reality of freedom itself in a concrete, palpable form, and so presumably a social world that was not characterized in any way by beauty—a world that was prosaic through and through—would be a source of constant frustration and tension.[14] For this would be tantamount to presenting sensuous intuition with an *absence* of freedom, with a domain characterized primarily by finitude, limitation, fragmentation, and instrumentality. If there were a political state that was in principle committed to recognizing and realizing the freedom of its individual citizens, but which, in its actual, concrete, and sensuous side, afforded individuals only with the prosaic unfreedom of daily needs and work life, presumably the capacity of individuals to fully appreciate the freedom their state affords them would be limited or impoverished thereby, and so presumably their more immediate, intuitive relation to their environments would be in tension with their "inward" relation to their freedom.[15] I will eventually argue that, on Hegel's account, even the modern, prosaic state cannot do without some appeal to the aesthetic intuition of beauty in establishing itself, but first we must come to terms with why it is that Hegel thinks that everyday life in the modern state is itself largely devoid of beauty.

As part of his argument that artworks, rather than any natural or spontaneously occurring phenomena, constitute the privileged site for the embodiment of beauty, Hegel makes a point of singling out the actual practical life of humans as one of those naturally occurring, spatiotemporal phenomena that are incapable of adequately embodying beauty.[16] Broadly speaking, the actual practical realm is thoroughly plagued by finitude, with the result that individual human actions are always functions of, or responsive to, external forces that they themselves did not put into play.[17] Beautiful artworks, in contrast, manifest a kind of superlative independence and self-sufficiency as concrete individuals, insofar as they are essentially self-determining, original wholes that articulate their own parts and their own internal terms of reference, showing no adherence to external forces or standards. And, this self-sufficiency and self-determining character is manifest specifically in an immediate, intuitively apprehensible form, as, for instance, in the way the various colors on the surface of a painting visually cohere with each other to make manifest to the eye a unified lighting scheme throughout, such that we experience the painting as a kind of self-standing visual domain of its own.[18] Indeed, rather than simply being one among many other physical objects, each of which stands in the light of this room and thus depends for its visibility on this light, the painting has, in addition, an *inner light of its own* that is independent of the lighting of the room itself; this individual stands out as being its own visual world and is in that sense not straightforwardly determined by the physical world that surrounds it.[19] In comparison, individual human actions never fully stand on their own as complete, self-determining wholes but are always to some extent occasioned by, or otherwise dependent upon, external circumstances or the actions of others. As such, they can only be understood in reference to what is ultimately external to them, and this fact alone makes any beauty they might have inherently impoverished compared to works of art.

Hegel suggests that, from an aesthetic point of view, things are no better in the case of an individual's life within a well-governed modern state, and this despite the fact that the state organizes human actions so as to realize a collective unity among them. Within the state, argues Hegel, there is no escaping the fact that what we as individuals do is inevitably grounded upon, and so a sort of repetition of, the actions of other agents or of the state itself. For in this context the very situations we face, the norms and imperatives operative in them, along with the resources we have to address them, are provided by institutionalized forces that far exceed our capacities as individual agents and that are at bottom indifferent to us as the particular individuals we are. Within the life of the state, extraordinary, unprecedented judgments may sometimes be required by certain accomplished individuals, as in the case of a court justice presiding over a peculiar case that perhaps reveals an unforeseen inconsistency between existing laws, or in its singularity defies assimilation to any prior precedents. Such an action does lay claim to being a self-sufficient, self-determining whole, at least insofar as the free, creative judgment of the individual constitutes its backbone. But even in such a case the individual is positioned to act only in virtue of the institutions that authorize her, and that provide her with the resources and the overall context and goals in the first place.[20] Moreover, though the judge might be extraordinary at what she does, the abilities that qualify her for the job are essentially universal ones that others might in principle also possess, and so her individuality is in no way essential to the matter at hand.[21] Not only could others substitute for her, but if she for some reason proved corrupt, and let her individuality exert undue influence on her judgment, there are mechanisms in place to appeal or otherwise address such corruptions, restoring the universality and neutrality that are characteristic of such institutions. As such, even such decisive actions fall short of the sort of individual self-sufficiency and wholeness that Hegel thinks are required for beauty and aesthetic intuition. They are inevitably mere instantiations or repetitions of laws or institutional arrangements that are stably in place prior to them.

This ultimate tension between universality and individuality seems to be structurally unavoidable in the political realm, despite the various institutional mechanisms that the state develops in order to mediate this tension.[22] Particularly in the case of the modern state, Hegel argues that there is necessarily a privileging of certain kinds of reality—above all, the objective reality of law, along with the state's constitutional structure and legally recognized standing institutions—that in their very form are premised precisely upon their *independence* from all determinate, concrete realities.[23] Though objective, law is essentially ideal and universal in its reality, and so any finite, individuated, historical expression of it will be inadequate to establish or manifest it fully: as universal, it necessarily transcends every particular manifestation of it in concrete word or deed, and its sovereign authority is not in any way tied to its particular manifestations or instantiations; certainly its authority is not tied to any particular individual, for from its universal point of view every individual is essentially substitutable by others, as we've seen in the case of the judge.[24] While such institutions of course exist nowhere other than in the various individual actions that instantiate them, and so their objectivity is, in effect, the actuality of collective practical life, neither any one action nor any collective of actions is sufficient on its own to make the underlying universality of law apparent: one needs to grasp the law in a manner that is, at bottom, independent of any of its concrete instantiations. Just as no series of individual, visible triangles can be sufficient on its own to make manifest the one essence of triangularity that governs them all (for, of course, all visible triangles will necessarily have particular, contingent elements that are inessential to their triangularity as such and cannot on their own account differentiate between the essential and the contingent);[25] so too, none of one's actions in conformity to law, nor the collective of such actions, will be sufficient to manifest all that the law involves. Like the essence of triangularity, the laws, it seems, must ultimately be grasped by an internal act of thought that is, at bottom, independent of the empirical domain, and so with reference to an ideal, rational domain that has its own internal necessity. Only thus do the sovereign laws' essential power to override all individual claims prevail in and for individuals themselves.

It is this fundamental separation between individuality and universality, and between concrete lived experience and thought, that helps to explain Hegel's aesthetic judgment that the various dimensions of life in the state, and particularly within the state's civil sphere, fail to reveal its unity directly to concrete intuition.[26] When we are walking about in a busy city, for instance, we can easily be struck by the absence of any apparent sense of unity that joins the various people and projects we see into a meaningful, self-defining whole: we tend to be caught up in particularities, including our own, and so are most immediately alive to the externality, and often the indifference, between the different projects on view, as well as to their indefinite and exhausting proliferation. Aside from the various private individuals, the pedestrians, drivers, and store clerks, we also see distinct manifestations of public life, for instance, the street itself, police officers, the public park, the diverse architectural choices of the buildings, and the commercial billboards; but here too we are alive most to these forces in their particularity and in their contingent, finite roles, with the result that here too no fundamental unity or harmony is immediately apparent among them.[27] For many, this experience of endless particularity in its proliferation can be overwhelming and alienating at an immediate, affective, and even aesthetic level; that is, the experience of the frustrating finitude of prosaic social life is not itself aesthetically neutral, but rather an experience of a deficiency of aesthetic value. Of course, we can, nevertheless, find order and unity among this multiplicity, but this seems to require rising above the concrete individuals we find before us, and grasping *in thought* the universality that underlies them: for instance, our intellectual, theoretical grasp of economic systems and the complex interconnections of the multiple forces that are at play in them, as well as the government regulations and agencies that limit and enable them, might allow us to see regularity and even socially essential processes at play in the apparent chaos and contingency; but this order does not appear concretely to intuition in and through the individuals themselves, and is especially not apparent to us while we are in the midst of the fray, engaged by our particular practical projects and perceiving the world around us through them.[28]

Hegel notes that, both at the individual level and at the level of a society's various particular groups and agencies—even among the particular branches of government itself—there is a general tendency for particularity to overshadow its rootedness in the universal and its orderly, organic relation to other particularities, to the point of becoming at odds with it.[29] It seems that this absence of a direct, concrete, and intuitive manifestation of the universal is relevant for understanding how it is that individuals come to feel at odds with the universal; for, if their immediate, practical world persistently announces its endless particularity and externality and finitude, and itself offers little indication of a collective universal that underlies and organizes this sphere, we are faced—aesthetically, as it were—with a constant reminder of the ultimacy of finitude. Unlike the well-composed painting all of whose distinct elements cohere into a visually apparent unity, the cityscape presents us with the primacy of fragments and mutual externality.

Furthermore, Hegel notes that we tend to lose sight of the fact that various particular freedoms we enjoy, such as our capacity to walk the streets safely at night, are the effect of universal state institutions, rather than just being the way the practical world is in its natural immediacy.[30] This habitual trust and the sense of order that one thus relies upon in the carefree, unthinking way one takes an evening stroll, is, in a way, a practical demonstration of one's trust in the state itself and its well-functioning; and, indeed, one's own carefree walking is part of what helps to *constitute* the dimly lit streets as safe, at least to the extent that one's being at ease projects around it a safe world and announces to others something of the reality of that world. However, to the extent that the streets just appear naturally welcoming to our individual walking, as though they were always already there for our particular use and enjoyment, we lose sight of the fact that this ease is *actively maintained by the collective*—ultimately, the state—of which we are participating members.[31]

Because we are in this way embedded in particularity, and so are not directly alive, from within our projects themselves and their particular practical exigencies, to the universality and collectivity that underlies and informs them throughout, one of the conditions for the possibility of the rise of the state, in Hegel's view, is that ways be developed of linking the practical exigencies of concrete, practical life with the essentially universal demands of the state, conceived of as that encompassing collective reality, the concrete universal, that is an end in itself. This way, work done by individuals and for the sake of their particular interests come to be, at once, work for the sake of recognizing and reproducing the state itself, and so the universality of the state's demands gets a concrete practical grip on individuals, rather than remaining something merely inner and ideal.[32] However, the task of reconciling the particular with the universal is a never-ending one, requiring constant attention and never guaranteed of success. That is, the balance is itself finite and contingent; the unity of the particular and the universal, of the concrete and the law, is not itself granted with law-like regularity.

It is essentially this constitutive discrepancy between the universal and the particular that seems to rule out the possibility of beauty playing any essential role in the political sphere. For beauty, on Hegel's account, is premised upon the fundamental, inextricable unity between the universal and the particular, between meaning and its concrete embodiment: rather than being a relation of instantiation between a law that pre-exists its concrete expression and the concrete individual that expresses it, beauty confronts us with a universal or a law that comes to life above all in its exemplary embodiment in concrete form, and it is this fittingness between the universal and the individual that constitutes the core of beauty.

Beautiful Individuality

As we have seen, on Hegel's account, there are fundamental ways in which actual practical life fails to manifest beauty. It is this deficiency, and along with it the deficiencies inherent in all finite, natural objects, that brings Hegel to consider the domain of human-made artworks as better suited to the realization of beauty and its intrinsic demands for the presentation of a self-sufficient, self-determining individual whole. However, as he goes on to offer an account of the ideal forms in which beauty can be made manifest in artworks, Hegel comes to focus primarily on the drama of human action as a privileged site for the manifestation of beauty: that is, despite its constitutive finitude of practical life, it nevertheless stands out among other phenomena in the natural, empirical world as an exceptionally rich "material" for artistic rendering.[33] What is at issue here is how it is that artworks *idealize* action by eliminating or downplaying the aspects of finitude and dependence inherent in them, and thereby transform them into a site in which the self-determining, infinite movement of spirit can come to appear in a concrete, intuitive form.

For instance, one way to idealize our practical reality is by depicting a gesture of *withdrawal* from it. Hegel gives the example of Murillo's painting *The Toilette* (1670–75), which depicts a boy who, despite his squalid social conditions, appears turned inward to the domain of his own subjectivity, suggesting his enjoyment of the infinite interiority of the subject and its ultimate freedom from all practical life.[34] Far from being simply determined by his circumstances, then, the boy appears to be located instead in the self-sufficient, self-determining realm of his own interiority. Artworks might also depict agents as absorbed in otherwise alienating daily work, as though this work were a full-fledged end itself rather than merely a finite means of answering to the needs of life. One might consider Vermeer's *The Milkmaid* (1660) as a good example here: in virtue of the maid's tender and relaxed attentiveness to the trickle of milk pouring slowly out of her jug, it is as though the rest of the world falls away, as though, rather than being a servant in the midst of a day's tiresome tasks, answering to the demands of her employer, she were finding an infinite, self-sufficient value in the quiet stillness and purity of her simple act. Thus artistic idealization works to relinquish the practical world of its jarring finitude and relativity, so as to let it appear in its serene self-sufficiency.

But for Hegel, these are hardly the sorts of scenarios that provide art with the most suitable occasions in terms of which to make the scope, efficacy, and potentially self-determining character of human practical life most fully manifest. Much better to focus on the heightened, momentous deeds of the passionate, fully engaged hero, argues Hegel, deeds that respond to some fundamental ethical controversy about what it is to be human and how humans ought to comport themselves in the face of their natural and social worlds.[35] Much as in Kant's account of moral autonomy, for Hegel it is precisely when action aims at realizing what is most noble in human life—that is, in bringing into play the unconditioned and universal ethical and political forces that underlie and give normative articulation to all human endeavor—that it is itself genuinely free and self-determining. Whereas everyday acts, for instance, those that cater to natural needs, can be made by an artist to signify something of the timeless movement of spirit, it is the dramatic ethical act, in which the hero puts all on the line to stand up for something expressly spiritual in character—an ethical force that would not prevail but for the will's free and active commitment to it—that freedom, and so beauty, are made most fully evident to us, argues Hegel.[36] What is typically at issue in the sorts of high-stakes actions Hegel has in mind is not just some relative, local matter, but the very capacity of human spirit to make itself at home in the world, our very capacity to give rise to a "spiritualized world" in which justice and right and free will—and not merely the contingency of nature—prevail. Thus in Sophocles's *Antigone* (to take one of Hegel's recurring examples), Antigone risks all for the sake of the right of the human dead to be properly memorialized, rather than being simply obliterated by ravaging dogs and birds: it is spirit's capacity to respond meaningfully to, and to incorporate within its domain, death itself—rather than death remaining something contingent that "merely happens" to individuals—that is on the line in her determination to disobey Creon.[37]

One of the core features of the beautiful heroic action, as Hegel conceives of it, is that it stands on its own as a kind of self-determining, complete—and so infinite—whole. Like the act of Vermeer's milkmaid, which is presented in its quiet purity as though it were an absorbing end in itself and as though it were the central focus of the world around it, the heroic act is typically portrayed as though it were the central focus of the social-cultural world in which the agents live. But whereas the act of pouring milk, by itself, is but one of many possible *instantiations* of freedom—following Hegel's discussion of Dutch genre paintings, we might see such an act in the light of the hard-won freedom of the Dutch spirit in its overcoming of the various opposing forces of nature and political challenges[38]—the heroic action is typically a singular act upon which the fate of the agent's whole world is quite literally at stake: the act typically responds to or brings to a head a fundamental structural conflict that puts into question the very coherence of the social-cultural world in which the agent lives, and so what is at issue in the action is the restoring of this disrupted coherence. So, even though this act is finite and relative like every other, for instance, in that its specific occasion arises only as a result of the contingent natural occurrences or the actions of others, the singular, heightened character it takes on as a result of its "world-restoring" (or "world-forging") role makes it such as to stand on its own as a self-articulating, free whole: rather than simply being one among many actions occasioned and made possible by the social-cultural world in which it takes place, the heroic action is singled out as the hinge upon which this very world as a whole depends, and so it can be viewed, to some extent, as coming from *beyond* this world and its everyday, empirical conditions. That is, rather than being a *repetition* or *instantiation* of an already prevailing law, the action at issue is tasked with actually giving force to the law, sometimes for the very first time and in a way that would stand as a precedent.[39] Similarly, rather than simply being relative to this or that local affair, it is as though this action were directly the affair of everyone in the community insofar as it is the very stability of their community that is on the line. In the *Antigone*, for instance, this communal stake is manifest in the chorus's keen concern in the affair, in the ruling-class status of the agents involved, and in the prospect that, if Polyneices's corpse is unceremoniously defiled by the dogs and birds, Thebes itself would be under threat of divine justice. Antigone acts alone—and it is in part because of this isolation, because it all comes down to this one will, that her action stands out with such beauty and poignancy—but she acts on behalf of an essentially collective concern, and, in a way, no spectator (whether within the play or in the audience) can take himself to be merely neutral, as though he were not in some way implicated in the substantive matter stood for.

It is this aesthetic privileging of the decisive act's singular status as world-forming or world-preserving that allows us to see why it is that Hegel also privileges the *stateless* hero (for instance, epic figures such as Achilles or Odysseus), or heroes living in a domain in which the formation and maintenance of a stable state is either very primitive or fundamentally contested (as in Creon's Thebes). What most distinguishes such "beautiful individuals" from the state-bound agent is that they are, in their individuality, the exclusive conditions upon which hinge the laws and ethical forces that preside over a people: in an absence of developed state institutions that ensure, as a matter of course, that justice will be served, and that are often so resilient that they can even withstand the negligence or corruption of the particular individuals that are entrusted to administer them, the *only* way justice will be served in this stateless domain is through the contingent resolve, confident energy, and unrelenting perseverance of the individual who is willing to risk all for its sake.[40] In part it is this contingency of the individual will—the fact that, in the end, it is ultimately up to us as individual agents to make ourselves the vessels and exemplars of the universal good—that is crucial for the experience of beauty, for such contingency and its decisiveness is what enables the sort of ontological freedom central to beauty to manifest itself in a concrete, temporal form for intuition.[41]

The Modern State in Its Concrete Individuality

Beauty, as rooted in intuition, is always focused on concrete individuals. Rather than experiencing the individual as an instantiation of a universal, as in the case of the theoretical attitude, aesthetic intuition thoroughly immerses itself in the individual (as, for instance, in the way we immerse ourselves in a particular painting or piece of music) and finds universal meanings at play precisely within this individuality and in its concrete way of manifesting itself to us in intuition.[42] This helps to explain why Hegel's poetics of the beauty of art ends up focusing on the drama of the heroic individual in his or her extraordinary actions: the claim is that human individuals, and in particular human agents in the midst of realizing themselves through action—that is, in the midst of freely individuating themselves, for it is through actions that individuals distinguish themselves from others—are, despite their finitude, the richest sorts of individuals to be found in the empirical world, richest from the point of view of their capacity to make palpable to us the movement of spirit in its self-determination. And it is precisely when such individual actions stand on their own as being of interest in themselves, rather than presenting themselves as one among many instantiations of preexisting, universal institutions, that their individuality attains its highest aesthetic power. This featuring of individuality also explains why the stories we find most compelling tend to be focused on the lives and characters of one, or at most a small handful, of individuals and their concrete interactions, rather on larger collectives from the point of view of which no particular individuals or particular dramas come to be emphasized or privileged: in art, we come to care about universal concerns only to the extent that we can dig in to certain particular characters who embody them, and ideally these individuals are well-rounded, such that their actions come across, not merely as the mechanical instantiations of laws they have arbitrarily committed themselves to, but as living, organic outgrowths of their complex, individual lives.

As we've seen, it is precisely this partiality for the individual and the compelling character of its extraordinary actions that make the scenes of modern life within an established state less capable of manifesting beauty on Hegel's account. While Hegel is steadfast in affirming that we, as essentially thinking, rational beings, cannot but will the state and its laws as an essential condition of our own freedom, and so cannot but affirm that situation in which all of our actions are in effect grounded in and contextualized by state institutions that support and recognize us as individuals, he acknowledges that, from an aesthetic point of view, we cannot quite let go of our fascination with the stateless hero and with the self-sufficient, self-determining, and, indeed, world-forging character of her action.[43] That is, Hegel seems to admit that what reason itself demands, in its underwriting of the necessity of the modern sovereign state, is somewhat at odds with the truth that beauty, in its peak forms, discloses to us: namely, the self-sufficiency of the individual, the capacity of the individual to take the law into her own hands, as it were, and forge an ethical world through her own extraordinary example. To the extent that the beauty of such intensive individual freedom still compels us moderns, presumably there is reason to think that beauty, at least in this its peak forms, is not only inessential to modern state life but at odds with it.[44] But is it the case, then, that the modern state has no place left for such outward, incarnate beauty, and so must resign itself to the prosaic?

In light of this question, we might consider the possibility that there are other forms of individuality, besides the heroic individual and his or her momentous action, that might serve as a comparable material for the intuition of beauty within the modern state. As we've seen, the universality of the state does not itself appear in a concrete, intuitable form in the plurality of the finite, contingent actions of its citizens; the unity underlying all individuality and all particular agencies can perhaps be *thought*, but it does not offer itself as such in an immediate, individuated form. More, when the state is functioning smoothly, such that everyday actions are for the most part in conformity with the demands of state institutions, and trust in the state's efficacy is well entrenched in habit, the universality of the state recedes into the assumed background of everyday life and is not singled out or targeted as such. Just as the fish presumably does not notice the water it swims in, so much as the various particular things that appear to it through this medium and which, in their particularity, set the specific terms of its particular projects and exertions, so too do we tend not to notice the state or its universality as such, so much as the particular, finite projects it enables and which set the concrete terms of our lives.[45] The universality of the state most typically presents itself within experience, then, only as something *negative*, as something that is *not present in its own right* but only as a background element through which particular things present themselves. Indeed, this background character is arguably an essential aspect of the state's infinite and all-comprehending nature, for in this role it is never merely one object in our experience among others, but is *always* presupposed as context whenever something particular appears to us as soliciting our action or our freedom in the first place.

But because this universal element of our lives does not constitute the shared background context for all humans but only those of the particular nation in which we live, it too is necessarily something exclusive and thus individual in nature. And, in its individuality and historical specificity the state does not *merely* recede as the negative background or invisible element underlying the particular and visible, but arguably comes to pronounce itself as such in and to experience. We see a hint of this in Hegel's account of the nature of state constitutions.

In discussing the sovereignty of a state's fundamental constitution, Hegel draws attention not just to its universality but to its inescapable individuality as well. It is universal in that, like a mathematical theorem whose significance transcends the historical acts of discovery that first introduced it to the world, the constitution itself ought to appear as transcending its own historical institution. As he writes, the constitution "should *not* be regarded as *something made*, even if it does have an origin in time. On the contrary, it is quite simply that which has being in and for itself, and should therefore be regarded as divine and enduring, and as exalted above the sphere of all manufactured things."[46]

To say that its authority has a being "in and for itself" is to say that this universal grounds and authorizes itself, that it is, like the unconditioned nature of reason itself, self-determining and self-establishing, and so is in no way beholden to its concrete origination, or, indeed, to any external standard: just as reason, insofar, as it is the presupposition of any particular act of justification, cannot itself be justified by anything but itself, so too the state, as the sphere that is necessarily presupposed whenever any particular interest lays claim to recognition in the public sphere, cannot itself be justified on the grounds of anything particular. And, as with the case of reason itself, it is the inherently universal, self-reflective form of *thought* that is best suited to revealing law's truth and necessity to us.

However, Hegel notes that the constitution is also inherently individual and that this individuality is not irrelevant from the point of view of the establishment of its authority and sovereignty: for a people must immediately experience the constitution as distinctly *its own*—this is why it is not possible to impose a constitution on a people, however rational it might be—and this compelling sense of ownness, which necessarily comes with a sense of exclusiveness, cannot itself be accounted for in terms of its universal dimension and so in terms of *thought*, but only by its rootedness in the *particular* history and character of a *particular* people and by these citizens' capacity to identify themselves, in their individuality, with this unfolding history and character.[47] It seems, then, that the constitution, while it is in certain key respects indifferent and negative toward the individuals and individual acts that instantiate it, must also be accessible in *its* concrete individuality, and in this sense the constitution cannot be *merely* something universal and ideal, cannot be merely something for thought, but must manifest itself concretely, in an individuated, spatiotemporal form—that is, in a form that is most naturally accessed in and through the immediacy of concrete, lived experience, or sensuous intuition. But how does this individuality, which is essentially a collective individuality, or the individuality of a collective, appear, in its individuality, to the various citizens who identify with it—particularly given that in everyday life the most prominent thing that seems to appear is precisely the various finite particulars of practical life in their externality to one another? Presumably the answer to this would be the key to seeing how the sort of sensuous intuition characteristic of aesthetic experience might still have a role to play in the formation of the state and its sovereignty.

Arguably, Hegel's answer comes in his account of those extraordinary moments in which the everyday life of the state is disrupted so fundamentally that the otherwise firm boundaries between individuals and between the particular agencies of the state become negated or blurred: it is such crisis moments, Hegel argues, and above all in times of war with other states, that the otherwise negative reality of state sovereignty, as that which underlies all particular forms of life in their particularity, comes to affirm itself as such. In times of war, Hegel writes, "the state's absolute power over everything individual and particular, over life, property, and the latter's rights, and over the wider circles within it, gives the nullity of such things an existence and makes it present to the consciousness."[48] The palpable presence to consciousness of this nullity of the particular is complex and requires some elaboration. This nullity is, at bottom, that of the finitude of practical life itself in its particularity. Formerly, in the smooth functioning of everyday life, this finitude was effaced, and the particularities of life were embraced as something positive or absolute, that is, in their capacity to set the ultimate terms of practical life; thereby, the universal, the collective way of life that underlies them and makes them possible, is obscured and relegated to an assumed background. But in the singular and disruptive event of war, Hegel argues, such particularity is finally revealed in its truth, namely as something "null" in its own right, something that only is what it is in virtue of the inherently collective context that makes it possible.

As Hegel says, this nullity is itself brought into existence and thereby made present to consciousness. I take it this requires a concrete disruption of the ways of seeing and behaving that are typical of habitual, everyday life, such that individuals can come to experience this nullity directly for themselves, rather than being blinded by the particular exigencies of their more local situations. For instance, the state might take extraordinary measures to require its citizens to join the war cause: in extreme cases, it might force them to work in munitions factories, pay extra taxes, grow their own food to make up for shortages, or draft them into the military. Through such measures, individuals can come to have a firsthand experience of their own particularity—their time, their work, their property, indeed their very lives—as something that is not absolute and permanently fixed, and as something that is not simply a positive and complete reality in its own right, but that is, rather, a merely finite and passing expression of the overall way of life that transcends it and that alone makes it possible. In demanding my property for our collective war effort, the state demonstrates to me that this property was never absolutely and exclusively mine in the first place, that it was only mine insofar as various collective institutions kept it in place. While the state has no right to take my property arbitrarily, now that these collective institutions are themselves under threat, I can be brought to see and even to *affirm for myself* how insignificant and ephemeral my particular property is in comparison to this inherently collective "property." As Hegel writes, "War is that condition in which the vanity of temporal things and temporal goods—which tends at other times to be merely a pious phrase—takes on a serious significance, and it is accordingly the moment in which the ideality of *the particular attains its right* and becomes actuality."[49]

The "ideality of the particular" is precisely that which overcomes the externality of particulars to one another, so as to reveal their fundamental interconnectedness as expressions of the same one social whole. Hegel calls this realization the "willed evanescence" of the finite,[50] and this "negative" will comes hand in hand with an affirmation of, and identification with, the essential priority of the collective over any of its particular, finite expressions.

Note that without a living appreciation of the extraordinary and unsettling context of war, in virtue of which alone these collective institutions are under real threat, the state's demand for me to give up my property is still liable to come across as merely external to me as I continue to cling to what I take to be most my own. It seems, then, that part of what brings home to me the legitimacy of the state's sovereign demand in this case is precisely the crisis moment itself. Indeed, Hegel speaks of war itself—and not simply the state itself in its everyday legislative capacity—as what properly has the "agency" required to break the stagnation of our typical clinging to the finite.[51] Thus, it is above all in the face of an extraordinary threat to the state that the peculiar conditions are opened up for citizens themselves to affirm the finitude of their own particularity and thereby the absolute sovereignty of the "substantial individual."

War is premised upon the state being faced with the threat of its own otherness, its own becoming-other, the threat posed by what is external to its own sovereign domain—most typically *another state*, though presumably civil unrest can also be considered a threatening other in this context. Part of what is key here is that this external relation, this threat of dissolution, "assumes the *shape of an event*, of an involvement with *contingent occurrences* coming *from without*."[52] It is precisely in being immersed in a concrete event in which one is directly faced with the real prospect, not only of one's own death and the death of one's fellow citizens, but the death of the independence of one's state, that the identification of one's individuality with the individuality of the state achieves its highest possible pitch—indeed, Hegel calls this the "state's own highest moment."[53] So, it is precisely in and through the experience of the concrete event of war that the state, as what had been a stable, reliable, habitually repeated background of life, becomes *directly* and *palpably present* in its *concrete individuality*. Presumably, then, it is only through immediate intuition—as that which alone grasps individuality and its concrete, dramatic unfolding in time—that we can come to have access to this "highest moment." Though the state does not manifest itself in the obvious form of some natural individual—for here, it is not merely a matter of protecting a monarch or other ruler but of protecting the underlying constitution and collective institutions that have made up one's independent way of life—it is nevertheless the case that, in war, a decisive moment can be reached in which there is either victory or defeat, and so in which the state itself and its sovereignty either live on or die. Only something fundamentally individuated, only something tied in essential ways to concretely occurring bodies or actions—in other words, only something that is not merely ideal and inward and that as such can in principle transcend all finite particularity, but that has become *incarnated* and thus *intuitable*—can presumably face the brink of historical finality in this way.

While the drama here is not that of the stateless individual hero, but of the state itself in its collective individuality, the parallels to Hegel's account of the distinctive aesthetic power of the hero are striking. Indeed, there is even a sense in which the state's entanglement in war involves entry into a sphere of statelessness much like that of the stateless hero. While, of course, the state's sovereignty still applies to its own citizens in times of war—indeed, it can be more pronounced and thorough in its claims on individual action, particularly for soldiers within a standing military that itself comes to evolve various laws and codes and tribunals[54]—as we have seen it is also the case that, having entered into war, the state itself ultimately gives itself over to the judgment and sovereignty of something that exceeds it: the sovereignty of the event, the sovereignty of history itself. For, while the state has absolute authority within its domestic terrain, in which all relevant particularity is in principle always already managed by it, in war it finds its whole fate hinges on contingent events over which it *cannot* have an absolute say. Victory would no doubt be a profound and dramatic reaffirmation of its independence and sovereignty, and Hegel goes so far as to suggest that a state can come to will war precisely so as to have a stage upon which to make its sovereignty more pronounced, thereby locating even war itself within the rational circuit of its domestic policies; as he says, from this point of view, while war or other crises inevitably are sparked by contingent occasions, they are, in fact, a rational and even essential part of the self-establishment of sovereignty.[55] However, in appealing to such a concrete, palpable self-presentation, and thus to the essentially *dramatic* form of being brought back from the brink, the state necessarily exposes itself to the vulnerability of not being guaranteed victory in advance, and so to the contingency and final decisiveness of the historical event itself. That is, the state affirms its universality *only in and through the particular and contingent*, concentrating its whole reality into the dramatic turn of the event itself. As we have seen, it is such incarnation of the universal into the contingency of the concrete and individual that constitutes a core dimension of beautiful individuality in Hegel's account.

It is true, there is no one individual—neither monarch, nor military strategist, nor brave warrior—who comes to embody the whole of the state that is in crisis. So, unlike the case of the beautiful individual of epic poetry or drama, there is no one protagonist whose character provides an aesthetic point of access to the universal issues that are at stake. As we have seen, the individuality here is essentially a collective individuality, a "we" that joins various single individuals into a collective historical fate. But to the extent that citizens share a common lived experience of being in an extraordinary, crisis situation happening here and now, insofar as they are aware that their collective way of life is concretely on the line, this shared individuality must be making itself directly manifest to intuition.

In the *Aesthetics*, Hegel seems to acknowledge such intuitions of collective individuality and accords them a place in the appearance of beauty. For instance, Hegel sees the paintings of such Dutch masters as Rembrandt, Van Dyck, and Wouwerman as "fired by a sense of . . . vigorous nationality," insofar as what we see in them is not merely the prosaic events of everyday life in their particularity, but rather expressions of the ways in which the Dutch as an individual people have managed to affirm their freedom and their spirit over the considerable adversities that they faced.[56] That is, here the scenes of everyday life, artistically rendered, come to make vivid and palpable to us the inherently collective spirit of the individuals depicted, enabling them to appear as agents of a collective historical event or drama (namely, the establishment of the Dutch state). Similarly, Hegel argues that an essential part of what is made present in epic poetry is the collective world of the people to whom the poem belongs, and in epic more so than in painting there is particular focus on a decisive event that brings this world into relief: "the whole worldview and objectivity of a national character [*Volksgeistes*], gone past [*vorübergeführt*] in its self-objectifying shape as an actual event, makes up the content and form of real epic."[57] Thus, though the focus of epic is typically the action of a "beautiful individual," there is nevertheless a sense in which this action serves above all to make palpable the collective world that the individual exemplifies. In other words, part of what is beautiful in the appearance of the beautiful individual's action seems to be the way in which it enables the *appearing of the collective individual* as such. And Hegel highlights that in epic poetry too it is especially in crisis situations of war, when the nation confronts something foreign to its sovereignty, that "the whole has an inducement to answer for itself," and so reveal its true colors.[58]

Conclusion

Of course, it is one thing to intuit the collective individuality of a people in the context of a beautiful artwork but quite another to be faced with an actual war in one's own state. The claim at issue here is certainly not that war is itself beautiful in any straightforward sense. But if such heightened events do provide artists with an especially fitting subject matter for the creation of beautiful artworks—if, indeed, they share much in common with Hegel's ideal figure of the beautiful individual, as I have been suggesting—it must be because such phenomena, in their decidedly non-prosaic, extraordinary character, take us out of our everyday ways of seeing and behaving and thereby allow something more profound to appear: namely, on Hegel's account, the collective individuality of the nation, in the dramatic moment of its attempt to affirm itself against dissolution. I have been arguing that the striking, dramatic appearance of this collective reality, specifically in its concrete, individuated, and so intuitable form, *is* beautiful, according to the terms that Hegel develops in the *Aesthetics*. Crisis moments allow for something to show itself that would not otherwise appear in its own right, and the compelling power of this extraordinary appearance—its gripping, intuitive character—is, in the end, a fundamentally *aesthetic* phenomenon, rather than something we grasp primarily by way of rational *thought*, as is the case in our relation to the state's standing laws. To the extent that Hegel regards such extraordinary moments to be essential to the state's re-establishment of its sovereignty, then, we can see that the sort of intuition at stake in the apprehension of beauty may after all have a key role to play in his account of modern political life.

Abbreviations

LFA   Hegel, G.W.F. *Aesthetics: Lectures on Fine Art*, vols. 1 and 2, trans. T. M. Knox (New York: Oxford University Press, 1975) / *Vorlesungen über die Ästhetik* (vols. 1–3), *Werke* 13–15 (Frankfurt am Main: Suhrkamp, 1970). Volume and pages of the English edition will be given, followed by the volume and pages of the German edition. Cited passages will be drawn from the Knox translation, unless otherwise noted.

PhR   Hegel, G. W. F., *Elements of the Philosophy of Right*, ed. Allen Wood, trans. H. B. Nisbet. Cambridge: Cambridge University Press, 1991/ *Grundlinien der Philosophie des Rechts*, *Werke* 7 (Frankfurt am Main: Suhrkamp, 1970). All references are to Hegel's section numbers, and any references to the Remarks or Additions to these sections are indicated by "R" and "A," respectively. Cited passages will be drawn from the Nisbet translation, unless otherwise noted.

PhS   Hegel, G. W. F., *Philosophy of Mind, Part Three of the Encyclopaedia of the Philosophical Sciences* (1830), trans. William Wallace (New York: Oxford University Press, 1971) / *Enzyklopädie der philosophischen Wissenschaften, Dritter Teil, Die Philosophie des Geistes*, Werke 10 (Frankfurt am Main: Suhrkamp, 1970). All references are to Hegel's section numbers, and any references to the Remarks or Additions to these sections are indicated by "R" and "A," respectively. Cited passages will be drawn from the Wallace translation, unless otherwise noted.

PhH   Hegel, G. W. F., *The Philosophy of History*, trans. J. Sibree (New York: Dover Publications, 1956)/ *Philosophie der Geschichte* (Stuttgart: Philipp Reclam, 1961). Pages of the English edition will be given, followed by the volume and pages of the German edition.

Notes

1 See *LFA* 1:103; 1:42, where Hegel says that, despite our appreciation of the excellence of artworks, we moderns "bow the knee no longer."
2 See *LFA* 1:102; 1:141.

3   See *PhH*, Part II, Sections 1 and 2, to see how Hegel structures his historical account of the Greek practical and cultural life in terms of the concept of beautiful work of art.
4   As Hegel writes, with the Reformation "religious ideas were drawn away from their wrappings in the element of sense and brought back to the inwardness of heart and thinking" (*LFA* 1:103; 1:142). See also *PhS* 556 and 565 for Hegel's contrast between the immediate, outward-directedness of *Anschauung* (appropriate to beauty) and the inward-turning, reflective character of *Vorstellung* and *Glauben* (appropriate to revealed religion).
5   Compare Hegel's discussion of romantic artworks that depict Christian martyrs in their affirmation of inner faith and their complete renunciation of the worldly (*LFA* 1:544–48; 2:160–66). An irony here is that the spirit that martyrs and ascetics embody, and which is the focus of these artworks that depict them, must presumably renounce such worldly objects (i.e., the beautiful artworks themselves) as inessential to faith.
6   See *LFA* 1:103; 1:142.
7   See, for instance, *LFA* 1:526; 2:138. Hegel here goes so far as to construe the most crucial historical event of Christianity—namely, the incarnation of Christ—as an essentially prosaic phenomenon. For a helpful and more extensive discussion of the fate of art in the face of the transformations brought about by Christianity, see Stephen Houlgate's "Hegel and the 'End' of Art," *Owl of Minerva* 29, no. 1 (1997): 1–21.
8   See *LFA* 1:518; 2:129, where Hegel speaks of romantic art's focus on the "spiritual beauty of the inner in and for itself [*an und für sich Inneren*]" (my translation).
9   See *PhR* 260 and A, where Hegel discusses the distinctive standpoint of modern states, in contrast to ancient states. Hegel's remark that "the state is not a work of art" (*PhR* 258A) can also be understood in terms of this contrast, for in his account the ancient Greeks (for whom the state *could* be considered on the model of a work of art) had generally speaking not yet attained to the stage of reflection and conscience (see *PhH* 250–53; 354–58).
10 See *PhR* 270R.
11 See *PhS* 483 and 545.
12 *PhR* 324 and R.
13 See *LFA* 1:179–94; 1:236–55.
14 On the basic link between beauty and freedom, see, for instance, *LFA* 1:97–102; 1:134–41.
15 Hegel at one point argues that the state's conception of freedom must be consistent with the people's *religion* and *its* particular perspective on freedom. He draws attention to the untenability of a situation in which a well-conceived, rational constitution is imposed upon a nation whose existing religious faith and practices (for instance, Catholicism in the context of the French Revolution) were at odds with some of the basic tenets of this constitution; as Hegel writes, "a free state and a slavish religion are incompatible" (*PhS* 552R), so a political revolution, without a corresponding religious reformation, is destined to face internal contradiction. Hegel does not to my knowledge address the possibility I am laying out here, namely that a state might be at odds with the relationship to freedom and to spirit embodied in people's *aesthetic* experience, though I am suggesting here that, as in the case of religion, this is something that his thought does warrant us in exploring.
16 *LFA* 1:145–52; 1:192–202.
17 *LFA* 1:93, 99; 1:129, 136–7.

18 See *LFA* 2:843-4; 3:75-6 for Hegel's discussion of how distinct colors come to be reconciled with one another in painting so as to make their harmony apparent to the eye.
19 *LFA* 2:809; 3:31-2.
20 The preceding discussion draws from Hegel's extended account of the essentially prosaic character of modern life at *LFA* 1:181-183, 193-4; 1:238-40, 253-5.
21 *PhR* 291-2; see also *LFA* 1:181-3; 1:238-40.
22 The striking critique of political life laid out in the *Aesthetics* has not received much attention in the secondary literature, perhaps because it seems to be at odds with what is taken to be Hegel's more authoritative justification of the state in its liberating character, given in the *Philosophy of Right*. The most notable exception here is John McCumber's insightful study of this political critique, in his *Poetic Interaction: Language, Freedom, Reason* (Chicago: University of Chicago Press, 1989), ch. 4. I find McCumber's thesis that, for Hegel, aesthetic experience is inherently at odds with the political ends of the modern state, convincing, though I think there are more sides to Hegel's conception of the relation between aesthetics and politics than McCumber acknowledges.
23 Hegel sees the ultimate task of legislators as that of determining "the will which has being in and for itself—i.e., reason," and this requires "insight into the nature of the state's institutions and needs," which are in their basic character essentially independent of the more particular, empirical concerns of this or that group (*PhR* 301R).
24 It should be acknowledged that, for Hegel, there *is* one individual in the modern constitutional state who is essentially non-substitutable by others: the monarch. However, Hegel does not see the monarch as an independent individual authority whose own personal character, insights, and decisions are to determine, from the ground up, the shape and direction of the whole social sphere. Rather, the monarch decides on the basis of the proposals and advice of relatively independent, constitutionally necessary government agencies, and so is, like the judge, wholly constrained by institutional forces and resources; see *PhR* 279A and *LFA* 1:193; 1:253.
25 Hegel also appeals to geometric examples to illustrate the essential opposition between the universal and the individual; see *LFA* 1:96; 1:132-3.
26 See *LFA* 1:149; 1:198.
27 Jay Lampert asks why Hegel does not take up the city as a legitimate object of aesthetic experience; see his "Why is There No Category of the City in Hegel's *Aesthetics*," *British Journal of Aesthetics*, 41:3, 2001, 312-24. I suspect that it is ultimately such experience of fragmentation and of the proliferation of particularity—an experience that Hegel links to civil life generally—that underlies this omission. As Hegel says in describing the aesthetic possibilities of complex civil life, "the whole appears only as a mass of details" (*LFA* 1:149; 1:198; my translation).
28 Drawing on Hegel's account of the beauty of nature, I elaborate upon the difference between *intuiting* and *thinking* the unity of a system in my "Embodied Meaning in Hegel and Merleau-Ponty," *Hegel Bulletin*, 38:1, 45-66.
29 See *PhR* 302.
30 *PhR* 268A.
31 Hegel notes in the context of his example of how people take collective institutions for granted, that "habit blinds us to the basis of our entire existence" (*PhR* 268A).
32 See, for instance, Hegel's discussion of "corporations," which are conceived as a means of connecting the individual worker in a given sector of the economy to the underlying universality that makes her way of life possible in the first place (*PhR* 250-56, 302).

33 See *LFA* 1:177–244; 1:233–316.
34 *LFA* 1:170; 1:224.
35 Hegel regards the Greek statues of the gods as among the most successful embodiments of beauty, but what these statues, in their serenity and self-possession, lack, is precisely the "difference and struggle of opposition" (*LFA* 1:177; 1:233). It is this deficiency that leads Hegel to focus the bulk of his discussion of the ideal of beauty on *action*, which is essentially characterized by the movement of opposition and its overcoming. (Incidentally, Hegel sees the Murillo boy as possessing a serenity and detachment much like the Greek statues, and so presumably as sharing in their aesthetic deficiency.) I discuss this aesthetic privileging of action in more detail in my "Hegel and the Phenomenology of Art," in *Phenomenology and the Arts*, edited by Peter Costello and Licia Carlson (New York: Rowman and Littlefield, 2016), 297–322.
36 See *LFA* 1:220–5; 1:286–92.
37 *LFA* 1:221; 1:287. For a more extensive discussion of the significance of Antigone's act, see also Hegel's *Phenomenology of Spirit*, trans. A. V. Miller (New York: Oxford, 1977), paragraphs 451–53.
38 *LFA* 1:169; 1:222–23.
39 See *LFA* 1:185; 1:244.
40 *LFA* 1:185–89; 1:243–48.
41 This theme is discussed at more length in my "Hegel and the Phenomenology of Art."
42 *LFA* 1:37–38; 1:58–60.
43 As Hegel says, "The interest in and need for such an actual individual totality and living independence [of the beautiful, stateless hero] we will not and cannot sacrifice, however much we may recognize as salutary and rational the essential character and development of the institutions in civilized civil and political life" (*LFA* 1:195; 1:255).
44 The worry that our aesthetic enjoyment of the individual hero is in tension with our participation in modern life seems to be premised on the notion that we somehow identify with the individual hero and at some level develop a desire to assume his or her unalloyed freedom for ourselves, in our own actual lives. It is this notion that structures McCumber's reading of the tension between art and politics in Hegel's thought (*Poetic Interaction*, 100–5). This notion also informs Julia Peters's thesis that the aesthetic ideal of the beautiful individual is something that Hegel intends as a practical ideal or model of ethical life (though Peters is not concerned to show how this ideal is at odds with modern politics per se); see her *Hegel on Beauty* (New York: Routledge, 2015). However, I find little evidence in Hegel of the claim that our aesthetic experience of such virtuous heroes has, or ought to have, any direct, practical ramifications in such a straightforward way. Indeed, if art is a realm of Absolute Spirit, and thereby autonomous with respect to practical life, this straightforward translation of aesthetic ideals into practical ideals must involve a *betrayal* of beauty, not a faithful working out of its implications. The liberating feature of aesthetic experience arguably has to do with our broader, metaphysical relations to reality as a whole (that is, beauty's truth gives us perspective, for instance, on the absolute relation between spirit and sensuous nature, or the universal and the particular, as such) and is not limited to the freedoms peculiar to practical life as such, even when such overtly practical contents as the idealized hero are the focus of our aesthetic experience.
45 Compare *PhR* 147, where in the context of discussing the individual's trust in the collective backdrop of life, Hegel describes the ethical substance of a people (which includes the state and its laws) as that in which the individual "lives as in its element which is not distinct from itself."

46 *PhR* 273R.
47 "The wish to give a nation a constitution *a priori*, even if its content were more or less rational, is an idea which overlooks the very moment by virtue of which a constitution is more than a product of thought. Each nation accordingly has the constitution appropriate to and proper to it" (*PhR* 274R). In lectures on this passage (*PhR* 274A), he goes on to say that, rather than being merely made, the constitution is inevitably "the work of centuries," drawing attention to the inherently historical dimension that mediates a nation's relation to its own constitution.
48 *PhR* 323.
49 *PhR* 324R; Hegel's emphasis.
50 *PhR* 324R.
51 Ibid.
52 *PhR* 323; the first two emphases are added.
53 *PhR* 323.
54 See *PhR* 328.
55 See *PhR* 324R.
56 *LFA* 1:169; 1:223.
57 *LFA* 2:1044; 3:330, my translation.
58 *LFA* 2:1059; 3:349.

Bibliography

Ciavatta, David. "Embodied Meaning in Hegel and Merleau-Ponty." *Hegel Bulletin* 38, no. 1 (2017): 45–66.

Ciavatta, David. "Hegel and the Phenomenology of Art." In *Phenomenology and the Arts*, edited by Peter Costello and Licia Carlson, 297–322. New York: Rowman and Littlefield, 2016.

Hegel, G. W. F. *Aesthetics: Lectures on Fine Art*, vols. 1 and 2, translated by T. M. Knox. New York: Oxford University Press, 1975. German version: *Vorlesungen über die Ästhetik* (vols. 1–3), *Werke* 13–15. Frankfurt am Main: Suhrkamp, 1970.

Hegel, G. W. F. *Elements of the Philosophy of Right*, edited by Allen Wood, translated by H. B. Nisbet. Cambridge: Cambridge University Press, 1991. German version: *Grundlinien der Philosophie des Rechts*, *Werke* 7. Frankfurt am Main: Suhrkamp, 1970.

Hegel, G. W. F. *The Philosophy of History*, translated by J. Sibree. New York: Dover Publications, 1956. German version: *Philosophie der Geschichte*. Stuttgart: Philipp Reclam, 1961.

Hegel, G. W. F. *Philosophy of Mind, Part Three of the Encyclopaedia of the Philosophical Sciences (1830)*, translated by William Wallace. New York: Oxford University Press, 1971. German version: *Enzyklopädie der philosophischen Wissenschaften, Dritter Teil, Die Philosophie des Geistes*. *Werke* 10. Frankfurt am Main: Suhrkamp, 1970.

Houlgate, Stephen. "Hegel and the 'End' of Art." *Owl of Minerva* 29, no. 1 (1997): 1–21.

Lampert, Jay. "Why is There No Category of the City in Hegel's *Aesthetics*." *British Journal of Aesthetics* 41, no. 3 (2001): 312–24.

McCumber, John. *Poetic Interaction: Language, Freedom, Reason*. Chicago: University of Chicago Press, 1989.

Peters, Julia. *Hegel on Beauty*. New York: Routledge, 2015.

3

Bildung and the Novel in Hegel's Lectures on Aesthetics

Timothy L. Brownlee

Hegel's remarks concerning the novel seem to be wrought with internal tensions. Hegel offers us no theory of the novel. While his aesthetic thinking—at least, his account of the particular parts or moments of the beautiful—is oriented around the distinction into different genres, he does not treat the novel as a self-standing genre. In part for this reason, it can seem that Hegel's thinking about the novel is underdeveloped.[1] At the same time, Hegel does seem, even if half-heartedly, to find a place for the novel within his genre theory, apparently identifying it as a species of epic poetry. We can therefore identify a first tension: On the one hand, Hegel does not offer us a theory of the novel akin to the ones that he offers of other genres and forms. On the other hand, he seems to identify the novel as a form of epic. However, when we attend to his account of the novel as a form of epic, we find a second tension. Whenever Hegel considers the novel in the context of an account of epic poetry, he immediately identifies a number of ways in which the novel fails to possess the same formal qualities that he argues the epic proper does (his ultimate models here are the Homeric epic poems). If Hegel conceives of the novel as a kind of epic, it is unclear why he would stress its failure to possess so many of the characteristics that he deems distinctive of epics. The specific ways in which the novel is distinct from the epic point to a third tension, inherent in the form itself. Hegel defends a social account of the meaning of art, holding that works must be understood in relation to the cultural context—the configuration of *Geist*—from which they emerged. However, he claims that, due to its "prosaic" character, the modern world, in which the novel is properly at home, is unsuited to the production of epic poetry.[2] This lack of fit gives rise to a whole range of further tensions: the prosaic character of the modern world exists in a basic tension with poetic forms more broadly; the modern world is one that has its own continued existence, and does not stand in need of founding or setting up, which Hegel believes was among the primary social functions of ancient epic poetry; and finally, as a result, there is no room in the modern age for the epic hero, whose action is that of founding.

Given these tensions, we might be inclined to think that Hegel had a low estimation of the novel and its aesthetic prospects. In this, he would not be alone, since the novel had been, in his own lifetime, an object of derision, both as a mere popular form, inadequate to the designation of "fine art" and as an idle, "feminine" pastime, unsuited to the seriousness required by philosophical consideration. In short, Hegel's relative silence on the novel might itself be an indication of a critical attitude on his part. Indeed, some interpreters are explicit in claiming that Hegel offers us a "critique of the novel."[3] However, these apparent intimations of a critical attitude themselves stand in tension with what we know about the role that novels played in Hegel's philosophical writing outside of the aesthetics lectures and in his own life. Speight points to Hegel's "own significant appropriation of [novelistic literature] for the limning of essential moments of the development of the world-historical spirit," and he has argued convincingly that it is novels—most centrally Diderot's *Le neveu de Rameau* and Jacobi's *Woldemar*—that provide the foundations for Hegel's account of decisive moments of the development of spirit in the modern age in the early *Phenomenology of Spirit*.[4] Whether a popular form or not, Hegel's appropriation of novels suggests that he thinks they are important objects of consideration for philosophy. Vieweg points to Hegel's high opinion of the humor of Theodor Gottlieb von Hippel, which suggests that he did not think of novels as below his own appreciation and interest.[5]

My primary aim in what follows is to argue that interpreters have overstated the extent to which the lectures on aesthetics provide the basis for a criticism or dismissal of the novel as an artistic form. First and foremost, I argue that the grounds for holding that Hegel thought that the novel should be understood as a form of epic are much weaker than is typically believed and that we are better off approaching Hegel's remarks on the novel without the assumption that novels are modern epics. Instead, I argue that we should take seriously the claim that Hegel seems not to have a theory of the novel. However, rather than engage in speculation as to why Hegel does not treat the novel as its own genre, I argue that we should approach Hegel's discussions of the novel and novels in the lectures in light of his broader claims about the nature and purpose of art. In this connection, I attend to a resonance between Hegel's remarks on the modern novel—in particular Goethe's *Wilhelm Meister*—and his treatment of civil society in the *Philosophy of Right*. I argue that the novel is particularly suited to the achievement of the task of *Bildung*—formation or "culture"—that Hegel holds is central to civil society, and that Annemarie Gethmann-Siefert has argued is central to Hegel's account of the role of art in the modern age.[6]

A quick word concerning my approach: In general, I share Gethmann-Siefert's conviction that the lectures present us with a significantly different picture of Hegel's philosophy of art and aesthetics than does Hotho's text.[7] By consequence, my account rests most directly on the published texts of the lecture transcripts. While it is true that Hotho was likely among the foremost experts on Hegel's philosophy of art during his lifetime, we have good reason to doubt the authenticity of much of the additional material contained in the 1835 text for which we find no reference in any of the many lecture transcripts now published. (There are now two published editions of transcripts from the 1820/21, 1823, and 1826 lectures, and one published edition from the 1828/89 lectures.[8]) As I hope to demonstrate in what follows, many of the ideas that have been central to interpretations of Hegel's conception of the novel—in particular of the relation between the novel and the epic—are anchored in claims whose basis in the lectures is very slim.

* * *

I would like to begin by setting out what I take to be the more significant claims that Hegel makes about the novel in the lectures on aesthetics. We can distinguish two broad sorts of claims concerning the novel. In the first, Hegel links the novel to romantic art more broadly. In the second, he considers the relation between the novel and the epic. We find the first instance of the first sort of remark in the 1820/21 lectures, in which Hegel considers the novel in a discussion of the "formalism of subjectivity" in his treatment of the romantic form of art. Here, Hegel traces the rise of the modern novel from the chivalric romance. In particular, Hegel argues that the concept of knighthood central to those romances is itself inherently contradictory, since it sets up merely subjective characteristics as though they were "ethical." In the work of Ariosto and Cervantes, Hegel thinks we find the sublation of this contradiction in the revelation of the merely formal character of knighthood:

> With [Ariosto and Cervantes], the truly romantic ends itself; in *Don Quixote* one sees the decline of a powerful nature, that climbs to the height of insanity. [T]he whole is a mockery of knighthood, to which a series of un-romantic novellas [*Novellen*] are connected. There is genuine irony in *Don Quixote*, and he remains certain of his matter [*Sache*] in spite of all mistakes, and this certainty is, considering the substantial [matter] thoroughly noble. The dissolution of the most beautiful romantic itself occurs with the dissolution of knighthood; the end [*Ende*] of the romantic is what we call the novel [*Roman*]. Here is the emergence of knighthood, but shaped according to contemporary circumstances. In *Don Quixote* it has already become chimerical, the world has shaped itself into a fixed state constitution, and the individual now relates themselves to it, it is fixed against the arbitrary will [*Willkür*] of the individual, against the willing of the individual. [T]he end can only be that the individual must give up their subjectivity and unify themselves with the state. Each begins with ideals, and finds a disenchanted [*verzauberte*] world before them, finds infinite difficulties and proceeds to knock a hole [*Loch*] in the world; what is achieved through this effort is that [the individual] becomes a human being like others, or, to express it with a popular expression, becomes a Philistine like others.[9]

We find a similar remark in the 1823 lectures, only now with a new emphasis on the role that the exploration of the hero's subjectivity plays in the novel:

> It is the novel that follows [the chivalric romance] and is familiar as a particular art form. It is the romantic [*die Romantik*] that is placed here in our age and relations. The basis of the novel is no longer [the] contingency of external existence, which has here been transformed into the higher order of the state. All relations that are lacking in knighthood are fixed. The novel has its basis where the chief moments of ethicality are fixed, the ethical life no longer rests on arbitrary will [*Willkür*], whose extent [*Umfang*] is now small. This small extent is the particular interest of an individual in general, the standpoint that individuals take in the world; the interest of their heart comes here to language. The individual as free subject, knowing itself in the objective world, emerges in contrast to their imagination [*Einbilden*] and plans, which [it] makes from itself or from its activity in the world, its ideals, which it undertakes to

realize. These can be [in part] of a universal kind, in part a particular content. The individual sets forth in a knightly way, and wants to bring about good for the world, to satisfy their ideal of love. They clash in struggle with the fixed actuality, and the end can only be this, that the individual does not make the world into something else; instead the individual sows their wild oats [*sich seine Hörner abläuft*] and capitulates to the objective. The end will be that the individual enters into the chain of the world [*die Verkettung der Welt*], secures a family, a position [*Standpunkt*], and a wife who is—however highly she was idealized—a wife, no better than most others.[10]

These remarks are echoed in the 1826 lectures, in a way that seems to sharpen them to the point where they approach criticism:

In *Don Quixote*, knighthood, in an implicitly noble nature, becomes insanity. Our novel is connected to a specific distancing from this character. Knighthood is in itself chimerical. The novel has a knight as its object, who has as his aim the entirely customary [*gewöhnliche*] purposes of common life, [for example] winning a young lady for his wife; it only becomes fantastic [*phantastisch*] through the supplementation [*Aufschrauben*] of fantasy, [which] has raised [these customary purposes] to something immeasurable [*etwas Unermeßlichen*]. Difficulties are opposed to achieving this customary purpose; there are laws, police, state, etc.; the young person is the knight who takes these rights, which are to be respected, as limitation on his infinite purpose; they seem [appear] to him only as a disenchanted [*verzauberte*] world, which stands against him as something wrong [*Unrecht*] and against which he struggles. This struggle is nothing other than [that which Goethe called] apprenticeship, [and when this] is completed, the purpose comes to an end; he has secured the young lady, she becomes his wife, he becomes a human being [*ein Mensch*] like others, as in Goethe's *Wilhelm Meisters Lehrjahre*. Then come children, and the whole hangover of life, he becomes a Philistine, when he earlier struggled against Philistinism.[11]

This passage immediately precedes Hegel's account of the decay [*Zerfallen*] of romantic art into the opposed poles of subjectivity and objectivity, of exploration of the subjectivity of the artist in humor, and the naturalistic portrayal of the prosaic that we find in Dutch genre painting. The novel seems to anticipate this decay, since it is central to Hegel's account here that the modern world of the novel is "small," "fixed," and "customary," and not the flux on which the hero comes to impose an order through their deeds. Instead, the hero "capitulates to the objective" and "becomes a Philistine." If the central character of the novel is to be the knightly hero, its subject matter is simply unsuited to its prosaic world ("our age and relations").

Finally, the remarks on the novel in the account of romantic art in the 1828/29 lectures recapitulate many of the same ideas. Now, in contrast to the fantastic works of Ariosto and Cervantes, in which "the human is woven together with unnatural and irreconcilable relations,"

in the novel the true natural character of the human being and relations of the world are contained in the present. The relations are fixed, so that, in the novel, there is only a small field for action. If the state is fixed, the adventure of the knight ceases to exist. Only the subjective interest of the individual remains. The knight in the novel has his interests and purposes to execute, whether it is passion or the purpose of love; forces [*Gewalten*] present themselves against him, with which he must struggle. These forces are the will of the father, of aunts, etc. The knight must replace these relations with their purpose. He must create a hole [*Loch*] in the state of things, in order to come to his goal and to achieve his particularity. The end is that the individual emerges into the chain of these relations, and the subject recognizes [*erkennt*] their own purpose as something useless.[12]

In addition to this first set of remarks on the novel in his account of romantic art, we find a second set of remarks linking the novel and the epic. Beginning in the 1826 lectures, Hegel returns to the novel in the discussion of the "particular parts" of art, specifically in his account of epic poetry:

Another form is connected to the epic: The novel, our so-called modern epic. The hero of the novel cannot be the hero of an epic poem, because the ethical and the right have become fixed relations; in this world the individual acts in accordance with these; what remains for the hero to do is their own subjectivity.[13]

Of course, if the novel is to be the modern epic, it is unsuited to the requirements of that form. The Homeric epics, the "summit" of the form, are distinctive in the way in which they give expression to the *Geist* of a people: "Such an epic falls in time where a people emerges into consciousness and the *Geist* feels itself to be powerful enough to produce [its own world] and to know [itself] as being at home [in that world]."[14] The epic hero plays a special role here. In the absence of a preexisting, fixed order, it is the hero's actions that are decisive for instituting that order. By contrast, in these passages, Hegel argues not only that the *Geist* of the modern world is distinct from that of the classical but that this also transforms the role that the hero can play. The modern hero cannot institute a world through their actions because their world is already "fixed." As we have seen, Hegel thinks that the hero of the novel "capitulates" to the objective rather than transforming it. Instead, all that remains for them is the exploration of their subjectivity, either in contrast to the fixed, objective world as fantasy or in their humdrum engagement in it.

As I have mentioned, some readers have interpreted these and other remarks to form the basis for a *criticism* of the novel on Hegel's part. If novels are to be understood as epics, then they are bound to fail according to their constitutive norm. According to Bungay, "The self-understanding of modern civil society cannot be articulated in epics. . . . The attempt to articulate the total self-understanding of society can still be made, but in the modern state it will be necessarily particular and subjective. It will be the author's view, with no guarantee that it be shared by anyone else."[15] Weiss argues that, due to the prosaic character of the modern world, the novel is not only bound to fail when it is measured against the standpoint of the epic in particular. Rather, by Hegel's standards, novels are condemned to fail as artworks of any kind. Weiss argues that the *Geist* of the modern world is itself prosaic, and so allergic to the unification through fantasy that, on his account, Hegel believes is essential to artworks generally: "The novel is therefore an artwork that is directed against the 'proper character of the artwork.'" Hegel thus comes to a shocking [*unerhörten*] aesthetic discovery: *The artworks of the modern age are directed against art itself*."[16]

These criticisms depend on some basic claims about what novels are in particular, and about the more general relation between art and its subject matter, specifically the ways in which art can concern itself with *Geist*, with the shared social world in its breadth and depth. In the following two sections, I aim to challenge what I take to be the two basic claims on which these accounts depend: first, that Hegel thinks that novels are epics; and second, that the prosaic character of the modern age makes it unsuited to artistic treatment of any kind. Instead, I am to show that, once we drop the assumption that novels are epics, we can identify some important ways in which the novel in particular can engage with the prose of everyday life and so can contribute to one of the essential tasks that Hegel sets for art, *Bildung*.

* * *

That Hegel understands the novel to be a form of epic is commonplace. Hegel's remarks in this connection provided a powerful impetus for Lukács's early account of the novel.[17] And the claim that novels are epics was a common one in the modern era as well. For example, in the "Preface" to *Joseph Andrews*, Fielding calls the novel "a comic-epic poem in prose."[18]

Indeed, if we base our account on Hegel's formulations in Hotho's text, the case seems to be simple. There, we find the claim that "matters are entirely different in regard to the *novel*, the modern *bourgeois* epic [*dem* Roman, *der modernen* bürgerlichen *Epopöe*]."[19] Many interpreters have taken this claim to provide the basis for their accounts of Hegel's view of the novel. However, I believe that we should have less confidence that Hegel actually thinks of the novel in these terms. As we have seen, this claim does not appear in the 1820/21 or 1823 lectures. We can therefore start by examining the lecture notes that come from hands other than Hotho's. When we consider the 1826 lectures, we do not find the full-voiced assertion that we do in Hotho's text. In Kehler's notes, the specific terms expressing the relationship between the novel and the epic are absent.[20] However, in the von der Pfordten notes, this apparently straightforward identification is significantly weaker: "Another form is connected to the epic: The novel, our so-called modern epic."[21] Finally, the 1828/29 lectures assert no specific connection between the novel and the epic. Instead, Hegel there claims that it is the idyll that "completes" the epic. He contrasts the simplicity of the world, action, and characters of these idylls with the novel: "From the ballad, we pass over immediately into the novel, where there are fixed relations, raw necessity appears as rational, and the human being appears in a narrow sphere, love, and recognizes necessity."[22]

If we base our interpretation on the available published textual evidence, only one of the four texts identified here, Hotho's, includes this direct identification of the novel as an epic. None of the others provides specific support for holding that *Hegel* believes that that identification is justified.

The claim that the novel is only a "so-called modern epic" admits of alternative interpretations, for example, that Hegel is citing familiar and common claims like that of Fielding, rather than endorsing them outright. Such an interpretation is justified in part because it helps us to make sense of the claims about the novel that immediately follow them. In several of the texts under consideration—Hotho's edited text, as well as the von der Pforten and Kehler notes—Hegel identifies a possible relation between the novel and the epic, but then goes on to stress specific ways in which novels fail to meet the standards constitutive of the epic. As we have seen, in 1826, he immediately claims that "the hero of the novel cannot be the hero of an epic poem, because the ethical and the right have become fixed relations; in this world the individual acts in accordance with these; what remains for the hero to do is their own subjectivity." Hotho's text includes the claim that, like the epic, the novel presents the "total world" of a people. However, we find no such claim in any of the available lecture notes. And even in Hotho's text, the author immediately turns to stress that the modern world is unsuited to epic treatment: "What is missing is the *original* [*ursprünglich*] poetic condition of the world, from which the epic proper emerges. The novel in the modern sense presupposes an actuality that has already been ordered *prosaically* [*eine bereits zur* Prosa *geordnete Wirklichkeit*]."[23] Finally, such an explicit contrast between classical epic and the novel is completely absent in the Heimann notes from 1828/29. If Hegel wanted us to consider the novel as a form of epic, we would expect him to pause for at least a moment to make the case for the fit between these two forms. If, in these remarks, Hegel is not offering a criticism of the novel form itself, how are we to make sense of their apparently critical tone? As we have seen, the claim that novels are epics was familiar in Hegel's time. On the interpretation I am offering here, we can account for the critical tone of Hegel's remarks by seeing them as directed against those other critics who count the novel as a form of epic, rather than against the novel itself.

Of course, if Hegel does not situate the novel as a genre within his account of the "particular forms" of art, we might well wonder what sort of art he considered it to be. But the fact that he does not straightforwardly so identify it does not automatically entail that he dismisses it or thinks it insignificant.[24] Acknowledging that Hegel does not offer a complete theory of the novel, as so many commentators do, by no means entails that he dismisses it as an insignificant genre or believes that it is condemned to insignificance. As we have seen, even though he never explicitly situates it within his account of the particular parts of art, he does come to devote increasing attention to the question of what sort of form the novel is from his reflections on the distinctive features of the *Quixote* dating from the first lectures in 1820/21, to those on *Wilhelm Meister* and the explicit remarks on the relation between the novel and the epic in 1826. In short, there is an equally plausible story that we can tell to the effect that Hegel's thinking on the novel is under development throughout the 1820s, a development belied by the comprehensive and systematic appearance of Hotho's 1835 text.[25]

Accepting this account of Hegel's taxonomy of the novel requires a significant break with the interpretive orthodoxy, an orthodoxy that has only been strengthened by Lukács's Hegel-inspired treatment of the novel as the modern epic. However, it also opens up space for construing Hegel's remarks on the novel along the lines of other critics who reject the claim that novels are best understood as epics, most notably, for my purposes at least, Bakhtin.[26] Indeed, the rejection of the novel-as-epic thesis marks the first of several points of concord that I shall argue we find between Hegel's and Bakhtin's theories of the novel.

* * *

The first criticism that we've considered indicts the novel on the grounds that it fails as an instance of a particular artistic genre, that of the epic. By contrast, the criticism of the novel that stresses the prosaic character of its subject matter aims to demonstrate that the novel fails not simply as an instance of a specific genre but rather as a work of art generally. As we've seen, in his remarks on *Don Quixote* and *Wilhelm Meister's Lehrjahre*, Hegel argues that the modern novel no longer fits the model of the chivalric romance. The world of the modern novel is one that is already fixed, a "disenchanted" world, and that world is not profoundly changed by the action of the novel. Instead, the hero of the modern novel "capitulates" to the existing world. And instead of documenting their great deeds, the novel can only explore the subjectivity of the hero. It might seem as though Hegel is a critic of the novel due to its failure to acknowledge these characteristics of the modern world and of the relationship of subjectivity to it. From the standpoint of that world, the aspirations of the hero who dreams of fundamentally transforming it through her own deeds must appear merely "fantastic," a product of subjective imagination bound to be frustrated. Likewise, the hero of the novel couldn't but appear as a hypocrite, who formerly rejected capitulation to the "customary purposes" of the world as Philistinism, but who ends up themselves capitulating, and so becoming a Philistine, whose life can only appear as a "hangover" that follows a period of youthful intoxication.

Hegel's remarks on *Wilhelm Meister* are instructive in this connection. Wilhelm does not triumph over the perceived injustice in the world, or place his own individual stamp on it, for example, by fulfilling his dream of founding a national theater. In light of this failure, the action of the novel might appear quaint when we compare it to the initial high hopes and aspirations of its hero. And Hegel's claim that the novel can only explore the hero's subjectivity, rather than document their divine deeds, seems to fit the suggestion that Hegel is critical of the novel. However, when we consider the specific way in which Hegel characterizes the action of the novel, we can see that he otherwise agrees with the way in which *Wilhelm* portrays the confrontation between the subjectivity of the hero and the objective reality of the social world. In particular, his remarks on the novel recall the critique of the standpoint of "virtue" in Chapter VB of the Jena *Phänomenologie des Geistes*. There, Hegel argues that the standpoint of a virtue that sees itself as elevated above the social world, which it treats merely as an instrument for the achievement of its own self-given purposes, is basically unstable: in order for the world to be the site of the realization of virtue, the virtuous agent learns that "the way of the world" cannot be so radically opposed to its purposes, a stance that undermines the radical understanding of the distinction between itself and the world on which its stance is based.[27] When we return to the lectures on aesthetics, we see that Hegel is claiming that the modern novel presents exactly this same picture, where the hero begins with an elevated sense of the importance of their own purposes, conceiving the world as fallen (an *Unrecht*). However, the novel presents just the same reality that Hegel believes "virtue" finds in its experience: instead of triumphing over the world, the hero of the novel finds that they become a part of it. It might seem as though Hegel is *criticizing* the hero for being a "Philistine," for coming to engage in the shared social world, rather than working to transform it in accordance with their own fantasy. But, when we consider the account of the aesthetics lectures in relation to other of Hegel's texts, we should remind ourselves that this sort of engagement is precisely what a life of rectitude (*Rechtschaffenheit*) or virtue (*Tugend*) requires.[28] Instead of offering a criticism of the hero, we should read Hegel as offering a criticism of others who can conceive of this engagement only as Philistinism (which he identifies, we may recall, in the 1820/21 lectures as a "popular expression," not necessarily one of his own). The life that Wilhelm takes up only looks like a "hangover" from the standpoint of the unrealistic aspirations from which he begins. But the text by no means obliges us to hold that Hegel thinks that Wilhelm is a Philistine.

In short, we can make sense of the critical tone of Hegel's remarks on the novel by seeing them as directed not against the novel itself as a genre, but against other critics' claims about the novel's appropriate genre, or against an unjustified aspiration expressed in the attempt to elevate the subjectivity of the hero over the objectivity of the social world. By contrast, in the novels to which Hegel attends most closely in his discussions—*Don Quixote, Wilhelm Meisters Lehrjahre*—the reader sees the unsustainability of that attitude and is compelled instead to consider the dynamic of a subjectivity that is essentially worldly, engaged in the otherwise-mundane or prosaic practices that characterize modern social life. On this interpretation, Hegel is not criticizing *the novel* for entrenching a false conception of subjectivity, whose high aspirations could only be frustrated by the established character of the social world. Instead, he is criticizing those *critics* who hold that the novel's task lies in the exploration of the hero's subjectivity as completely independent of its realization within the world. Of course, at this point, the criticism of the novel as a work of art (not simply as a form of epic) would seem to return with renewed force: How can a work of art engage with the inescapably prosaic character of the modern world and remain a work of art?

The impression of a critical aspect to Hegel's remarks seems only to be strengthened when we compare them to the high praise that F. W. Schlegel lavishes on *Wilhelm Meister* in his review. However, when we consider the details of Hegel's account here, his view is actually much closer to Schlegel's both in substance and in tone than we might initially be inclined to think. First, Schlegel argues that the novel is actually better understood as a sort of hybrid form, the product of a playful assembly of elements of diverse genres. So Schlegel rejects the claim that the novel should be understood to be subject to the norms governing epics. And I have argued that Hegel shares this view in an important way, since he too argues that important aspects of the novel are resistant to classification as an epic. Of course, Hegel does not issue the same high praise to the form that we find in Schlegel, and he does not point to its hybrid character. But I believe that both share the view that it is a mistake to take our orientation to understanding novels from assumptions about the nature of epics. Second, on Schlegel's interpretation, among *Wilhelm*'s central concerns is a presentation of the *Bildung*, the formation, of its main character. He is particularly interested in the way that the novel's form can itself mirror that development.²⁹ To be sure, Hegel neither expresses such a high opinion of the distinctiveness of the novelistic form as does Schlegel nor conceives of the task of *Bildung* in the same exalted terms.³⁰ However, since he understands the novel to be about the ways in which individuals come to be competent agents within the world, with a particular focus on the different configurations of individual subjectivity within that engagement, there remains significant space for him to advocate for a tight connection between the novel and individual *Bildung*. And, on this account, which I shall defend in the remainder of this chapter, it is a feature—and not a bug—of the novel that it can address itself to the prose of everyday life.

* * *

Wilhelm Meisters Lehrjahre explores the issues that are at the center of Hegel's consideration of the novel—art, *Bildung*, the prosaic character of modern social life— in complex ways. The novel itself is an artistic portrayal of Wilhelm's own *Bildung* and development. It addresses directly the role that art plays within that development, since Wilhelm's formation turns essentially around his engagement in the theater. The novel depicts the struggle of art against the prosaic character of the modern world, in the opposition it establishes between Wilhelm's devotion to the theater and his pursuit of business as a vocation, in the conflict between the aspiration to establish a national theater and the pursuit of a life devoted to money-making. At the same time, it considers the ultimate dependence of art on the prose of everyday life in its depiction of the humdrum matters that are involved in establishing and sustaining a theater company. Finally, it portrays art and art-making as themselves bound to issues and concerns that might seem base in comparison to Wilhelm's high aspirations, in particular in its description of the ill treatment that the theater company receives at the hands of its "noble" patrons, among whom we might expect a superior appreciation for art. It is not accidental that Hegel focuses so much attention on this particular novel. I've argued that he characterizes its central action in terms that express broad agreement with how it portrays reality, namely, the instability of the attitude of virtue that considers itself superior to and separate from the prosaic world. However, the terms in which he characterizes the resolution of the novel suggest that he thinks that the novel portrays a process of *Bildung* or formation that is successful on the terms that he sets out in his practical philosophy. In particular, it is significant that Hegel claims that we find the resolution of the novel at the point when the hero "enters into the chain of the world [*die Verkettung der Welt*]"³¹ and "becomes a human being like others."³²

These remarks suggest that Hegel conceives of a tight link between the novel and civil society. First, it is in the treatment of "Civil Society" in the *Philosophie des Rechts* that we find the most significant account of *Bildung* in Hegel's mature practical philosophy. In that account, Hegel aims to defend the importance of *Bildung* against two competing positions, according to which *Bildung* is unimportant or even pernicious because of the way that it compromises a natural condition of innocence, and according to which the individual's needs exist as an absolute purpose in which *Bildung* appears merely as a means for the achievement of those needs. In contrast to these positions, Hegel instead treats *Bildung* as essential to the contribution that it makes to a person's freedom. As Hegel sometimes portrays it, freedom is a condition of being with oneself in what is other, a condition in which one experiences what is other not as a limitation or alien imposition, but rather as something in which they are "at home" (*einheimisch*).[33] *Bildung* is central to civil society because it enables the individual to be "with themselves" both in the customary institutions and practices of a market society and in their relations to one another.

Specifically, Hegel conceives of *Bildung* as the "process" (*Prozeß*) by which the individual can surpass the limitations of their own "particular" standpoint—"the immediacy of desire, the subjective vanity of sentiment, and the arbitrariness of preferences"—and to assume a standpoint that is "universal": "*Bildung* is thus in its absolute determination *liberation* and the *labor* of higher liberation, the absolute point of departure to the substantiality of ethicality that is no longer immediate and natural, but spiritual [*geistigen*], the infinite subjective substantiality raised to the shape of universality."[34] In part, the work of this process is unconscious, and it is effective regardless of whether the individual acknowledges it or not. That is, even if the individual continues to think of herself as a merely "private person, who has [her] own interest as [her] purpose," the achievement of those purposes requires that she engage in social practices, and so relate to others, not merely according to the wishes of her own private purposes, but according to the requirements of shared "universals": because the individual's purpose "is mediated through the universal, that *appears* to them as a *means*, this purpose can be achieved by them only insofar as they determine their knowing, willing, and deeds in a universal way, and make themselves into a *link* in the chain of this *connection* [*sich zu einem* Gliede *der Kette dieses* Zusammenhangs *machen*]."[35] On this account, *Bildung* is the process of "raising the individuality and naturalness of the consciousness of [the] participants in civil society . . . *to formal freedom* and formal *universality of knowing and willing, of forming* [bilden] subjectivity in its particularity."[36] It is through this process that the individual is "elevated" to the status of being a "human being" (*Mensch*), in distinction from the circumscribed and given sphere of needs and desires that constitute animality.[37]

Several aspects of this characterization are worthy of note. First, Hegel portrays the social result of the process of *Bildung* in basically the same terms as he does the resolution of *Wilhelm Meisters Lehrjahre*. In both cases, the individual overcomes a separation from others and comes to assume a "universal" standpoint by means of developing an institutionally mediated relation to them: they become a "link" in a "chain" joining them. Hegel seems to thinks that the novel considers, in a distinctive way, the relations that individuals bear to one another within a specific set of institutions and practices constituting civil society. Second, the effect of the process of *Bildung* on the individual is the same as the one we find at the resolution of Goethe's novel: Wilhelm ceases to be an individual separate from others, and becomes a *human being*, the specific status or standing that Hegel thinks is proper to the members of civil society. As I have argued earlier, Hegel shares Bakhtin's conviction that we misunderstand the novel if we interpret it in terms of the norms and standards governing the epic. Here we see a second great point of agreement between them: Hegel fits within Bakhtin's characterization of the task of the *Bildungsroman*, in which the novel plays a significant role in portraying the process by which individuals come to find a place in modern civil society. In Bakhtin's words, "A man must educate himself or re-educate himself for life in a world that is, from his point of view, enormous and foreign; he must make it his own, domesticate it. In Hegel's definition, the novel must educate man for living in bourgeois society."[38] At the same time, for Hegel, the novel not only *portrays* this process but actually helps to contribute to its achievement. Annemarie Gethmann-Siefert has argued that the "'*Bildung*' of human beings" is among the primary roles that Hegel ascribes to art:

> But it achieves this *Bildung* in the framework of the enlightened world and before the forum of "rationality-demanding reason" in the form of alternative *proposals* regarding world-significance and action, not in the form of *rules* and *commands* with the final claim to validity of religion. . . . Through alternative intuitions of the world and representations of human action, art forms [*bildet*] toward critical reflection: it is "formal *Bildung*."[39]

At the same time, when we consider the account of *Bildung* that Hegel offers in the *Philosophy of Right*, Gethmann-Siefert's claims might seem either too strong or misguided. That is, if the proper place of *Bildung* is civil society, why would art be necessary or important in the way that she suggests it is? I would like to conclude by showing that Hegel thinks that modern civil society in particular stands in need of the distinctive sort of work of which art is uniquely capable.

* * *

While engagement in the institutions and practices of civil society plays an essential role in individual *Bildung*, Hegel stresses that it contributes merely to the "formal freedom" of its members. Among the limitations that Hegel links to this merely formal freedom is the fact that the process of *Bildung* can happen outside of the "consciousness" of the individual.[40] It is true that my successful integration within civil society requires that I actually develop and change in such a way that, for example, my abilities can address the wants and needs of others in some way. However, Hegel considers this to be a merely "formal *universality of knowing and willing*" because it remains possible for me to consider both civil society itself and the others to whom I am related through it as (mere) "*means*" (*Mittel*).[41] But in this case the individual's particularity can be formed *in fact* through her integration within civil society, even if the meaning and significance of that transformation are not explicit *for her*, so that she retains the initial, instrumental attitude toward ethical institutions. This instrumental attitude, however, is potentially dangerous. On Hegel's account, civil society is "the system of ethicality lost in its extremes, that constitutes the abstract moment of the *reality* [*Realität*] of the idea, which here is only as the *relative totality* and *inner necessity* in this external appearance."[42] We have already seen one implication of the idea that in civil society we find only the extremes of ethicality, namely the fact that "in civil society, each is a purpose for herself, and everything else is nothing for her," when individuals treat their own particularity as the only thing that matters. However, this attitude toward oneself is equally the source of an instrumental attitude toward the institutions and practices of ethical life. When Hegel points to the mere "reality" (*Realität*) of civil society, he is identifying the way in which ethical institutions can come to appear as mere empty, humdrum appearances, and not as themselves essential for our highest aims. This characterization should recall the way in which, in the lectures on aesthetics, he identifies the "prosaic" character of modern life.

At the same time, in one of the most direct and powerful statements of the purpose of art that we find in the lectures, Hegel argues that the essential work of art is to cut through this mere empty reality and to show us what is true in the social world:

> The sensible present is reality [*Realität*]; the mode of presentation of art we call shine. . . . What is true in the sensible present are the powers therein, the spiritual [*Geistige*], ethical; these universal eternal powers [*Mächte*] are what is presented through art. Thus what is called appearance in art is that common reality [*gewöhnliche Realität*] is sublated. And the shine in it is a much truer, higher form in comparison to the form in which we are accustomed [*gewohnt*] to see the ethical. The ethicality of the common world [*gewöhnlichen Welt*] we call common reality. It is the chaos that we call reality; but the chaos is much more only in shine, and it is the powers in the chaos which art brings to appearance.[43]

On this account, art "sublates" the mere common reality, the prosaic way in which we are accustomed to encounter the social world, and instead shows us the "powers" that are really active therein: "The shine of art is thus not to be repudiated, rather it is common reality which appears as the inauthentic in comparison to it [that is to be repudiated], and [this shine] is a much higher mode of appearing than reality."[44] Given the predominance of this lower mode of appearing in civil society, it would seem that that ethical sphere is one that particularly requires artistic presentation, which brings to light the essential "powers" that are really true in it.[45]

How could art, and, in particular, the novel, do this? In the introductions to the lectures, Hegel assigns an essential ethical task to art, specifically in its role in the awakening and purification of the emotions, ultimately contributing to the achievement of liberation. In the 1826 lectures, Hegel claims it is "an essential power and activity of art" that it: "completes [*ergänzt*] the experience of our actual life, and through these excitations [*Erregungen*] we are made more able [to feel more fundamentally and deeply] in particular conditions and situations, or [we are prepared], so that [external circumstances] awaken these sensations, which was first made possible through these mediations in the intuition of art."[46] To be sure, Hegel points out that art can awaken passions of all kinds, including bad passions and for this reason such awakening of passions must serve another aim, namely their "purification," so that we no longer experience them immediately and overwhelmingly. Instead, when the passions are awakened through the engagement with works of art, we experience them in an objective way. Indeed, Hegel identifies "the highest final purpose of art" in its capacity to purify our passions, since this process of objective presentation can itself come to be a "power" that opposes passion in its subjective form.[47]

In the 1823 lectures, Hegel describes this process as one of the "tempering" (*Milderung*) of the "barbarism" (*Barberei*) of the passions. On this account, art sublates the "rawness" (*Roheit*) of the "drives, inclinations, and passions" by "forming" (*Bilden*) them.[48] This "rawness consists in a direct self-seeking of the drives, in desire, that seeks its satisfaction. . . . [D]esire is more raw the more that it, as individual and limited, takes over the whole human being, and the human being has not divided itself as individual from this determinacy."[49] By presenting these emotions in an objective, external form, the work of art weakens the hold that they have on the individual, so that the individual can stand in a relation of "freedom" to them.[50] But Hegel describes the process of *Bildung* in essentially the same terms in the *Philosophy of Right*, namely as the elimination of the "rawness" (*Roheit*) of subjectivity.[51] If artworks contribute to the mitigation of the barbarism of the passions, then they make an essential contribution to the *Bildung* that life in civil society ultimately requires.

The novel plays a particularly significant role in uniting these two strands of Hegel's account. Specifically, because of its subject matter, the novel can present directly the ethical *world* considered objectively, that is, as a set of customary institutions and practices, and, as a work of art, it can contribute to the "sublation" of the mere reality of that world, presenting the ethical "powers" that are true in it. At the same time, the novel can equally engage with the subjectivity of its characters, considering their individual "standpoint" and the process by means of which they come to be a "human being," the status that we come to enjoy as participants in civil society. Hegel's claim that in the novel, in contrast to the ancient epic, "what remains for the hero to do is their own subjectivity" might seem to be laden with a tone of dismissiveness. However, on his account of the moral purpose of the work of art, this exploration of subjectivity contributes in an essential way to the achievement of the final purpose of the work, liberation from the barbarism of the passions.

This is a distinctive account of the contribution that the novel can make to life in the institutions of modern civil society. In *The Structural Transformation of the Public Sphere*, Habermas identifies a central role for novel reading in contributing to the conditions for participation in the bourgeois public sphere. Habermas, too, thought that participation in market society was importantly limited, arguing that by itself it was not sufficient for achieving the sort of education and formation that is required for a public sphere. Instead, he pointed to the practice of novel reading as significant because of the contribution that it made to enlarging the individual's subjectivity, enabling them to empathize with others, and to assume their standpoint, both necessary abilities for the engagement in public reasoning. Indeed, Habermas holds that the cultivation of subjectivity that happens through novel reading broadens the individual's outlook beyond the narrow confines of bourgeois concern, expanding it to a concern with "*Humanität*" as such.[52] Hegel's account is similar, in that his remarks on the novel indicate that it can correct an important deficit within civil society. However, instead of stressing the role that the novel plays in establishing the right sorts of relations to *others*, Hegel instead points to two distinct contributions that the novel might make: First, as a work of art that can consider directly the "prose" of life in modern institutions, it can contribute to drawing out what is essential in those institutions, the "divine powers" that animate them, and thus to the sublation of the form of mere "reality" that plagues them in civil society. Second, while the novel engages with the subjectivity of the hero in direct and significant ways, this engagement does not, in the first instance, establish a different relation to *others*, but instead contributes to establishing the right sort of *self*-relation, namely one in which the individual is no longer subject to the constraints of her particular standpoint and perspective, specifically to her own particular passions and drives. Rather, as a work of art concerned with subjectivity, the novel can help to temper the rawness of the passions, and to enable the individual to assume a free relation to them, which, we have seen, Hegel thinks is the essential aim of *Bildung*, that is, the passing over from a particular point of view to a universal one.[53]

Conclusion

Where does this account of the novel leave us? Given the way that the novel came to assume even greater prominence in the course of the nineteenth century, not only in terms of its popularity but also in terms of its distinctive achievement as an aesthetic form, Hegel's account in the lectures may be particularly disappointing. It seems likely to me that one of the reasons that the novel-as-epic interpretation has assumed the stature that it has (aside from the interpretive basis for it in Hotho's text) lies in the fact that accounts like Lukács's create space for an aesthetically ambitious conception of the novel within a (more-or-less) Hegelian framework. Since my account of the lectures, which rejects the strict identification of the novel with the epic, undermines this conception, we might be worried that we are again condemned to disappointment with Hegel's remarks on the novel. Even if he is not a critic of the form as such, we might be concerned that his conception is uninspired or uninspiring, and of little importance when it comes to understanding the significance of the form. However, I believe that this disappointment need not be our fate. First, as I've suggested throughout, the novel-as-epic account is by no means the only or even most exciting one on offer. In drawing attention to some possible links between Hegel's rejection of the novel-as-epic thesis and Bakhtin's, I have hoped to show that my account of the lectures opens up some new territory for exploring the distinctive character and achievement of the novel as a literary form. Second, as Gethmann-Siefert stresses, in contrast to Hotho's monumental text, consideration of the lecture notes presents us with a picture of Hegel's aesthetic thinking as a project underway, rather than as a single, complete, coherent system. Indeed, I have worked to point to some ways in which Hegel's own thinking on the novel in particular seems to develop and change throughout the 1820s in Berlin. Instead of seeing our primary task as figuring out where the novel fits within Hegel's apparent system of the arts, we should instead work to consider what conceptual resources Hegel offers us for thinking about the novel, even if those resources are not all put to best use within the lectures themselves.[54]

At the same time, I do believe that Hegel's account of novels like *Wilhelm Meisters Lehrjahre* indicates one important direction that we should take in thinking about the meaning and significance of the novel and novels. It is central to Hegel's remarks about Goethe's novel that it be understood in relation to concrete *social forms*, in particular in relation to civil society, about the distinctive status that we enjoy as participants in civil society—that of the "human being"—and about the struggles we face in achieving reconciliation within civil society—of overcoming the oppressive character of the seemingly empty *Realität* of modern institutional life, of negotiating the relationship between individual ideals and social reality, and of achieving just relations to others who are to enjoy the same human status as ourselves. This centrality of society to the novel in Hegel's account is significant for a number of reasons. However, if we are concerned with the vitality and relevance of Hegel's account of the novel, we would do well to work to appreciate the distinctive picture that we find in Hegel's lectures.

Abbreviations

Works by G. W. F. Hegel:

Ä *Vorlesungen über die Ästhetik* I-III, *Theorie Werkausgabe* 13–15, edited by Eva Moldenauer and Karl Markus Michel. Frankfurt am Main: Suhrkamp, 1970. Cited by volume and page number.

Ä 1820/21. *Wintersemester 1820/21 Nachschrift Wilhelm von Aschenberg und Willem Sax Van Terborg*. In *Vorlesungen Über die Philosophie der Kunst*, edited by Niklas Hebing. *Gesammelte Werke* 28, 1. Hamburg: Meiner, 2015.

Ä 1823a. *Vorlesungen über die Philosophie der Kunst*, edited by Annemarie Gethmann-Siefert. Hamburg: Meiner, 2003.

Ä 1823b. *Sommersemester 1823. Nachschrift Heinrich Gustav Hotho*. In *Vorlesungen Über die Philosophie der Kunst*, edited by Hebing. *Gesammelte Werke* 28, 1. Hamburg: Meiner, 2015.

Ä 1826a. *Philosophie der Kunst, Vorlesung von 1826*, edited by Annemarie Gethmann-Siefert, Jeong-Im Kwon, and Karsten Berr. Frankfurt am Main: Suhrkamp, 2004.

Ä 1826b. *Philosophie der Kunst oder Ästhetik. Nach Hegel. Im Sommer 1826. Mitschrift Friedrich Carl Hermann Victor von Kehler*, edited by Annemarie Gethmann-Siefert, Bernadette Collenberg-Plotnikov, with Francesca Iannelli, and Karsten Barr. Munich: Wilhelm Fink, 2004.

Ä 1828/29. *Vorlesungen zur Ästhetik. Vorlesungnsmitschrift Adolf Heimann (1828/1829)*, edited by Alain Patrick Olivier and Annemarie Gethmann-Siefert. Munich: Wilhelm Fink, 2017.

PhG *Die Phänomenologie des Geistes*, edited by Hans-Friedrich Wessels and Heinrich Clairmont. Hamburg: Meiner, 1988. Cited by paragraph and page number.

PR *Grundlinien der Philosophie des Rechts*, *Theorie Werkausgabe* 7. Cited by section and page number.

Notes

1 According to Stephen Bungay, Hegel "does not fully theorize" the novel. Bungay, *Beauty and Truth: A Study of Hegel's Aesthetics* (Oxford: Oxford University Press, 1984), 163. On Speight's account, "Despite the profusion of novelistic literature in his own time and his own significant appropriation of it for the limning of essential moments of the development of the world-historical spirit, Hegel's official *Aesthetics*

hardly presents what one could claim to be an especially worked-out *theory* of the novel." C. Allen Speight, "Lukács and Hegel on the Novel," *Bulletin of the Hegel Society of Great Britain* 62 (2010): 23. Weiss argues that, in spite of the centrality of the novel among the early romantics, the novel seems to "elude" (*entziehen*) Hegel. János Weiss, "Die Theorie des Romans in Hegels Ästhetik," in *Hegels Ästhetik als Theorie der Moderne*, ed. Annemarie Gethmann-Siefert, Herta Nagl-Docekal, Erzsébet Rósza, and Elisabeth Weisser-Lohmann (Berlin: Akademie Verlag 2013), 67.

2 I consider the elements of this discussion in detail below.
3 See, for example, the discussion of Hegel's "critique of the novel" in Benjamin Rutter, *Hegel and the Modern Arts* (Cambridge: Cambridge University Press, 2010), 257–65. While I disagree that Hegel is a critic of the kind that Rutter claims, his treatment of the relevant issues is otherwise excellent.
4 Speight, "Lukács and Hegel on the Novel," 23, and Speight, *Hegel, Literature, and the Problem of Agency* (Cambridge: Cambridge University Press, 2001).
5 Klaus Vieweg, "Komik und Humor als literarisch-poetisch Skepsis—Hegel und Laurence Sterne," in *Skepsis und literarische Imagination*, ed. Bernd Hüppauf and Vieweg (Munich: Wilhelm Fink, 2003), 64.
6 It is a limitation of my account that I focus on what would come to be known as the *Bildungsroman*, *Wilhelm Meisters Lehrjahre* in particular. I do not consider "subjective humor" and Hegel's remarks concerning Jean Paul.
7 For the factors contributing to the assembly of Hotho's 1835 text, see Annemarie Gethmann-Siefert, *Einführung in Hegels Ästhetik* (Munich: Wilhelm Fink, 2005), 15–24 esp.
8 The forthcoming volume 28, 2 of the *Gesammelte Werke* will include editions of the 1826 and 1828/29 lectures. There are, as yet, no published versions of the lectures Hegel delivered in Heidelberg in 1818.
9 *Ä* 1820–21, 112. Unless otherwise noted, all translations from the German are my own.
10 *Ä* 1823a, 197–98.
11 *Ä* 1826a, 170.
12 *Ä* 1828/29, 125.
13 *Ä* 1826a, 240.
14 Ibid., 232–33.
15 Bungay, *Beauty and Truth*, 163.
16 Weiss, "Die Theorie des Romans in Hegels Ästhetik," 78.
17 Georg Lukács, *The Theory of the Novel*, trans. Anna Bostock (Cambridge, MA: MIT Press, 1971). On the relation between Hegel and Lukács on the novel, see Speight, "Lukács and Hegel on the Novel," and Niklas Hebing, *Unversöhnbarkeit. Hegels Ästhetik und Lukács' Theorie des Romans* (Duisburg: Universitätsverlag Rhein-Ruhr, 2009).
18 Henry Fielding, *The History and Adventures of Joseph Andrews and His Friend Mr. Abraham Adams* (1742; London: George Bell and Sons, 1908), 2.
19 *Ä* III, 392.
20 "[Unser] modernes Epos [ist] der Roman." *Ä* 1826b, 217.
21 "Eine andere Form schließt sich ans Epos an: der Roman, under sogenanntes modernes Epos." *Ä* 1826a, 240.
22 *Ä* 1828/29,197.
23 *Ä* III, 392.

24 Of course, it is also possible to *overstate* the significance of the novel for Hegel. While intriguing, Weiss's claim that the novel amounts to the repressed "unconscious" of Hegel's philosophy of art overstates the significance of the novel in the lectures. Ultimately, I disagree that the novel presents the sorts of challenges to comprehension that Weiss suggests it does.
25 On this score, I agree with Gethmann-Siefert's claim that we should consider the lectures to be a "work in progress," rather than a finished, systematic account of art.
26 See especially "Epic and Novel," the first essay in M. M. Bakhtin, *The Dialogic Imagination*, ed. Michael Holquist, trans. Caryl Emerson and Holiquist (Austin: University of Texas Press, 1981).
27 See Hegel's account of the conclusion of this dialectic in *PhG* 391/258.
28 *PR* §150, R, 298–300.
29 "Without arrogance and noise, as the *Bildung* of a striving spirit silently develops, and as the becoming world quietly emerges out of its inner, the clear history begins." Friedrich Schlegel, "Über Goethes Meister," in *Athenäums-Fragmente und andere Schriften*, ed. Andreas Huyssen (Stuttgart: Reclam, 1998), 143.
30 "Individuality is the primordial and eternal in human beings. . . . To drive toward the *Building* and development of this individuality as the highest task would be a divine egoism [*göttlicher Egoismus*]." Schlegel, *Ideen*, in *Kritische-Schlegel-Ausgabe* II, ed. Ernst Behler, Jean-Jacques Anstatt, and Hans Eichner (Paderborn: Ferdinand Schoeningh, 1958–), 262 (#60).
31 *Ä* 1823a, 198.
32 *Ä* 1826a, 170.
33 "Only in this way is spirit *at home* and *with itself* [bei sich] in this *externality* as such." PR §187R, 344.
34 PR §187R, 344–45.
35 PR §187, 343.
36 Ibid.
37 PR §190, R, 347–48.
38 From "Forms of Time and the Chronotope in the Novel" in Bakhtin, *The Dialogic Imagination*, 234. In situating Hegel's position in relation to Bakhtin's account of the novel, my aim is not to offer an interpretation of the aims or implications of *The Dialogic Imagination* as a whole.
39 Annemarie Gethmann-Siefert, "Einführung," in *Ä 1826a*, 35–36.
40 *PR* §187, 343.
41 Ibid.
42 *PR* §184, 340.
43 *Ä* 1826b, 25.
44 Ibid. It merits noting that the German term that I have translated as "shine," *Schein*, has a distinctive significance. *Schein* is a category of Hegel's essence-logic and is initially contrasted with what is essential as "mere" appearance. In the lectures on aesthetics, however, Hegel is explicit about the sense in which "shine" is itself essential to art: "Shine [*Schein*] is therefore the mode of externality of art. But what shine is, what relation it has to essence, regarding this it is to be said that all essence, all truth must appear [*erscheinen*], in order not to be an empty abstraction. . . . Shine is nothing inessential, but rather an essential moment of the essence itself. In spirit, the true is for itself, shines in itself, exists [*ist da*] for others." *Ä* 1823a, 2.

45 I present a more extensive account of this passage and its significance for Hegel's aesthetics in Timothy L. Brownlee, "Hegel on the Need for a Philosophy of Art: An Ethical Account," in *The Necessity of Freedom in Hegel: Logic, Phenomenology and History*, ed. Emilia Angelova (Toronto: University of Toronto Press, forthcoming).
46 Ä 1826a, 56.
47 Ibid., 57.
48 Ä 1823a, 27.
49 Ibid.
50 Ibid., 28.
51 *PR* §187$, 344.
52 Jürgen Habermas, *Strukturwandel der Öffentlichkeit* (1962; Frankfurt am Main: Suhrkamp Verlag, 1990), 112. For Habermas's account of the function of novel reading more broadly, see §6 of this work.
53 I think it's not unreasonable for Gethmann-Siefert to stress the more Habermasian idea that works of art expose one to alternative viewpoints, and I don't think that account is *inconsistent* with Hegel's. But it does merit notice that his primary focus in the lectures is on the role that artworks can play in establishing the right self-relation, which happens through the objective presentation of the particular, subjective passions and drives to which one is otherwise unfreely bound.
54 And, of course, there is a place for interpreters like Speight and Hebing, who look for links between Hegel's account of the novel and that of thinkers like Lukács.

Bibliography

Other Sources

Bakhtin, M. M. *The Dialogic Imagination*, edited by Michael Holquist and translated by Caryl Emerson and Michael Holquist. Austin: University of Texas Press, 1981.

Brownlee, Timothy L. "Hegel on the Need for a Philosophy of Art: An Ethical Account." In *The Necessity of Freedom in Hegel: Logic, Phenomenology and History*, edited by Emilia Angelova. Toronto: University of Toronto Press, Forthcoming.

Bungay, Stephen. *Beauty and Truth: A Study of Hegel's Aesthetics*. Oxford: Oxford University Press, 1984.

Fielding, Henry. *The History and Adventures of Joseph Andrews and His Friend Mr. Abraham Adams*. 1742. London: George Bell and Sons, 1908.

Gethmann-Siefert, Annemarie. "Einführung." In G. W. F. Hegel. *Philosophie der Kunst, Vorlesung von 1826*, edited by Gethmann-Siefert, Jeong-Im Kwon, and Karsten Berr. Frankfurt am Main: Suhrkamp, 2004.

Gethmann-Siefert, Annemarie. *Einführung in Hegels Ästhetik*. Munich: Wilhelm Fink, 2005.

Habermas, Jürgen. *Strukturwandel der Öffentlichkeit*. 1962. Frankfurt am Main: Suhrkamp, 1990.

Hebing, Niklas. *Unversöhnbarkeit. Hegels Ästhetik und Lukács' Theorie des Romans*. Duisburg: Universitätsverlag Rhein-Ruhr, 2009.

Lukács, Georg. *The Theory of the Novel*, translated by Anna Bostock. Cambridge, MA: MIT Press, 1971.

Rutter, Benjamin. *Hegel and the Modern Arts*. Cambridge: Cambridge University Press, 2010.

Schlegel, Friedrich. *Ideen*. In *Kritische-Schlegel-Ausgabe*, II, edited by Ernst Behler, Jean-Jacques Anstatt, and Hans Eichner, 256–72. Paderborn: Ferdinand Schoeningh, 1958–.

Schlegel, Friedrich. "Über Goethes Meister." In *Athenäums-Fragmente und andere Schriften*, edited by Andreas Huyssen, 143–64. Stuttgart: Reclam, 1998.

Speight, C. Allen. *Hegel, Literature, and the Problem of Agency*. Cambridge: Cambridge University Press, 2001.

Speight, C. Allen. "Lukács and Hegel on the Novel." *Bulletin of the Hegel Society of Great Britain* 62 (2010): 23–34.

Vieweg, Klaus. "Komik und Humor als literarisch-poetisch Skepsis—Hegel und Laurence Sterne." In *Skepsis und literarische Imagination*, edited by Bernd Hüppauf, and Vieweg, 63–76. Munich: Wilhelm Fink, 2003.

Weiss, János. "Die Theorie des Romans in Hegels Ästhetik." In *Hegels Ästhetik als Theorie der Moderne*, edited by Annemarie Gethmann-Siefert, Herta Nagl-Docekal, Erzsébet Rósza, and Elisabeth Weisser-Lohmann, 67–82. Berlin: Akademie Verlag, 2013.

4

On Art, Religion, and Recognitive Communities

Philip T. Grier

Introduction: On a Functional Definition of Art

In the "Introduction" to her influential edition of the Hotho transcript of Hegel's 1823 lectures on the philosophy of art, Annemarie Gethmann-Siefert observed that "Hegel takes for his model and standard not *works of art* but instead a *function of art* within the culture."[1] Moreover, she argued that Hegel's treatment of the function of art varied, depending upon the historical timeframe and the culture in question. She views Hegel's lectures on aesthetics as a historicallybased phenomenology of art in terms of its cultural functions, and not as a systematizing imposition of the concept upon the raw materials of art history, which is the impression sometimes gained from Hotho's editing of both original *Werke* editions of the *Aesthetics*.[2]

To be sure, there is a striking passage in Hotho's transcript of Hegel's 1823 lectures on the philosophy of art that may appear at first glance to support the claim that Hegel's aesthetics should indeed be seen as "a systematizing imposition of the concept upon the raw materials of art history." It reads:

> The procedure in aesthetics is like the procedure in natural science, where one must not establish subdivisions according to what is simply there; instead, the concept must be established and the particular cases must arrange themselves in accord with the concept. It is then evident that many of the particular cases are not commensurate with the concept, and this is not the concept's fault. We cannot be definitive about these hybrid natures. The fables of Aesop are one such hybrid form.[3]

Two points should be made here. First, Hegel's reference to procedure in natural science can presumably be assimilated to his account of empirical science in the *Encyclopedia Logic*, where he emphasizes that scientific understanding cannot be grounded in mere perception alone, because, as he states, "Perception as such is always something singular that passes away, but cognition does not stop at this stage. On the contrary, in the perceived singular it seeks what is universal and abides; and this is the advance from mere perception to experience."[4] Empirical cognition takes place then not merely at the level of perception ("what is simply there"), but in terms of "universal notions, principles and laws" *suggested by* perception.[5] *Experience* is then a *reformulation* at the level of abstraction of the contents of mere perception. However, such notions, principles, and laws are presumably always subject to revision in the light of the further deliverances of perception. There would be no basis for thinking of these abstractions as *a priori* concepts simply being *imposed* upon perception.

Second, in the passage just quoted Hegel observes that "the concept must be established," implying likewise, that such a concept is not an *a priori* imposition of some abstract metaphysical category, but an attempt at a rational ordering worked out from the study of a wide range of specific examples—which is essentially what the *Aesthetics* appears to be (among other things). The categories of Hegel's *Logic* are sometimes viewed as products of some sort of purely abstract exercise in theory construction, but there are good reasons for thinking of them as no less *a posteriori* than *a priori*, grounded in the contingencies of finite experience, even though such contingencies are presented in the *Logic* (as opposed to the *Realphilosophie*) as already sublated in thought. According to Errol Harris, "The Logic is that phase of human thought in which finite experience of the world and of human affairs becomes aware of itself as the self-awareness of the world through human experience."[6] If this is right, then the categories of Hegel's *Logic* must also be seen as being ultimately grounded in the experience of finite human beings. And if cultural histories present us with a great variety of objects, many bearing some but not all the marks that we have concluded must be exhibited by paradigm instances of true works of art, that is not proof of an illegitimate "imposition" of an *a priori* category. It would rather be an illustration of the commonplace observation that any attempt to apply a discrete definitional category to an indefinitely large and boundlessly varied population of possible instances of a phenomenon would almost certainly produce borderline cases: hence, Hegel's "hybrid forms" of aesthetic objects.

Continuing in the spirit of Gethmann-Siefert's focus upon the *function* of art as its most significant defining characteristic in Hegel's view, I propose to reconsider Hegel's account of the development of art by focusing especially upon its functions within religious experience, as depicted in the *Lectures on the Philosophy of Religion*, particularly in the relatively neglected middle part on *Determinate Religion*,[7] in addition to the more usual source, the *Lectures on Aesthetics*. Paying attention to both sources simultaneously should serve to underscore the centrality of this fundamental connection between art and religion in Hegel's thinking and likewise to further highlight the paramount religious function of art throughout most of its history in Hegel's conception of it.

That function, stated in the most basic terms, is to serve as one of the means whereby spirit distinguishes itself from nature, producing itself as freely acting subjectivity, existing *for* itself as well as *in* itself, developing through successive stages to reveal its ultimate actuality as inwardly self-determining, self-differentiating, self-unfolding thought—infinite, Absolute Spirit producing its own other in the forms of nature and finite spirit. Absolute Spirit actualizes itself by entering into the sphere of the finite as its own self-manifestation, and returning to self as infinite spirit, now also embracing the finite, hence fully actual. This is essentially Hegel's philosophical account of the development of the Divine (God being conceived as a representation of Absolute Spirit), and it overlaps his account of the development of art in crucial respects.

However, the histories of religion and art are not coextensive in his view; the phenomenon of religion is significantly older than the phenomenon of fine art (though not of art in a more general sense, symbolic art). Hegel divided the history of religions into three basic phases: (1) the immediate, or nature religions, (2) the religions of spiritual individuality or freedom, and (3) the consummate, or Christian, religion, that is, religion *so consummated* as to correspond to its concept.[8] The first of the three basic forms of religion encompasses everything from religions of magic (the earliest, borderline cases, possibly not deserving of the description "religion") to the religions of ancient China and India.

Hegel's Histories of Religion and Art

A common feature of all the nature religions, even the earliest according to Hegel, is that while they conceive God as spirit in some sense, the highest reality for human beings, and do not simply take some external, physical object to be God,[9] they, nevertheless, all conceive the spiritual to be united in some fashion with the natural, meaning that spirit is not yet free, not yet grasped in its subjectivity, not yet actual as spirit.[10] On the other hand, human *self-consciousness* in some form is present throughout all the determinate religions, including the earliest nature religions, and human self-consciousness is in essence the presence of spirit.[11] Thus the spiritual is present from the beginning, even when not yet recognized in its truth. At the same time, the progression of these finite religions is a precondition for religion to arrive at its absolute truth, for spirit coming to be for spirit, for the relationship of spirit to spirit, which is itself a condition for the attainment by spirit itself of its truly infinite determinateness.[12]

Across the four sets of lectures Hegel delivered on the philosophy of religion (1821, 1824, 1827, and 1831), he continued to rearrange the precise sequencing of the religions composing his history, apparently never settling on a final version before his death. These changes particularly affected his account of the transition to the second of the three major forms of religion—that is, the religions of spiritual individuality or freedom—as well as the sequencing of religions within that form. For example, depending upon which lecture series we are attending to, ancient Judaic religion (the "religion of sublimity") is either the first or the second of the religions of spiritual individuality, alongside ancient Greek religion. Alternatively, it constitutes a transitional form already *within* the category of the religions of freedom, grouped with the ancient Persian and ancient Egyptian religions. Similarly, he treats the religion of ancient Egypt either as a transitional form of nature religion *leading to* the religions of spiritual individuality or as a transitional form already *within* that second category.

However, from the standpoint of the history of art, Hegel seems much more settled in his view that Egyptian religion supplied the immediate transition to the "religion of beauty" of the ancient Greeks, and hence the emergence of fine art proper. In the context of Egyptian religion, we encounter subjectivity for the first time in the form of representation.[13] This he attributes to the figure of Osiris. Osiris dies (a negation), yet is perpetually restored to life (a negation of a negation pertaining to his very essence), which places the god beyond the realm of the merely natural and finite. Consequently, he is regarded as ruler of the dead as well as of the living, representing an elementary form of subjectivity.[14] This ancient Egyptian attempt to distinguish spiritual subjectivity from the merely natural and finite, to keep the forces of nature at bay even in death, and finally, to depict this entire conception of reality for themselves, took the form of vast architectural constructions: the pyramids, temples, the labyrinth, etc., involving extraordinary masses of labor.[15]

> This colossal diligence of an entire people was not yet in and for itself pure fine art; rather it was the impulsion toward fine art. Fine art involves the characteristic of free subjectivity; spirit must have become free from desire, free from natural life generally, from subjugation by inner and outer nature; it must have become inwardly free, it must have the need to know itself as free, and to be free, as the object of its own consciousness.[16]

This impulsion or craving for fine art visible especially in the domain of Egyptian architecture was thus merely evidence of a *craving* in Hegel's judgment; the beauty of fine art itself had not yet emerged as such, because spirit had not yet succeeded in raising itself above nature.[17] Egyptian art thus remained in the initial *symbolic* phase, falling short of the achievement of "fine art" that defined the *classical* phase.

Fine art proper enters this historical narrative fully only when the religions of "spiritual individuality" or "freedom" arise. It enters particularly in the form of the *cultus* of ancient Greek religion. Every religion, even nature religion, is described as having some form of *cultus*, in which finite human consciousness collectively encounters the divine (in whatever conception it possesses) and recognizes an essential relation between itself and the divine, expressed in some form of worship or devotion. In the 1821 Manuscript, Hegel described the main features of the *cultus* of the nature religions as consisting of (1) abstract devotion, and (2) concrete devotion or *cultus* in the proper sense, including the activities of daily life, ritual sacrifices, and productive labor. Strictly speaking, there are two kinds of life, religious life and ordinary, everyday life, but the two sides may not be distinguished; everyday life may simply be a life lived routinely in relation to religion. The *cultus* would thus be a community of finite human beings conducting their everyday lives in relation to their own representations of their gods.[18]

The emergence of the "religion of beauty" in ancient Greece marked the inception of genuine art because the Greeks took their sculptures of the individual gods, conceived with human-like forms, as the focal objects of worship within their *cultus*, a development that signified the emergence of a concept of spirit in its *subjectivity* or *spiritual individuality* (though in a somewhat limited form, to be sure). "The distinctively novel relationship, however, is the standpoint of *art*, i.e., of *fine art*. This is the precise point where art must emerge in religion, and where it has a necessary role."[19] He acknowledges that art can be merely *mimetic*, but then it is not *fine* art, "not truly divine, not what is truly needed for religion; where it *is* that, where it *emerges* as it essentially *is*, it pertains to the very concept of God . . . Genuine art is religious art."[20] The gods of Olympus were, to be sure, quite limited by comparison to the God of Christianity: their subjectivity was abstract, they were finite in their random multiplicity, and constrained by necessity or fate, but their representations in the sensuous materials of sculpture achieved an ideal of beauty, an expression of subjectivity in sensuous form.[21]

Beauty, the ideal, the highest achievement of art, is conceived by Hegel as the complete unity of content and form in the work of art, where the content is the universal element, the contribution of spirit, while the form is what is realized in the sensuous medium. To achieve beauty, the determinate being, the immediacy, of a work of art (as a human production) must be wholly determined by spirit, where "all externality is completely characteristic and significant, is determined from within as from what is free." "The natural moment must be mastered everywhere in such a way that it serves only for the expression and revelation of spirit."[22] Beauty is realized when "Form and content are absolutely one and the same with neither aspect predominating, with the content determining the form and the form determining the content: oneness in pure universality."[23] Speaking of the history of art as a whole, Hegel observed succinctly that the beautiful is at first *sought after*(the symbolic), is *achieved*(the classical), and then *transcends* the achievement(the romantic).[24]

In the first stage of art (the symbolic), divinity is still conceived in relation to natural objects, and genuine art has not yet been achieved, only sought after. In the second stage (the classical), the divinities are thought to be present in the form of works of art (sculptures of the Olympian gods). They are conceived as *subjectivities*, and thus religion and art coincide, are coextensive. This intersection of the two in ancient Greece realized the ideal of artistic beauty in Hegel's view. In the third stage (the romantic or Christian), the content surpasses the form, requiring more than the artistic depiction is capable of providing.[25] The divine, conceived as infinite spirit, can only be grasped in thought; no sensuous representation is possible. As Hegel made clear in his treatment of the Judaic religion of sublimity, God, Absolute Spirit conceived independently of the incarnation, cannot possibly be sensibly presented: the pure Absolute is thought, and only for thought.

The Transition from Nature to Spirit

In its initial manifestation, however, spirit is limited to human consciousness gradually becoming aware of itself, beginning to distinguish itself from the finite realm of nature:

> What we can say at this point is that the universality of the need for art involves none other than the fact that human beings are thinking, are conscious. In being consciousness, one must place before oneself what one is and what, on the whole, exists; one must have these as one's objects. Natural things just *are*; they are just onefold, just simply exist (*sind nur einfach, nur einmal*). Yet as consciousness, human beings double themselves; they simply *are*, and then are *for themselves*.

They bring before themselves what they are, intuiting themselves, standing before themselves, and are consciousness of themselves. They simply bring before themselves what they are. So the universal need for the work of art is to be sought in a human being's thought, since for a human being the work of art is a way of bringing before oneself what one is.[26]

Making basically the same observation from an explicitly religious perspective, Hegel claims that "the need to make the subject visible through art can arise only when the moment of natural immediacy is overcome in the concept by the moment of freedom—or when the essence of God begins to be essentially free and self-determining."[27]

At one point, Hegel discussed the process of spirit's emergence from nature in practical terms as the moderation of barbarity, as taming the passions and savagery of the natural condition, and he acknowledged this as one of the valid purposes of art, though a subsidiary one. We presumably also view this as a subsidiary purpose in the contemporary world; however, the closer to the natural condition we imagine humanity to be, presumably the more significant we assume this function of art to be. (And, perhaps, the more concerned we happen to be about an innate savagery being revealed in contemporary human beings, the more likely we are to view this function of art as being of permanent importance.) To live within the merely natural condition is to be ruled by desire, by a direct selfishness of the impulses, to live in a condition of coarseness. "Coarseness" refers to living in the complete selfishness of immediate impulses, aimed at the entire satisfaction of self to the exclusion of the interests of all others, indeed converting others into mere instruments for the satisfaction of one's own desires.[28]

To continue living in such a natural condition is to fail to recognize the intrinsic freedom of one's own subjectivity as the capacity to will purposes other than those demanded by one's immediate natural condition, to resist or negate the promptings of immediate passion and desire.

The contribution of art to transcending this situation is through truthful portrayals of the natural passions and impulses themselves, thus turning those same passions and impulses into an object for human beings, depicting what one is. Such depictions serve as a force for moderation, enabling humans to examine their own baser instincts, now rendered external to them, with greater detachment, freeing them to reject such instincts.[29]

The complex of natural human feelings, inclinations, and passions contains both what is higher and what is lower, both good and evil alike. Art can inspire humans to seek what is higher and discourage the pursuit of the lower passions. People are freed to search for a higher purpose, one involving something existent in and for itself.[30] The proper subject matter of genuine art is just these same essentialities, which are existent in and for themselves. In this way art can contribute directly to liberating us from the merely natural condition and, through the promotion of self-consciousness, to disclosing the free subjectivity of spirit inherent in our true being.

Hegel's depiction of the immediacy of the singular individual's relation to the sensuous object of desire—that it simply uses it, consumes it, maintains itself by sacrificing the other—reflects the unthinking nature of this relation. The singular individual confronts the singular object of sensuous desire as a matter of purely individual, natural interest. The alternative to such a relation he describes as taking up what constitutes the universal in singular thingsas opposed to their singularity, their immediate, determinate being; rather, choosing them for the sake of some "universal" determination.[31] But this is possible only for the individual who has begun to grasp the universality inherent in his or her own being. The transformation from immediacy, the state of nature, to spirit depends upon the human capacity for thought, the capacity to take ourselves inwardly as objects for thought. "Thinking is knowledge of the universal."[32] "The unending drive of thinking is to transpose what is real [i.e., the true universal] into ourselves as something that is universal and ideal [i.e., transcends the merely finite]."[33] As a result we cease being merely natural, cease living in our immediate intuitions, drives, and satisfactions. We restrain our drives, interposing representation, thought, the ideal, between the urgency of the drive and its satisfaction.[34] We formulate purposes grounded in thought, entertaining objectives that we contemplate prior to executing them, choosing options for action based upon such objectives.

> The specific objective can be something wholly universal if one posits what is wholly universal as one's purpose. The most boundless universal is boundless freedom. Human beings can posit this freedom as their aim or purpose.... [W]hat constitutes the abstract wellspring of human nature as such is thinking, the being of humans as spirit, as I; this constitutes the principle by which spirit is spirit.[35]

The defining characteristic of spirit, the ultimate aim of this transition from nature to spirit, is thus freedom, the freedom that can be possessed only by self-creating, self-knowing subjectivity, which is at the same time substance, actuality, what exists in and for itself, transcending the realm of finitude.

"Immediate" versus "Universal" Singularity

The passage in the Hotho transcript distinguishing the immediacy, the singularity, of the natural condition from the universality of the spiritual condition may be regarded as a foreshadowing of a more full-blown version of the same distinction that Hegel elaborated in *The Berlin Phenomenology* (1825), that is, the distinction between "immediate singularity" and "universal singularity."[36] The former characterizes the individual living in a merely natural condition: "Self-consciousness in its immediacy is *singular*, and constitutes *desire*."[37] Such individuals, "fixed in the being-for-self of desire are said to be barbarous. This raw state exists in so far as man is bent upon his desire as a single being."[38] In this case "the immediate singularity of my self-consciousness and my freedom are not yet separated. I am unable to surrender anything of my particularity without surrendering my free independence."[39] In recognizing another as a free being, I lose my own freedom.[40] Such is the condition of the singular self-consciousness in its natural immediacy; to remain thus isolated from others in this condition is ultimately evil. To escape this condition, it is necessary for the individual to transcend the particularity of desire to which its self-consciousness has previously been restricted and elevate the self-consciousness of its own freedom into universal self-consciousness (reason).[41] For this to occur, self-consciousness must "give itself determinate being in another consciousness, i.e., be recognized by another," which is to say, find its being objectively reflected in another free and independent self-consciousness.[42]

Hegel was of the opinion that the only way this transformation could be brought about in the natural condition was through force, through a life-and-death struggle for recognition that ended in establishing one individual as lord over a great many others who become bound in servitude to the lord, or vassals, that is, the origin of the state. ("Force is then necessary and justified, and heroes have founded states by using it."[43]) The details of Hegel's account of the struggle for recognition are well known and needn't be rehearsed here. What is important for now is his characterization of the ultimate outcome: the condition of "universal singularity" or universal self-consciousness.

> *Universal self-consciousness* is the affirmative knowing of one's self in the other self. Each self has *absolute independence* as a free singularity, but on account of the negation of its immediacy or desire, does not differentiate itself from the other. Each is therefore universal and objective, and possesses the real nature of universality as reciprocity, in that it knows itself to be recognized by its free counterpart, and knows that it knows this in so far as it recognizes the other and knows it to be free.
>
> This universal reflectedness of self-consciousness is the Concept, which since it knows itself to be in its objectivity as subjectivity identical with itself, knows itself to be universal. This form of consciousness constitutes not only the *substance* of all the essential spirituality of the family, the native country, the state, but also of all virtues—of love, friendship, valor, honor, fame.[44]

The resulting condition is "the unmediated universality and objectivity of self-consciousness,—reason, and, as that which gives itself determinate being, as consciousness, *reason is spirituality*."[45] Thus the transition from "immediate singularity" to "universal singularity" is nothing less than the transition from the natural condition to spirit. The institutions of family and state, law, ethical duty, virtue, love, and friendship are grounded in the spiritual substance of mutually recognitive community, and genuine art, fine art, aims at portraying these as existentinandforthemselves, as what is substantial.

It is worth noting that Hegel does not appear to conceive of humanity living in the finitude of nature as a phenomenon restricted to the dawn of civilization, something inevitably overcome by the emergence of states and the substantial ethical powers intrinsic to them. Rather, he appears to believe that remaining in this state of sheer finitude is a permanent possibility for human beings at any stage of history. Describing three possible spiritual states at the outset of his discussion of the romantic art form, he lists them as (1) the human figure directly known as having divinity within itself, namely, Christ; (2) the human being beginning from itself as finite, natural spirit, originating not from God but instead from finitude, yet elevating itself to God, relinquishing the natural state;[46] (3) also beginning apart from God but *not* elevating itself to God, instead remaining situated in finitude. This third, natural state is something evil, something finite.It is something purely contingent, not valid in and for itself, but instead is the kind of natural state in which spirit does not discover its own existence.[47] The ultimate form of finitude is of course death, and this third state would represent something close to it: a perpetually moribund state of spirit. We will re-encounter this possibility in Hegel's description of the "modern" condition.[48]

Art and the Fixity of Ethical Life

The spiritual condition resulting from this mutual reciprocal recognition lifting us out of the natural condition is thus necessarily *communal*. The life of spirit is a life lived within recognitive community. The first and most fundamental such recognitive community, in which self-consciousness achieves objectivity, is the state (whether primitive or modern) and life within a state, the life of the state, constitutes the primary form of objective spirit, the form in which spirit is first actualized in the world. In a set of lectures delivered in 1823, Hegel described membership in the state in the following terms:

> The living power of the state in individuals is what we have called *ethical life*. The state, its laws and institutions, are theirs, are their right; so also are their external possessions in nature—the soil, mountains, air, and waters—as their land, their native land. The history of this state, its deeds and the deeds of their forefathers, are theirs; it lives in their memory as having brought forth what now exists, what belongs to them. All this is their possession, just as they are possessed by it; for it constitutes their substance and being. Their way of thinking (*Vorstellung*) is fulfilled within it, and their will is the willing of the laws of their native land. This spiritual totality constitutes a single essential being, the *spirit* of a people.[49]

The various elements of ethical life—that essential power which "constitutes their substance and being"—are the institutions of law, morality, duty, virtue, and so forth, achievements of spirit, which make of the state the objectification of (a form of) freedom. Such elements of ethical life as these are existent inandforthemselves, which is to say they are *substantial*, transcending the condition of mere finitude, of merely contingent being. What is merely finite is inevitably subject to death, the ultimate mark of finitude. "Death takes from people what is temporal and ephemeral in them, but has no power over what is in and for itself."[50] Indeed, humans have within themselves "a region that is in and for self,"[51] which is to say, that which transcends finitude, is not subject to natural contingency, but shares in the substance of the concrete universal, which will ultimately be identified as Absolute Spirit.

The task of the artist is to depict these elements of spirit, of what exists inandforitself. They constitute the proper subject matter of genuine art, art that is a product of the free subjectivity of the artist. In this respect, art shares with religion and philosophy the task of "expressing and bringing to consciousness the divine, the highest demand of spirit."[52] In the case of the Greeks, the gods were first recognized as these substantive powers transcending what was merely external or contingent. Duties, justice, knowledge, civic and political life, family relationships—these were recognized as what is true, what is valid in and for itself, as the substantive bonds that hold the world together.⁵³ In depicting these gods, the artists were depicting their people's own customs, their ethical life.⁵⁴ Athena was both the city and also the goddess, that is, the spirit of the people, their living, actual, present spirit represented in its essentiality, its universality.⁵⁵

> The free artist is internally resolute and must also be technically prepared. He always has for his object a content that is existent-in-and-for-itself, for there is an ideal that is suited to the concept. The concept is determined in-and-for-itself and so too is the shape. This rules out caprice on the artist's part because the content is present at hand for the artist, who comes upon it, and the artist is only the subjective activity of portraying, is formative as such.⁵⁶

The spiritual, the true subject matter for the artist, is not created by the artist; it already exists inandforitself as what is substantial, universal. The artist's task is to portray it as it is.

From Classical to Romantic Art

The recognitive community within which spirit first achieves objectivity, that is, the state (whether primitive or modern), is also the context in which the freedom intrinsic to spirit is first institutionalized, made objective. "In the actuality of law, for example, my rationality, my will and its freedom, are indeed recognized; I count as a person and am respected as such."⁵⁷ However, even as a citizen of a genuine state, the individual still remains trapped in a kind of finitude, because the principle of which the state is the realization "is nevertheless *one-sided* and inherently abstract."⁵⁸ "It is only the rational freedom of the *will* that is explicit here. It is only in the *state*, and again, only in this *individual* state—thus within a *particular* sphere of existence and its isolated reality—that freedom becomes actual."⁵⁹

> In this connection, what man, entangled with finitude on all sides, seeks, is the region of a higher, more substantial truth, in which all the oppositions and contradictions of the finite can find their ultimate solution, and freedom, its complete satisfaction. This is the region of truth in itself, not of relative truth. The highest truth, truth as such, is the solution of the highest opposition and contradiction.⁶⁰

Such an ultimate form of freedom is potentially achievable only in the context of the religious community, specifically in the Christian *cultus*, the outlook of which was expressed through what Hegel terms "Romantic art," that is to say, primarily European (Catholic) religious art of the medieval and Renaissance periods.⁶¹ This art "has above all to make the Divine the center-point of its presentations,"⁶² a remark that could pertain in some respects to all three stages of Hegel's history of art: the symbolic, the classical, and the romantic (and in a certain extended sense, even the postromantic).

However, in this particular passage, it is clear that Hegel was referring to the third stage, the romantic art of the medieval and Renaissance Christian era. Of course, strictly speaking, the Divine itself, "grasped explicitly as *unity and universality*, is essentially only for thought and, as inherently imageless, [is] deprived of all images and shapes of the imagination."[63] In this respect, God necessarily transcends any possibility of visual representation. Nevertheless, the Christian tradition made available a potentially endless realm of visual imagery through which events in the life of God incarnate (Christ) could be depicted, along with imagery of the Mother of God, the holy family, lives of the disciples and saints, and so on. Painting was peculiarly suitable for expressing the deepest religious feelings, for stimulating the religious imagination, and it was destined thus to become the dominant art form of the romantic period.

Hegel was an attentive student of various national traditions of religious painting—the Italian, the Flemish, the German, and the Dutch in particular—and formed detailed judgments concerning the successes and failures of each. These comparative judgments were of course limited by the range of paintings and works of art to which Hegel had access in his travels (which did not extend to Italy, Greece, Spain, or England). On the other hand, he was able to view firsthand some of the greatest works of art in the museums and cathedrals of Paris, Vienna, Amsterdam, Berlin, and several other German cities.[64] In his view, Christian religious art reached its zenith in the great Italian masters (Raphael, Correggio) of the early sixteenth century,[65] though each of the national traditions, he thought, achieved some notable superiority in at least one sphere.[66]

Hegel's conception of the situation of the artist in the context of romantic art is thus doubly fixed: the artist's identity is first of all fixed by his or her cultural context. The *ethical life* of each such cultural community is shaped by the laws and institutions of its political state, by the history of that state, including memories of the deeds of its founders and the inhabitants' forefathers. The particulars of external nature form the backdrop of all these events, constituting one's native land: "the soil, mountains, air and waters."[67] This cultural identity is further specified in terms of its heritage of distinctive architecture (religious and secular), songs, dances, musical traditions, and well-known works of arts by its sons and daughters. The boundaries of such cultural communities might be identical with the territory of some modern state; but more likely, in the period of the High Renaissance that Hegel had in view, they would have been identical with a territory we now regard as a mere *region* of some larger modern nation-state. And at the time, such regions might have been subject to the rule of the Holy Roman Empire, the Hapsburgs, and so on, but not of a unified nation-state. Thus Hegel's references to "Italian" or "German" art of the Renaissance must be taken as more generalized cultural designations and not specifically political ones. The second "fixity" in question involves the subject matter of the artist's work. As described earlier, the proper concern of the artist is with what transcends mere finitude, what exists in and for itself, the *substantive*, those elements of shared spiritual life that constitute what is divine: duties, justice, knowledge, civic and political life, family relationships, the substantive bonds that hold the ethical world together. Hegel allocated the content of romantic art into two basic categories: the religious domain (the life of Christ, religious love, and the spirit of the religious community) and chivalry (honor, love, fidelity). In depicting such subjects, the artist is depicting the customs, the ethical life, the religious tradition of his or her own people. And this subject matter is not created by the artist; it is "something already complete on its own," and the artist merely works on it, portraying it sensuously.[68] Thus in Hegel's conception, at the height of fine art's historical development, the *identity* of the artist is specified by the cultural community to which he or she belongs. Furthermore, the *subject matter* suitable for artistic depiction is already given, fixed by the ethical customs and religious traditions of that same community. This subject matter represents the divine element, spiritual substance, what exists inandforitself, transcending the merely finite. By depicting such subjects in creative ways, the artist deepens religious feelings, heightens the religious imagination, and enhances the community's comprehension of its own collective spiritual identity.

Toward Subjectivity: The Transition from Romantic to Modern Art

Such is Hegel's account of art functioning as a direct expression of a specific community's self-conception, of its collective understanding of its own spiritual being, as well as of its prevailing conception of the divine—in short, art functioning in accordance with its "highest *calling*."[69] However, Hegel observes that "in the continuing development of every nation there comes a time when art points beyond itself."[70]

> Thus, for example, the historical elements of Christianity, Christ's appearing, his life and death, have given to art, especially to painting, manifold opportunities for cultivation, and the church itself has promoted art, or let it be. However, when the drive for knowledge and inquiry and the need for inner spirituality brought forth the Reformation, the representation of religion was withdrawn from the element of sense and returned to the inwardness of feeling and thought. . . . We may still find the statues of the Greek gods excellent, and the presentations of God the Father, Christ and Mary worthily and perfectly done—it does not help: we no longer bend our knee.[71]

Thus the Reformation marks the terminus of art in its "highest calling." Since romantic art was characterized by the supremacy of painting, and the centrality of such painted images for religious devotion in the Catholic world, one supposes that Hegel was responding in part to the Protestant tendency to strip the walls of their churches bare of such images and likewise to remove religious statuary from their interiors. In any event, Hegel declared that given these developments, "art, considered in its highest calling, is and remains for us a thing of the past."[72]

In Hegel's conception, the Protestant Reformation marked the beginning of "modern" art and not (as has so often been asserted) the end of art.[73] In the modern period, the situation of the artist changes markedly; religion and art are no longer intrinsically connected; the artist's own cultural identity no longer plays a decisive role in shaping the forms "appropriate" for his or her art; and there is consequently a vastly greater range of possible subject matter available for artistic treatment:

> With this, we have arrived at the conclusion of romantic art, at the standpoint of the current age, a peculiarity of which we may find in the fact that subjectivity of the artist stands above its content and technique of production, in that he is no longer ruled by the given conditions of a pre-determined circle of content, as well as of form, already given in itself. Rather, both the subject matter and the shaping of it remain entirely within his power and choosing.[74]

Hegel did not claim that the transition in art from the romantic to the modern took place with the same historical abruptness as the Protestant Reformation itself. Rather he viewed it as the culmination of a process that had begun much earlier within the context of romantic art itself, and only reached its terminus sometime later, in the changed spiritual atmosphere of Protestant Europe. The change in question concerned the presence and the treatment in works of art of trivial everyday objects: those finite, ephemeral objects having no greater, objective (substantive) significance in themselves. Such elements may be present in even the most representative works of romantic religious art, alongside the substantive, the objective, alongside those elements that exist inandforthemselves and thus transcend the level of mere finitude. For example, "in connection with the birth of Christ and the Adoration of the Kings, neither the oxen and asses, nor the crib and straw can be left out."[75] However, even in romantic painting, the artist on occasion may depict "the content of ordinary, daily life which is not grasped in its substance—wherein the ethical and the divine is contained—*but in its variability and finite transitoriness.*"[76] Where objects of daily life are being painted in such a way as to suggest their substantiality (i.e., the ethical/divine element represented in them), Hegel refers to such subject matter as *objective*. However, when the artist finally fills the canvas entirely with the finite, transitory, "trivial" items of everyday experience, the nature of art has changed fundamentally. Its subject matter is no longer "objective" but "subjective." The *subjectivity* of the artist has become the prime focus of attention, and this is the situation of art in the modern period.

The consequences of such a transformation are several. First, the artist is now freed to depict absolutely any subject matter whatsoever. It is only the subject matter of "objective" (e.g., romantic) art that is provided to the artist as something already given, prescribed by the circumstances of his or her native culture and its religious tradition. Once the artist is released from the expectation (or "duty") of depicting such prescribed subjects in their "objectivity," a universe of "secular" subject matter is opened up: "the more secular art becomes, the more it gathers in the finite things of the world, prefers them, grants them complete validity, when it depicts them as they are."[77] From Hegel's point of view, however, a significant question arises in the aftermath of such a fundamental transformation: do these productions featuring the merely *subjective* perspective of the artist still deserve to be called works of art? A strong case can be made for the negative:

> If we thereby have before our eyes the concept of true works of art in the sense of the art of the ideal, and it must have on one side a not inherently accidental and

transitory subject matter, and on the other, not portray such subject matter in a poorly-corresponding fashion, then the art products under consideration in our contemporary stage surely fall short.[78]

However, he seizes on another feature of this changed artistic practice in order to argue that there remains an adequate basis for calling such productions genuine works of art. That other feature is that the artist, given this extraordinary freedom to select anything whatever as subject matter, must necessarily reveal something essential concerning his or her own spirit *via* the work of art. It is possible that such a work will reveal an extraordinary degree of wit, of imagination, of coherence of artistic vision, combined with exceptional skill in execution.

> Then, as well, there is the subjective liveliness with which the artist, with his spirit and feeling, enlivens, in terms of their whole inner and outer shape and appearance, the entire existence of such objects, presenting them to us with this ensoulment. In this regard we may not deny to productions of this type the name of works of art.[79]

In the modern period, it is poetry and painting in particular that lend themselves especially well to this new practice of art.

In Hegel's understanding of the history of art, the dissolution of romantic art is not the first time that the emergence of *subjectivity* marked the terminus of an artistic epoch. Hegel associates the emergence of subjectivity with *humor*, and he saw the emergence of the satirical humor of Aristophanes, with its glaring subjectivity, as marking the terminus of classical (Greek) art. Correspondingly, Hegel views the emergence of subjectivity in modern art as the re-emergence of humor as the dominant mode of artistic practice. "In so far as this subjectivity [of the artist] no longer affects merely the external means of presentation, but rather the *content* itself, art has become thereby the art of caprice and humor"[80] He observed that much artistic activity in his contemporary world could be put down to "subjective" humor—a dwelling on the particular, the trivial, as a reflection of the ever-shifting mental perspectives of the lesser writers and artists, of which the audience usually tires in short order. On the other hand, he identified a few authors as engaging in "objective" humor, numbering among them the Persian poet Hafiz and Hegel's own contemporary Goethe, author of the *West-Östlicher Divan*.

> Above all, in such depictions of objects and feelings the poet must no longer remain imprisoned in immediate wishes and desires, but must in the freedom of thought have raised himself above them, so that only the satisfaction given by imagination as such concerns him. This serene freedom, this broadening of the heart and satisfaction in the conceptual, gives, e.g., to many of the songs of Anacreon, as well as to the poems of Hafiz, and Goethe's *West-Östlicher Divan*, the most beautiful charm of spiritual freedom and poetry.[81]

Though "objective humor" does not seem to be a particularly engaging or significant way of designating the dominant tradition of contemporary art, Hegel appears to believe that it marks a genuine path toward the further development of spirit in the form of a deepened understanding of our shared, universally human spirit, or *Humanus*.

> In this going out of itself, however, art is just as much a return of man into himself, a descent into his own breast, through which art strips away every fixed limitation to a determinate conception and circle of contents, and makes *Humanus* into a new holy of holies—the depths and heights of human feeling as such, the universally-human in its joys and sorrows, its strivings, deeds, and fates. With this, the artist acquires his subject-matter within himself, and becomes the human spirit actually self-determining and considering, devising and expressing the infinity of his feelings and situations. Nothing living in the human breast can remain alien.[82]

And if genuine fine art "has above all to make the Divine the center-point of its presentations,"[83] a remark Hegel made in reference to romantic (religious) art at its most developed, there is a (possibly attenuated) sense in which this same declaration could be seen to apply to "objective humor," the fine art of Hegel's modernity in that the *spirit* of universal humanity would be, in Hegel's view, not merely human but necessarily also divine.

Hegel's Ambivalence and Our Own

Notwithstanding Hegel's willingness to declare the subjective art of "modernity" a genuine form of art, potentially capable of contributing to the further development of freely self-determining spirit (finite as well as infinite), many commentators have been struck by an essential ambivalence in Hegel's attitude toward the contemporary art of his day and its future prospects. If it is true that "one can well hope that art will always rise higher and reach perfection,"[84] it is equally true in his view that "the form of art has ceased to be the highest need of spirit."[85] The subjectivity of "subjective" art poses a distinct problem: if it should *remain merely* subjective in every sense, it presumably would not contribute in any way to the further development of spirit, because "spirit" for Hegel is intrinsically *objective*—something existing inandfor itself, the substantive. We are apparently being asked to conceive of certain artists as so large in spirit, so generously gifted with imagination, intelligence, and insight, that in their "subjective" presentations of freelychosen subject matters others are led to see extensions of their own spiritual experience as something intrinsically objective. But if a deepening comprehension of *Humanus* was to be the primary vehicle of such spiritual development, Hegel's enthusiasm for that endeavor seems curiously muted.

In Hegel's view, the contemporary world did not otherwise provide much scope for the validation of subjective viewpoints, especially in the realm of ethical life. The steady development and bureaucratization of states everywhere had drastically diminished the prospects for "heroically" imposing one's subjective view of moral necessity upon the world at large. Hegel's remarks on the *Bildungsroman* as a literary genre (e.g., *The Sufferings of Young Werther*) made clear that the sufferings of young moralists and idealists determined to reform the world would have no effect upon the settled institutions of family, civil society, state, laws, or the settled ways of the professions. "Now, however, in the modern world, these struggles are nothing more than the apprenticeship, the education of the individual into the actuality of the present,"[86] Where freedom and reason have already been institutionalized in the realm of objective spirit, the individual is reduced to being either a willing or an unwilling functionary of the universal, alongside millions of others similarly situated.

At a deeper and still more serious level, Hegel was well aware that in his contemporary world, the situation of religious belief itself had become increasingly precarious. Given his convictions about the connections between fine art and religion, this would have presented the most worrying threat of all. He was acutely aware of the "hollowing out" of philosophy and theology that had occurred in the aftermath of Humean skepticism and the Kantian critical philosophy and the negative influence of both on religious belief in his own time. His entire philosophy can be viewed as an intellectual struggle to overturn Kant's enormously influential rejection of the possibility of rational knowledge of God, the soul or the world, and, in particular, to reverse the "hollowing out" of theology that had followed in the wake of Kant's work.[87] Given the widespread conviction that knowledge of God is beyond humanity's reach, and that the truths of Christianity are merely historical ("we know and cognize nothing of God, having at best a dead and merely historical sort of information"),[88] in his view the threat of meaninglessness looming over European civilization was stark:

> When everything is done in this way, and the moral man is satisfied in his reflection and opinion, his conviction, in his finitude; when every foundation, security, the substantive bonds of the world, have been tacitly removed; when we are left inwardly empty of objective truth, of its form and content—then one thing alone remains certain: finitude turned in upon itself, arrogant barrenness and lack of content, the extremity of self-satisfied dis-enlightenment.[89]

In such circumstances, the prospects for a genuine recognitive community capable of continuous deepening and growth, of development toward the infinite, would appear to be greatly diminished, and with it, any real prospect for the development of spirit or for genuine art.

During his own lifetime, he could not have harbored any certainty about the ultimate outcome of the competition for public influence between his standpoint and the Kantian one, whatever private hopes he may have entertained. Thus, while, on one hand, he was confident that in his works he had decisively undermined the authority of both Hume's skepticism and Kant's (less than fully) critical philosophy for anyone who carefully followed his reasoning, on the other, he was clear-eyed about the massive influence of skepticism and the "critical" philosophy on the culture of "modernity" in his own time, and documented its consequences with penetrating insight and no small element of despair. Thus, one may suppose that had Hegel, *per impossibile*, been able to learn of the reinvigoration of the Kantian viewpoint that took place over the final quarter of the nineteenth century, initially in Germany, and its eventual dominance over so much of subsequent philosophy, he would have been bitterly disappointed, but not entirely surprised. In his descriptions of the tendencies of "modern" art, there is little evidence that he anticipated any major reversal of the trends already underway in his day.

Richard Eldridge, as have others, distinguishes between "accounts of art that focus on identification of the varieties of art and those that focus on the critical elucidation of art's functions and values."[90] Obviously, Hegel's theory of art belongs decidedly in the second camp. Eldridge cites Nietzsche's *Birth of Tragedy* as endorsing a similar view: "Individually and collectively, human beings come to *represent* their world and experiences not simply for the sake of private fantasy . . . but as an expression of a common selfhood, 'as the complement and consummation of [the] existence' of human subjectivity, 'seducing one to a continuation of life' as a subject."[91] Eldridge also cited Richard Wollheim's claim that the making and understanding of art somehow involve "the realization of deep, indeed the very deepest, properties of human nature."[92] Eldridge further comments that "it is desperately difficult to say, clearly and convincingly, both what these deep properties or interests of human nature that are realized in art might be and how, specifically, different works achieve this realization."[93]

Hegel's theory of art is surely one of the most heroic attempts in the modern period to specify more fully what those deep properties or interests of human nature might be. And even if we step back somewhat from some of the specific details of Hegel's philosophy of art, his focus on mutually recognitive communities as the immediate ground from which springs our common spirituality strikes me as a profoundly important insight. Art's contribution to this process is surely one of the reasons it has been taken so seriously over the centuries. And any conception of the function of art as elucidating our essential human nature, which failed to come to grips with this aspect of Hegel's thought, would be of less value for that reason in my view.

Notes

1. G.W.F. Hegel, *Lectures on the Philosophy of Art: The Hotho Transcript of the 1823 Berlin Lectures*, together with an introduction by Annemarie Gethmann-Siefert, ed. and trans. Robert F. Brown (Oxford: Clarendon Press, 2014), p. 85. Hereafter: Hegel, *Aesthetics: Hotho*.
2. She states, "The specific shape of the phenomenology of art Hegel developed . . . becomes, in Hotho's editing of the Aesthetics, just as unrecognizable as are Hegel's explanations closely connected materially with this reasoning and its method, which are reflections on the cultural-historical function of art. This explosive point naturally shows, above all, that the thesis of the end of art within the framework of Hegel's as well as Hotho's, systematic aesthetics has to be revised." "The thesis of the 'end' of art . . . is therefore understandable only within a framework characterizing the forms of art." Ibid., 83–84.
3. Hegel, *Aesthetics: Hotho*, 302.
4. G.W.F. Hegel, *The Encyclopedia Logic*, trans. T. F. Geraets, W. A. Suchting, and H. S. Harris (Indianapolis: Hackett Publishing Co., 1991), §38 Addition.
5. Ibid.
6. Errol E. Harris, *An Interpretation of the Logic of Hegel* (Lanham: University Press of America, 1983), 295. For a more extensive discussion of these matters, see my essay

"Reading Religion into the *Logic*," *The Owl of Minerva*, 49, no. 1–2 (2017–18): 59–82, esp. sections VII and VIII.
7   See Hegel's *Lectures on the Philosophy of Religion*, 3 vols., ed. Peter C. Hodgson (Oxford: Oxford University Press, 2007), Vol. 2, *Determinate Religion*.
8   Hegel, *Philosophy of Religion*, 1:363.
9   Ibid., 2:531.
10 Ibid., 2:519.
11 Ibid., 2:293.
12 Ibid., 2:516.
13 Ibid., 2:629.
14 Ibid., 2:625–27.
15 For an illuminating discussion of this topic, see Jon Stewart's excellent essay, "Hegel's Analysis of Egyptian Art and Architecture as a Form of Philosophical Anthropology," *Owl of Minerva*, 50, nos. 1/2 (2019): 69–90.
16 Ibid., 2:634–35.
17 Ibid., 2:637.
18 Ibid., 2:109–20.
19 Ibid., 2:373.
20 Ibid., 2:373–74.
21 Ibid., 2:662–69.
22 Ibid., 2:260.
23 Hegel, *Aesthetics: Hotho*, 214.
24 Ibid., 282.
25 Ibid.
26 Ibid., 192–93.
27 Hegel, *Philosophy of Religion*, 2:374.
28 Hegel, *Aesthetics: Hotho*, 205–6.
29 Ibid., 206.
30 Ibid., 205.
31 Ibid., 198, 199.
32 G.W.F. Hegel, *Lectures on the Philosophy of World History*, 2 vols., ed. and trans. Robert F. Brown and Peter C. Hodgson, with William G. Geuss (Oxford: Clarendon Press, 2011), 1:148.
33 Ibid.
34 Ibid., 148–49.
35 Ibid., 149–50.
36 See G.W.F. Hegel, *The Berlin Phenomenology*, ed. and trans. M. J. Petry (Dordrecht: D. Reidel Publishing Co., 1981),Part B. Self-consciousness, §§424–37.See also the important discussion of this distinction in Robert R. Williams, *Hegel on the Proofs and the Personhood of God: Studies in Hegel's Logic and Philosophy of Religion* (Oxford: Oxford University Press, 2017), 180–83.
37 Hegel, *Berlin Phenomenology*, §426, p. 65.
38 Ibid., §433, p. 85.
39 Ibid., §431, p. 77.
40 Ibid., 77.
41 Ibid.
42 Ibid., 79.
43 Ibid., §433, p. 83.
44 Ibid., §436, p. 91.

45 Ibid., emphasis added. The condition of achieved spirituality is thus the outcome of successfully realized mutual recognition. This should help to demystify Hegel's cryptic pronouncement in the 1805 Jena *Philosophy of Spirit* that "Being-recognized [*Annerkanntsein*] is the spiritual element" (*Hegel and the Human Spirit: A Translation of the Jena Lectures on the Philosophy of Spirit (1805–06) with Commentary*, by Leo Rauch [Detroit: Wayne State University Press, 1983], 173).
46 See the important discussion of Hegel's conception of "the elevation to God" found in Chapter 2 of Williams, *Hegel on the Proofs and the Personhood of God*.
47 Hegel, *Aesthetics: Hotho*, 333–34.
48 See section "Hegel's. Ambivalence and Our Own."
49 Hegel, *Philosophy of World History*, 100–1.
50 Hegel, *Philosophy of Religion*, 2:293.
51 Ibid.
52 Hegel, *Aesthetics: Hotho*, 184.
53 Ibid., 479.
54 Ibid.
55 Ibid.
56 Ibid., 312. In the Hotho transcript, Hegel goes on to point out that Greek artists took their subject matter from popular religion, while the Christian artists Raphael and Dante represented what was present in the church.In this sense, their subject matter is something already complete on its own.
57 Hegel, *Aesthetics*, *Werke* 13:136 (Moldenhauer and Michel, eds., Suhrkamp, 1970). All translations from the *Werke* are my own.For convenience, the corresponding passages in *Hegel's Aesthetics*, trans. T. M. Knox (Clarendon Press, 1975), 2 vols., will be cited as here: [*Knox* 1:99].
58 *Werke* 13:137. [*Knox* 1:99].
59 Ibid. [Ibid.].
60 Ibid. [*Knox* 1:99–100].
61 Though we should note that this claim becomes an ambiguous one at best in the context of "modernity" as Hegel presents it.
62 *Werke* 13:230. [*Knox* 1:175].
63 Ibid.
64 See Stephen Houlgate, ed., *Hegel and the Arts* (Evanston.: Northwestern University Press, 2007), xii, xiii.
65 For example, Hegel wrote: "Nevertheless, when we compare these Flemish paintings with the masterworks of the Italian painters, we are more attracted to the latter. Given the more complete inwardness and religiosity of the Italians, they render more prominent a spiritual freedom and beauty of the imagination. The Flemish figures indeed delight us by their innocence, naiveté, and piety; to be sure, in their depth of feeling they in part excel the best Italians. However the Flemish masters have not been able to equal their beauty of form and freedom of soul; in particular, their images of the Christ-child are ill-formed." *Werke* 15:125. [*Knox* 2:814].
66 Hegel thought that the German painters excelled in making the transition from "from [a] quieter, reverential piety to the depiction of martyrs, to the ugliness of reality in general."The North Germans excelled in painting "the brutality of the soldiers, the malice of the mockery, the barbarity of their hatred for Christ"; in the Passion story. *Werke* 15:126. [*Knox* 2:883–84].
67 Hegel, *Philosophy of World History*, 101.
68 Hegel, *Aesthetics: Hotho*, 312.

69 *Werke* 13:25.[*Knox* 1:11].
70 *Werke* 13:142. [*Knox* 1:103].
71 Ibid., [Ibid.]
72 *Werke* 13:25 [*Knox* 1:11].
73 Stephen Houlgate has been helpfully emphatic in making this point.See Stephen Houlgate, ed., *Hegel and the Arts, xxii* ff.
74 *Werke* 14:231. [*Knox* 1:602].
75 *Werke* 14:221–22. [*Knox* 1:594].
76 *Werke* 14:222. [*Knox* 1:595]. Emphasis added.
77 *Werke* 14:221. [*Knox* 1:594].
78 *Werke* 14:223. [*Knox* 1:596].
79 *Werke* 14:224. [*Knox* 1: 596].
80 *Werke* 14:229. [Knox 1:600].
81 *Werke* 15:459. [*Knox* 2:1145].
82 *Werke* 14:237–38. [*Knox* 1:607].
83 *Werke* 13:230. [*Knox* 1:175].
84 *Werke* 13:142. [*Knox* 1:103].
85 Ibid.
86 *Werke* 14:220. [*Knox* 1:593].
87 On this theme, see especially Williams, *Hegel on the Proofs and the Personhood of God*, ch. 1.
88 Hegel, *Philosophy of Religion*, 3:159.
89 Ibid., 3:160.
90 Richard Eldridge, *An Introduction to the Philosophy of Art*, 2nd ed. (Cambridge: Cambridge University Press, 2014), 20.
91 Ibid., 6–7. The internal quotes are from Friedrich Nietzsche, *The Birth of Tragedy and the Case of Wagner*, trans. Walter Kaufmann (New York: Random House, 1967), 43.
92 Eldridge, *An Introduction*, 10. The Wollheim quote is from Richard Wollheim, *Art and Its Objects*, 2nd ed. (Cambridge: Cambridge University Press, 1980), 234.
93 Eldridge, *An Introduction*, 10.

Bibliography

Eldridge, Richard. *An Introduction to the Philosophy of Art*, 2nd ed. Cambridge: Cambridge University Press, 2014.

Harris, Errol E. *An Interpretation of the Logic of Hegel*. Lanham: University Press of America, 1983.

Hegel, Georg W.F. *The Berlin Phenomenology*, edited and translated by M. J. Petry. Dordrecht: D. Reidel Publishing Co., 1981.

Hegel, G.W.F. *The Encyclopedia Logic*, translated by T. F. Geraets, W. A. Suchting, and H.S.Harris. Indianapolis: Hackett Publishing Co., 1991.

Hegel, G.W.F. *Hegel's Aesthetics: Lectures on Fine Art*, in 2 vols., translated by T. M. Knox. Oxford: Clarendon Press, 1975.

Hegel, G.W.F. *Lectures on the Philosophy of Art: The Hotho Transcript of the 1823 Berlin Lectures, with an Introduction by Annemarie Gethmann-Siefert*, edited and translated by Robert F. Brown. Oxford: Clarendon Press, 2014.

Hegel, G.W.F. *Lectures on the Philosophy of Religion*, in 3 vols., edited by Peter C. Hodgson, translated by R. F. Brown, P. C. Hodgson, and J. M. Stewart with the assistance of H. S. Harris (Oxford: Clarendon Press, 2007). Vol. 1: *Introduction and the Concept of Religion*. Vol. 2: *Determinate Religion*. Vol. 3: *The Consummate Religion*.

Hegel, G.W.F. *Lectures on the Philosophy of World History*, in 2 vols., edited and translated by Robert F. Brown and Peter C. Hodgson, with the assistance of William G. Geuss. Oxford: Clarendon Press, 2011, Vol. I: *Manuscripts of the Introduction and the Lectures of 1822–23*.

Hegel, G. W. F. *Werke in zwanzig Bänden*. Redaktion Eva Moldenhauer und Karl Markus Michel. Frankfurt am Main: Suhrkamp Verlag, 1970.

Houlgate, Stephen, ed. *Hegel and the Arts*. Evanston: Northwestern University Press, 2007.

Williams, Robert R. *Hegel on the Proofs and the Personhood of God: Studies in Hegel's Logic and Philosophy of Religion*. Oxford: Oxford University Press, 2017.

Williams, Robert R. *Tragedy, Recognition, and the Death of God: Studies in Hegel & Nietzsche*. Oxford: Oxford University Press, 2012.

Part II

Art's Persistence and Authority

5

Hegel on Romantic Art and Modernity

John Russon

It is always the case that we live with realities the nature of which we have never explicitly comprehended. At the very least, this is a consequence of the fact that we grow up into an already developed world, and our development is most fundamentally a matter of learning quickly to navigate with the terms of this already established world: that these things exist is given, and our task is to accept them and to adapt to them functionally, a task that does not wait upon our working out the exact nature of each and every thing from first principles. We thus learn how to operate within the terms of a money economy, parliamentary democracy, traffic laws, and department stores well before grasping the inherent nature of any one of these. And, of course, most fundamentally we deal with ourselves and with other people all within the surrounding context of rocks, plants, and animals, and surely these realities of nature and human nature will remain at root mysterious to us forever. It is important to remember this broad context of ignorance that permanently defines all of our experience and, more specifically, to recognize that many of the realities that are most familiar to us—that we most take for granted—are ones that we have not truly understood: in the terms that Socrates introduces at the opening of Plato's *Republic*, these are ways of recognizing what surrounds us that we have inherited, but not earned.[1]

Three particular realities with which we are generally familiar are philosophy, religion, and art. From childhood, typically, we have come to associate some phenomena with the term "art"—perhaps the coloring we do in the classroom or the framed images on the walls of our family home—and we have come to associate some behavior with the term "religion"—perhaps the church attendance of our neighbors or the assertion of claims about God by our parents or our schoolmates. "Philosophy" is a term that we typically "pick up" a bit later, perhaps associating it with the code one lives by or the practice of explicit reflection upon something otherwise taken for granted. At a later time, these initial associations may be supplemented by further phenomena that complicate one's initial sense of these terms: abstract paintings or works from another culture may seem not much like the pictures one initially took as exemplary of art; practices from other religions or careful theological claims may sit uncomfortably with what one has understood religion to be; a university course in which one studies symbolic logic or Aristotle's account of the difference between a nutritive and a sensitive soul may seem not to have much to do with what one had initially imagined philosophy to be. It is by no means obvious that these different associations are, in fact, compatible with each other and, whether they are or not, the sense we associate with each of the terms "art," "religion," and "philosophy" will typically be a very rough-and-ready way of holding these associations together without ever going through a rigorous process of collecting, organizing, and evaluating the relevant data and subsequently producing a careful definition. In this way, then, art, religion, and philosophy, *if they are realities at all*, are typically realities we have inadequately comprehended, and our recognition of various phenomena through these terms is typically a fairly thoughtless way we have taken over some inherited sense and set of associations rather than something we have earned.

One of the most powerful aspects of Hegel's work is his very careful and precise study of art, religion, and philosophy and his rigorous articulation of the distinctive nature of each. In order to grasp and appreciate Hegel's work, though, we need first to recognize about ourselves that we have not done this work and that we do not, in fact, know what art, religion, and philosophy are. Or, said otherwise, Hegel's work has the capacity to transform our understanding of what these realities are, in part by revealing the presumptions, confusions, and naïveté in our familiar views about them. Probably the most pivotal assumption that Hegel's analysis challenges is that art, religion, and philosophy are clearly distinguishable realities. Indeed, Hegel's argument is that the gradual, historical change in human *political* life more fundamentally reflects precisely the gradual process of art and philosophy slowly distinguishing themselves from religion, a change that itself reflects a transformation within religion itself.

I will explore in particular Hegel's argument that it is precisely the historical reality of the Christian religion and its attendant interpretation of art that make possible the emergence of the modern secular world. More specifically, I will investigate how the Christian religion makes it for the first time both possible and necessary to distinguish clearly between art and religion; in other words, it is in the art of the Christian religion— what Hegel calls "Romantic" art—that art as such truly becomes fully autonomous as a field of human experience.[2] We will then see that philosophy, and the sense of the rational autonomy of the individual subject—the hallmark of modern secularity—is itself the direct result of this development within the history of art and religion.

Absolute Spirit

We always deal with a profoundly *specific* world. I live at this time, in this place; I have these friends and this career; I see these flowers and hear these car horns; and so on. Our world is intensely particular, manifesting itself in the unique, irreducible, and full determinacy of the sensory flow that constitutes the ongoing happening of our experience.[3] And, indeed, I *am* this determinate flow, this determinate perspective. It is this irreducible *finitude* of our perspective that inspires skeptical philosophies: Is it not the case, these philosophies propose, that I am *only this*? Such skepticism is the core of the phenomenological method, for, like phenomenology, skepticism insists on the principle that we must limit our claims to what is actually attested in experience, in other words, our claims in principle can never have a meaning that exceeds a description of what is actually happening in and as our experience. This principle is sound, but in fact there is a telling feature in our experience that inherently speaks against these skeptical claims, namely, that, though our experience is always intensely finite and particular—intensely *specific*—we (humans, apparently unlike other beings) always experience that finite particularity *as real*.⁴

To experience something *as* real is to experience it as participating in the fabric of reality; it is to experience it, that is, as a part of the self-existing domain of what *is* as such. To experience something as real is precisely to experience it as *not* defined by our experience of it. The finite and particular is inherently relative—the finite is always defined by its limited relationship to other finite beings, the particular by its limited relationship to other particularities—but the real *qua* real is not relative to anything beyond itself: the real is the absolute.

That our experience is of the real is a significance *given in* our experience. The very meaning of this significance, however, is that it exceeds the finite significance of our experience, that is, it is a significance that cannot be justified by—cannot be derived from—the finitude of our experience. Were meaning limited to finitude—the skeptical claim—we could never have this experience; the fact that we do have this experience reveals that our experience is not limited to its finitude. This is the point of Kant's famous remark in the *Critique of Pure Reason*: "Though all our knowledge begins with experience, it does not follow that it all arises from experience."⁵ We *find ourselves* already engaged with meanings that cannot be *derived from* our experience. We find ourselves *already* passively engaged with the absolute, or, as Hegel remarks in the "Introduction" to the *Phenomenology of Spirit*, "the Absolute" is "with us, in and for itself, all along."⁶

The absolute—the real as such—is given as a meaning—indeed, as the *ultimate* meaning—in all of our experience. It is given pervasively and irreducibly, but it is never given *as such*, that is, the absolute is always given *in* and *as* the relative. Consequently, the experiential meaning of the absolute is always an imperative: it is always the imperative to recognize the finite as not merely finite, the particular as not merely particular, and so on. We experience this cognitively in the imperative to *understand*: we grasp the meaning of "What?" and "Why?" which are the imperatives we face always to grasp the limited within the context of the whole, and we recognize that these questions are themselves unlimited, that is they intrinsically project us toward the ultimate, the absolute.⁷ Our experience of the absolute is not simply cognitive, however; we experience it *practically* in and as the imperatives of morality: as Kant demonstrates in *The Groundwork for the Metaphysics of Morals*, we *find ourselves* answerable to the categorical imperative to do what is good as such, and our action is always experienced by us in light of this absolute.⁸ And, more fundamentally than either of these, we experience it *existentially* in our recognition of ourselves—of our very being—as not self-caused but as emerging from a defining source that eludes our grasp.⁹

The experiential meaning, therefore, of the "presence" of the absolute—or, more exactly, the presence of its absence, of the impossibility in principle of its presence as such—is the experience of the imperative to "recognize" that absolute, not in the sense of "notice," (though that is no doubt true too), but in the sense of "grant due recognition to," to *behave* in a way that acknowledges. Thus, as Derrida writes in *Memoirs of the Blind*, in the context of his interpretation of the ancient Hebrew story of Tobit, relating to one's experience truly is

> less a matter of telling it *like it is*, of describing or noting what one sees (perception or vision), than of *observing* the law beyond sight, of ordering truth alongside the debt, of ordering truth from the debt, of giving thanks at once to the gift and the lack, to what is due, to the faultline of the "il faut."[10]

The intrinsic character of our experience, in other words, is a call to us to attest to the presence of the (absent) absolute. This definitive human activity—actively acknowledging our passive relation to the absolute—is what Hegel calls "absolute spirit," and this acknowledging of the absolute, Hegel argues, is the essential and defining character of each of art, religion, and philosophy.[11]

As I noted at the start, we all presumably have some pre-philosophical familiarity with each of these realities—art, religion, and philosophy—but our grasp of them is skewed, not just by the fact that we typically have only an idiosyncratic, empirical grasp of them, but even more fundamentally by the fact that whatever experience we have of them is *within* the perspective of contemporary, capitalist society: we experience them, in other words, as they exist in this particular culture when in fact each of these realities has a very charged and, in a sense, challenged, relationship with this culture. We will go on to consider this relationship in more detail, but we can notice first the misleading contemporary perspective on these as realities of *individual* life.

In identifying these practices of "absolute spirit" as our most distinctively human practices, Hegel is also recognizing that these are first and foremost *social* realities, that is, they are the way the human *community* attests to the absolute. Thus, before being an individual act of expression, an individual act of faith, or an individual statement of reasoned theses about the nature of reality—before being, that is, optional matters of personal judgment and choice—art, religion, and philosophy are the practices by which a human community enacts *in ways that are founding of the very nature and identity of that community* its grasp of "what ultimately is"—"the absolute"—and does so through emotionally provocative expressions, through acts of devotion, and through expressly articulated theses. As such founding acts of communal life, art, religion, and philosophy are not simply disconnected practices, but are themselves three intimately related facets of a single collective process. And, inasmuch as this single process is the practice of affirming the commanding power of the absolute, religion is its most fundamental realization.[12]

We are accustomed to identifying art, religion, and philosophy as three distinct and autonomous spheres of activity—indeed, spheres so autonomous that they commonly appear to be in conflict with each other, art and philosophy being secular rather than religious, philosophy and religion being about truth unlike imaginative art, philosophy being conceptual unlike art and religion that rely upon images and stories. The reality of this autonomy and opposition, however, is only a rather late development in the historical reality of each of art, religion, and philosophy, and, in origin, art and philosophy are not explicitly differentiated from religion. In other words, in their origins, art is religious art and philosophy is a form of devotion. It is the gradual separating out of these three practices that precisely characterizes the history of religion, a process we can in fact understand most effectively through Hegel's analysis of the history of art in his *Aesthetics*. Hegel identifies art's history as developing through three distinct formations—symbolic art, classical art, and romantic art—and it is understanding the difference between these formations that allows us to understand the autonomy of art, religion, and philosophy as those exist in the contemporary world.

Art History

The history of art—as of religion and philosophy—is the history of the changing grasp of "the ultimate": it does not just vary with that grasp—it *is* that grasp. Effectively, human culture has to forge for itself the means to *say* what it means in affirming the absolute. Now, as we already noticed in our remarks on skepticism, it is the very nature of our existence that we have only finite and relative resources available to us, and yet the purpose to which we need to put these resources is precisely the affirmation of the infinite and absolute. Consequently, the most basic affirmation—and the context within which any more developed affirmations take place—is a "self-negating" use of those finite resources, that is, the finite must express that "the finite is not everything." "Symbolic Art" is Hegel's name for this inaugural use of expressive media to affirm the absolute, and, while it can exist in any cultural context, it is most definitively the art of the most ancient cultures. This founding artistic gesture—the founding act that is gesture itself—is precisely the act in which some natural material becomes a medium expressive of the absolute.

There is a kind of "sacrificial" logic inherent to artistic materials, that is, to function as art and affirm the absolute, artistic materials must give themselves over, in and as a gesture of acknowledgment, to that which is their source. Sacrificial rituals themselves no doubt accomplish many other social, political, and psychological functions, but most fundamentally they are a gesture by which an authoritative "beyond" is affirmed by the negation of the terms of everyday, instrumental life. In sacrificing coconuts, goats, and so on, the members of a culture take instrumentally useful goods and, by sacrificing them—smashing the coconuts or killing the goats—affirm that they, the sacrificers, are not defined by quotidian need[13]: the sacrifice affirms simultaneously a higher reality to which the community and the world must answer and, by virtue of their involvement with that reality, that community's own higher purpose—their own superiority to nature (or to any other human group that fails to recognize that higher reality). It is precisely *by the negation* of the natural reality—the coconut or the goat—that that which transcends nature is affirmed. Perhaps this has something to do with why fire is such a profound medium for such religious affirmations, whether in Zoroastrianism, for which fire is what is most definitively sacred reality, in the Vedic culture, in which the householder's maintenance of the sacred fire is the fundamental duty, or in the ancient Hebrew religion, in which fire is the most common symbol for God[14]: fire is the natural world apparently sacrificing itself, as if on its own nature were affirming its subordination to the higher "beyond." Thus *Exodus* 3:2: "There the angel of the Lord appeared to him [Moses] in flames of fire from within a bush." In these cultures, it is precisely in and through these *articulations*—the sacrifice or the fire—that the absolute is grasped.[15] The recognition of the absolute is the content of what we would call the "religion" of these cultures, but this recognition is equally the creative taking up of these natural realities—coconut, goat, and fire—*as* expressions of the absolute, and they are thus simultaneously inaugural developments of art. It is this gesture of announcing the beyond in and through the negation of the finite, Hegel argues, that is developed with greater focus and refined in, for example, the architecture of Egypt, in which massive works of stone rise from the sand to announce the presence of something much more than sand, or in the poetry of the ancient Hebrews, such as *Job* 38, that uses the description of the natural world to induce wonder in the face of that natural world.

These symbolic expressions are simultaneously articulate and inarticulate: they use the world of nature to affirm the existence of a reality beyond nature, a reality to which nature is answerable, but aside from this basic "definition" as "absolute"—that is, as source and goal (beginning and end), as *definiens* rather than *definiendum*—there is no further positive significance of the absolute expressed. This absence of determinacy, however, is not a failing, but is itself a profound revelation: symbolic art affirms the absolute as the *mystery* of reality. Thus God asks Job in *Job* 38:4, "Where were you when I laid the earth's foundations?" and being thus addressed is surely the familiar experience we regularly have in engaging now with these ancient works, whether great, stark architectural works like Stonehenge or the pyramids at Giza, the wildly imaginative figures of many-headed or many-armed creatures from ancient India, or the provocative part-human, part-animal gods of ancient Egypt: it is as if, as Hegel says, we are "walking through problems [*Aufgaben*]," for these figures, sphinx-like, seem to pose to us a question—a challenging question about our own reality—that we cannot answer.[16] Indeed, some version of this founding experience of art is very much the experience most of us have today when we are confronted with any of the so-called "great works" of art, or when we are confronted with contemporary, more abstract work: we tend to sense that it is "art" precisely when we experience the work as mysterious and strangely "beckoning," as promising an important meaning we cannot quite discern.

This articulation of the inarticulable is not, however, the only form of artistic experience, even in everyday life, for, on the other hand, when we hear a popular song or watch a "great movie," we are absorbed in the experience and find it inherently satisfying—as "self-fulfilling," so to speak. Like the common experience of the "mystery" announced by great artworks in general, this common attitude of fulfilled absorption is largely "subjective," in the sense that it is primarily a reflection of one's personal taste, education, and so on; nonetheless, these two popular experiences attest to two fundamentally different kinds of experience that a work of art can induce. Just as the former subjective experience corresponds roughly to the historically "objective" reality of symbolic art, the latter experience corresponds roughly to the experiences of what Hegel calls "Classical" art.[17]

Classical art, of which the art of ancient Greece is exemplary, is the art of beauty.[18] Whereas symbolic art is effectively the art of the sublime, for it affirms the reality of a transcendent "beyond" by using the finitude of nature to express its own negation, classical art uses the experience of beauty to affirm the *immanence* of that very absolute.[19] In his "great speech"—the *palinode*—in the *Phaedrus*, Socrates describes beauty as the "shine" (*pheggos*) here of "there"[20]; it is precisely the way that we feel the presence of a deeper reality *within* the very specificities of our everyday world of nature. In the experience of beauty, we recognize the *presence* of a richer, greater reality than our everyday instrumental world—our world of "slavish economizing," as Socrates says[21]—and we recognize ourselves as *in* that world. In the experience of beautiful art, in other words, we experience ourselves—naturally existing human beings—as *already there with* the absolute. The experience of beauty is thus, effectively, the experience of the harmony of the divine and the natural, and it is in making the world into a beautiful place and in being beautiful ourselves that we make the divine present. Greek sculpture is exemplary of this classical gesture: whether in the Riace bronzes (460–459 BC), for example, which portray perfect individuals in an eternal stance of relaxed readiness for action, or in the (Hellenistic) Hermes of Praxiteles (330 BC), with his flawless and effortless posture of almost liquid erotic perfection, the human form is removed from the realm of idiosyncrasy and indigence and made a vehicle for the presentation of self-sufficient completeness, a perfect harmony of principle and realization. The absolute is expressed, in other words, as being present precisely in and as the beauty that is the human realization of the divine. In the so-called "mythology" of the Greeks—that is, in what is precisely the Greek *expression* of the divine in poetry, vase painting, and sculpture—the divine, more than simply an alien mystery to which we are inherently subordinate and to which we must, uncomprehendingly, submit, is present in the meaningfulness that informs rule (Zeus), marriage (Hera), war (Ares), technology (Hephaistos), and so on. This is not a reduction of the divine to the human, but, on the contrary, the recognition that the divine must be *livingly present* in and as the meaningfulness—the value—that informs human culture. Indeed, one might say in general that Greek classical art takes culture as its expressive medium, rather than nature, as is the case in symbolic art. In our experience of works of classical art, we are not impelled to lose ourselves in the mystery of a beyond—a beyond that, by definition, we cannot bring into meaningful, direct contact with any specificities of our immediate existence—but to rise to the call of beauty and to take pleasure in our own enactment of communion with the determinate forms of the divine.

Just as symbolic art is the art *of* particular cultures, that is, it is not an optional form of decoration but is *expressive* of the grasp of the absolute that is formative of all the basic institutions of that culture, so is classical art the art *of* a specific culture: cultures that grasp the absolute as a reality that can only be expressed symbolically are cultures that implicitly experience humanity itself as a reality *subject* to rule—which, practically speaking, means rule by despotic god-kings—whereas the culture that grasps the absolute as realized in beautiful expression is a culture that experiences humanity itself as a reality *participant* in the divine rule of nature, that is, as a reality capable of taking on for itself the authority to *legislate* how humans *should* exist. Thus classical art is of a piece with the *political* revolution that is the emergence of the self-governing *polis* of ancient Greece.[22] The founding developments in art, in other words, are integral to broader cultural revolutions that are expressive of our basic human grasp of who and what we are as human beings, that is, they are integral parts of our collective, historical process of articulating who we are in relationship to the ultimate nature of reality as such, a process of articulation that is as much religious and political as it is artistic. Yet neither the grasp of the absolute—the ultimate—that is expressed in symbolic art and theocratic despotism nor the grasp of the absolute that is expressed in classical art and Greek democratic politics is itself the last—the ultimate—word on the nature of the absolute. Beyond the artistic, religious, and social revolutions exemplified in each of symbolic and classical art, there is a third cultural revolution in our human relation to the absolute which is exemplified in what Hegel calls "Romantic" art.

I noted earlier two familiar experiences we have of art, namely, a sense of inspiring mystery and a sense of pleasant fulfillment. In both of these subjective cases, and in the analogous, historically objective experiences of symbolic and classical art, the "work" of the artwork is the experience it thus induces in us, that is, the art really only "happens" in being experienced as such by the human witness, but within these experiences the work is nonetheless experienced as something other than the experience itself, that is, it is grasped as a sublime or beautiful *object*, and, as such, it remains statically indifferent to the witnessing subject. Beyond these experiences of mystery and satisfaction, though, another experience—another *kind* of experience—is possible that does not leave the terms of the relationship between subject and object unchanged. This is the experience—the uncomfortable experience—of feeling personally called by the artwork to transform oneself.

Sometimes a tune—perhaps the first of Eric Satie's *Trois Gymnopédies*—catches one "off guard," and one finds oneself emotionally gripped by the compelling weight of a sad memory and a sense of guilt for not communicating well with a dear friend; or perhaps a painting—for instance, *The Massacre of the Innocents* by Peter Paul Rubens— raises one's moral ire at the inhuman treatment of others and one feels the urgency to protest injustice; again, a poem—maybe *The Love Song of J. Alfred Prufrock*, by T.S. Eliot—fills one with the sense of the conformity and passivity of one's own behavior and with the sense that "you must change your life," as Rilke writes in *Archaic Torso of Apollo*.[23] This experience is neither simply the "awe" of encountering a sublime mystery nor, indeed, is it the simple satisfaction of an experience of beauty; this is experience of being "called" by the artwork to rise to an imperative that is intrinsic to one's very reality as an experiencing being. This is the distinctive form of the experience of what Hegel calls "Romantic" art.

As an historical, revolutionary development in art and culture, romantic art is integral to the emergence of Christianity that corresponded with the collapse of the Greco-Roman world and became the religious-cultural context for our contemporary world. As an affirmation of the absolute, Christianity differs from the other religious cultures we have considered because it thematizes the irreducible role—the absolute status—of the individual within the reality—the realization—of the absolute itself. We already saw, with classical art, the sense that the human practices are forms of communion with divinity, but those are all matters of our "species-being," as Marx says, that is, they are the forms of human *social* life; in Christianity, however, the communion of human and divine is a matter of and for the *individual*. According to Christianity, the absolute exists *as* the imperative force of the ultimate good, commanding one's allegiance from within the inherent nature of one's subjectivity: one must *convert* and personally recognize the absolute as a compelling reality already alive within one's own experience.[24] In this sense, the absolute is not simply an alien "object" but is, on the contrary, the fabric of one's very being as an individual subject. Romantic art is the expression of this nonobjective absolute—an absolute that, as Schelling writes, exists not as a being but as a *revelation*.[25]

The defining character of romantic art is that it precisely expresses the denial of the ultimacy of the alienation of subject and object. In other words, like symbolic art and in opposition to classical art, romantic art is fundamentally a negative expression. Unlike symbolic art, however, romantic art does not simply affirm the transcendence of nature by its (objective) source: it affirms the transcendence of the opposition between subject and object by a source that is as much immanent to subjectivity as it transcends it. In symbolic art, the artwork is in principle insufficient to portray that which it expresses—the absolute—because it has only natural means to express that which is beyond nature. Romantic art faces an analogous but importantly different challenge: in romantic art, the artwork in principle is insufficient to portray that which it expresses because it has only alienated, objective means to express that which is in principle is not alien and objective. In other words, as we anticipated earlier, romantic artworks only exist as the imperative to the witness to transform his or her relationship to him- or herself and to find the transcendent absolute immanent to his or her subjectivity, an imperative that itself exists only in and as the act of recognizing it.[26]

Inasmuch as art, by its nature, is an *expression*, a meaning "outed" in materiality—whether stone, paint, sound, or bodily movement—the artwork always has an inherently "objective" reality, and this is as true of the artistic expressions of the absolute as understood in the romantic art of the "revealed religion" as it is of the absolute as affirmed by symbolic and classical art: as Hegel writes, "Absolute subjectivity as such, however, would elude art and only be accessible to thinking if it did not, in order to be *actual* subjectivity corresponding to its concept, also step into external existence [*äußere Dasein*] and, out of this reality, gather itself into itself" (*Aesthetics* I, p. 519/II, p. 130). Yet, inasmuch as that expressed by the artwork—the meaning—is precisely the denial that objectivity is ultimate, the very meaning of romantic art is the non-ultimacy *of art*. In classical art, beauty is precisely recognized as the adequate expression of the absolute and art—enacting the beautiful (objective) harmony of the infinite and the finite, the divine and the human—is thus the ultimate form of witness to, the ultimate grasp of, the absolute. Romantic art, on the contrary, is precisely the artistic affirmation that art *cannot be* the ultimate witness to the absolute—the ultimate form of "absolute spirit"—because, qua objective, it is *inherently insufficient* to grasp—to express—the absolute. romantic art, in other words, has as its message its own transcendence: romantic art affirms the need for superior—subjective—modes of witness to the absolute. One cannot adequately bear witness to the absolute in any *thing*—one must, rather, bear witness to the absolute in and through the taking up of one's own subjectivity.

It is with romantic art, therefore, that *art itself* affirms the distinction between art and religion. The cultural acknowledgment of the absolute that is Christianity is as much a matter of art as it is a matter of religion, and this distinction of *form* is itself part of the *content* of this very acknowledgment. And, as we shall see, inasmuch as this acknowledgment of the absolute is an affirmation of the necessity of a subjective recognition of the absolute—"faith"—the recognition of philosophy is also integral to the content of this acknowledgment. In other words, the distinction we make between art, religion, and philosophy as distinct modes of Absolute Spirit is itself the way art, in its own unfolding history, *distinguishes itself* from those other forms of witness.

Romantic Art and Modernity

Like symbolic art and classical art, romantic art is the art of a *culture*, and a culture defined by the distinctive form of its collective grasp of the absolute. Hegel writes,

> The form of romantic art is determined . . . by the inner concept of the content [*Gehalt*] that art is called to exhibit [*darzustellen*], and so we must first of all try to clarify to ourselves the principle peculiar to the new content [*Inhalt*], which now, as the absolute content [*Inhalt*] of truth, comes to consciousness in a new worldview [*Weltanschauung*] and art form [*Kunstgestaltung*].[27]

The "distinctive principle of this new content" is the recognition that the domain of "subjective inwardness" rather than the domain of objectivity is the site for the revelation of the absolute, and the culture that makes this recognition—Christian culture or, in the language of the *Phenomenology of Spirit*, the culture of the "revealed religion"—itself develops through different stages in its gradual process of grasping the significance of this, its founding insight.[28]

Like Christian culture, the cultures of symbolic and classical art were themselves not "monolithic" realities, but were dynamic and ever-deepening engagements with that reality made manifest through their artistic-religious practices. In the *Aesthetics*, Hegel documents the increasing depth and complexity that characterizes the historical development of symbolic artistic practices from the earliest stirrings of cultural affirmations of a "beyond" to nature to the highly developed religious world of ancient Egyptian culture. In the *Phenomenology of Spirit* especially, Hegel is similarly articulate in his analysis of the gradual but systematic transformations within ancient Greek art (from the earliest developments in Greek architecture and sculpture through the most refined developments of Greek tragic and comic drama) that reflect and enact the process by which that culture digested its own animating principle as the historical reality of the *polis* moved from a revolutionary affirmation of the possibility of human freedom in roughly the eighth century B.C. to the demonstration of the limits of that grasp of freedom in the trial and execution of Socrates in Athens in 399 B.C.[29] But, whereas these developments in the religious-political cultures of symbolic and classical art are the determinate characteristics of ancient and alien cultures, the developments in Christian culture are the developments of *our own* culture, and the real importance of Hegel's analysis is its ability to transform our perception of our *present* cultural reality.

As we noted earlier, the Christian religion and culture begins with recognition of the irreducible and ultimate value—the "absolute" status—of the self-conscious individual who converts: in other words, the question of "what is ultimate?" cannot be satisfactorily answered without reference precisely to the individuals who ask that question. Initially, this focus on subjectivity has an otherworldly trajectory, inasmuch as it is the affirmation of the call to turn oneself away from the worldly terms in which one defines oneself and to turn oneself toward "there." Inasmuch, however, as it is always oneself—one, in one's concrete particularity—who must make this turn, the very fact of personal answerability implies the essentiality of the finitude *from* which one is turning, that is, from which one responds. It is not *qua* finite that one's particularity is "saved," however, but *qua* answering to the infinite. The call, in other words, is ultimately the imperative *to live one's finitude as* a recognition of and response to what is ultimate. Consequently, the history of the Christian revelation is the history of the gradual transformation of an anti-worldly otherworldliness into an anti-reductive secularity.

In contrast to the sublime, monolithic temple that is exemplary of symbolic art or the beautiful, plastic sculpture of the god that is exemplary of classical art, it is the ugly, painted crucifixion that is the exemplary work of romantic art. In romantic art, the ultimate is portrayed as an intensely finite person—the unique individual—who must sacrifice his finitude in order to allow divinity to be realized. The image, in other words, is not of the independent, perfect ideal (as in classical art), but of the suffering, imperfect, and pointedly nonuniversal individual who must, in pain and suffering, *live out* the affirmation—the recognition—of the absolute, as, for example, in *The Crucifixion* (c. 1400) of Stefano da Verona (c. 1374/5–after 1438) (Figure 1).

This large painting shows the emaciated body of Christ (an emaciation emphasized by its elongation) uncomfortably draped on a cross to which it has been aggressively nailed, attended by suffering, worshipping individuals, each with a distinct—an *individual*—expression of grief, and each—the virgin Mary and St. John standing and Mary Magdalene desperately hugging the cross—gracefully posed with luxurious and richly colored garments, further emphasizing the awkward impropriety of Christ's posture and situation; four angels, whose symmetrical positioning, elegantly turned bodies, and beautiful garments further underscore the ugly reality of Christ's situation, also each individualistically display grief in their overseeing of the scene. Christ himself is not at all portrayed as polished and beautiful (like a classical statue) but is a coarse-featured, ruddy-complexioned, everyday individual—a peasant rather than a noble.

Unlike the methods of symbolic and classical art, the method here for portraying the absolute is to portray the suffering subjectivity that recognizes the absolute: whereas symbolic art invokes a mysterious ultimate reality through the limitations of natural reality, here, similarly, the absolute "as such" cannot be made present, but it is in and as our *suffering* that the absolute is presented to us. The Christian focus on the "death of God" means that it is a mistake to imagine that God could ever be present (in some other time or place); the proper recognition of the absolute, rather, is precisely the recognition that God can only be present in and as "revelation," only in and as appealing to "subjective inwardness." And in the romantic artwork, the absolute is presented *as* unpresentable precisely *through* the "unpresentable" (i.e., nonclassical) Christ: it is not humanity in its perfect objectivity but humanity in its imperfect subjectivity that provides the image of divinity. The absolute as such cannot be "shown," and the thematization of suffering, whether in Christ or in the witnesses, is an exhortation

Figure 1 Stefano da Verona. *The Crucifixion* (ca. 1400). Tempera on wood, gold ground, 33 ⅞ × 20 ⅝ in. The Metropolitan Museum of Art, New York. Credit Line: Purchase, Álvaro Saieh Bendeck Gift; Gwynne Andrews Fund; Charles and Jessie Price Gift; Philippe de Montebello Fund; Gift of Mrs. William M. Haupt, from the collection of Mrs. James B. Haggin, Bequest of Lillian S. Timken, and Gift of Forsyth Wickes, by exchange; Victor Wilbour Memorial Fund; funds from various donors and Gifts of the Marquis de La Bégassière and Cornelius Vanderbilt, by exchange; Marquand Fund; and the Alfred N. Punnett Endowment Fund, 2018.

to you to "see along with them"—to follow where they are pointing. Indeed, the very image of the crucifixion is the image of the pointer: all that can be portrayed is the real "crossed out" and the "crossing out" or denial of "the real" is exactly what a pointer is, just as my pointing finger essentially says "this is not a finger (but a sign, a signifier invoking a signified)."[30] Indeed, even the medium of the artwork—paint—has taken a step back from the "reality" of architecture and sculpture that are typical of symbolic and classical art, respectively, in that it is a medium that requires the viewer to "see it as" what it portrays and pointedly not to notice its physical reality as pigment on wood; in other words, the medium itself makes the same point as the image.[31] The romantic artwork itself, and the meaning it communicates, is distinctive in its insistence that *you* must *perform* the recognition simultaneously of that to which it points and of it as a pointer.

In the romantic artwork, then, the finite individual attests of itself to the insufficiency of the finite: it is the *self*-sacrifice of the finite, the finite attesting to its own self-transcendence, and this is an image of what the one witnessing the work must *do*. But this attestation, therefore, whether in the witness portrayed in the work or in the witness of the work, is itself *of* the finite and thus the essential place of the finite is necessarily maintained even as its subordination to the infinite is affirmed. Thus Hegel writes,

> The existence [*Dasein*] of God, however, is not the natural and sensuous as such, but the sensuous brought to non-sensuousness, to spiritual subjectivity, which, instead of losing the certainty of itself as the absolute in its external appearance, first obtains present and actual certainty of itself exactly through this reality. God ... puts himself in the middle of the finitude and external contingency of existence [*Dasein*] and yet knows himself therein as a divine subject that in itself [*in sich*] remains infinite and makes this infinity explicit for himself [*für sich*].³²

Because the absolute is portrayed in romantic art as the finite making its own reality into the affirmation of the absolute that uniquely reveals itself to finite individuals—because it portrays *witnessing*—the initial, explicit focus on the absolute as such is, consequently, implicitly a focus on our finite worldliness. Not our finite worldliness "in its own right," however, but *as* the inescapable site for the enacting of the recognition of the absolute. But *you are* this "finite"; in other words, for one to recognize the absolute is to do something to one's own experience—it is actively to experience oneself *as* personally called upon in one's most intimate being to answer to the absolute imperative that one cannot evade because it is intrinsic to one's reality as a subject. What is at stake, in other words, is not some "other world," but how we take up this world: do we, wrongly, reductively treat this world as "just" its own finitude or do we, rightly, anti-reductively recognize this world as the site for the occurring of absolute value—which is, indeed, precisely the theme with which we began in our comparison of skepticism and phenomenology. Romantic art and the Christian religion of which it is the expression are the affirmation of the absolute as the call performatively to bear witness to the resurrection of this world, to enact the "transfiguration of the commonplace" (in the language of Danto) as the site of the appearing of the absolute.³³ Indeed, this is one of the most powerful of the sayings of Jesus:

> Then he said to them all: "Whoever wants to be my disciple must deny themselves and take up their cross daily and follow me. For whoever wants to save their life will lose it, but whoever loses their life for me will save it."³⁴

In the preface to the *Philosophy of Right*, Hegel, discussing the primacy of the here and now, quotes the ancient saying: "here is Rhodes, here is your jump."³⁵ Analogously, romantic art says to each of us, "Here is your cross."

It is through this thematizing of "here" as the ultimate site for the contestation of good and evil—as "Armageddon"³⁶—that Christianity brings into being for the first time our familiar experience of the world of secular objectivity. Thus, though the Christian religion—like any religion—testifies to the answerability of "this world" to that which is absolute, it is nonetheless fundamentally a *validation* of the unique significance of humanity—of "this world"—as the proper site for the appearing of the absolute; for this reason, the artistic tradition that begins with the portrayal of the ruined body of Christ itself naturally develops into the "humanism" of the Italian Renaissance and the subsequent celebration of the everyday human world found in Dutch "genre painting" from the period of world-historical ascendancy, economically and politically, of the Dutch.

The Renaissance in Italy was a time of emerging science, industry, and culture. Through figures such as Giovanni di Bicci de'Medici and Cosimo de'Medici in the late 1300s and 1400s, the modern world of capitalist trade and finance was born, and with it the cultural transformations introduced by the expanding intercultural communication that accompanied growing international trade, developments that dovetailed with the emerging science of the 1500s.[37] These developments together reflect the human use of our "divine" capacities—our self-transformative rationality—to "transfigure" the world, from its simply "given" form to a form that reflects the primacy of those, our gifts. And the artistic developments that are so definitive of this new culture are themselves *about* this culture. The continuing development of painting makes this clear. Thus the great portraitists, for example—Leonardo da Vinci, Michelangelo, and Titian, for example, but also the great portraitists of the North, such as Jan van Eyck, Albrecht Dürer, and Hans Holbein (the Younger)—pointedly portray *individuals*. These are typically powerful economic and political figures, so of course these works are manifestly "propagandistic" works for wealthy patrons, and so on. But what is being celebrated is what the *individual can do* (rather than the divinity of the human *community*, as in Greece); these are precisely the individuals who have "used their gifts," (as Hegel says in "Virtue and the Way of the World").[38] In other words, it is not just *any* aspect of the human that provides the content of these paintings: it is the human being as the *rational individual*. These distinctive powers of human subjectivity are almost comically put on display in the "portrait" of Philip IV of Spain by Diego Velazquez, familiarly known as *Las Meninas*[39]: in this work, Velazquez portrays Philip IV *by portraying what he* (Philip) *sees*, that is, he portrays Philip's *subjectivity*. Perhaps impudently, this amounts to Velazquez's own self-portrait as a painter, since what Philip sees is Velazquez painting his portrait. Velazquez thus both slyly portrays the primacy of subjectivity and puts on display the distinctive power of art (which is the power of his own subjectivity) to magically bring life—to bring subjectivity itself—out of the otherwise dead materiality of oil, pigment, and canvas. And the very method of painting—especially through Alberti's articulation of the method of one-point perspective in 1435[40]—itself reflects the scientific developments in optics, that is, that emerging scientific perspective by which humans use their gifts to transform nature itself becomes the very medium for artistic presentation: in its very *form*, painting, more than ever, reflects the "rational" subject. These themes are especially pronounced in the paintings of the Northern (Dutch) Renaissance.

In the 1600s, the Netherlands—and Amsterdam in particular—became the world center for economic "progress," largely through the invention of the joint-stock company, developments in banking, and the correlated growth of the Dutch empire worldwide. In experiencing themselves as "the cutting edge" of contemporary culture, the Dutch furthered the Renaissance perception of the "mission" of humanity: the use of our distinctive (rational) powers to transform the world into a proper home for those powers. Indeed, the Protestant developments within the Christian church of that time in various ways emphasize the importance of making the kingdom of God on earth (with capitalism as a duty to cultivate and grow). And painting, too, advanced in its own right with a focus exceeding even that of the Venetians on color and visible brushstroke rather than design and polish as the media for painterly expression. Within this context, so-called Dutch "genre" painting especially captures the sense—perhaps even the mystery—that within this human spirit there lie waiting the powers of transformation and progress that are bringing about the "new world."

The Harvesters (1565) by Pieter Bruegel the Elder (Figure 2) exemplifies well this benevolent affection for human individuals as the vehicles for the cultivation of the world, for it centrally portrays a group of tired workers relaxing during a break in the process of bringing in the harvest of ripe wheat. Like Christ in Stefano's painting, the individuals here are pointedly unidealized and they are displayed in their most "finite" way, namely, enjoying rest, bread, and friendly companionship. Frans Hals's *Merrymakers at Shrovetide* (1616–17) (Figure 3) amplifies this sentiment of honoring individuals in their moment of leisure.

Hals brings us inside the most drunken, carnivalesque moment of a party of theatrically clad individuals (including a boy dressed as a woman), portraying the sense of self-indulgent, erotic enthusiasm of individuals enjoying the last chance to partake of fine foods before the forty days of fasting for Lent.[41] Indeed, with no larger contextualizing scene, the compressed space and the intense focus on the individuals bring us almost uncomfortably close to their experience and the painter's embrace

Figure 2 Pieter Bruegel the Elder. *The Harvesters* (1565). Oil on wood, 46 ⅞ × 63 ¾. The Metropolitan Museum of Art, New York. Credit Line: Rogers Fund 1919.

Figure 3 Frans Hals. *Merrymakers at Shrovetide* (ca. 1616–17). Oil on canvas, 51 ¾ × 39 ⅛ in. Metropolitan Museum of Art, New York. Credit Line: Bequest of Benjamin Altman, 1913.

of the sensuality and idiosyncratic finitude of individual experience is so "non-ideal" that the painting is almost grotesque—an exposure to the intimate reality of human subjectivity that typically stays "in private." Further, the thick impasto gives the surface an unrefined and almost "fleshy" appearance, in contrast to the smooth and austere polish of, for example, a portrait by da Vinci—indeed, one might even refer to the image's "texture," to communicate the way the painting seems to appeal as much to touch as to sight. This celebration of the unadorned sensuality of human individuals is perhaps taken to its most intense form in Jan Steen's *The Dissolute Household* (c. 1663–64) (Figure 4).

Though this painting has an almost "classical" finish, in content it is virtually the antithesis of classical art. It is a pointedly *interior* scene—it is within the walls of the family house, not out in the public world—and, within that setting, virtually all of the norms of "proper" life are transgressed: the family pet is given free access to the family's meal, the furniture is in disarray, a bible is being stepped on, and a beggar is being turned away from the door while drunkenness and lust are given free rein. Like Christ on the cross, this is a portrayal of what, by classical standards of beauty, is precisely *ugly*, but the painting resists the classical denigration of individuality and idiosyncrasy and instead affirms that we are "saved," so to speak, *to the depths of our finitude*.

Starting with Bruegel's *The Harvesters*, these Dutch paintings push to its limits the "humanism" we witnessed in Italian Renaissance painting; indeed, these paintings are almost a challenge to the institutionalized form of the Christian church, much like that offered by Jesus as portrayed in *Luke* 7:34-47:

> The Son of Man came eating and drinking and you say, "Here is a glutton and a drunkard, a friend of tax collectors and sinners." . . . When one of the Pharisees invited Jesus to have dinner with him, he went to the Pharisee's house and reclined at the table. A woman in that town who lived a sinful life learned that Jesus was eating at the Pharisee's house, so she came there with an alabaster jar of perfume. As she stood behind him at his feet weeping, she began to wet his feet with her tears. Then she wiped them with her hair, kissed them and poured perfume on them. When the Pharisee who had invited him saw this, he said to himself, "If this man were a prophet, he would know who is touching him and what kind of woman she is—that she is a sinner." . . . Then [Jesus] turned toward the woman and said to Simon, "Do you see this woman? I came into your house. You did not give me any water for my feet, but she wet my feet with her tears and wiped them with her hair. . . . Therefore I tell you, her many sins have been forgiven—as her great love has shown. But who has been forgiven little loves little."[42]

Whereas for Sublime art and the religious perception to which it is wed all of nature is effectively nothing, equally derivative and insubstantial, in the face of the absolute to which it is subordinate, and for classical art and religion it is only perfected, beautified nature that is worthy of recognition, for romantic art and the revealed religion *all* of the finite is "saved" in its uniqueness and individuality—validated as the one and only site for the appearing of the absolute. In an almost Nietzschean sense, these Dutch paintings are resolute in their defense of the dignity and irreducible worth of the human subject in all its particularity, thus answering to and completing the artistic and religious exhortation inaugurated in the image of the crucifixion.

The history of romantic art demonstrates the way in which Christianity simultaneously recognizes the ultimacy of finite, human actuality—"here"—as the site of "the final judgment," as *where* "it is really happening," and the *intrinsic* worth—the intimate relation to what is ultimate—that is definitive of each human individual. Each human individual, in her or his finitude, has within her- or himself simultaneously the possibility of and the responsibility for accomplishing a relationship with the absolute that already implicitly defines her or him. This, initially, is the definitive Christian insistence on religious conversion—"faith." But this inherently subjective affirmation of one's intrinsic relation to the absolute is equally the definitive reality of *science*, that is, of *philosophy* itself.

We are familiar with the imperative to "think for yourself," which most typically and definitively we associate with Socrates and his philosophical practice, and as modern individuals we are also very familiar with the sense of rational self-responsibility, cognitively and morally, that we associate with Descartes and Kant, respectively; further, it is this rational self-responsibility that is the foundation for the notion of rights that we associate with Locke and that is at the foundation of our modern conception of liberal democracy. The notions of rights and self-responsibility are precisely the hallmarks of secular modernity—of modern secularity. What we should

Figure 4 Jan Steen. *The Dissolute Household* (ca. 1663–64). Oil on canvas, 42 ½ × 35 ½ in. The Metropolitan Museum of Art, New York. Credit Line: The Jack and Belle Linsky Collection, 1982.

recognize is that they are all themselves species of the Christian interpretation of our human nature—the very recognition worked out in and through the developments in romantic art.

Romantic art—and likewise the Christian religion—is the recognition of the human individual as the finite site of the happening of infinite meaning: we are, as it were, "lightning rods," uniquely able to "channel" powers that precede and exceed us. The recognition of this initially emphasizes that "exceeding power" but the fuller recognition must acknowledge the inescapable essentiality of our finite context of reception of that power, and it is this fuller recognition that is progressively worked out in romantic art and, indeed, in the history of the "Christian" culture of the West.[43]

Conclusion

We typically live our modern, secular subjectivity as if it were the opponent of religion (this is the opposition Hegel studies in the section on "Enlightenment" and its struggle with "Faith" in the *Phenomenology of Spirit*).[44] What our analysis here shows, though, is that this orientation misrepresents both "faith" and "reason." Our critical, secular stance presumes the self-sufficiency of the rational individual, and concomitantly treats art, religion, and philosophy as optional choices of private subjectivity, without seeing that this individuality is itself a *product* of art and religion. In fact, however, our modern ability to grasp ourselves *as* finite subjects who harness the infinite powers of what we commonly call "rationality" is itself a form of cultural self-interpretation that began with the revolutionary emergence of Christianity, a mode of self-interpretation made possible only through its articulation in the rich cultural tradition of romantic art.[45] In thus imagining itself to be independent of art and religion, modern subjectivity precisely misrepresents its own foundations, portraying what are its non-evadable causes as if they were its optional effects. Learning the history of the emergence of individuality through art and religion allows us to see that art and religion are not enemies of individual rationality but precisely the conditions that must be preserved if rational individuality is itself to exist.

And contemporary art is itself precisely the critical articulation of this (our) cultural misapprehension of the nature of art and its founding necessity for our very experience of subjectivity. Art, far from being an entertaining adornment, is in fact the very medium by and through which we come to *think*—to form an intelligent grasp on our world and ourselves—but our modern capitalist, technological world, which "religiously" presumes the ultimacy of the finite, rational individual, though dependent on the deeper powers of art, in fact suppresses that deeper meaning. Indeed, the trivialization of art is powerfully performed by the modern institution of the art museum, which, though it is "officially" the institutes that defend the "higher value" of art, effectively "quarantines" art, removing art from its living role in shaping cultural perception and, as it were, putting the dead carcasses of works on display like the anatomical specimens in a surgical laboratory. Far from being neutral, in other words, art museums are in fact vehicles of cultural interpretation and, indeed, dangerous such vehicles.

From April 4, 1992, until February 28, 1993, Fred Wilson rearranged the works in the Maryland Historical Society's collection, demonstrating the suppression of Maryland's black history: the suppression both of the history of slavery and of the accomplishments of its black population. In "Mining the Museum," Wilson rearranged objects (for example, juxtaposing slave shackles with fine serving vessels, under the heading "Metalwork, 1793–1880"), orchestrated lighting (on the portrait of Henry Darnall III by Justus Engelhardt Kühn to draw attention to the black man with a metal collar around his neck who was otherwise allowed to slip perceptually into the background), added audio soundtracks to "give voice" to those whose voices were otherwise excluded from the collection, and prominently exhibited the works of black individuals, such as the journals of Benjamin Banneker. Wilson's work demonstrated the implicit narrative that defines the work of the museum and its rhetorical affect, here with respect to matters of race, class, and history; but, even more fundamentally, such narrative effects are true of the museum's portrayal of art as such, and "institutional critique" has been a prominent focus of contemporary art at least since the "Futurist Manifesto" of 1909, but it especially characterizes much of the most vibrant art since the 1960s.[46]

The challenge to the "institutionalizing" of art is often a matter of demonstrating positively the living significance of art, and not allowing art to be comfortably portrayed as something "safely" removed from everyday life. Throughout the 1960s and 1970s, members of the "Fluxus" network challenged the authority of the museum to determine the nature and limits of art and to bring the living experience of art to people directly. Works by Fluxus artists often encouraged participation—such as in Ben Vautier's *Total Art Match-box* (1965), a box of matches with a label indicating that the matches inside should be used to burn artworks—or took the form of performances—such as Benjamin Patterson's *Paper Piece* (1960), a musical work in which the instrumentation is various pieces of paper (fifteen sheets and three bags per performer) that have been distributed to five performers who are to "play" the paper according to an established "score," and that became (after its first performance and despite its original written instructions) a matter of audience participation; or Joseph Beuys's "How to Explain Pictures to a Dead Hare" (1965, documented in photographs by Ute Klophaus), in which Beuys covered his head with honey and gold-leaf, put on one shoe with a felt sole and one with an iron sole, and first sat and then walked through the Galerie Alfred Schmela in Düsseldorf (where his own drawings were on display), explaining the works there to a dead hare that he carried with him. Like romantic art generally, the works of Fluxus resist the model of art as a matter of exhibition and contemplation and insist instead on art as a medium and context for action, and specifically revolutionary action that liberates one from the static and oppositional terms in which art and individuals have come to be defined in modern society.

Hegel argues that romantic art, in portraying its own insufficiency to portray the absolute, precisely makes way for a new form of religion—the revealed religion—which itself makes way for philosophy: it makes possible the experience of the modern subject—each of *us*—for whom art, religion, and philosophy are autonomous spheres of experience. In thus defining itself as "past," as Hegel says, art does not, however, diminish its own continuing significance; it indicates, rather, that it is inescapably *up to us* to *performatively recognize* what is of absolute worth.[47] Art, in other words, expresses the imperative that we become active in "owning up" to the constitutive parameters of meaning in our experience rather than accepting the institutionally prefabricated identities that our modern culture offers us. Hegel's philosophy is thus particularly powerful in allowing us to understand the living significance of art today.

Notes

1 Plato, *Republic*, I.330a, 3rd edition, trans. Allan Bloom (New York: Basic Books, 2016).
2 For Hegel's basic distinction between "Symbolic," "Classical," and "Romantic" art, see G. W. F. Hegel, *Vorlesungen über die Ästhetik*, 3 vols., ed. Eva Moldenhauer and Karl Markus Michel (Frankfurt: Suhrkamp, 1970), I:106–14, translated into English by T. M. Knox as *Aesthetics: Lectures on Fine Art*, 2 Vols. (Oxford: Clarendon Press, 1975), I:75–81. Subsequent references to this work will be to *Aesthetics*, followed first by the volume and page number in the English translation and then by the volume and page number of the German text. All translations from this text are my own. Compare G. W. F. Hegel, *Philosophy of Mind*, trans. William Wallace (Oxford: Clarendon Press, 1971), §§561–62.
3 Compare the opening of Hegel's discussion of "Sense-Certainty," in G. W. F. Hegel, *Phänomenologie des Geistes*, ed. H.-F. Wessels and H. Clairmont (Hamburg: Felix Meiner, 1988), especially 69–70; in English Hegel, *Phenomenology of Spirit*, trans. A. V.

Miller (Oxford: Oxford University Press, 1977), §91. Subsequent references to this text will be to *Phenomenology of Spirit*, followed by the paragraph number in the English translation (M) and the pagination in the German text (W/C); hence, this reference would be to M91, W/C 69–70.
4. *Phenomenology of Spirit*, M73, W/C 57–58. This phenomenon of "experiencing *as real*" is the central organizing principle of Immanuel Kant's *Critique of Pure Reason*, trans. Norman Kemp Smith (New York: Palgrave Macmillan, 2003). I have discussed various aspects of this theme in Kant and in Hegel's *Science of Logic* in "Subjectivity and Objectivity in Hegel's *Science of Logic*," in *Infinite Phenomenology: The Lessons of Hegel's Science of Experience* (Bloomington: Indiana University Press, 2016), 256–70, and in "Hegel and the Philosophy of Mind," in Michael Baur (ed.), *Hegel: Key Concepts* (New York and London: Routledge, 2014), 44–58.
5. Kant, *Critique of Pure Reason*, B1.
6. *Phenomenology of Spirit*, M73, W/C 58.
7. Ibid., M132–34, 143–44, W/C 93–94, 100–02. I have discussed Hegel's analysis of understanding more fully in "Understanding: Reading and *Différance*," Chapter 3 of *Infinite Phenomenology*, 57–73.
8. This theme runs throughout the first two sections of Immanuel Kant, *Groundwork for the Metaphysics of Morals*, trans. Allen W. Wood (New Haven and London: Yale University Press, 2002), especially 33.
9. The existential experience of our own definitive limitation is the experience of "the unhappy consciousness," *Phenomenology of Spirit*, M206–31, W/C 143–57. For an interpretation of this experience and its role in Hegel's *Phenomenology of Spirit* in particular, see "The Call of the Beyond: Unhappy Consciousness and the Structure of Hegel's Argument," Chapter 7 of *Infinite Phenomenology*, 126–42.
10. Jacques Derrida, *Memoirs of the Blind*, trans. Pascal-Anne Brault and Michael Naas (Chicago: University of Chicago Press, 1993), 29.
11. *Aesthetics* I:92–104/I:128–44, especially 93–94/130–31: "The absolute itself becomes *object* [*Objekt*] of spirit, as it steps onto the level of *consciousness* and *distinguishes* itself in itself as *knowing* and conversely as the absolute *object* [*Gegenstand*] of knowledge.... From this point of view... it is immediately clear that art belongs to the same territory as religion and philosophy. In all the spheres of absolute spirit, spirit delivers itself from the restrictive limits of its existence, developing from the contingent circumstances of its worldliness and the finite content of its aims and interests to the contemplation and accomplishment of its being in and for itself."
12. I have discussed this theme more fully in "Expressing Dwelling: Dewey and Hegel on Art as Cultural Self-Articulation," *Contemporary Pragmatism* 12 (2015): 38–58. On the primacy of religion, see *Philosophy of Mind*, §554.
13. On this theme, compare Georges Bataille, *Erotism: Death and Sensuality*, trans. Mary Dalwood (San Francisco: City Lights, 1986), 8, 21–22, 67–68, and 81–82; and *Theory of Religion*, trans. Robert Hurley (New York: Zone Books, 1989), 44.
14. On fire in Judaism, see Hannah K. Harrington, *Holiness: Rabbinic Judaism and the Graeco-Roman World* (New York and London: Routledge, 2001), 13–14.
15. See *Aesthetics* I:316/I:409–10 for the idea that Zoroastrianism and fire are "pre-artistic" in that there is not a separately fashioned symbol/art-object.
16. *Aesthetics* I:308/I:400.
17. Symbolic art and classical art are matters of a culture's grasp of the ultimate nature of reality, rather than appropriations of this or that particular subject matter, and they are matters, not of personal taste, but of the very development of art itself—of what

18 *Aesthetics* I:436–38/II:25–27.
19 For the general correlation of the sublime and the beautiful with symbolic art and classical art respectively, see *Philosophy of Mind*, §561. For Hegel's more precise use of the notion of the sublime in relation to symbolic art, see *Aesthetics* I:362–77/I:466–85, especially 363–64/467–69, 371–73/478–80.
20 Plato, *Phaedrus*, trans. Stephen Scully (Newburyport MA: Focus, 2003), 250b.
21 *Phaedrus*, 256e.
22 This human "usurpation" of powers formerly reserved for divinity is expressed, for example, in the founding Greek myth of Prometheus stealing fire from the gods; the parallel "hubris" of political self-legislation is powerfully expressed especially in Sophocles's *Antigone*. I have discussed the relationship between Greek art, politics, and religion somewhat more fully in "Expressing Dwelling" and in "The Phenomenology of Religion: Freedom as Exposure to the Absolute," Chapter 13 of *Infinite Phenomenology*, 228–55.
23 In *Ahead of All Parting: The Selected Poetry of Rainer Maria Rilke*, ed. and trans. Stephen Mitchell (New York: Modern Library 1995), 66–67.
24 This theme runs throughout Paul's epistles in the *New* Testament; see, for example, *Romans* 2:14–15, 28–29, *Galatians* 2:14-19. Compare *Aesthetics* I:518–24/II:128–36.
25 "For God never *exists* [*ist nie*], if the existent *is* that which presents itself [*sich darstellt*] in the objective world ... but he continually *reveals* [*offenbart*] himself" (F. W. J. Schelling, *System of Transcendental Idealism*, trans. Peter Heath (Charlottesville: University Press of Virginia, 1978), 211). Hence Hegel's designation of Christianity as "the revealed religion" in the *Phenomenology of Spirit*; on this issue, see Quentin Lauer, *A Reading of Hegel's Phenomenology*, 2nd ed. (New York: Fordham University Press, 1993), 262n4.
26 For romantic art as the art of "subjective inwardness," see *Aesthetics* I:519/II:129–30.
27 *Aesthetics* I:517/II:127.
28 *Aesthetics* I:519, 522–23/II:129–30, 133–34.
29 *Phenomenology of Spirit*, Chapter VII, Part B, "The Art Religion," M699–747, W/C458–88.
30 Analogous themes are of course raised by René Magritte, "The Treachery of Images (*La Trahison des Images*)," 1928–29.
31 See about the romantic arts generally *Aesthetics* II:794–95/III:14 : "Now the *subjective* inner ... in order to be able to shine forth as inner, will in fact efface the spatial [*räumlich*] totality of this material ... and transform it from its immediate, oppositional existence into a show [*Schein*] produced by *spirit*"; and II:801/III:22, about painting in particular: "Namely, its sensuous element, that in which it moves, is distribution in surface and form through the particularization of colours, through which the form of objectivity as it is for intuition is transformed into an artistic show self-posited by spirit in place of the material shape. It lies in the principle of this material that the external shall no longer maintain final validity on its own account [*für sich*] in its ... actual existence [*wirklichen Dasein*], but in this reality must be denigrated to a mere show of the *inner* spirit, which wants to behold itself on its own account [*für sich*] as spiritual."
32 *Aesthetics* I:520/II:130–31.
33 Arthur C. Danto, *The Transfiguration of the Commonplace: A Philosophy of Art* (Cambridge: Harvard University Press, 1981).

34 *Luke* 9:23–24.
35 *Elements of the Philosophy of Right*, trans. H. B. Nisbet and ed. Allen W. Wood (Cambridge: Cambridge University Press, 1991), 21.
36 *Revelation* 16:16; cf 6:15-17, 11:15, 14:14-16, 21:3.
37 I have discussed this history in greater detail in Chapter 3 of *Sites of Exposure: Art, Politics, and the Nature of Experience* (Bloomington: Indiana University Press, 2017).
38 *Phenomenology of Spirit*, M381–93 W/C 251–59, especially M385–86, W/C 254–56.
39 I have analyzed the significance of this work in greater detail in *Sites of Exposure* (Bloomington: Indiana University Press, 2017), 14–16. It is also the subject of Michel Foucault's famous analysis in *The Order of Things*, trans. Alan Sheridan (New York: Vintage, 1994), 3–16.
40 Leon Battista Alberti, *On Painting*, trans. Rocco Sinisgalli (Cambridge: Cambridge University Press, 2013).
41 On the theme of carnival, see Gregory Kirk, "Bakhtin, Dewey, and the Diminishing Domain of Shared Experience," *Contemporary Pragmatism* 12 (2015): 216–31.
42 Compare also *Luke* 23:32-43, *Matthew* 9:10-17, and especially *Matthew* 21:31: "The tax collectors and the prostitutes are entering the kingdom of God ahead of you."
43 I have given a fuller analysis of this cultural and political history in Chapter 3 of *Sites of Exposure*.
44 *Phenomenology of Spirit*, M527-73, W/C 348–78.
45 I refer to "what we commonly call 'rationality'" to indicate the rich critique of a narrow conception of "reason," a critique introduced in Hegel and subsequently developed throughout the major writers of subsequent "Continental" philosophy.
46 For a helpful collection, see *Institutional Critique: An Anthology of Artists' Writings*, ed. Alexander Alberro and Blake Stimson (MIT Press, 2009).
47 *Aesthetics* I:11/I:25: "In all of these respects, art, in terms of its highest determination, is and remains for us a thing of the past [*ein Vergangenes*]." For the interpretation of this passage, see Stephen Houlgate, "Hegel's Aesthetics," *The Stanford Encyclopedia of Philosophy*, ed. Edward N. Zalta (Spring 2016 Edition), https://plato.stanford.edu/archives/spr2016/entries/hegel-aesthetics/, section 6.2.4.

Bibliography

Alberro, Alexander and Blake Stimson, eds. *Institutional Critique: An Anthology of Artists' Writings*. Cambridge, MA: MIT Press, 2009.

Alberti, Leon Battista. *On Painting*, translated by Rocco Sinisgalli. Cambridge: Cambridge University Press, 2013.

Bataille, Georges. *Erotism: Death and Sensuality*, translated by Mary Dalwood. San Francisco: City Lights, 1986.

Bataille, Georges. *Theory of Religion*, translated by Robert Hurley. New York: Zone Books, 1989.

Danto, Arthur C. *The Transfiguration of the Commonplace: A Philosophy of Art*. Cambridge: Harvard University Press, 1981.

Derrida, Jacques. *Memoirs of the Blind*, translated by Pascal-Anne Brault and Michael Naas. Chicago: University of Chicago Press, 1993.

Foucault, Michel. *The Order of Things*, translated by Alan Sheridan. New York: Vintage, 1994.

Harrington, Hannah K. *Holiness: Rabbinic Judaism and the Graeco-Roman World*. New York and London: Routledge, 2001.

Hegel, G. W. F. *Aesthetics: Lectures on Fine Art*, 2 vols, translated by T. M. Knox. Oxford: Clarendon Press, 1975.

Hegel, G. W. F. *Elements of the Philosophy of Right*, translated by H. B. Nisbet and edited by Allen W. Wood. Cambridge: Cambridge University Press, 1991.

Hegel, G. W. F. *Phänomenologie des Geistes*, edited by H.-F. Wessels and H. Clairmont. Hamburg: Felix Meiner 1988.

Hegel, G. W. F. *Phenomenology of Spirit*, translated by A. V. Miller. Oxford: Oxford University Press, 1977.

Hegel, G. W. F. *Philosophy of Mind*, translated by William Wallace. Oxford: Clarendon Press, 1971.

Hegel, G. W. F. *Vorlesungen über die Ästhetik*, 3 vols, edited by Eva Moldenhauer and Karl Markus Michel. Frankfurt am Main: Suhrkamp, 1970.

Houlgate, Stephen. "Hegel's Aesthetics." In *The Stanford Encyclopedia of Philosophy* (Spring 2016 Edition), edited by Edward N. Zalta, Available online: https://plato.stanford.edu/archives/spr2016/entries/hegel-aesthetics/, section 6.2.4.

Kant, Immanuel. *Critique of Pure Reason*, translated by Norman Kemp Smith. New York: Palgrave Macmillan, 2003.

Kant, Immanuel. *Groundwork for the Metaphysics of Morals*, translated by Allen W. Wood. New Haven and London: Yale University Press, 2002.

Kirk, Gregory. "Bakhtin, Dewey, and the Diminishing Domain of Shared Experience." *Contemporary Pragmatism* 12 (2015): 216–31.

Lauer, Quentin. *A Reading of Hegel's Phenomenology*, 2nd ed. New York: Fordham University Press, 1993.

Plato, *Phaedrus*, translated by Stephen Scully. Newburyport: Focus, 2003.

Plato, *Republic*, 3rd ed, translated by Allan Bloom. New York: Basic Books, 2016.

Rilke, Rainer Maria. *Ahead of All Parting: The Selected Poetry of Rainer Maria Rilke*, edited and translated by Stephen Mitchell. New York: Modern Library 1995.

Russon, John. "Expressing Dwelling: Dewey and Hegel on Art as Cultural Self-Articulation." *Contemporary Pragmatism* 12 (2015): 38–58.

Russon, John. "Hegel and the Philosophy of Mind." In *Hegel: Key Concepts*, edited by Michael Baur, 44–58. New York and London: Routledge, 2014.

Russon, John. *Infinite Phenomenology: The Lessons of Hegel's Science of Experience*. Bloomington: Indiana University Press, 2016.

Schelling, F. W. J. *System of Transcendental Idealism*, translated by Peter Heath. Charlottesville: University Press of Virginia, 1978.

6

A View from an Apartment

Hegel on Home and Homelessness in Romantic Art

Shannon Hoff

In the introduction to his lectures on aesthetics, Hegel states that "the human being as spirit *duplicates* itself": the human being is "*for* itself, looks at itself, envisions itself, thinks," and "only through these forms of active being-for-self is spirit."[1] In thinking, he observes, we bring ourselves before ourselves, developing and bringing to consciousness our sense of ourselves and all that moves us,[2] and in acting we render what is outside of us into matter that is hospitable to us, responsive to and affirmative of us. Through these activities, we imprint ourselves in what is outside ourselves, and thereby both discern our nature and make that externality suitable to it. We and the world are stripped of foreignness and come into sight, becoming familiar to ourselves and others.[3] Whereas initially the object is "simply found," and we encounter a "mere 'ought' in realizing the good" and "narrowness in knowing,"[4] the activity of life, the activity of duplication, overcomes this immediate alienation, and through these activities the subject comes to be at home in objectivity. In dealing with human reality, we are always dealing with this interpenetration and entanglement of inner and outer, of meaning and being. Reality, insofar as it includes this kind of being, is always two-sided in this way; external reality is never simply external; internal reality is never simply internal.

Because this activity is essential to human beings as such, the externality of any individual's starting point—the "found" object—is already thoroughgoingly human, intensely cultivated, and integrated, insofar as others have already worked to render it hospitable to them. Further, the results of our doubling activities, in their externality, are also for others; they are not simply confined to private experience. The activity of the external and persistently externalizing human being is essentially shareable; others interact with it and its products, basing their own doubling activity upon its doubling activity. The doubling activity of each one of us is tied up with that of others, and Hegel broadly designates as "spirit" the "bricolaged" result: a multiplicity of activities and orientations having a rough unity insofar as they are all informed by the shared context we find at hand and tied to each other by virtue of their mutual responsiveness. Spirit, that is, is this "double" we are all engaged in producing and in which we all find ourselves. Spirit is the amalgamated outcome of the activity of doubling, inspiring specific forms of continued engagement in the activity of doubling. Human beings have made reality over into something that is expressive of them, and they live inside of its terms, finding their active, self-expressive, meaningful reality supported and propelled by these terms.

Spirit, both the platform and the amalgamated effects of doubling activity, itself admits of differentiation, which it is essentially the point of this chapter to explore. Hegel uses the terms "objective spirit" and "Absolute Spirit" to articulate one key distinction internal to spirit: it is the difference between making the world, the "objective" domain, into a hospitable site for the basic, finite activities of human life, and making it into a site appropriate for the kind of being that engages in the open-ended activity of understanding and illuminating the nature of its existence *as* spirit.[5] In other words, each of these forms of doubling activity is a matter of coming to be at home in the object and in the world, but each has different concerns at stake: the one arranges and organizes the external environment as the necessary context in which human life unfolds, dealing with objects and subjects in their capacity to affect each other externally, while the other pursues the interpretation and production of *meaning* and *insight*, engaging with objects and subjects in their capacity to express and pursue meaningfulness, to affect each other internally. We will see that, whereas objective spirit essentially involves making our specific location over into a home for ourselves and thus requires a kind of exclusionary stance with regard to people and objects, Absolute Spirit implicitly affirms our essentially unhomely character or our capacity to be at home anywhere, adrift in a meaningful cosmos, so to speak, and involves an essentially open stance that permeates our interaction both with people and with objects. The first involves a specific place, exclusive access to things, and interaction with a specific set of others; the second, however, involves a kind of transcendence of or indifference to place in the name of a fundamental capacity to belong in a sense anywhere, as well as the capacity for interaction with indefinite others about content that is in principle shareable. I will begin by exploring this distinction between objective and absolute in general, following which I will investigate the specific and unique character of *art* as Absolute Spirit. Since my interest is specifically in the difference between objective and Absolute Spirit, I will investigate the character of romantic art in particular, as Hegel construes it, and by extension the art of our time, since this art, I will argue, is specifically animated by the very tension between objective and Absolute Spirit. That is, romantic art "recognizes" that the subjectivity with which it is occupied is at odds with externality, and presents it as withdrawing from the world, but it also "learns" that this finite domain is the only place that can be a home for subjectivity and thus reconciles itself with the tension between inwardness and externality, embracing as its vocation the expression of this two-sided character of the human being. At the end of the chapter, I will turn to a more or less contemporary piece of art, Jeff Wall's *A View from an Apartment* (2004–05), to illustrate this two-sided character of romantic art.

Home and Homelessness

We live inside of distinct political domains, locally meaningful structures that are more or less integrated with each other and that answer in different ways to basically similar human demands. Local external reality—the "objective" aspect of objective spirit—is organized in response to the specific demands we make upon it and reflects in its structure the diversity of our needs. The degree to which we can effectively shape it and render it answerable to us, of course, changes from person to person and community to community, given that the means for doing so are unequally shared, and given that one of the strategies that has contributed to the success of some in the activity of world-shaping is the exploitative harnessing of the agency of others as instruments with which to do so. Nevertheless, every human life gives evidence of the fact that we are able to be who we are, to enact our character as free subjectivity, because we live in a specific context that we and other human beings have attempted to shape in such a way that it answers to us in our basically free subjectivity. The fact that some, for instance, can outstrip the powers of others does not change the persistent fact that free subjectivity is a real possibility for us because of the historical efforts of others.

This is the essential meaning behind communities organized politically: their institutions and legal mechanisms reflect to some degree the priority of human empowerment, agency, and interaction, as does their cooperation with each other. Their structure is one of answerability to the general human demand that the agency of their members be supported, that it be a home for those lives, even though the degree to which they actually do so ebbs and flows. Further, insofar as political structures and institutions reflect the decisions and developments of a historical humanity, this humanity is carried along in them. These structures and institutions reflect what a specific, human "we" has learned and decided, and any individual person who fills a role in them can never herself perfectly grasp the specific meaningfulness to which they are a response, which they in their very existence have "grasped." This captures the "spirit" aspect of objective spirit: these institutions and structures reflect insight, ideas, and principles—they are not simply material—and they are a result of a significant history of sharing by which the significance of single individuals and their accomplishments is generally superseded. Established social and political practices allow the "mere ought" in pursuit of the good to be overcome, insofar as these practices embody collective, historically developed insight into the good, rendering it real and actually effective.[6] The development of scientific understanding is comparable: in it, the world becomes transparent and receptive to human action; objects lose their mysterious, recalcitrant character and become capable of being handled, malleable and available in relation to our existence. In living *within* these structures of knowledge and practice, we are living in some sense *with* historical humanity, having our own agency and interaction propelled by the agency of that humanity, finding our power multiplied by the power of the context and all the living decision and insight it reflects, for better or worse. We are living inside of human insight, which has demystified external reality, rendered it open to being meaningfully integrated into human activity, and established it as a home. Only on the basis of this home is any individual person able to accomplish her basic humanity; we can only be fully human as a "we." To be human is to be integrated in a world with others, with a system of organization on the basis of which we can have access to the resources necessary for a functioning life.[7]

No matter how necessary such a world is, however, it will always also be constrictive in an essential way. This is not the superficial constriction that we might associate, for instance, with not being allowed by law to do something; laws exist, at least in principle, to shape a world in which we can do more than we otherwise would be able to do, so this superficial constriction reflects a deeper empowerment. They may very well not operate according to the principle behind them, but that is a different story. There is, however, a constriction essential to the operation of objective spirit, and that is found in the *exclusionary specificity* of the shapes that it takes. It is not simply the principle of law that we live with, for instance; it is specific laws, specific decisions about how to arrange a shared life—decisions, for instance, about the distribution of social and economic resources, about the amount of money that will be required in taxes or spent on social infrastructure, about traffic regulations, about the distribution of public and private property and space, about immigration, and so on. It is not simply generic people that constitute politically organized domains such as the nation-state; it is people with a specific linguistic competence and political history, people with particular cultural practices and religious beliefs and not others, people for whom certain things seem and do not seem "normal," and so on. It is not simply generic land that we live on; it is rather certain formations of land, such as mountains, fertile soil, dry desert, cold and rocky terrain, and so on, and their specific character affects the kinds of lives and undertakings available to us. We require a home, and that home will always take on a specific shape, answering to a specific set of needs and requirements and not others. This specificity is a necessary condition of the worlds we inhabit, and it is constrictive in the sense that, while we have the capacity to relate to other possibilities of life as meaningful, the specific form of life we inhabit cannot in fact answer to this open capacity effectively; it *must* be specific, determinate, and exclusionary.[8] Objective spirit is not dedicated explicitly to registering the openness of our capacity to experience meaning, to reflecting the truth as such back to us, to bringing the infinity of possibility home to us. If it were to do so, it would lose its capacity to answer to the ways in which we have essentially local demands that must be locally met.

But there are other domains of experience dedicated specifically to the exploration of this infinity of meaning and the ongoing possibility of experiencing new forms of meaning and truth: according to Hegel, they are religion, philosophy, and art.[9] These are also activities of doubling—Hegel says that "the need from which art" springs, for instance, "finds its origin in this, that the human being is *thinking* consciousness—that is, that he makes out of himself and *for himself* what he is and what generally is"[10]— but the environment we produce around us in engaging in these activities does not have the same essentially specific and limited character as our political environments do. While we will always need to make a home in a specific environment, and while it cannot be anything but specific, it is nevertheless the case that we also relate to a reality beyond this environment, insofar as we have the capacity as human to relate to the openness of meaning, to the possibilities beyond those actualized in our specific environments, and to the open-ended reality—signified, for instance, by the notions of good, truth, and beauty—that is beyond our capacity to fully grasp.[11] Our experience also points us to a "beyond" that is beyond the specific domain in which we live, the things with which we interact to pursue our basic existence there, the relationships, institutions, and practices in which we are embedded. There are activities that, even while they result in specific objects or products, and even while they are cultivated by particular traditions, are unconstrained by the specificity of needs and expose us to a field of significance that seems open-ended; they emerge as a result of our engagement with questions about what is true, good, and meaningful. In exercising powers of intelligence and creativity, we manifest tendencies toward unhomeliness, toward transcending our specific, limited, worldly domains. While our artistic, religious, and broadly philosophical activities—our attempts to create meaning and to understand reality as such—will always bear the traces of home, they are also projects of transcendence, assertions that *this* home will never fully enclose and incorporate us, and that therefore we will never be completely at home in it.[12] Or that is, they assert that our home is essentially the world or reality as such, which we inhabit with others as such, even while inhabiting a specific "somewhere." As Kant similarly observes, the proper political domain for a being with reason is one without boundaries limiting the operation and development of this reason: the exercise of reason finds its proper home in a cosmopolis, even while the human being also requires specific, local government to answer to its specific, necessarily local, and finite needs.[13] To be a citizen of a country, to be implicated in a specific culture with a specific way of life, to be situated in a specific family and community: this gives our identities, actions, habits, and desires a kind of blueprint, yet we live also with a tendency toward transcendence of this blueprint, potentially engaged with what is not simply reducible to it. In identifying these two distinct trajectories of the human being, toward home and homelessness, toward social life, and toward what he calls "the absolute," Hegel shows that human life is characterized by a tension between living in a specific home and being involved in activities that thrust us outside of the specificity of home.

Notwithstanding the also specific character of artworks and aesthetic experience, art is one of these domains that involve us in transcendence of home. In aesthetic experience, we are drawn beyond the demands of everyday life to relate to what is meaningful as well as to the possible transformation of our conventional modes of expression. "In all the spheres of absolute spirit," Hegel writes, "spirit divests itself of the restraining limits of its existence, developing out of the contingent circumstances of its mundanity and the finite content of its aims and interests to the contemplation and accomplishment of its being in and for itself."[14] While these contingent affairs and finite content support and substantiate the free human life, they do not answer or address themselves to our possible engagement in the pursuit of meaning.

While it is true of all art that it does this, romantic art—or so I will show—makes the very relation between existence in externality and liberation from it into its specific theme. In other words, the essential point of romantic art, as Hegel portrays it, is to display the necessary tension between, and thus the necessary coexistence of, being at home and being homeless, insofar as it makes a mark in externality while communicating *both* that this mark cannot capture the subjectivity expressed through it *and* that subjectivity is nothing, so to speak, without this mark. While art in general is the expression of a content in a form—the wedding of objectivity and meaning, of materiality and expression—romantic art makes this very activity (and its oddness) its focus. To be human is to be inward, yet also to be perpetually outside of oneself and drawn to register and develop what is implicit in one's inwardness by making a mark in externality. Romantic art is thus essentially a reflection on the human condition as such as well as a self-reflexive activity, implicitly devoted to consideration of the nature of aesthetic experience as such, as the two-sided relationship of externality and meaning. Let us turn now to a discussion of art in general, after which we will discuss romantic art in particular, as that domain in which we find exactly the tension between objective and Absolute Spirit thematized.

Art

Hegel writes that the task of art "is to bring the highest interests of spirit to consciousness"[15]: "the *divine*, the deepest interests of human beings, and the most comprehensive truths of spirit."[16] In works of art, he says, "nations have recorded their richest inner intuitions and visions" about what is highest.[17] Art is one of the few domains in which the ultimate meanings operative in reality are explored. Who are we? To what priorities do and should we answer? Upon what basis does our existence unfold? What is the meaning of reality? This kind of activity renders it essentially similar to religion and philosophy: indeed, "fine art is often the key, and for some nations the sole key, to understanding [their] wisdom [*Weisheit*] and religion,"[18] insofar as in making a mark in external reality art *records* their interpretation of the absolute for others to see. As one of the central ways in which history is recorded, this sensible existence is integral to our contemporary awareness of past worlds.

Although art shares the characteristic of grappling with "the highest" with religion and philosophy, it differs from them insofar as it displays this grappling sensuously.[19] While in all the forms of Absolute Spirit, spirit "divests itself of the restraining limits of its existence,"[20] art's uniqueness in doing so lies in the fact that it employs precisely this externality itself in pursuit of liberation from these "restraining limits." Like the other absolute-oriented activities, art is essentially an activity of liberation, engaging not with the finite issues of concern that arise within the confines of finite existence, but with what exceeds them, but it does so by employing finite material, by making "a sensuous presentation of the absolute itself."[21] Art communicates its sense of the meaningful in an external product; it is an *expression* in externality. Its liberating activity uses finite materials to express the human capacity to live beyond finite specificity in the dimension of meaning.

This is a singular kind of activity. To use an object to express an inward meaning is to take up a unique relation to the objective domain. The "objects" of artistic experience are not like other objects: they are not for physical sustenance; they are not exhausted in their consumption; they are open to being integrated into the experience of more than one individual. Insofar as the object is something that reflects and expresses *meaning*, it is the expression of and resource for an experience, as well as that through which the human being implicitly claims that a life defined merely in terms of interaction with one's own possessions, objects of immediate consumption, or tools for the sustenance of life is inadequate.[22] In fact, insofar as art is one of the modes by which we *interpret* who we are, and since these interpretations shape our interaction with and sense of the meaning of objects, the art-object logically precedes and situates the ordinary object.

Let us linger with one of these characteristics in particular. We typically relate to objects by appropriating them as simple possession or as property, and if one of us uses or owns it, then others have lost at least temporary access to it. Insofar as the art-object expresses a meaning, however, one's engagement with it, whether as perceiver or artist, makes something for others as well; meaning potentially gives of itself over and over through this kind of object. While an artwork, like an ordinary object, is specific, it is *not* exclusive in the same way that ordinary objects are; as an attempt to grasp and express, originally, the meaning of things, it is equally available in principle to other beings who live in the dimension of meaning, and indeed exists precisely because other beings live in this dimension. Like the authentic religious or philosophical idea, it is not the kind of reality that suffers from being shared. Art is a way of making the world over into a home for the human being, but its activity of doubling, its externalization of meaning, answers not to a need to live as a specific being but to a need that is universal and rational, as Hegel describes it.[23] Art is in principle shareable by other beings who live in the dimension of reason and meaning, no matter who or where they are, even while their modes of access to it are likely to be different. The external products of expressive activity are specific in a way that has universality as its essential horizon (a horizon, of course, that is never simply reached), insofar as they do not need to exclude other specificities but can relate meaningfully to them, empowering rather than undermining their activity.

The meanings in works of art are capable of being interpreted by others because these meanings emerge from *experience*, and anyone who experiences has the potential to access and interpret such meanings. A work of art is an active interpretation or "grasping" of the character of experience that imaginatively and uniquely aims to express something true, and insofar as it does so it has the capacity to change the way anyone sees or grasps reality (this is why, as I said earlier, it precedes and situates ordinary objects). Indeed, it *calls for* interpretation and thus carries its answerability to others within its very being. From the point of view of those who engage in the production of this expressive specificity, there is also sharing: even though art is in principle interpretable by all who undergo human experience, it is also the activity of a *culture*, not simply an individual, and through the artistic activity of others our own capacity and concrete possibilities for such activity are empowered. From this discussion we should have a good sense of why art counts as a sphere of Absolute Spirit. It inhabits a domain that operates in terms irreducible to those of any given, local environment. It is an engagement not with matters of finite concern but with what exceeds them, with matters of potentially ultimate concern—with issues of proliferating meaning rather than with issues of local need. And works of art are not ordinary objects insofar as they are not exhausted in their use or by appropriation of them, but in principle are shareable and give of themselves infinitely.

Hegel distinguishes the human history of artistic experience into three general periods: symbolic, classical, and romantic. The first grapples essentially with the meaning behind nature, underplaying its own active status; the second celebrates the self-making character of humanity considered collectively and thus also precisely its own significance as a making; and the third asserts the character of the human being as subjective inwardness and grapples with its relationship to its finite world, acknowledging the alien yet necessary partnership of the two.[24] To provide the interpretive context in which the specific character of romantic art will be clear, and to conclude this basic explication of the character of art, let us briefly discuss each of these.

Symbolic art is the name Hegel gives to the beginning of art, that form of art that is essentially a symbol, insofar as it is fashioned to point to a meaning beyond it. It takes itself as incapable of manifesting the meaning it points to immediately, insofar as this "real thing" is taken to be the ground of external reality in general. This form of art is thus essentially religious and begins in wonder at the mysterious character of reality,[25] which it takes as beyond explication or understanding and thus as an object of reverence. Insofar as the meaning that is revealed here is revealed as "unrevealable," to experience symbolic art is to experience oneself as "wandering among problems."[26] Centered on the idea that nature is not self-sufficient but has a deeper ground, this form of art unfolds in interaction with natural objects, identifying their non-self-sufficiency: Zoroastrianism, for instance (only a precursor of art, Hegel says, since it does not actually fashion its objects), separates fire from its immediate natural reality, interpreting it instead as the means by which the Absolute reveals itself[27]; Hinduism brings natural objects together in nonnatural ways so as to attest to the division between the divine and the natural; in Egypt, animal and human elements are blended in forms such as the Sphinx, pyramids are built as dwellings for the immortal soul, and so on. In all of these forms, what is meant or pointed at remains obscure; the artwork does not aim to *clarify* this meaning but to reverentially honor it in its mysteriousness. Even though, over time, different forms of symbolic art come to give increased articulation to their communicated meaning, they are still occupied with the distant character of the relation between natural finitude and the divine infinite, and they still construe the absolute as beyond, "as the universal, all-pervasive *substance* of the entire phenomenal world."[28] Islamic and Hebrew poetry are Hegel's examples of symbolic art becoming more articulate about the nature of the divine and yet still taking the "pointer" to be inadequate to that to which it points. John Russon demonstrates this point in relation to the book of Job: "the phenomena of nature are powerfully presented precisely so as to point to their non-self-sufficiency. The very existence of these natural realities serves as a pointer to the power of their origination . . . for which they cannot on their own account."[29] Job 38 asks who "commanded the morning," "shut in the sea with doors," "cut a channel for the torrents of rain," and "loose[d] the cords of Orion"[30]: the natural object (and Job, the one being addressed) is used to point to God's power, which ultimately transcends it. There is indeed much to be said, and said powerfully, about that which transcends and causes nature, but it is said negatively: namely, how much more powerful than nature is the one who has made nature and harnesses its power?

Classical art no longer points beyond to a transcendent God; rather, what is ultimate is construed as operative "right here," in the activity of the human community—indeed, the very constitution and nature of the gods is worked out in and through artistic practice. In ancient Greek sculpture, the god is sculpted, but with the form of a perfect human body, in the form of "immaculate externality."[31] In tragedy, the tragic characters act in terms of *pathos*, moved to act on behalf of forces and powers that are not idiosyncratic and specific but of ultimate significance; these characters embody and express what is ultimate in their action, which is thereby not simply individual. Antigone, for instance, acts on behalf of the gods and their laws, taking herself to be subordinate to them and expressing through her nonreflective fidelity the powerful idea that we live on the basis of a reality—divine and familial—that we could never make.[32] The gods are rendered present in the human domain and their greatness is expressed in human action; human lives become the platform where what is significant makes itself manifest. Indeed, the gods of Greek religion are linked to the various aspects of existence to which human beings must answer if they are to live well.[33] The multiplicity of the gods is also relevant: what is ultimate is not the human as individual, but the human construed in a specifically social way. It is *we* who are doing the work of the gods in cultivating and governing ourselves, not a mere collection of individuals. In developing and celebrating the magnificence of the human community as a coherent whole, art and religion go hand in hand with a specific political vision: that of collective self-governance. This is a self-making human community composed of citizens who, while "independent and free" in themselves, are so "without detaching themselves from the universal interests of the actual state and the affirmative immanence of spiritual freedom in the temporal present."[34] We are free because *we* (citizens) are free; we have a rich cultural and social world because *we* do. When oriented together to the universal interest, together doing the work of the gods, we in our developed culture will be of great value and significance. And indeed it is: the culture of ancient Greece is unprecedently and uniquely creative and politically consequential.

A very different aspect of the human is asserted in romantic art, and with it emerges a newly critical orientation to the social and external aspects of human existence. While romantic art is still implicitly a veneration of the human, it is a very different side of the human that is thematized here than in classical art. Specifically, it is the human being as subjective inwardness, not humanity construed collectively and embedded together in a "beautiful," external cultural home.[35] Christianity initiates this vision of art, according to Hegel, and the figure of the crucified Christ, presented, for instance, in Hans Holbein's *The Body of the Dead Christ in the Tomb* (1521–22), illustrates the picture perfectly: the body is no longer beautiful but emaciated, suffering, and ugly, and its surroundings are greatly reduced. What is portrayed here, however, is that which cannot be portrayed: Christ on the way to withdrawing from the limitations of the body and the finite world. The portrayal of his body and environment as restricted brings to light the incomparable significance and fundamentally alien nature of the soul. What Christ proclaims to all is the importance of personal, inward conversion to a new life unbound by bodily suffering, communal ties, and finitude—the ultimacy of what is *within* subjectivity. Art's newly emerging goal is "to bring to view in this human form not the immersion of the inner in external corporeality, but conversely the withdrawal of the inner into itself, the spiritual consciousness of God in the subject."[36] Through its external mark, art registers subjective withdrawal from externality, the irreducible chasm between subjectivity and objectivity. Art and religion are still integrated here, at the beginning of what Hegel calls the romantic era; they circle around the same theme and meaning, which in a religious vein we might call the state of the soul. At this point, romantic art simply takes the content of Christianity as its own content, using Christianity and its themes and images to express its content. Thematized in

Christianity is the subjective, inward orientation of the human being to God, which occurs in the domain of the soul and is thus not externally manifest or verifiable, and does not admit of external evidence.[37] Subjective inwardness, however, once broached, offers a vista of infinite depth, and the history of romantic art in general is the history of the plumbing of this depth, the history of the ongoing artistic exploration, and indeed, co-fabrication of this newly emerging reality. Just as classical art contributes to the development and shapes the content of Greek religion, so also romantic art contributes to the fashioning of subjective inwardness.

The category "Romantic art" encapsulates substantial developments in art, but their thematic focus is the same, according to Hegel: the character of subjective inwardness. In its initial, religious emergence, this idea thrusts the human being out of the concrete, physical, human world: Christian art declares that what is of ultimate significance is not here in the world or body or community, but in the soul. What is at issue is the inward state of the soul, or whether or not one has allied oneself with God. While this emphasis on the state and orientation of the soul remains—"you must recognize your character as subjectivity, your irreducibility to the finite world, and actively assume this identity!"—the perception of the nature of human inwardness and its relation to the world changes over time.[38] While the inward state of the soul remains primary, Christianity itself gradually discovers that this cannot entail neglect of the world, insofar as the world provides itself as the very site in which the "kingdom of God" can be made real.[39] And so, emerging from the very orientation to the otherworldly is a renewal of efforts in this world (seen, as Hegel notes, in the chivalric tradition[40]). Finally, although romantic art is essentially an exploration of inwardness and thematizes its irreducible difference from the external world, it culminates in a kind of reconciliation with that world, insofar as it reflects the recognition that this object, this place, this environment is where subjective inwardness lives, where it can be itself.[41] Romantic art works out a new reconciliation with objectivity that is distinct from the classical insofar as it is the very finitude of objectivity that inspires this reconciliation, not its character as the expression of the divine. It develops the idea that *this world* is where we live out our otherworldliness, that the very infinity of inwardness only expresses itself in the finite domain, that to care for subjectivity is to care for the specific content of its experience, its attachment to a local environment, its expression as expression in and through the world.[42] "The absolute inner expresses itself," Hegel writes, "in actual existence" and "in a human mode of appearance, and the human connects with the entire world; thereby is there established at the same time a wide multiplicity both in the spiritually subjective and in the external, to which spirit relates as its own."[43] Romantic art concludes in a doubled or two-sided vision: the other side of the infinity of subjective inwardness is finite specificity as "its own." Neither is what it is without the other: the ordinariness of externality is where we express the extraordinary; the object is the occasion and location for a "sensitive self-feeling of the soul."[44] To explain how this vision might make itself manifest in romantic art, let us take a close look at a particular work of contemporary art.

The distinctive character of this late development in romantic art as Hegel understands it is well demonstrated by Jeff Wall's *A View from an Apartment* (Figure 5). Upon initial observation, several things stand out. The first is that there is a lot of

Figure 5 Jeff Wall, *A View from an Apartment*, 2004–05, transparency in lightbox, 167 × 244 cm. Courtesy of the artist.

material in this small scene: magazines and newspapers strewn on various surfaces; folded and unfolded clothing; various containers (laundry basket, water bottle, vase, tea pot, cups, plant pots); furniture; a TV with accompanying DVDs or video games below it; lights; paintings on the wall; water, ships, trees, buildings, and electrical lines outside. The scene inside is very full; all of the surfaces are in use, whether they are occupied by people or by things. And the scene outside, similarly, is highly developed and articulated: in the distance we see an urban center with high rises, cranes, a harbor, and ships, a city with its implied urban activities and industries, and also with the means for interaction and communication with the outside world. Closer to the window, the electrical wires show the connection of the apartment to an organized system of utilities, and the tree reminds us that the world outside is also natural, that the apartment is embedded in a natural world. The title of the artwork identifies the interior we are seeing as the interior of an apartment, implying the nearby character of other apartments and their inhabitants. This is a highly developed and mediated space; there is a lot of *information* in it, so to speak—information about the layers of experience, about the phenomena that lend themselves as means to a functional human existence, about the world outside of the apartment by which it is situated.

Second, one's attention is drawn, of course, to the people in the space. Each of the inhabitants is engaged in an ordinary domestic activity: the one in ironing and folding pieces of cloth, the other in reading a magazine. They are not interacting with each other, although it seems apparent—given their degree of absorption in their activities and their relaxed interaction with the space—that they are comfortably familiar with the space and with each other. They appear to be deeply absorbed in their own experience, to the degree that their attention is spent on themselves and not on any piece of the outside world beyond the scope of their activities. The title of the piece marks the absorption of the apartment's inhabitants in themselves and their activities: they are emphatically *not* looking at the "view" from the apartment, not engaging with the outside world. Rather, they display a kind of comfortable obliviousness to the external conditions of their existence, showing instead what it is like to be a human being: engaged with oneself, absorbed in the stuff of one's environment. Even though the specific inward life they have is supported and enabled by this highly mediated external reality—even though the outside world makes its way into this intimate domain, as suggested by the television, magazines, plants, books, fabric, and art—what is inside of this intimate domain also marks itself as separate from this external reality through its absorption with itself and its preoccupations. Insofar as being inside of one's living space encourages a kind of nonreflective comfort with the things within that space, to display this comfort is to display subjectivity unperturbedly living in and through the things of its environment without explicitly thematizing them.

Third, one would also probably notice that there is nothing out of the ordinary in such a view; there are innumerable similar views all around the world, at any moment. This point is underlined, again, by the title of the piece: the indefinite articles "a" and "an" express the nondescript, non-remarkable character of the view and the apartment. There is nothing extraordinary to see here—nothing like the gods, as in classical art, or the ultimate truths by which human existence is oriented—*besides* the fact that someone has put this view on display in the form of an artwork. Insofar as this ordinary view is turned into a work of art, we are invited to see the significance of the ordinary; the artwork asks the observer to pay attention to the depth of significance available in the ordinary, to how much a careful observation of the ordinary world allows us to notice, to see. The artwork directs us to *pay attention* to the ordinary in putting it on display and in implicating us in this display—to not allow the ordinary to pass us by.[45] Further, insofar as the scene does not seem particularly noteworthy, the photograph calls attention to itself as a gesture; in other words, what seems the only difference between this view and another view like it is that someone thought to say about this one: "look at this!" The difference between a view that is unidentified as such by the artwork and a view that is identified by the artwork lies not exactly in the reality identified but in the person who chooses to call attention to it and in the activity of calling attention to it, and so we pay attention here to the artist's capacity to attend to something, his own subjectivity. Further, the observer's capacity to notice something also calls attention to itself here—the observer's status as another attentive subjectivity engaged in pursuing the question of the meaningfulness of the artwork. If a person were in the presence of this work of art, she would experience its large size—it is almost 5½ feet by 8 feet, which makes it almost true to life. To experience the artwork, then, would involve implicitly experiencing oneself being integrated into it, insofar as one would be on its level; the observer and the observer's activity are implicitly placed in the scene, set in the room. The existence of both artist and observer is also invoked by the artwork insofar as it is called "A View from an Apartment," since they, and *not* the inhabitants, actually attend to the view from the apartment in observing the scene.

These three observations converge in a single point: the reality of subjectivity, manifest in the women, the artist, and the observer, is highly mediated and supported by its external world, and yet it is different from this externality—it is the experience of a self-absorption independent of that world, the experience of its own unique capacity to pay attention, to be absorbed. In the women, it manifests itself both as essentially different from the world from which it turns its face and as freed for nonreflective dwelling precisely by this world. The external environment is supportive of subjectivity such that it can be free for self-absorption; while what are viewed from the apartment are essentially its conditions of possibility, subjectivity can ignore the view. Similarly, the attending to the ordinary performed by the artist and the observer is presented as essentially different from the ordinary, as that which is capable of turning the ordinary into the extraordinary, into something worth noting. Thus it is in and through our way of taking up our home that our inward "conversion"—actively taking up our character as subjectivity—is accomplished: conversion *is* our experiencing our familiar environment as the site for the happening of the extraordinary, as the site of the absolute.

This artwork underlines Hegel's conception of romantic art. First, it displays the break between inwardness and external reality. Second, it manifests a deep satisfaction with the ordinary—indeed, a sense that the ordinary can contain great depth and significance. Third, what we view in the view from the apartment is an external world that is both alien to subjectivity and yet that very means by which it is empowered to be caught up with itself in its character as alien from externality. While the artwork displays subjectivity explicitly in its home, it shows that subjectivity as also far away, so to speak—absorbed in itself and freed by the home to be indifferent to it. With this last point, let us turn finally to the issue of the relationship between romantic art and the distinction between objective and Absolute Spirit: those human activities by which we make a specific home for ourselves, and those human activities by which we show our status as essentially living beyond that home.

Romantic Art and the Distinction between Objective and Absolute Spirit

In his artwork, Jeff Wall displays an apartment and the external realities of, for example, industry, energy, urban life, and shipping that empower specific human lives to unfold in that apartment. The lives that unfold there, however, are not particularly concerned with these external realities and do not take up the "view," but inhabit their own private, inward depths. The artwork portrays a double-sided reality: inwardness unfolding in its inaccessible depths within a mundane externality, or the infinity of subjectivity at home in finitude. This same two-sided character of human life is captured by the distinction between absolute and objective spirit: like these two women, we need to cultivate, inhabit, and have protected for us a home in the world, and yet we who are at home here have the capacity for thought, imagination, and a general receptivity to meaningfulness that entails that we may always be moved beyond our specific environments. Yet, while the home we make has limitations and intrinsic forms of one-sidedness that can always entail critique of or separation from it, a separation that these two women manifest in their absorption with themselves, we cannot depart from specificity as such. *There is* a view, and what is seen in the view as well as in the apartment supports the capacity to live beyond it; we live this inward subjectivity in *this world* and must care for it as the site of the happening of the absolute.

This odd status human beings have in relation to their environments is, in fact, it turns out, the very meaning central to romantic art. What Hegel designates as the romantic era acknowledges an intimacy between the objective and the absolute; they are not simply different from each other, but two aspects of one reality. As art, romantic art makes a mark in objectivity, rendering some piece of objectivity expressive, and witnesses about the objective that it is both that through which something *else* is expressed and the very opportunity for its expression. In other words, *you* have to do something, both to "get" the art and to make your world a good place—*you* have to convert, which means taking up your world *as* a place in which the inherently homeless character of humanity is to be accommodated. This specific form of art, therefore, is not simply one form of Absolute Spirit, but also a recognition of the intimacy of objective and Absolute Spirit. Romantic art grapples with the coexistence and co-unfolding of objective and Absolute Spirit: subjectivity and externality do not quite fit, and yet they are always together. We must realize our existence objectively—in the specific forms that political and cultural life takes—but our political and cultural existence will never on its own be sufficient for us: we need the domain of Absolute Spirit to "make a home" for those aspects of ourselves that exceed the forms of externality, and yet they will always be enacted in the forms of externality. We must care for our finite environments as the home for our homelessness.

We began with a reflection on the importance of art for fulfilling our human needs, and we conclude here by showing that art itself makes this point. Art in its historical development into romantic art attests to the human need for the reality of Absolute Spirit. It shows that, while we must together make a finite (political) home in the world, that home will be inadequate to us unless we *live* it as a site for enacting the absolute. The key to romantic art is its insistence upon the ambiguity of the human being as a being who lives both in externality and in meaning—both in a spatially determinate and historically specific location and in reason and the imagination, which perpetually lead off in all manner of spatially and historically unrestricted directions, which live perpetually elsewhere, in relation to which our homes will never be absolutely satisfying. In its very externality, or in the external conditions of its production, art reminds us of our necessary externality, and in its exploration of the unlimited dimensions of free subjectivity, romantic art continually reminds us of our ambiguous relationship to this externality. Our "elsewhere" is nowhere "else" than here: it is only in our inhabiting of this world that this recognition of ourselves as elsewhere can be accomplished. If romantic art recognizes that our elsewhere is *here*, then it motivates a concern for this here. Indeed, the ongoing persistence of art precisely asserts about specific forms of externality that this is where we live. In art, the external is a presentation of the inner, and this relationship is one that cannot be severed: the artistic content needs the external in order to be expressed and cannot be indifferent to it. Art's ongoing dignifying of the object makes it one of the key sites in which our necessarily concrete and material character makes its importance known. In the domain of concrete finitude, our spiritual character can be expressed and defended, insofar as this domain is uniquely open to being rendered expressive. Thus romantic art has the capacity to help us keep sight of how significant this two-sided character is for us, and art asserts for itself an ongoing significance as the site in which that two-sided character is powerfully expressed, even while it itself can become vulnerable here, since the focus on subjective inwardness can lead to disavowal of our reliance on a richly developed and articulated world that is in turn necessary for the cultivation of artistic expression.[46]

This necessarily two-sided character of reality claims an authority for art: expression and the human relationship to meaning entail that our interaction with external reality will take shape on the basis of our creativity and does not therefore answer absolutely or solely to the specifications of external reality. The history of Wall's production of *A View from an Apartment* also shows that art is formative of reality and not simply secondary to it. Wall does not use a camera to record a preexisting scene; rather, he himself produces this mundane scene, insofar as he asked the woman pictured as ironing to move into the apartment and to behave as if the apartment were her own, and gave her a budget with which to furnish it as she liked.[47] His artistic intentions thus precede the domestic activity he "records," even though these intentions are essentially joined and carried out by another, the woman who inhabited the apartment. Through this artwork, we witness art's ongoing intimacy with mundane reality, the imbrication of objective and Absolute Spirit: art underlies the development of ordinary reality insofar as reality unfolds, double-sidedly, as meaning, and art actively shapes that meaning.

Notes

1 G. W. F. Hegel, *Vorlesung über die Ästhetik* (henceforth *VA*), 3 vols., ed. Eva Moldenhauer and Karl Markus Michel (Frankfurt am Main: Suhrkamp, 1970), 1:51. All translations are my own. The reader can also consult the English translation most commonly used, which is G. W. F. Hegel, *Aesthetics: Lectures on Fine Art*, 2 vols., trans. T. M. Knox (Oxford: Oxford University Press, 1975).

2 *VA* 1:51.

3 Robert Pippin cites the *Phenomenology* for analogical points: "Ethical self-consciousness now learns from its deed the developed nature of what it actually did" (G. W. F. Hegel, *Phenomenology of Spirit*, trans. A. V. Miller (Oxford: Oxford University Press, 1977), §469) and "an individual cannot know what he is until he has made himself a reality through action" (Hegel, *Phenomenology of Spirit*, §401). He argues that "in the same way, Hegel is trying to say that we do not, cannot, know who we are, what we are up to, until we have found some way to externalize some version of this knowledge or activity, in art among other enterprises, and (to speak highly metaphorically) have found a way to contest with each other and settle on some authoritative view . . . art-making is not an . . . *expression* of an already achieved self-knowledge, any more than action is the result of or expression of a distinct

inner intention. Art *is* an achieved form of self-knowledge." Robert Pippin, "The Absence of Aesthetics in Hegel's Aesthetics," in *The Cambridge Companion to Hegel and Nineteenth-Century Philosophy*, ed. Frederick C. Beiser (Cambridge: Cambridge University Press, 2009), 410–11.
4 *VA* 1:129.
5 "In all the spheres of absolute spirit, spirit divests itself of the restraining limits of its existence, developing out of the contingent circumstances of its mundanity and the finite content of its aims and interests to the contemplation and accomplishment of its being in and for itself" (*VA* 1:131).
6 For instance, the requirement of public education is implicitly an expression of the idea that human beings require care and cultivation, and commitment to it is moral in nature; in living a world with public education, we already live in a morally responsive context (although the degree to which public education actually answers effectively to this idea fluctuates).
7 For extended treatment of the theme of our integration in a specific world with others, see David Ciavatta, *Spirit, the Family, and the Unconscious in Hegel's Philosophy* (SUNY Press, 2009); and Shannon Hoff, "Rights and Worlds: On the Political Significance of Belonging," *Philosophical Forum* 45, no. 4 (2014): 355–73.
8 This is essentially the issue that occupies Derrida in *Rogues*, motivating his discussion of democracy: its principle requires of it a kind of infinite openness, but in order to care for its actual citizens it must be closed, limited, specific. Jacques Derrida, *Rogues: Two Essays on Reason*, trans. Pascale-Anne Brault and Michael Naas (Stanford: Stanford University Press, 2005).
9 "Due to its occupation with truth as the absolute object of consciousness, art too belongs to the absolute sphere of spirit, and thus in its content stands on one and the same ground as religion, in the specific sense of the word, and as philosophy" (*VA* 1:139).
10 *VA* 1:50–51. Hegel need not be taken to mean here that this doubling activity is simply an externalization of a preexisting reality. While he does not speak in particular about the way in which expression is a key ingredient of the activity of thought or creative activity—in contrast, for instance, to Dewey in *Art as Experience* and Merleau-Ponty in *Phenomenology of Perception*—he criticizes the idea that nothing is itself learned or accomplished in the externalization of action in the section called "Spiritual Animal Kingdom" in the *Phenomenology of Spirit*, and his argument here could easily be reiterated in the domain of artistic activity.
11 Hegel captures these two sides in the following:
At a higher level, the life of the state as a whole constitutes a self-consummated totality. . . . The *principle* itself, however—the actuality of which is the life of the state and wherein the human being seeks its fulfillment—is . . . again *one-sided* and abstract in itself. It is only the rational freedom of the *will* that is expounded herein; it is only in the *state*, and in turn only in this *single* state, and thereby once more in a *specific* sphere of existence and its individualized [*vereinzelte*] reality that freedom becomes actual. Thus the human being also feels that rights and duties in this area and their mundane and again finite modes of existence are not sufficient: that they in their objectivity as well as in their relation to the subject need a still higher confirmation and sanction.

What the human being seeks, ensnared as it is by finitude on all sides, is the region of a higher, more substantial truth [*Wahrheit*], in which all oppositions and contradictions of the finite can find their ultimate solution, and freedom its full fulfillment. This is the region of truth in itself [*Wahrheit in sich selbst*], not relative truth [*relativ Wahr*] (*VA* 1:137).

12 Heidegger's *Hölderlin's Hymn "The Ister"* is very similar. One of his aims is to illuminate the way in which we come to dwell in a locality: our dwelling has the character both of aiming to become at home there and as moving. To be human is to be becoming homely and to be unhomely, like the river: the river is "the locality of journeying and the journeying of locality." Martin Heidegger, *Hölderlin's Hymn "The Ister,"* trans. William McNeill and Julia Davis (Bloomington: Indiana University Press, 1996), 33.

13 This distinction arises in Kant's essay on cosmopolitanism. It is only the state that can offer concrete, local measures such as education, which are required in order that its citizens be cultivated into the willingness for international relations and the capacity to conduct them well: in the Seventh Thesis, Kant notes that "a long internal process of careful work on the part of each commonwealth is necessary for the education of its citizens," which is the condition of possibility of the development of the "*morally mature*" Immanuel Kant, "Idea for a Universal History with a Cosmopolitan Purpose," in *Kant: Political Writings*, ed. H. S. Reiss (Cambridge: Cambridge University Press, 1991), 49. The Fifth Thesis asserts that "the greatest problem for the human species . . . is that of attaining a civil society which can administer justice universally"; this is the only context that can attain for human beings "the development of all natural capacities" (Kant, *Political Writings*, 45); the Eighth Thesis asserts, similarly, that a "perfect political constitution" is "the only possible state within which all natural capacities of mankind can be developed completely" (Kant, *Political Writings*, 50). Kirsten Jacobson describes a similar tension in discussion of Plato's *Crito*, Derrida's *Of Hospitality* and *Rogues*, and Heidegger's lecture course, *Hölderlin's Hymn, "The Ister."* She argues that each of these texts captures this specific two-sided character of the human condition and identifies how these two sides can be integrated in one way of life. Socrates, for instance, attests in the *Crito* to his dependence on the laws of the city, which have constituted him, and yet in his opposition to his prosecutors demands that the law be open "to the inherent demands of critical self-consciousness" (49). Kirsten Jacobson, "Socratic Hospitality: Heidegger, Derrida and the Primacy of the Guest," *Studies in Humanities and Social Sciences* 33, no. 1 (2016): 36–54.

14 *VA* 1:131.
15 *VA* 1:28.
16 *VA* 1:21.
17 *VA* 1:21.
18 *VA* 1:21.
19 *VA* 1:21.
20 *VA* 1:131.
21 *VA* 1:100.
22 Dewey similarly distinguishes the art-object from other kinds of objects in Chapter Five of *Art as Experience*. John Dewey, *Art as Experience* (New York: TarcherPerigee, 2005), 85–109.
23 *VA* 1:52.
24 Martin Donougho nicely illustrates the logic of their development out of each other thus: "symbolic art will reveal the truth (content, *Inhalt*) implicit in nature, as classical art reveals the tacit content of symbolics (humanity, intentionality), or romantic art reveals the true content of classical form (the bifurcation of human and divine existence, subjectivity, and the world). . . . Art begins with symbolism—the pretense

that signs are natural when in fact they are intentional—and proceeds to a fusion of nature and culture, sensuous shape (the human body) and intellectual meaning (the Ideal)—signified in sculpture and epic deed—and then on to the aesthetic distinguishing of spirit from nature, and finally to a reflection on the whole semiotic process." Martin Donougho, "Art and History: Hegel on the End, the Beginning, and the Future of Art," in *Hegel and the Arts*, ed. Stephen Houlgate (Evanston: Northwestern University Press, 2007), 185.

25 VA 1:408.
26 VA 1:400.
27 VA 1:409.
28 VA 1:415.
29 John Russon, "Expressing Dwelling: Dewey and Hegel on Art as Cultural Self-Articulation," *Contemporary Pragmatism* 12 (2015): 48.
30 Job 38:12–31, New Revised Standard Version.
31 VA 2:83.
32 "Antigone honors the ties of blood, the subterranean gods" (*VA* 3:544).
33 Hegel writes that "their content is extracted from the human spirit and existence and is thereby the human breast's very own" (*VA* 2:78). To give several examples, this content is the importance of desire, associated with Aphrodite; of self-discipline, associated with Artemis; of the fertility and cultivation of nature, associated with Demeter; of justice, associated with Zeus; of social integration, associated with Dionysus; of strategy in war, associated with Ares, and so on.
34 VA 2:25.
35 A related and central difference between classical and romantic art has to do with the centrality of art as a practice: it was artistic practice that was largely responsible for producing the content of Greek religion, but it has no such role in Christianity, which can in principle unfold entirely in the inward domain of subjectivity. The Christian God, as Stephen Houlgate writes, "does not need to be given aesthetic expression in order to become determinate and intelligible for us, but can be fully comprehended within religious feeling and faith.... Christianity is thus independent of art in a way that Greek religion is not." Yet Christianity is open to art insofar as it "also holds that God's love is incarnated and made visible to believers in the life and death of Christ (and of the Virgin Mary and the other saints). Christian love and spirituality thus remain capable of being given sensuous, visible expression in art." Stephen Houlgate, "Introduction: An Overview of Hegel's Aesthetics," in *Hegel and the Arts*, ed. Houlgate, xx.
36 VA 2:131. Terry Pinkard captures this withdrawal in his claim that "romantic art thus begins with the conviction that what we mean by our actions is not completely disclosed by what we do and that there is therefore an 'inwardness' which must be discovered or uncovered if we are to find out who we really are." Terry Pinkard, "Symbolic, Classical, and Romantic Art," in *Hegel and the Arts*, ed. Houlgate, 18–19.
37 Paul's treatment of circumcision throughout his letters reflects this. In Romans, for instance, he writes: "For a person is not a Jew who is one outwardly, nor is true circumcision something external and physical. Rather, a person is a Jew who is one inwardly, and real circumcision is a matter of the heart—it is spiritual and not literal. Such a person receives praise not from others but from God" (Romans 2:28-29, NRSV). In Galatians, he speaks even more strongly: "Listen! I, Paul, am telling you that if you let yourselves be circumcised, Christ will be of no benefit to you. Once again I testify to every man who lets himself be circumcised that he is obliged to obey the entire law. You who want to be justified by the law have cut yourselves off

from Christ; you have fallen away from grace. For through the Spirit, by faith, we eagerly wait for the hope of righteousness. For in Christ Jesus neither circumcision nor uncircumcision counts for anything; the only thing that counts is faith working through love" (Galatians 5:2-6, NRSV).

38 "Romantic art first deepened spirit in its own inwardness" (VA 2:232).
39 As Hegel writes, "When, however, the kingdom of God has won a place in the world and is active in penetrating and thereby transfiguring mundane aims and interests, when father, mother, brother are together in the common domain, then the mundane also for its part begins to take and assert its right to validity in making claims" (VA 2:170).
40 In this context, the inwardness of subjectivity gains its greatness because of its contrast to the underdeveloped world: "In the condition of statelessness, however, the security of life and property rests solely on the singular power and courage of each individual, who has to care for his own existence and also for the preservation of what belongs and is due to him. . . . This occurs in the so-called Heroic Age, which appears as a time in which virtue, in the Greek sense of ἀρετή, constitutes the ground of action" (VA 1:243). Hegel's reference to the chivalric era in particular is found a page later: "In the Christian West, feudalism and chivalry are the basis for free heroism and self-reliant individualities. The heroes of the Round Table are of this sort, as is the circle of heroes of which Charlemagne was the centre" (VA 1:245).
41 With its development through and beyond Christianity, art begins to assert its independence of religious content and becomes freer to take up its own self-defined activity. Between Christianity and mundanity, Hegel writes, this form of romantic art "can be, as it were, a freer beauty. For it stands here in the free midpoint between the absolute content of separately [für sich] fixed religious views and the motley particularity and narrowness of finitude and mundanity" (VA 2:172). We should notice here that it is only in the later developments of this romantic era that art takes on the character with which "we moderns" are familiar. For most of its history, art did not occupy this independent position but was fundamentally entangled with religion and even philosophy, and so we are instructed by Hegel's text to avoid importing our own limited ideas about what art is about and what it is like. Indeed, the history of art teaches us that insofar as art is a reshaping of meaning, a discovery of new meaning, its very own meaning or the character of the role it takes in a given social world is also unstable; "art" is a fundamentally and necessarily heterogeneous category. As Martin Donougho notes, "there simply is no supra-historical term 'art' instantiated in various cultural formulations" (Donougho, "Art and History," 194). Nevertheless, contemporary artistic experience is as much as at other times a reckoning with what is absolute, with what is of highest interest, though in the contemporary context this absolute is subjective inwardness. The absolute simply ceases to be construed as "outside of" subjectivity and so ceases to be that to which we would "bow the knee" (VA 1:142). Thus while in some sense it is of correct to say, as for example, Houlgate does, that "art is no longer the space in which 'the Divine, the deepest interests of mankind, and the most comprehensive truths of the spirit' find their adequate expression; those interests and truths are now fully articulated in religion (and philosophy) alone" (Houlgate, "Introduction," xxi), we could also simply say that the ultimacy to which art pays credence is dramatically transformed in character. What is absolute has become that which is also most common yet also diverse and unshared (in the sense that the subjectivity of each is irreducible to that of others)—not exactly divine but still culturally invoked as an absolute.

42   The reconciliation of subjectivity with externality is often presented by romantic art as a challenge, insofar as subjectivity shows itself to be of a different dimension than externality. Here the content of Shakespeare's tragedies is especially emblematic: Macbeth and Hamlet each struggle with a lack of fit between their inwardness, their "great soul[s]" (*VA* 3:564), and the external domain available for the actualization of that inwardness. Yet romantic art's ultimate development is full-fledged recognition of the irreducible character of subjectivity, as well as the recognition that subjectivity itself points to the contingent domain of determinate becoming as that site in which it lives and makes itself real, and so it culminates in a "sensitive self-feeling of the soul [*Gemüt*] in the object" (*VA* 2:240).

43   *VA* 2:132.

44   *VA* 2:240. Hegel characterizes "this positive finding and willing of himself in his present" as the conclusion of the development of romantic art, in which the individual "delves into himself" (*VA* 2:196). Pinkard captures this development in the following: "Romantic art begins as religious art, as the aesthetic exhibition of religious (and eventually theological) truths; but its own dynamic drives it to develop out of itself a conception of the truth of humanity as individuality, as each person having a rich inner life, an 'infinite subjectivity' that eventually detaches itself from its religious origins and comes to be concerned with itself in its prosaic, mundane world" (Pinkard, "Symbolic, Classical, and Romantic Art," 19).

45   In an analysis of Hegel's account of Dutch painting, Benjamin Rutter calls attention to the significance of the Dutch painter's absorption of *himself* into the situation he is observing. He writes that "the painter performs a sort of attentiveness and interest that suggests it [the ordinary situation observed] may deserve our own attention in ways we had not expected." Benjamin Rutter, *Hegel on the Modern Arts* (Cambridge: Cambridge University Press, 2010), 97–98.

46   This line of thinking should be a guide for interpreting Hegel's suggestive yet nonconclusive comments about the end of art. With the focus on individual inwardness, art, as engagement with externality and propped up by worldly cultural practices, becomes vulnerable; there could or could not be art, depending on where the priorities of subjectivity lie. The focus on subjectivity entails disavowal of the existence of practices, traditions, and cultural habits designed for the cultivation of artistic expression. In this reality, art is vulnerable. When the content of art is no longer a culturally shared meaning construed as transcending our individual existence and in the face of which all individuals are subordinate but a matter of the expression of intimate individuality, then we as individuals can choose to neglect it; culture must "bow the knee" (*VA* 1:142) to individual subjectivity. As Pippin has noted, the important consideration here is *how* art matters: "Hegel's claim is thus not about the end of art, however much he is associated with that phrase, but the end of a way of art's mattering, something he thinks he can show by presenting a kind of history and logic and phenomenology of anything mattering to human beings, within which art plays a distinct and changing role. . . . Again, the claim is not that there will not be art, or that it won't matter at all, but that art can no longer play the social role it did in Greece and Rome, in medieval and Renaissance Christianity, or in romantic aspirations for the role of art in liberation and *Bildung*." Robert Pippin, "What Was Abstract Art? (From the Point of View of Hegel)," *Critical Inquiry* 29, no. 1 (2002): 3–4.

47   Andrew Pulver, "Interview: Photographer Jeff Wall's Best Shot," *The Guardian*, May 5, 2010, https://www.theguardian.com/artanddesign/2010/may/05/photography-jeff-wall-best-shot.

Bibliography

Ciavatta, David. *Spirit, the Family, and the Unconscious in Hegel's Philosophy*. Albany: SUNY Press, 2009.

Dewey, John. *Art as Experience*. New York: TarcherPerigee, 2005.

Donougho, Martin. "Art and History: Hegel on the End, the Beginning, and the Future of Art." In *Hegel and the Arts*, edited by Stephen Houlgate, 179–215. Evanston: Northwestern University Press.

Hegel, Georg Wilhelm Friedrich. *Aesthetics: Lectures on Fine Art*, translated by T. M. Knox, 2 vols. Oxford: Oxford University Press, 1975.

Hegel, Georg Wilhelm Friedrich. *Phenomenology of Spirit*, translated by A. V. Miller. Oxford: Oxford University Press, 1975.

Hegel, Georg Wilhelm Friedrich. *Vorlesung über die Ästhetik*, edited by Eva Moldenhauer and Karl Markus Michel, 3 vols. Frankfurt am Main: Suhrkamp, 1970.

Heidegger, Martin. *Hölderlin's Hymn "The Ister,"* translated by William McNeill and Julia Davis. Bloomington: Indiana University Press, 1996.

Hoff, Shannon. "Rights and Worlds: On the Political Significance of Belonging." *Philosophical Forum* 45, no. 4 (2014): 355–73.

Houlgate, Stephen, ed. *Hegel and the Arts*. Evanston: Northwestern University Press, 2007.

Houlgate, Stephen. "Introduction: An Overview of Hegel's *Aesthetics*." In *Hegel and the Arts*, edited by Stephen Houlgate, xi–xxviii. Evanston: Northwestern University Press.

Jacobson, Kirsten. "Socratic Hospitality: Heidegger, Derrida and the Primacy of the Guest." *Studies in Humanities and Social Sciences* 33, no. 1 (2016): 36–54.

Kant, Immanuel. "Idea for a Universal History with a Cosmopolitan Purpose." In *Kant: Political Writings*, edited by H. S. Reiss, 41–53. Cambridge: Cambridge University Press, 1991.

Merleau-Ponty, Maurice. *Phenomenology of Perception*, translated by Donald A. Landes. New York: Routledge, 2013.

Pinkard, Terry. "Symbolic, Classical, and Romantic Art." In *Hegel and the Arts*, edited by Stephen Houlgate, 3–28. Evanston: Northwestern University Press.

Pippin, Robert. "What Was Abstract Art? (From the Point of View of Hegel)." *Critical Inquiry* 29, no. 1 (Autumn 2002): 1–24.

Pulver, Andrew. "Interview: Photographer Jeff Wall's Best Shot." *Guardian*, May 5, 2010. https://www.theguardian.com/artanddesign/2010/may/05/photography-jeff-wall-best-shot.

Russon, John. "Expressing Dwelling: Dewey and Hegel on Art as Cultural Self-Articulation." *Contemporary Pragmatism* 12 (2015): 38–58.

Rutter, Benjamin. *Hegel on the Modern Arts*. Cambridge: Cambridge University Press, 2010.

"The Absence of Aesthetics in Hegel's Aesthetics." In *The Cambridge Companion to Hegel and Nineteenth-Century Philosophy*, edited by Frederick C. Beiser, 394–418. Cambridge: Cambridge University Press, 2009.

Hegel's Symbol and Symbolic Art: Revisiting Ambiguity?

Olga Lyanda-Geller

Introduction

In his *Aesthetics*, Hegel defines the place of symbolic art and symbols in general in relation to signs. On the one hand, Hegel's definition of the beautiful as *das sinnliche Scheinen der Idee*[1] implies a symbolic interpretation of the beautiful. On the other hand, the symbol, an organic unity of the spiritual (the meaning or sense) and the sensuous (the image or shape), is taken to belong to pre-art only, awaiting a transition to classical art. There are at least two different meanings of Hegel's concept of the symbol.[2] One refers to a type of artistic contemplation (and is analyzed in detail in the discussion of the historic stage of artistic development that Hegel labels "Symbolic"), the other is a concrete means of representation of the meaning (and extends beyond the properly "Symbolic" historical type). For the sake of convenience, let us describe these two meanings as "relative," or defined within a certain system, here, the system of Hegel's symbolic art form; and "absolute," or independent from a particular system, that is, applicable to any stage in Hegel's *Aesthetics* and beyond. These two meanings of the concept of the symbol can operate in overlapping but different problematic contexts, and the dialectic of these two different "symbols" is developed differently: due to the ambiguity of symbols, the symbolic stage, as pre-art, is to be surmounted in the classical stage, that is, art in the proper sense. However, it is less clear how, or even if, the ambiguity of symbols themselves is to be overcome. It is quite common to charge Hegel with failing to respond to the challenges of the symbol and symbolic language, primarily because of his view of the symbol's ambiguity as an obstruction to thought. This chapter revisits Hegelian mistrust of symbols and of the symbolic by looking at the subject that performs the symbolic act as *homo admirans*, the wondering man. Such a perspective allows us to re-evaluate Hegel's "symbol" both as a theoretical construct and in its political and historical concreteness—in particular, by considering the symbolism of Prometheus. Hegel evokes the myth of Prometheus on various occasions and admits that myths about the Titans are not "lacking in symbolical meaning," despite the fact that they do not belong to the symbolic type. However, Hegel does not attempt to analyze the figure of Prometheus as a symbol, as it is usually depicted in the world art and culture. I aim to show that Hegel has the requisite elements for a comprehensive theory of the symbol that he leaves largely undeveloped; such theories were later constructed by twentieth-century theorists of the symbol, in some cases under Hegel's direct influence.[3] I will illustrate this point by discussing the theory of symbols by the Russian philosopher Aleksei Losev and by analyzing the symbolic nature of the Promethean myth.

The Symbol and the Symbolic in Hegel's Aesthetics

One of the key questions of aesthetics is defining the beautiful. In his *Lectures on Aesthetics*, Hegel notably defines beauty as "das sinnliche *Scheinen* der Idee"—the sensuous appearance, or manifestation of the idea.[4] By offering philosophical grounds for his theory of art, Hegel seeks to demonstrate that art is not merely entertainment for the mind, nor is it just a means of moral instruction or moral betterment, but can be treated scientifically. Reflecting on common ideas about art, Hegel observes that the work of art is a product of human activity and is drawn from the sensuous sphere. Its genuine goal is to discover and represent the Ideal: "Art is intended to reveal the truth in the form of sensuous artistic composition. . . . Because other purposes, such as instruction, purification, improvement, financial gain, pursuit of fame and honor, do not concern the work of art as such, and do not determine its idea."[5] Hegel systematically discusses the five major arts: architecture, sculpture, painting, music, and poetry, in their historical progression from the symbolic art form through classical to romantic. It is interesting to note that, as Paul de Man stated, "in Hegel's well-known and in essence unchallenged division of the history of art in three phases, two of these phases are designated by historical terms—the classic and the romantic (which in Hegel designates any post-Hellenic, that is, Christian art) whereas the third period is designated by the term 'symbolic,' which we now associate with linguistic structures and which stems not from historiography but from the practice of law and of statecraft. The theory of the aesthetic, as a historical as well as a philosophical notion, is predicated, in Hegel, on a theory of art as symbolic."[6]

For Hegel, art begins with the symbolic phase marked by searching, fermentation, mysteriousness, and sublimity. Here the idea in its indeterminacy is being made the content of artistic shapes: "The Idea has not yet found the form in itself and thus only remains the struggle and pursuit of it . . . the meaning cannot be entirely actualized in the expression and, despite all the efforts and striving to conquer the incompatibility between the Idea and shape, it still remains unconquered."[7] The symbolic shape is imperfect "for, on the one hand, in it the Idea enters consciousness only as abstractly determined, or undetermined, and, on the other hand, because of this, the correspondence between meaning and shape must always remain deficient and abstract by its nature."[8] Hegel finds a characteristic example of this prevalence of form over content in Ancient Eastern architecture, particularly in the art of Egypt, with its manifestation of the obscure meaning in the creations of those times. The next stage, the classical art form, eliminates this double defect of the symbolic form due to its "free adequate embodiment of the Idea in the shape that is peculiar to the Idea itself in accordance with its very nature. Thus, the Idea can reach the free and perfect harmony with its shape. Therefore, only the classical art-form produces the completed Ideal and presents it as actualized."[9] An example of this adequate embodiment in the idea in the appropriate shape can be seen in beautiful ancient Greek sculpture, for this is where Hegel finds this particular harmony of the content and form. The romantic art form starts for Hegel with Christianity, when, for the first time, art forsakes the self-limiting classical ideal of perfection and responds to the need of expressing a higher spiritual content: "[It] again abolishes the completed unification of the Idea and its reality . . . the romantic form of art again abandons the unseparated unity of classical art because it has gained a content which goes beyond the classical form of art and its mode of expression . . . at this third stage, free concrete spirituality constitutes the object of art."[10] Romantic art is not homogeneous: it starts with Christianity, then exceeds its religious boundaries in the chivalric period, and finally liberates the artist from all dependency on the past, as demonstrated, for example, in poetic masterpieces of modern Europe.

Let us now focus on the symbolic art form and address in particular Hegel's theory of symbol at the stage of "conscious symbolism of the comparative art-form," that is, at the stage when the artist creates a symbol with a deliberately significant idea, as opposed to the older periods of art when the process of symbolization is more spontaneous.[11] On the one hand, Hegel considers it a pre-art form and treats it as deficient for the reasons discussed earlier: "The symbol, in the meaning of the word that we use here, constitutes the beginning of art, both in accordance to the concept and as a historical phenomenon, and, therefore, should be considered, so to speak, as pre-art only."[12] On the other hand, the very definition that Hegel gives to the beautiful makes such an approach at least ambiguous. As I mentioned earlier, Hegel famously defines the beautiful as "the sensory [or sensuous] appearance [or manifestation] of the idea." But, as Paul de Man notices, this definition is tautological: the term *aesthetic* is derived from the Greek $αἰσθητικός$ meaning "of or for sensation or perception by the senses, sensitive, perceptive."[13] Hegel's definition, De Man continues, "does not only translate the word 'aesthetics' and thus establishes the apparent tautology of aesthetic art (*die schönen Künste* or *les beaux-arts*), but it could itself best be translated by the statement: the beautiful is symbolic."[14] Thus, in art forms the symbol acts as a necessary intermediate between the Idea and the reality.

Hegel makes several important distinctions in his account of the symbol. First, the symbol as a form of artistic expression that is present at all stages of art forms is not the same as the symbol of the symbolic art form as the first stage in the progression of art forms: "from the very beginning we must immediately differentiate between the symbol in its own independent originality, where it appears as the definitive type for artistic contemplation and representation, and that kind of the symbolic that is reduced only to an external dependent form."[15] Thus, the symbol and the symbolic have at least this dual feature of carrying their symbolic nature in general and in particular. Second, we should distinguish in the symbol itself "first, the meaning, and, second, its expression. The former is an idea or an object, regardless of the content; the latter is a sensuous existent or an image of some sort."[16] Therefore, the very nature of the symbol itself is dual, and Hegel points out to the gap between its two parts. It is not clear from how or even if the gap is to be surmounted in Hegel's exposition.[17] Third, Hegel distinguishes between a symbol and a sign, but this distinction will not satisfy later philosophy and semiotics. Hegel starts with identifying the symbol and the sign, claiming that "the symbol is primarily a sign. But in a mere designation, the connection between meaning and its expression is only an entirely arbitrary linking."[18] However, a symbol is also different from a sign because "the symbol is not an indifferent sign, but such a sign which in its externality already includes in itself the content of the concept which it unveils."[19] In other words, the symbol is different from the sign due to the nonarbitrary character of the connection between the meaning and its expression. Finally, this nonarbitrariness also has limits: "While the symbol, contrasting to the purely external and formal sign, cannot be absolutely inadequate to its meaning, nevertheless, in order to remain a symbol it should not be entirely commensurate to that meaning."[20] Looking at multiple examples of symbols in various areas, including myth, religion, art, language, and mathematics, Hegel concludes that ambiguity is an inalienable characteristics of the symbol.[21] This conclusion leaves him quite disappointed because this is not a productive ambiguity but rather an obstacle which is impossible to overcome because it lies in the very nature of the symbol and symbolic relations. Hegel considers the possibility of unequivocal symbols (for example, the triangle of the Trinity in Christian symbolism is quite unambiguous) and stipulates that their ambiguity may disappear when both the meaning and its shape are explicitly named and their relation is clearly articulated—but then the symbol will be reduced to an allegory, simile, or another trope. Thus the richer the symbol and its meaning, the more obscure it becomes, and the more frustratingly ambiguous it may appear. Moreover, Hegel deliberately refrains from extending symbolism to every sphere of mythology and art. Nor does he consider extending it further to other systems that make use of symbols, such as language or mathematics, in this part of his *Aesthetics*, because it is beyond the scope of his current aims. His goal is not to explore the limits of a symbolic interpretation of artistic forms but rather to see to what extent the symbolic can count toward an art form.

Therefore, on one hand, we see in Hegel's aesthetics a beautifully structured system of symbolic form(s)—in the way the later twentieth-century philosophers of the symbol, such as Ernst Cassirer, Aleksei Losev, and Susanne Langer, will continue to address the theory of the symbol and symbolic forms. On the other hand, this very system leaves its author and many of his followers and critics rather dissatisfied with its main concepts, the symbol and the symbolic—to the extent that Paul de Man, for example, following Péter Szondi, calls Hegel "a theoretician of the symbol who fails to respond to symbolic language" and effectively dismisses Hegel's account of the symbol as unproductive for modern thought.[22] However, these charges might be premature if we take a closer look at the role of the artist in the symbolic act and at the impulse that triggers symbolic appreciation: wonder. Hegel has this notion but does not consider it a potentially interesting direction of thought because of his mistrust of the symbol. Let us now address this issue and its implications.

Homo Admirans

It would be too easy—albeit not unheard of—to dismiss Hegel's theory of the symbol as outdated. However, it is worth bearing in mind that, while Hegel has all the right premises that later theories of the symbol develop, he prefers by choice not to pursue their implications. As he explores the laws of art, Hegel underscores art's special role as a means of comprehending the world and the role of the artist. He dedicates a special chapter to the figure and the role of the artist in symbolic relations, where he addresses the notion of the artist's genius and inspiration.[23] The artist finds inspiration, Hegel says, in the creative power of imagination. This is the power that allows the artist to have lived and experienced things that might not have been the artist's own and to grasp their essence. However, this insight remains undeveloped in Hegel's account. Nor does Hegel connect it to the point about the origin of creativity, which he makes in passing but which is very important for us.[24] Like Aristotle, Hegel believes that human creative thought starts with wonder:

> The artistic contemplation as such, as well as the religious one . . . and even scientific research, have begun with wonder. The man who has not yet known wonder still lives in ignorance and stupidity. He is not interested in anything, and nothing exists for him, because he has not yet distinguished himself for himself. Nor has he separated himself from objects and their immediate singular existence. On the other hand, he who no longer wonders at anything views the totality of external facts as something which he has already clarified for himself . . . and transformed the objects and their existence into a spiritual self-conscious intuition about them.[25]

According to Hegel, wonder is present when the human being breaks its usual and immediate connection with nature and perceives the universal in the trivial. This is an illuminating, wonderful moment, that is, one full of wonder but, unfortunately, Hegel does not elaborate this thought—again, due to its ambiguity: "Here the inkling of something higher and the consciousness of externality are still unseparated and yet at the same time there is present a contradiction between natural things and the spirit, a contradiction in which objects prove themselves to be just as attractive as repulsive, and the sense of this contradiction along with the urge to remove it is precisely what generates wonder."[26] Hegel views this impulse as a contradiction rather than an occasion for further debate and does not pursue it further. He does not consider the implications of wonder lying in the heart of what creates a symbol, both in general and at the symbolic stage of art. Although he was not a stranger to paradoxes, Hegel was not interested in exploring how they might be productive for his theory of the symbol in the way, for example, Schelling and later Losev did.[27] As Oleg Bychkov points out, Schelling introduces a "dialectic of the symbol," and Losev develops it further by

> addressing the problem of the essence in the form in which it is expressed and by discussing the correlation between the essence and its energy. In Schelling, the absolute in its self-affirmation and self-knowledge is disclosed in some form; this form is the form of identity of the absolute with itself. . . . Paradoxically, however, although every meaning has this form, the latter can never carry the entire fullness of the essence: this paradox is at the center of the symbolic connection.[28]

The paradox can only be seen and treated by the wondering person; let us call this person *homo admirans*. In Hegel's aesthetics, there is both the paradox and *homo admirans*, but Hegel does not bring them together, and this is not surprising. It is characteristic of childhood—and of primordial stages of human history—to be fascinated and taught by wonder. But already in the Kantian universe, the mind is more preoccupied with creating meaning than with discovering it. As Sam Keen demonstrates in his *Apology for Wonder*, from primeval societies through ancient Greek culture to the early Judeo-Christian world, there always was a place for mythopoesis, the mysterious, and wonder.[29] But over time *homo admirans* was replaced by *homo faber*.[30] And yet there is still a place for wonder in this world—even though the overall situation may not be welcoming for *home admirans* anymore. It is not surprising that wonder and miracle has been a subject of investigation in religious thought and literary studies, but it can also be found in unexpected places, such as analytic philosophy. Let us take a very brief look at some theories of miracle.

Western thought mostly echoes the early Hegelian account. First, Hegel himself returns to the question of miracles and wonders in his *Lectures on the Philosophy of History* when he examines Christianity. However, miracles and the miraculous for Hegel are not primarily a religious matter. He rejects the miraculous testimony of Christ in favor of the spiritual attestation, for "the spirit recognizes the spirit."[31] Miracles can help with divine recognition, but this is not their primary job: "A miracle is when the natural course of things is interrupted; but that which is termed the natural course is extremely relative, and the working of e.g. a magnet is just such a miracle."[32] For the rational mind, though, a miraculous event occurs when a fact is considered supernatural and until a scientific explanation is given. When explained, it ceases being wonderful.[33] This direction of thought is most clearly expressed by Ludwig Wittgenstein in his famous *Lecture on Ethics* (1929). In a characteristically Greek way, Wittgenstein's *homo admirans* first wonders at the very existence of the world, at the "what" of the world, and only after that at the "how" of it:

> Let me . . . consider, again, our first experience of wondering at the existence of the world and let me describe it in a slightly different way; we all know the like of which we have never yet seen. Now suppose such an event happened. Take the case that one of you suddenly grew a lion's head and began to roar. Certainly that would be as extraordinary a thing as I can imagine. Now whenever we should have recovered from our surprise, what I would suggest would be to fetch a doctor and have the case scientifically investigated. . . . And where would the miracle have got to?[34]

Wittgenstein asserts with utmost certitude that, examined from such an angle, "everything miraculous has disappeared; unless what we mean by this term is merely that a fact has not yet been explained by science which again means that we have hitherto failed to group this fact with others in a scientific system."[35] But scholars, according to Wittgenstein, do not approach facts as if they were miracles. Even if they distinguish between a relative and an absolute sense of the term "miracle," scholars do not look at their facts as miraculous in the absolute sense. Wittgenstein concludes his exposition of the experience of wondering by saying that it is precisely "the experience of seeing the world as a miracle."[36] As wonderfully as this conclusion sounds in Wittgenstein's ethics, the creative power of wonder is not explored further in his thought, nor is it applied to aesthetics. Much like in Hegel's system, we have both the miracle and *homo admirans* (as well as language and paradoxes), but they are not brought together in a creative symbolic act.

At the same time, the Eastern world, which is also greatly preoccupied with language and logos, approached this problem from a different perspective. Just one year after Wittgenstein's lecture had been delivered, Aleksei Losev, an outstanding Russian philosopher, published his brilliant work *The Dialectics of Myth*.[37] In this book he used his newly developed phenomenological-dialectical method, rooted in both the Eastern (Neoplatonic and Russian Orthodox) and the Western traditions (German idealism, primarily Hegel, and Husserlian phenomenology), to create his own philosophy of myth.[38] This last book of his famous eight-volume set of books published in 1927–30 brings together Losev's most important concepts: name, person, symbol, and myth.

As he examines myth in his unconventional way, Losev apophatically eliminates what myth is not, and then defines myth as (1) a miracle; (2) an image of a person; (3) a personal history given in words; and, finally, in an immanent dialectical formula, as (4) "an unfolded magical name taken in its absolute being."[39] Myth is neither an outdated nor artificial concept; neither a fiction nor a fairy tale nor a metaphor; it involves miracle and magic. It is not accidental that Losev starts his definition of myth with the miracle, which, in turn, receives an elaborate explanation in his system. Proceeding once again by elimination, Losev first shows what a miracle is not to be confused with. A miracle is not a mere manifestation of higher powers or a violation of "the laws of nature." The resulting formula describes the miracle as "(a) the encounter of two personalistic planes of being that (b) may exist within the same person; (c) these are the external-historical plane and the plane of inner design; (d) the forms of their union; (e) . . . the sign of the person's eternal idea."[40] The personalistic aspect and the personhood of *homo admirans* are of utmost importance, for a miracle is "a coincidence of an accidentally happening empirical history of the person with her ideal design."[41] Therefore, quite opposite to the picture described earlier, where wonder occurs when facts contradict our expectations, for Losev, a miracle is a coincidence of a fact with some ideal plan, or rather the fact's correspondence to its own higher purpose. So a miracle happens with the liveliest participation of *homo admirans* and may result in the production of a symbol because of the symbolic relations inherent in this entire process of interaction.

To conclude this part, in his aesthetics, Hegel has all the prerequisites for developing his "relative" theory of the symbol, which he confines mostly to the symbolic stage of art, into an "absolute" theory, which can be applied to other stages, in aesthetics and beyond. Moreover, Hegel even gestures in this direction but chooses not to pursue the issue any further. I will now consider a direction in which these premises could have been developed by discussing Losev's philosophy of the symbol and will apply them to analyzing the symbolic nature of the Prometheus myth.

Losev: Further Elaboration of Hegel's Discussion of the Symbol

Let us first recall some key points in Hegel's account of the symbol and the symbolic. Out of the three art forms in Hegel's schema, namely, symbolic, classical, and romantic, the idea remains undefined at the first stage. In symbolic art it is not expressed as such but rather appears as an image. The symbolic form is only pre-art and cannot yet fully express the idea, which it merely outlines. In his *Aesthetics*, Hegel pays more attention to the symbolic form than to the symbol itself, but when he does consider symbol per se, he concludes that it is in the nature of the symbol to remain ambiguous. Moreover, we cannot even always be sure what counts as symbol: "The view of a symbol immediately makes us doubt as to whether or not a shape should be taken as a symbol, even if we leave aside the further ambiguity with regards to the concrete meaning that a shape is supposed to actualize out of the several meanings it has, for it can often be used as a symbol of further contexts."[42] It is frustrating enough to realize that there are no clear guidelines provided as to whether something is a symbol, and it becomes even more so to think that, even when we are certain that we are dealing with a symbol, we cannot avoid this vicious ambiguity: "This uncertainty becomes even more apparent in the symbol as such because a shape endowed with a meaning is called a symbol only when this meaning is not specifically expressed or makes itself clear somehow otherwise, as it happens in comparison."[43] Hegel mentions that the ambiguity can be removed from the symbol when

> the connection between the sensuous image and the meaning becomes habitual, and transforms into something more or less conditional, which is a necessary requirement for simple signs.... Yet, even a particular symbol, due to its habitual character, is clear to those who exist in such a conventional circle of concepts, it happens altogether different for those outside of this conventional circle or for those for whom it is already in the past.[44]

It seems that Hegel strives to remove the ambiguity from symbol, but since this obscurity is in the symbol's nature, it can only be overcome in a conventional symbol (with its properties reduced to or shared with those of the sign) by the members of the same symbolic community, while those outside it will have to deal with the ambiguity. Is there a way out of this vicious ambiguity? Hegel leaves the situation the way it is, and if we keep thinking that dubiety in general is harmful, this uncertainty will remain merely frustrating. However, we do not have to think of ambiguity as of an obstacle. Following later philosophers of the symbol, in particular Losev, whose system and method were greatly influenced by Hegel, let us consider if it can be understood as productive for art and for symbolic relations.

Losev's interest in the symbol spans his entire life, from the early *Octoteuch* (the eight-volume series of books), including *The Philosophy of the Name* (*Filosofiia imeni*, 1927) and *Essays on Classical Symbolism and Mythology*, Vol. 1 (*Ocherki antichnogo simvolizma i mifolofii*, 1930), to his later *The Problem of Symbol and Realist Art*

(*Problema simvola i realisticheskoe iskusstvo*, 1976), with many monographs and articles on ancient and modern symbolism written during the decades in between. Losev's unprecedented eight-volume *History of Ancient Aesthetics* (*Istoriia antihcnoi estetiki*, 1963–94) deserves a special mention for its systematic analysis of the entire philosophy and aesthetic history of Antiquity, where the symbol and the symbolic play an important role. It should be noticed that the symbol in Losev's system does not stand alone and should be considered together with his other essential concepts: name, myth, number, and essence.

First, let us recall that the term *symbol* derives from the Greek σύμβολον (σύν, "together," and βάλλω "I throw, put," meaning "to throw together, dash together, to bring together, unite, collect, or come together.")[45] One of the oldest and arguably the most complicated concepts in the history of humanity, the term *symbol*, in the words of classical philologist Aza Takho-Godi,

> has kept in an amazing way, over thousands of years, the clarity and transparency of its original meaning. . . . Σύμ-βολοω is a verb that indicates a coincidence, confluence, meeting of two principles in one [thing], and σύμβολον as a result of this meeting and this joining, as their indication, as a sign of this union, with all the simplicity of its semantics is very far removed from that "symbol" which is deprived of this naïveté available to everyone and is linked in everyone's imagination with something mystical and mysterious.[46]

The presence of different principles brought together is an unalienable part of the symbol's structure.

Ontologically the symbol is a meeting point of the essence and the phenomenon where the essence is manifested due to the inseparable connection of symbolism and apophatism. This makes the symbol inexhaustible in its meanings because it comprises, to use Losev's terminology, the eidos incarnated in its *inobytie*, "other-being," due to "a limitless richness of the possibilities of its meaning."[47] The apophatic quality of this connection ensures the infinity of the meanings generated by the symbol, and dialectics allows the identity of the two opposite sides (namely, the *eidos* and its *meon*, or the meaning and its external manifestation[48]). That is why, according to Losev, the symbol can produce and incorporate diverging vectors of meaning without losing its integrity:

> The symbol lives by the antithesis of the logical and the alogical, of the stable and clear—and the eternally unstable, obscure; one can never make the transition in it from a complete incomprehensibility to a complete comprehensibility. In its eternally generated and vanishing semantic energies is all the power and significance of the symbol. . . . The symbol is the semantic circulation of the alogical power of the incomprehensible, the alogical circulation of the semantic power of cognition.[49]

Thus the ambiguity—or rather the polysemy, the σύν-βάλλω nature—of the symbol is its driving force; it should be nurtured, not surmounted. The symbol is intrinsically multivalent. And since it is "the arena of a meeting"[50] of different products of consciousness, the symbol needs the conscious, cognizant, and wondering person who will make the meeting possible. It is not only *homo admirans* who is present here; the wonder and mystery are also explicitly taking their place in the symbolism of the word. As Losev states, "The mystery of the word is exactly in the fact that it is the means of communication with objects and the arena of their intimate and conscious encounter with their inner life."[51] Therefore, Losev's "mystery of the word" is to be distinguished both from the tradition of identifying the word with thought and from the tradition of making the word an impersonal carrier of the thought. To explain how and why this understanding of the symbol works, Losev analyzes the category of the symbol with the help of his phenomenological-dialectical method, which, as I already mentioned, was developed under Hegel's influence. In a very general way, he treats the symbol in correlation with the ancient Greek and Schellingian tradition as "the indistinguishable identity of the universal and the particular, the ideal and the real, the finite and the infinite."[52] Echoing Hegel, Losev claims that the symbol is an advanced version of the concept *sign*. In Losev's dialectics, the sign and the symbol in the most general way are distinguished from each other by the degree of the complexity of the signified and symbolized objects. Therefore, all axioms of the sign are essentially the axioms of the symbol. Losev's complex sign-symbol axiomatics includes twenty-six items, the last ten of which are axioms of the symbol proper.

According to the dialectical definition rigorously elaborated by Losev, the sign is "1) the reflectively- 2) meaningful and 3) contextually- 4) demonstrating 5) function 6) of the thing (or reality in general), given as 7) a subjectively refracted 8) extremely generalized and 9) reversely-reflected 10) invariant 11) of the fluidly variable 12) indications 13) of the objective 14) information."[53] And since, as we have just seen, a sign can have an infinite number of meanings, it can become a symbol.[54] The symbol itself is also subjected to a meticulous examination resulting in nine principal semantic moments of its structure. According to Losev, the symbol of a thing is:

1) Its meaning that constructs and generates the symbol. This union is living and active.
2) Its generalization. And again, this generalization is not passive or abstract, but such that it is already present in the symbol and implicitly contains what is being symbolized, even if the latter were infinite.
3) Its law, but such a law that generates the meaning of things, while leaving their empirical concreteness untouched.
4) Its regular, ordered nature given as the general principle of its semantic construction.
5) Its internal-external expression formed in accordance with the general principle of its construction.
6) Its structure—albeit taken not in isolation, but charged with a finite or an infinite range of its manifestations.
7) Its sign that generates multiple and probably infinite individual structures.
8) Its sign, but not having to do with the immediate content of these singularities described here, but rather these singularities are defined by this general constructive principle.
9) The identity of the thing signified and of its signifying eidetic image.[55]

It would be appropriate to mention here that in his dialectical deduction of sixty-seven "moments" inherent in the category of the *name*, Losev explains the complexity of the result by ontological reasons: "It should not be forgotten that the word is born at the top of the scale of entities that comprise the living being, and that man must undergo a great evolution before he can meaningfully pronounce a sensible word."[56] And given that language is a symbolic system, one should not be surprised by the complexity of Losev's axiomatics of the symbol either.

His phenomenological-dialectical analysis of language leads Losev to viewing the word as both the form and the matter of rational thought. And although, like any other symbol, the word first arises as a sign, Losev demonstrates that the fact of it being a sign in the logical and epistemological sense is secondary with respect to its symbolic nature. This ability of the word to be a symbol is an entelechy of a kind that makes the word absorb external material and generate meaning from it. Returning to the importance of both symbolism and apophaticism for the nature of the symbol, Losev explains: "Only symbolism saves phenomena from a subjectivist illusionism and from a blind deification of matter, while affirming nevertheless its ontological reality; and only apophaticism saves the appearing essence from agnostic negativism and from rationalist-metaphysical dualism, while affirming nevertheless its universal significance and its irreducibly real nature."[57] In this claim, Losev underlines once again the inseparability of symbolism in the sense of a logical phenomenality of things and apophaticism in the sense of the hiddenness of the essence of things. The word is exactly this wonderful part of our materialistic consciousness that is both apophatic and symbolic by its nature. The paradox of the symbol consists in the fact that the apophatic character of the appearance of essence in it stipulates the increasing symbolism of the image that is being generated—the more so because the essence manifests itself in it.

The Symbol of Prometheus in Hegel and Losev

To illustrate the implications of Hegel's and Losev's respective theories of the symbol for the treatment of actual symbols in art, we can briefly turn to one of the most powerful and complex symbols in human history, the symbol of Prometheus.[58] Both Hegel and Losev repeatedly return to the image of Prometheus in their respective works on aesthetics, and Hegel's Prometheus seems to carry a different message than Losev's Prometheus. Let us compare this image as it is interpreted by the two philosophers, bearing in mind especially the point that they both make about the ambiguity of the symbol, with the aim to find a meaningful interpretation of the symbol. Depending on the sources from which we draw our knowledge of Prometheus, we receive very different images and different ideas behind the symbol. Hegel, for whom Prometheus is not a central character but only a means of illustration, speaks of at least three different figures of Prometheus: those of Hesiod, Protagoras, and the Scholiast. Losev, who devotes a chapter titled "The Historical Concreteness of the Symbol: The World Image of Prometheus" in his book on *The Problem of the Symbol*, derives its complex threads from dozens of sources, both ancient and modern.[59] Prometheus is mostly known as the Titan who brings people fire and is subsequently punished by the gods. However, the accounts of such things as Prometheus's motives—what else, if anything, he has to bring people along with fire; what exactly he is punished for by the gods; and the final result of the entire adventure—differ drastically from one tradition to another.

The Prometheus that Hegel takes from Hesiod primarily symbolizes hope. He is an ambivalent figure: on the one hand, he is friends with the gods, on the other hand, he helps human beings. He is a Titan but chooses to benefit people. This ambivalence does not make sense, notices Hegel, until Plato explains it.[60] Once Hegel has Plato's explanation and the illogicalities of the symbol are resolved, he is satisfied and proceeds further in his own investigation. In Protagoras, Prometheus is punished primarily for the theft but not for his rebellious deeds. This Prometheus did not give human beings ethical or legal laws. Overall, he is depicted as a strange Titan who was punished, but then he is freed and "he is constantly glorified."[61] This Prometheus does not exactly live up to Hegel's expectations, and his image remains largely unexplained. The Scholiast adds details about Prometheus's release. As Hegel states, "According to the myth, Prometheus was not doomed to endure his punishment forever but was freed from his chains by Hercules. In this story of the liberation there, too, appear some remarkable details, namely, Prometheus is released from his torment because he announces to Zeus of the danger to his rule that comes from his thirteenth descendant."[62] Here too, we get another "strange" Prometheus who buys his freedom in exchange for some important information, and the entire glory of his initial deed is lessened. Hegel does not create or reconstruct a comprehensive image of Prometheus; this is not his task. However, his use of it to illustrate various points about mythology at the symbolic stage of art suggests that he wishes to rationalize this complex symbol by bringing it to a common denominator: everything in this myth should make sense in some logical way. Hegel consistently dismisses parts of the myths and legends if, in his view, they are incoherent. As he notes elsewhere, "But since this assorted special material has lost its original meaning in the universality of the gods, we are left with gaudy and intricate stories that make no sense for us."[63] In Hegel's reconstruction of the myth, unless all parts of the story make some sense, the symbol will not function properly and will be reduced to an allegory at best.

By contrast, Losev treats Prometheus as a subject of special interest and investigation. Losev carries out a comprehensive analysis of various images of Prometheus from Antiquity to the modern day both in mythology and in art, and his main thesis is that any real symbol can exist only in history. Therefore, all symbols bear the mark of the epoch when they were created and of the author, if their creator is known. Like any other complex symbol, Prometheus is potentially inexhaustible in its connotations, but we can outline its primary meaning: as an image in world culture, it is a symbol of progressive civilization. The Greek Προμηθεύς is derived from the verb προμηθέομαι meaning "to use forethought," "to take care (of something)."[64] What makes Prometheus outstanding is that he brings humanity the idea of progress. Among the many versions of the myth Losev considers the three figures that we saw in Hegel's aesthetics, but Losev interprets Hesiod's Prometheus as the symbol of a struggle against the usurpation of power by the Olympic gods and in this sense the protector of human beings. Losev agrees with

Hegel that Hesiod's account is indeed confusing but, unlike the German philosopher, he does not mind the illogicalities in Hesiod's version of the story. "In Hesiod," Losev explains, "the superiority of Prometheus over Zeus is still given in a primitive form, so that Prometheus is simply the deceiver of Zeus, and for his deception he suffers a great punishment by being chained to a rock at the edge of the world."[65] Likewise, Losev notes, as did Hegel, that Protagoras's Prometheus fails to endow humanity with moral rules, but he finds Plato's explanation rather amusing. Prometheus's heroic deed is still worthy of respect but, strictly speaking, humanity receives the concept of conscience from Zeus, not from Prometheus, so the main emphasis is on Prometheus as the founder of a technological civilization. Since the symbol keeps generating new meanings, whose number is potentially unlimited, it can afford an interpretation that will be weaker than others or will fail to satisfy everyone, without undermining the symbol's integrity. As for the Scholiast, Losev provides an extensive commentary on this version. In particular, the Scholiast's comments contain information about Prometheus's origins, the reasons of his punishment, and his release (this last point was discussed by Hegel). In addition, the Scholiast lists various interpretations of the Prometheus myth showing that the philosophical interpretation of the myth dates back as early as the Peripatetic school. Losev discusses various versions of the story, some contradicting others, as told by the Scholiast, and finds this material fascinating. The only thing Losev regrets is that, although the Scholiast apparently survived all Neoplatonists, he refrained from any comments about them. It is the Neoplatonists' interpretation that would be the most interesting because, according to Losev, "they were the principal restorers of all mythological antiquity and tried to understand as deeply as possible the most ancient myths, discarding any rationalistic or allegorical interpretation of them."[66]

Losev carefully explores Promethean symbolism in the traditions of the Greeks and Romans, proceeds to highly interesting, unusual, and largely unknown Caucasian tales, then examines the Middle Ages, the Renaissance, the modern period, and, finally, the art of his own day. Over time, Losev demonstrates, the image of Prometheus has undergone some radical changes and its purely mythological component has been replaced with others: religious, artistic, or scientific. The symbolism of the myth has also altered considerably; St. Augustin, for instance, saw in Prometheus and his fire a symbol of wisdom and knowledge; Boccaccio's Prometheus was a symbol of science and scientific wisdom; in Voltaire, Prometheus lost all his universal and historical significance; and Goethe, the brothers Schlegel, and Johann Herder understood Prometheus as a symbol of an artist and creator. In general, the ancient cosmogonic component of the symbol has disappeared, with the exception of Vyacheslav Ivanov's Prometheus. In modern times, Losev writes, "Prometheus is neither a deity nor a demon nor a Titan in the ancient meaning of the term; he is just an ordinary human being, if an extremely wise or deeply knowledgeable one, or a great artist."[67] Losev starts with mythology and ends with art, which includes literature and other artistic forms, down to Alexander Skryabin's 1908–10 symphony *Promethée, The Poem of Fire*.

These examples show that the symbol is indeed inexhaustible. It is a mobile, living, polysemic, and polyvalent structure whose connections are multivalued. They are intertwined with one another and keep generating new meanings, without losing the central symbolic invariant. The artist, *homo admirans*, the creative principle behind both making the symbol and interpreting it, serves as a guarantor of symbolic communication and is unthinkable without it. Hegel does not explore the symbol very far and effectively stops at noting its ambiguity while denying the latter's creative potential. He does not find the symbol as a concept rigorous enough, but, remarkably, he has all the ingredients that could have been developed into a much richer theory. This is exactly what later philosophers and, in particular, Losev's philosophy of symbol has to offer.

Abbreviations

A   Hegel, *Aesthetics*, followed by a Roman numeral volume number and Arabic numeral page number.

VA Hegel, G. W. F. *Vorlesungen über die Ästhetik I*. Werke 13 (Frankfurt am Main: Suhrkamp, 1970), followed by a Roman numeral volume number and Arabic numeral page number.

Notes

1   This definition is present in the Suhrkamp edition of Hegel's Werke (*VA* I:211) and in many translations, including the Knox version (*A* I:111.). However, it might be considered controversial in Hegel, as it is not present in Hotho's manuscript of 1823; nor is it accepted by Gethmann-Siefert (cf. Annemarie Gethmann-Siefert, *Einführung in Hegels Ästhetik* [Paderborn: Wilhelm Fink, 2005], 89–94). For the purposes of this chapter, we'll use the Suhrkamp definition.
2   There was some interest in Hegel's theory of the symbol, in particular in the late nineteenth–early twentieth century, such as Johannes Volkelt, *Der Symbol-Begriff in der neuesten Äesthetik* (Iena: H. Dufft, 1876), ch. II, and Max Schlesinger, *Geschichte des Symbols* (Berlin: L. Simion, 1912), 65–94, 120–22, but it later subsided.
3   Among the most important theories of the symbol there should be mentioned Ernst Cassirer's philosophy of symbolic forms; Alfred North Whitehead's theory of symbols; Carl Gustav Jung's symbolic, or "deep" psychology (*Tiefenpsychologie*), Martin Heidegger's hermeneutic theory of symbols, Aleksei Losev's philosophy of the symbol, and Susanne Langer's metaphoric symbolism.
4   *VA* I:211. (*A* I:111.)
5   *VA* I:108. (*A* I:55.)
6   Paul De Man, "Sign and Symbol in Hegel's Aesthetics," *Critical Inquiry* 8, no. 4 (Summer 1982): 763.
7   *VA* I:146–148. (*A* I:76–77.)
8   *VA* I:148 (*A* I:77.)
9   *VA* I:149. (*A* I 77–78.)
10 *VA* I:151–54. (*A* I:79–80.)
11 *VA* I:723–816. Drittes Kapitel Die bewußte Symbolik der vergleichenden Kunstform, (*A* Chapter III, Conscious Symbolism of the Comparative Art-Form, 378–426.)
12 *VA* I:579. (*A* I:303.)

13 De Man, "Sign and Symbol in Hegel's Aesthetics," 764. See also Henry George Liddell and Robert Scott, *Greek-English Lexicon* (New York: American Book Company, 1897), 40.
14 De Man, "Sign and Symbol in Hegel's Aesthetics."
15 VA I:579–80. (A I:303.)
16 VA I:581. (A I:304.)
17 For example, in early twentieth-century Russian philosophy, Pavel Florensky calls this gap a "hiatus" (*ziyanie*) and explains how to overcome it: "There is no bridge from the reality to the picture. There is a hiatus here which is jumped over for the first time by the creative mind of the artist and then by the mind that co-creatively reproduces the picture in oneself." Florensky, "Obratnaya perspektiva," in *Sochinenia v 4 tomakh* (Works in 4 Volumes) 3, no. 1 (Moscow: Mysl', 1999): 71. Translations from Russian are mine, unless noted otherwise.
18 VA I:581. (A I:304.)
19 VA I:583. (A I:305.)
20 VA I:583–84. (A I:305.)
21 VA I:585. (A I:306.)
22 De Man, "Sign and Symbol in Hegel's Aesthetics," 765. See also Péter Szondi, *Poetik und Geschichtsphilosophie I* (Frankfurt am Main, 1974), 390–96.
23 VA I:536–72. (A I:280–98.)
24 Hegel's treatment of the imagination has left a few scholars dissatisfied; see, for example, John Kedney's remark made over a century ago: "I may remark that Hegel's treatment of imagination hardly amounts to a satisfactory definition. It is a synthetic, rather than an analytic procedure. He has given this name to a congeries of qualities and modes of activity." Kedney, *Hegel's Aesthetics: A Critical Exposition* (Chicago: S.C. Griggs and Company, 1885), 104–06.
25 VA I:602–3 (A I 314–15.) Cf.: "For it is owing to their wonder that men both now begin and at first began to philosophize; they wondered originally at the obvious difficulties, then advanced little by little and stated difficulties about the greater matters.... And a man who is puzzled and wonders thinks himself ignorant (whence even the lover of myth is in a sense a lover of wisdom, for myth is composed of wonders); therefore since they philosophized in order to escape from ignorance, evidently they were pursuing science in order to know." Aristotle, *Metaphysics*, 982b 12–20.
26 Ibid.
27 On paradoxes in Hegel see, for example, W. T. Harris, "Hegel's Four Paradoxes," *The Journal of Speculative Philosophy* 16, no. 2 (1882): 113–22.
28 Bychkov, "Introduction." Aleksei Fyodorovich Losev, *The Dialectic of Artistic Form*, trans. Oleg V. Bychkov, ed. Daniel L. Tate (München: Verlag Otto Sagner, 2013), 77. Bychkov refers to a paper by P.V. Rezvykh that explores the dialectics of the symbol in Schelling and Losev. See Rezvykh, "F.W.J. Shelling i A.F. Losev: Tezisy k postanovke problemy" (F. W. J. Schelling and A. F. Losev: Theses toward Outlining the Problem), *Bulleten' Biblioteki istorii russkoi filosofii i kul'tury "Dom A.F. Loseva"* (*Bulletin of the Library of history of Russian philosophy and culture "The House of A.F. Losev"*) 12 (2010): 97–109.
29 Sam Keen, *Apology for Wonder* (New York: Harper and Row, 1969).
30 Keen does not suggest returning to *homo admirans* or criticizing *homo faber*, but rather finding some room for wonder in modern society. He introduces his vision of a *homo tempestivus* who is aware of the challenges brought by the new era but can hear and respond to the echo of past as well.

31 G. W. F. Hegel, *Lectures on the Philosophy of History*, trans. Ruben Alvarado (WordBridge Publishing, 2011), 296.
32 Ibid., 296–97.
33 Konstantin Frumkin examines theories of wonder in the twentieth century (cf. Konstantin Frumkin, "Teorii chuda v epokhu nauki" ("Theories of miracle in the epoch of science"). *Epistemologiya i filosofiya nauki*. (*Epistemology and Philosophy of Science.*) No. 5 (2005): 153–72) and finds that Henri Bergson expresses a similar thought, only instead of the miracle he has *chance*: "When the wholly mechanical play of the causes which stop the wheel on a number makes me win, and consequently acts like a good genius, careful of my interests, or when the wholly mechanical force of the wind tears a tile off the roof and throws it on to my head, that is to say acts like a bad genius, conspiring against my person: in both cases I find a mechanism where I should have looked for, where, indeed, it seems as if I ought to have found, an intention. That is what I express in speaking of chance." Bergson, *Creative Evolution* (New York: Henry Holt and Company, 1911), 234. This paragraph from Bergson does not contain anything "wonderful" in the Hegelian sense, but it shows a mechanism of disruption in the usual course of affairs, be it of divine nature or just anything supernatural.
34 Ludwig Wittgenstein, *Lecture on Ethics*, ed. Edoardo Zamuner et al. (Hoboken: Wiley-Blackwell, 2014), 49.
35 Ibid., 50.
36 Ibid.
37 Olga Lyanda-Geller, "Aleksei Fedorovich Losev," in *Filosofia: An Encyclopedia of Russian Thought*, ed. Alyssa DeBlasio and Mikhail Epstein, February 2019, http://filosofia.dickinson.edu/encyclopedia/losev-aleksei/.
38 Aleksei Losev, *Dialektika mifa* (Moscow: Mysl', 2001); *The Dialectics of Myth*, trans. Vladimir Marchenkov (London and New York: Routledge, 2003).
39 Losev, *Dialektika mifa*, I–XI, XIII.
40 Ibid., XI.
41 Ibid., XI, 5 b.
42 *VA* I:585. (*A* I:306.)
43 *VA* I:587. (*A* I:307.)
44 *VA* I:588–89. (*A* I:308.)
45 Liddell and Scott, *Greek-English Lexicon*, 1456.
46 Aza Alibekovna Takho-Godi, "Termin 'simvol' v drevnegrecheskoi literature" ("The term 'symbol' in Ancient Greek literature"), *Obraz i slovo* (Image and Word) (Moscow: Izdatel'stvo Moskovskogo universiteta, 1980), 19.
47 Losev, *Filosofiia imeni* (Philosophy of the Name) (Moscow: Izdatelstvo MGU, 1990), 105.
48 For more detail about the structure of name and its relations with *eidos* and *meon*, see *Filosofia imeni*, II, "Predmentaia structura imeni" ("The Object-Structure of the Name").
49 Ibid., 93.
50 Losev repeatedly uses this metaphor; see ibid., 14–17, 49, and 59.
51 Ibid., 49.
52 Losev, *Ocherki antichnogo simvolizma i mifologii* (Essays on Ancient Symbolism and Mythology) (Moscow: Mysl, 1993), 20.
53 Aleksei Losev, *Problema simvola i realisticheskoe iskusstvo* (The Problem of the Symbol and Realist Art) (Moscow: Iskusstvo, 1995), 65.

54 Ibid., 104.
55 Ibid., paraphrased from pp. 46–47.
56 Losev, *Filosofiia imeni*, 161.
57 Ibid., 114.
58 Although, for Hegel, Prometheus would belong to the classical and not to the symbolical form of art, let us consider Prometheus as an actual symbol, without respect to its belonging to an art form.
59 "Istoricheskaia konkretnost' simvola. Mirovoi obraz Prometeia," Chapter VII of Losev's *Problema simvola*.
60 *VA* II:68. (*A* I:460.)
61 *VA* II:86. (*A* I:470.)
62 *VA* II:87. (*A* I:470.)
63 *VA* II:133. (*A* I:493.)
64 Liddell and Scott, *Greek-English Lexicon*, 1291.
65 Losev, *Problema simvola*, 192.
66 Ibid., 201.
67 Ibid., 217.

Bibliography

Aristotle. "Metaphysics." In *The Complete Works of Aristotle*, in 2 vols, edited by Jonathan Barnes, 1552–1728. Bollingen Series edition: Princeton University Press, 1984.

Bergson, Henri. *Creative Evolution*. New York: Henry Holt and Company, 1911.

De Man, Paul. "Sign and Symbol in Hegel's Aesthetics." *Critical Inquiry* 8, no. 4 (Summer 1982): 761–75.

Florensky, Pavel. "Obratnaya perspektiva" (Reverse Perspective), in *Sochinenia v 4 tomakh*. (Works in four volumes.) Moskva: Mysl', 1999. Tom 3 (1), 46–98.

Frumkin, Konstantin. "Teorii chuda v epokhu nauki." (Theories of miracle in the era of science.") *Epistemologiya i filosofiya nauki*, (*Epistemology and Philosophy of Science*.) No. 5 (2005): 153–72.

Gethmann-Siefert, Annemarie. *Einführung in Hegels Ästhetik*. Paderborn: Wilhelm Fink, 2005.

Harris, W. T. "Hegel's Four Paradoxes." *The Journal of Speculative Philosophy* 16, no. 2 (1882): 113–22.

Hegel, G. W. F. *Aesthetics: Lectures on Fine Art*, in 2 vols, translated by T. M. Knox. Oxford: Clarendon Press, 1975.

Hegel, G. W. F. *Hegel's Introduction to Aesthetics: Being the Introduction to The Berlin Aesthetics Lectures of the 1820s*, translated by T. M. Knox. Oxford: Clarendon Press, 1979.

Hegel, G. W. F. *Lectures on the Philosophy of History*, translated by Ruben Alvarado. WordBridge Publishing, 2011.

Hegel, G. W. F. *On the Arts*. Selections from G. W. F. Hegel's *Aesthetics or the Philosophy of Fine Art*, translated by Henry Paolucci. Griffon House Publications, 2001.

Hegel, G. W. F. *The Philosophy of Fine Arts*, in 4 vols, translated by F. P. B. Osmaston. London: G. Bell and Sons, LTD, 1920.

Hegel, G. W. F. *Vorlesungen über die Ästhetik I-III*. Werke in 20 Bänden. Bd. 13-15. Frankfurt am Main: Suhrkamp, 1970–86.

Kedney, John Steinfort. *Hegel's Aesthetics: A Critical Exposition*. Chicago: S.C. Griggs and Company, 1885.
Keen, Sam. *Apology for Wonder*. New York: Harper and Row, 1969.
Liddell, Henry George and Robert Scott. *Greek-English Lexicon*. New York: American Book Company, 1897.
Losev, Aleksei. *The Dialectic of Artistic Form*, translated by Oleg V. Bychkov and edited by Daniel L. Tate. München: Verlag Otto Sagner, 2013.
Losev, Aleksei. *The Dialectics of Myth*, translated by Vladimir Marchenkov. London and New York: Routledge, 2003.
Losev, Aleksei. *Dialektika khudozhestvennoi formy*. (The Dialectic of Artistic Form.) Akademicheskii proekt, 2010.
Losev, Aleksei. *Dialektika mifa*. (*The Dialectics of Myth*.) Moskva: Mysl', 2001.
Losev, Aleksei. *Filosofia imeni*. (*Philosophy of Name*.) Moskva: Izdatelstvo MGU, 1990.
Losev, Aleksei. *Ocherki antichnogo simvolizma i mifologii*. (Essays on the Ancient Symbolism and Mythology.) Moskva: Mysl, 1993.
Losev, Aleksei. *Problema simvola i realisticheskoe iskusstvo* (The Problem of Symbol and the Realistic Art.) Moskva: Iskusstvo, 1995.
Lyanda-Geller, Olga. "Aleksei Fedorovich Losev." In *Filosofia: An Encyclopedia of Russian Thought*, edited by Alyssa DeBlasio and Mikhail Epstein, February 2019. Available online: http://filosofia.dickinson.edu/encyclopedia/losev-aleksei/.
Rezvykh, P. V. "F.W.J. Schelling and A.F. Losev: Tezisy k postanovke problemy." ("Theses towards Outlining the Problem") *Bulleten' Biblioteki istorii russkoi filosofii i kul'tury "Dom A.F. Loseva* (*Bulletin of the Library of history of Russian philosophy and culture "The House of A.F. Losev"*) 12 (2010): 97–109.
Schlesinger, Max. *Geschichte des Symbols*. Berlin: L. Simion, 1912.
Szondi, Péter. *Poetik und Geschichtsphilosophie I*. Frankfurt am Main, 1974.
Takho-Godi, Aza Alibekovna. "Termin «simvol» v drevnegrecheskoi literature." ("The term 'symbol' in Ancient Greek literature.") *Obraz i slovo. Voprosy klassicheskoi filologii* VII (1980): 16–57.
Volkelt, Johannes. *Der Symbol-Begriff in der neuesten Ästhetik*. Iena: H. Dufft, 1876.
Wittgenstein, Ludwig. *Lecture on Ethics*, edited by Edoardo Zamuner et al. Hoboken: Wiley-Blackwell, 2014.

8

Hegel, Danto, Cavell, and the End of Art

Stefan Bird-Pollan

In this chapter I'd like to consider two philosophical provocations, the first is Hegel's claim that "art, considered in its highest vocation, is and remains for us a thing of the past," commonly known as Hegel's end-of-art thesis, and Stanley Cavell's claim that, for at least the brief period from the 1930s to the 1960s, film occupied the center of American public life.[1] My purpose in connecting these two theses is, in effect, to reflect on one surprising claim through another. Why does Hegel claim that art, in its highest vocation, is at an end yet to go on in his lectures for hundreds more pages explicating and art that he sees as superannuated? And how can Cavell, in a century reeling from the decline of representational art and the widespread understanding of art as something avant-garde, claim that film of all things is a "traditional" art, which can take its foundations for granted?[2] Hegel's claim, I shall argue, must be understood *phenomenologically*, that is, as a diagnosis of a current predicament rather than as a philosophical argument standing to the side of the practice of art. The controversial nature of Hegel's claim, and its staying power (versions of it are to be found in both Heidegger and Adorno), stems from the fact that it cannot be a merely definitional claim but must correspond to something we experience as we look around us. The argument here, though I cannot myself offer a reading of the history or current practice of art, depends on recognizing that what is being said must constitute a reflection of that history or practice. It is for this reason that I shall focus on writers who are *both* engaged in writing about art *and* are philosophers (Arthur Danto, Stanley Cavell, T. J Clark, Gregg Horowitz, T. W. Adorno), and I shall deal with philosophical debates that are more internal to Hegel only on the side.

I wish to understand the phenomenology of the experience of art by asking about what role art plays in helping us reflect upon the social institutions of which we are part. That is, I am asking about the way in which art, as part of what Hegel calls Absolute Spirit, allows us to understand what Hegel calls objective spirit. There are two general directions here, either art merely supplements our relation to objective spirit because the real work of making sense of our communal relation to *Sittlichkeit* is being done by another form of Absolute Spirit (religion or philosophy), or art continues to play a central role in allowing us to understand our relation to objective spirit, in which case art is not at an end. First, I shall argue that both tendencies are provided for in Hegel's text and constitute a tension. Second, I shall follow two interpretative strands, each of which takes up one variant. The supplemental interpretation of Karsten Harries and Arthur Danto takes it that Hegel is right that art is essentially over because it cannot do the conceptual work required by modernity. The dialectical interpretation of Adorno, Clark, and Horowitz, by contrast, argues that art continues and, furthermore, takes the fact that art continues as evidence of the failure of the "successor" form of objective spirit. Finally, I read Cavell's understanding of mid-twentieth-century Hollywood film as evidence of a real reconciliation between Absolute Spirit and objective spirit.

Absolute and Objective Spirit

Hegel locates the relation between objective and Absolute Spirit both systematically, by which I mean that Absolute Spirit is the genus of art, religion, and philosophy, and developmentally, in the sense of connecting each of the three types of art to different historical periods. By objective spirit, Hegel means the manifestation of the subject's inner freedom in the particular objective or social realm the subject happens to find itself in. The expression of freedom on the part of the individual takes the form of the political concepts of power and recognition.[3] I think we can say that Absolute Spirit is a way of thinking about freedom that goes beyond the determinate way in which objective spirit manifests itself in society. Absolute spirit is an idealized account of our origins, where we belong in the social structure, and our aspirations. Of art, Hegel says that it is the "concrete contemplation and mental picture of implicitly absolute spirit as the *Ideal*."[4]

By placing us within the domain of this ideal, art makes us feel at home:

> A surrounding world belongs to the subject the way a temple belongs to the god. This surrounding world is not something contingent but is instead an internally consistent, coherent totality. Human beings must be portrayed in relation to it, for they stand within this relationship.... Human beings must be at home in the world, making their home freely in it, finding themselves settled.[5]

The work done by Absolute Spirit is then to idealize our ordinary social lives, in the sense of showing us their true meaning. In this way, Absolute Spirit reveals that side of our freedom, which transcends the particular expression of freedom necessary for human social interaction. The central point I'd like to highlight in the relation between Absolute Spirit and objective spirit is that Absolute Spirit—art, religion, and philosophy—must always be understood as being *about* the problem of how freedom is to manifest itself in our social organization. By the same token, objective spirit must always be understood to be revisable under the ideal terms set out by Absolute Spirit. It is this revisability that will concern us throughout this chapter.

Two Dimensions of Absolute Spirit

Hegel thinks of the relation between absolute and objective spirit along two different axes: the systematic axis of different functions and the developmental axis of the sublation of one form by another. He puts the systematic point by saying that "nature and spirit are in general different modes of exhibiting its existence, art and religion its different modes of apprehending itself and giving itself appropriate existence. Philosophy has the same content and the same purpose as art and religion."[6] That is, for Hegel, Absolute Spirit represents three different modes of thinking about the relation between nature and spirit in human sociality. Hegel characterizes the different modes of consciousness of art, religion, and philosophy thus: "This relationship can be nothing other than (a theoretical one, a modality of consciousness, for it concerns the form, the objectivity as such.) [It has] the character (a) of immediate intuition, (b) of representation, (c) of thought in the strict sense of conceptual, speculative thought of what is true."[7] The Absolute Spirit's role of making us at home in our social conditions is also presented dynamically or historically as tied to the relative developmental level of objective spirit in a particular culture. Hegel thus understands the relation of objective to Absolute Spirit as a succession of these different relations. "The concept of spirit [as absolute] has its reality in the spirit. . . . The subjective and the objective spirit are to be looked on as the road on which this aspect of reality or existence rises to maturity."[8] The official form of this thought is that the various forms of Absolute Spirit correspond to different (historical) forms of objective spirit.[9] In art this means that the particular types of art Hegel delineates are also tied to particular, qualitatively different, conceptions of objective spirit's social organization. Thus, symbolic forms of art found in Egypt corresponded to the Egyptian political organization in which the ruler was a god.

The Greek polis corresponds to fine art as the appropriate form of Absolute Spirit. For Hegel, Greek art has two dimensions in which Absolute Spirit modulates objective spirit. On the diachronic axis, it is the relation of the Greek *polis* to its origins in nature and aspirations to freedom, and on the synchronic axis, the relation of the human (as finite) to the divine (as infinite). Art mediates both relations by representing the divine in human form in sculpture. Hegel thinks that this anthropocentrism is a virtue since it essentially belongs to human subjectivity to consider itself divine since this is the essence of spirit's aspiration of universal freedom.[10]

I'd like to submit that the dynamic or historical account is in tension with the systematic account. Hegel maintains that the different dimensions of Absolute Spirit are equivalent ways of mediating objective spirit but for different members of society, thus religion and philosophy perform the same function in modern society, for instance, but do so in different ways. In the *Lectures on the Philosophy of Religion*, Hegel writes: "Religion is for everyone. It is no philosophy, which is not for everyone. Religion is the manner or mode by which all human beings become conscious of truth for themselves."[11] At the systematic level, then, Hegel seems to be suggesting that there is an equivalence between the different modes of Absolute Spirit. Along the historical dimension, however, this equivalence is broken: Hegel claims, as we have seen, that in its highest vocation, art is a thing of the past. Along the historical dimension, then, Hegel conceives of the mode of art as being replaced by that of religion. But even this declared replacement seems doubtful because Hegel spends significant time in his lectures discussing what he calls romantic art, that is, postclassical art. It is thus fair to say, I think, that Hegel is deeply ambivalent about the question.

Hegel's ambivalence, I'd like to suggest, can be traced back to two currents in his thinking. On the one side, there is his perceptiveness with regard to what I've called the phenomenology of art, that is, the fact that fine art in his own day as well as in past ages, evidently, continued to play a central role in expressing the relation between our highest aspirations and the realities of the social world. On the other hand, Hegel is also committed to the idea that thinking progresses from immediacy to reflection, combined with the idea that since the paradigmatic experience of art is, for him, that of beauty (which does not admit of further reflection), art as a mode of thought can no longer play the central part that it seems to have done in ancient Greece.

Reframing the Question

What I'd like to do in the remainder of this section is to examine the historical narrative Hegel presents about the replacement of art by the two other forms of Absolute Spirit. The key point to understand will be in what way the different modes of thought offered by religion and philosophy can indeed properly replace art. I'd like to propose that we evaluate Hegel's phenomenological assessment of the continuing role of art in Christian culture against the story Hegel wants to tell about conceptual or rational development. This will put us in a position to understand the three proposed interpretations of Hegel later in this chapter.

The narrative we must follow in Hegel is the emergence of human subjectivity from nature, that is, from what Hegel calls immediacy and what in another vein we can call materiality. The criterion by which to evaluate Hegel's own thinking thus becomes what status we accord ourselves with regard to the project of extricating ourselves from nature. To follow the line in which art is a thing of the past is to believe that we have achieved a decisive step beyond nature and toward or into what Hegel calls philosophy but to hold to the claim that art continues to play a central role in our communal lives is to remain skeptical about the arrival of another, more rational, mode of thought. In order to better see what is at stake, I'd like to return to Hegel's texts and follow the official account of art's transition to religion and to philosophy.

Beauty as Freedom and Its Limitations

Greek art gives us freedom as beauty: "The business of art is to portray the appearance of . . . spiritual vitality outwardly in its freedom; to make the sensible appearance commensurate with the concept, to lead the indigence of nature, of the appearance, back to truth, to the concept."[12] That is, in artistic beauty, nature and spirit are unified in the concept that manifests itself as *appearance* (*Erscheinung*). In beauty the concept or the ideal is *visible* to us.

Yet with this characterization of Greek art as beauty we also arrive at what Hegel sees as the limitation of art's highest vocation, namely that the immediate unification of humanity with divinity in the Greek artistic manifestation of Absolute Spirit is limited to the sensible. Hegel writes that "the realm of beauty itself is still incomplete by itself, because the free concept is only sensuously present in it and has no spiritual reality within itself."[13] Spirit's essential freedom is limited when it expresses itself in sensuous form, that is, in beauty as the *immediate* unification of form and content in appearance. This immediate unification of form and content, however, ultimately turns out to be a lack of inwardness, as we see in the sequel.

The answer to the problem of the lack of unity between content and form in sensuous appearance is the development of inwardness in Christianity.[14] And with the concept of inwardness we have also finally arrived at the end-of-art thesis, the claim that, since art must forever be identified with the beautiful, the conceptual truth art can convey must remain limited to appearance. Because of the higher, reflective standard of Christian inwardness, art that is tied to appearance struggles to express freedom.[15] In terms of the dynamic view of the relation between absolute and objective spirit, this means that the Christian age has moved beyond the Greek age in the sense that it needs a more reflective way of understanding the subject's place in society. The appearance of that unity is no longer a central concern for Absolute Spirit, which now requires the *representation* rather than the *appearance* of unity as its concept or ideal. In his *Lectures on the Philosophy of Religion*, Hegel characterizes the transition from appearance to representation as the consciousness that the appearance, the picture, is merely the immediate hence not what is actually *meant*. This appearance, Hegel writes, seems to the observer to be the external.[16] The internal—that which is meant by the picture—is the relation between god and the world.[17]

Religion

The central problem with the arrival of Christianity for art is that, given Christianity's focus on the interiority of spirit, what makes aesthetic production possible—the relation between material and form *as* beauty—is now itself demoted to the category of mere materiality or content. The material of which art is made is now, in Christianity, more properly understood by giving it a *representational* form. This is another way of saying that in the absence of the immediacy of beauty in Greek culture, beauty, and with it, art, now appears *as* beauty and art for the first time. Beauty and art now become something to be reflected upon *as* representation.

This (partial) turning away from the material world in art constitutes a subjectivism: in her art, the artist creates a representation of the community but necessarily does so from *her* position in society. She seeks inclusion, we might say, in the mode of exclusion. The artist is constrained to work in a mode that she feels must be inadequate to express her relation to the divine. The artist, Hegel notes, stands in an ambivalent relation to the material she must work in, forever seeking to make fit what, by the standards of religious inwardness, can never achieve proper representation. Form and content are thus demoted to a less than necessary relation in art.

"Romantic art . . . can contain only a reflection of the soul's being-within-self and that is always a heterogeneous material, as opposed to what is true. Hence this heterogeneous material is set free to come forward in a personal (*partikular*) way. This is the abstract, basic concept of romantic art."[18] Another way to describe this tension, of course, is that in Christianity the artist is free.[19] By being tied to a superannuated mode of Absolute Spirit, the artist is "free," or perhaps forced, to be on the sidelines of the development of community's spirit. The real spiritual "action" concerns the understanding of human subjectivity as universal subjectivity in the figure of Christ and through the community. Let me be clear that I take this "advance" in Absolute Spirit to be an advance in the sense of making evident the higher power of representational thinking in us. But let me also note that this "higher" power of representational thinking comes at the cost of a turning away from nature. Nevertheless, according to the historical account, the development of religious consciousness is supposed to be an answer to the dissatisfaction of our immanent relation to nature in art.

Religion and Natural Science

Let me reinforce the plausibility of religion's inability to *generally* account for our communal relation to objective spirit by linking it to one other mode of explanation, which has equally failed to account for our communal relation to objective spirit: natural science. Linking religion to natural science will also be a way to transition to twentieth-century social theory in which the critique of religion prevalent in the nineteenth century gave way to a critique of natural science. The connection between religion and natural science is that in moving away from nature, they both are essentially subjective movements. The devaluation of nature in both does not only represent a move *away* from nature but also introduces the simultaneous project of a domination *over* nature and, consequently, as Hegel already points out in the Unhappy Consciousness section, over the as yet inchoate self.[20] Religious inwardness prepares the way for natural science's attempt to dominate nature.

What I am suggesting is that while Hegel's official account of inwardness is concerned with religious alienation from nature, this alienation can also be read (following Marx, Nietzsche, Weber, and, of course, Adorno and Horkheimer) as an account of domination as a masking of this alienation. As evidence of this claim, I can offer the close relation between the two modes of spirit's relation to nature in Hegel's treatment of the relation between the church and the *philosophes* of the Enlightenment.[21] There Hegel makes the claim that the mode of inquiry into nature employed by the philosophers of the Enlightenment, such as Diderot and La Mettrie, which consists in the complete separation of thing and observer, mirrors the alienation experienced by the religious mindset that, too, finds itself completely separate from its object of contemplation.

For Hegel, the move away from material nature both in its religious and in its scientific mode constitutes an alienation or the moment of subjectivity. While beauty was the immanent standard for the connection between spirit and nature for the Greeks, modern humans must develop their own standard. We have just seen that there are two ways of dealing with this alienation, one is to engage in yearning, as it exists in religious thought, while the other is to evade this yearning by substituting for it the attitude that humans are the measure of all things, as the Enlightenment's concept of utility makes evident.[22] In seeking to understand nature, we moderns have simply adopted the conception of god as having dominion over nature, substituting ourselves for god.

Philosophy?

The turning away from nature, which takes place in religion (and natural science), Hegel says, is necessary because it leads us to philosophy, which overcomes this alienation. Philosophy, which coexists with religion, Hegel argues, overcomes the negativity or inwardness of religion by uniting materiality and the concept. As he puts it:

> Philosophy not merely keeps [art and religion] together to make a totality, but even unifies them into the simple spiritual vision [*Anschauung*], and then in that raises them to self-conscious thought. Such consciousness is thus the intelligible unity (cognized by thought) of art and religion, in which the diverse elements in the content are cognized as necessary, and this necessary as free.[23]

So it is only in philosophy proper that nature can again be properly acknowledged as such. The tension between the dynamic and the systematic account is on display in this passage. For Hegel, now seems to be suggesting that rather than understanding religion as a completely adequate way of expressing the absolute it is really only in philosophy, as the unity (hence presumably as the sublation) of art and religion, that our proper relation to nature is achieved. Hegel here seems to conceive of philosophy developmentally with regard to religion rather than as merely a different mode of expression of the same thought. From the perspective of philosophy, at least in the *Encyclopedia* account, it appears that religion is itself merely a way-station like art. While art is too closely connected to the material, religion is too distant from it. Such a reading reinforces the impression that religion is to be taken as a subjectivism, which is not in the position of supplying and adequately understanding of our communal life.

It must, at this point, be said that Hegel's treatment of religion varies according to its different treatment. The *Phenomenology* itself contains two complementary treatments of religion, one as an account of alienation running from the Unhappy Consciousness to the account of deism in the Spirit chapter. The *Lectures on the Philosophy of Religion* for understandable reasons treat religion in a much more positive way, though there Hegel is at pains to reinterpret religion as essentially a thinking about the communal as he also does in Chapter 7 of the *Phenomenology*. As we have seen, the treatment of Christian religious art in the *Lectures on the Philosophy of Art* emphasizes Christianity's subjectivism with regard to nature. The main point here, however, is to raise some doubts about whether religion really constitutes a significant advance over art as the developmental account requires. If religion can be seen as a subjectivism and is therefore itself in need of sublation by philosophy, then, in the absence of the *general* attainment to the stage of philosophy, it becomes possible to imagine art continuing to play a part in our reflection on communal life.

Conclusion

In this section I've stressed that Hegel has two versions of Absolute Spirit's relationship to objective spirit. One in which Absolute Spirit is simply a mode of making us more at home in our objective social conditions and in which the three versions are essentially equal, each doing more or less the same thing and coexisting with one another. This is the version suggested both by some remarks in the *Encyclopedia* and by the detailed description of romantic art in the *Lectures on the Philosophy of Art*. The other version, the dynamic account, suggested again by remarks in the *Encyclopedia*, as well as by Hegel's famous dictum that art is, for us moderns, at an end in its highest vocation, is that the three moments of Absolute Spirit develop and express our different relations to the polis as we develop conceptually from the category of being tied to nature immanently through the concept of beauty in art, to that of a reflective turning away from nature in religion (and natural science), and finally to a mediated return to nature via the concept in philosophy.

In order to make sense of this ambiguity in Hegel's work, I've proposed looking to the phenomenon of modern life itself as a way of getting a purchase on what might be going on here. Modern social theory, from Marx through Weber to, say, Habermas and Foucault, confirms that Hegel is indeed tracking an important movement in calling our age one of alienation. That is, an age in which the human subject believes that it has released itself from nature and is now burdened with having to create a place for itself in nature, not as materiality, but as a second or social nature. Hegel himself speaks of this explicitly in his discussion of the figures of thought in the Spirit chapter of the *Phenomenology*. This suggests that we have indeed left behind the immanent view of life expressed by Greek art. However, and everything seems to depend on this, the claim that whatever has come after art is its rightful heir as a form of Absolute Spirit is predicated on us recognizing the new form as an adequate form. What I'd like to suggest is that the achievement of the sublation of art by whatever comes after it would mean that we found in that new form an adequate and satisfying expression of our communal relation to objective spirit. That is, given the parameters of the historical account, our current condition would have to appear to us as an expression of *philosophy*. The point is that for satisfaction to be achieved, we would have to be able to say that the alienation that I've traced in religion has come to a satisfactory resolution. And that resolution is called philosophy by Hegel. If this is acceptable, we can formulate the tension within Hegel's attitude anew: while the systematic account essentially remains pluralistic with regard to the different ways in which objective spirit can be made sense of from the side of Absolute Spirit, the dynamic account implies that the stage we have now reached is not religion but philosophy. The burden of this latter claim is that one must show that, whatever our current alienation consists in, it is a permanent and benign feature of modern life. I think we can now see that the choice between the systematic and the dynamic accounts is really a choice between a pluralist conception of Absolute Spirit and one that takes Absolute Spirit to have been achieved.

The Supplementary Interpretation

Let me begin by sketching the supplementary interpretation. This interpretation tries to understand the dynamic version of Hegel's narrative in which Absolute Spirit moves from one form of its self-expression to another. For Karsten Harries, this view depends on already seeing art as an inadequate carrier of the ideal. Harries suggests three theses that underlie Hegel's thinking of the superannuation of art:

(1) Genuine art transcends our conceptual grasp.
(2) Art reveals reality; it is tied to truth.
(3) Truth demands transparency; only what can be comprehended is real.[24]

The first thesis is a restatement of Hegel's basic claim that art represents a middle point between sensible nature and the idea but one that cannot be fully conceptually articulated.[25] But to have said this (thesis two) is equally to have said that art *does* provide us access to truth, just not fully conceptual truth or rather, art provides us access to a truth that cannot be fully articulated. But, the third thesis goes, truth requires full conceptual articulation, and so the inevitable conclusion, this conceptual articulation can only be found in something other than art, namely—by Hegel's lights at least—in philosophy. Note that this interpretation turns on the notion that truth is defined as something that must distance itself from the arbitrary nature of materiality. Harries writes that "to modern man the depth of the sensible is revealed by thought, not by art. This is not to deny that the turn to the sensible remains a possibility for the artist. But today this turn will lack necessity."[26] According to Harries, then, art is limited for us moderns because, since we possess a higher, more reflective type of truth, the truth that is presented to us sensibly is only one truth among many. This other type of truth then must presumably present itself to us with necessity. And yet, what is this other type of truth that has the force of necessity? Is Harries here thinking of the truth of modern natural science? Of some moral truth that is indisputable?

While Harries tells us only what Hegel might mean by his end-of-art thesis, Danto's employs Hegel's thesis in order to make sense of what, for him, is the loss of necessity or tradition in contemporary art. As he states, "The age of pluralism is upon us. It does not matter any longer what you do, which is what pluralism means. When one direction is as good as another direction, there is no concept of direction any longer to apply."[27] In turning to Danto's appropriation of Hegel, my interest lies first in how he conceives the transition from art to philosophy by employing a Hegelian model of development, the *Bildung* model. The second interesting point is that Danto admits that he himself is skeptical of his own solution. Danto finds that in the twentieth century each artistic movement or period "required a certain amount of quite complex theory in order that the often very minimal objects could be transacted onto the plane of art."[28] He noticed that art has become more and more theoretical until, as he puts it, "the objects approach zero as their theory approaches infinity."[29] Danto reaches for Hegel's end-of-art thesis to shed light on this phenomenon. Here it is Hegel's *Bildung* theory that interests Danto, not Hegel's metaphysics. For Danto, the *Bildung* theory, what I've called the dynamic relation between absolute and objective spirit, fits the bill in the sense that, unlike conventional progress theory, the *Bildung* model includes a way of thinking of transformation from one stage to another, something absent from the progress theory, which simply comes to an end in its own success. The *Bildung* theory makes it possible for art to internally exhaust itself and to be transformed into something else, namely theory, which was the thing Danto wanted to explain in the first place. Hegel's *Bildung* theory, as Danto conceives of it, says that one type of thought morphs into another in a developmental way just like a child turns into an adolescent and then into an adult. At each of these levels, there is not only a quantitative but also a qualitative shift. The person becomes someone different. The inner logic of the adolescent, we might say, ends in the birth of the adult from that adolescent. Using this model, Danto suggests that for art, "freedom ends in its own fulfillment."[30] The fact that art has morphed into theory means, according to Danto, that art's own internal drive is at an end. The importance of this move lies in the fact that, rather than assert the end of art as Harries has done, Danto works backward from the death of art, that is, from art's sublation by theory, back to a theory that could explain this. In this way Danto exhibits a properly phenomenological method, one that is called for in this case—especially since, as we shall see, the idea that art has been marginalized is hotly contested by other interpretations. While Danto's position seems to me an improvement on those that simply assume that Hegel is correct, his view remains unsatisfying insofar as it offers no way out of the crisis that he has diagnosed. Indeed, Danto doubts whether Hegel's claim that we have arrived at a stage of philosophical reflection in which, "there is no gap between knowledge and its object," is coherent at all.[31] If this conception is "fatally flawed," as Danto asserts, then we cannot look to *it* to provide evidence that spirit has moved from art to philosophy.[32] Nevertheless, Danto's argument has deepened our understanding of what is at stake by relating Hegel's thesis to the generalized phenomenon of twentieth-century art and by independently verifying, so to speak, through a reading of contemporary artistic practice, Hegel's own dynamic account of the superannuation of art. The *truth of the end of art thesis depends just as much on the conception of art as on what succeeds it*, and any claim about the demise of art must provide a reading of the history of art itself.

The Dialectical Interpretation

The dialectical reading picks up where Danto's argument left off, in doubts about philosophy's ability properly to extricate itself from the sort of thinking that is typical of art. But while I just criticized Danto for lacking a way to make sense of what comes after art, thereby confirming the death of art, the dialectical interpretation points to the inability of philosophy to formulate the end of art as a systematic failure of *philosophy* itself. Following what has been said in our discussion of Hegel, I'd like to read the claim for the continued existence of art in the midst of what is supposed to be the philosophical age of modernity as the result of the fateful replacement of the notion of truth with the notion of certainty as well as the persistence of the subjective turn, which goes hand in hand with certainty.

In turning to the dialectical interpretation, we also *eo ipso* turn to the philosophical critique of the scientific model of knowledge, the most influential example of which in the twentieth century can be found in the work of Heidegger, Adorno, and the later Wittgenstein. While these three thinkers differ in important respects, they all share the notion of a general loss of meaning, caused by the correspondence theory of truth typical of the scientific world view. The dialectical interpretation at issue here takes its departure from Adorno, while Cavell's work (see the final part of this chapter) is more indebted to Heidegger and, above all, to Wittgenstein.

The main move in the dialectical reading of the end-of-art thesis is to suggest that the immediate treatment of nature at the hands of art cannot be subsumed under the model of rationality employed by objective spirit as well as by later forms of Absolute Spirit. Further, proponents of the dialectical reading argue that the dialectic of concept and nature is itself *animated by* its inability to subsume nature (and hence art) under what counts as modern philosophical thinking. To put this in Hegel's terms, the fact that beauty continues to draw us in means that beauty has *not* been fully subsumed under our current mode of thought and that what Hegel announces as the culmination of Absolute Spirit in *Philosophy* has not yet been attained. As Adorno writes, "Hegel arrests the aesthetic dialectic by his static definition of the beautiful as the sensual appearance of the idea."[33] The characteristic movement of the dialectical interpretation is evident here: Adorno criticizes Hegel for having reduced the notion of the beautiful to the sensible, thereby putting a false philosophical gloss on something that is still ongoing. But, as Adorno also implies, that aesthetic dialectic is now less alive due to Hegel's pronouncement of its death. Adorno's move is to read as prescriptive what Hegel offers as a diagnosis.[34] Two tendencies in Hegel's thought are here played off against each other: the idea that something can be closed off, known in the mode of certainty, is juxtaposed with the notion of truth as process or development.

This dialectic is made explicit by T.J. Clark's claim that the relation between nature and thought which is expressed in art is continually under siege by the rationalization of thought by capitalist culture. As Clark put it, "It is just because the 'modernity' which modernism prophesied has finally arrived that the forms of representation it originally gave rise to are now unreadable."[35] This is so because modernism teeters on the edge of a full embrace of the forces that drive it—hence spreading itself almost unintelligibly thin—or of being fully conquered by those forces.[36] For Clark, then, modernist art exists in a precarious dialectic between what it seeks to depict, namely, our social relations under modernity, and the increasing impossibility of such representation due to the rapid rationalization of thought that stamps out the sorts of ambiguous signs needed for the representation of what something as ambiguous as nature is to us under modernity's austere gaze.

It is this dialectic, the development of *Geist* out of nature and the increasing difficulty of holding on to nature while undergoing this development, that Gregg Horowitz has made the central thesis of his reading of Hegel. Against the supplemental view, which simply accepts that spirit moves on from the particular relation between itself and nature, Horowitz argues that the key term "remains" in the phrase "art is and remains for us a thing of the past" is to be read as the continued pull of nature from which spirit cannot disengage itself. The "death" of art, Horowitz writes, haunts us.

> Spirit grows out of a dead nature that becomes ever more fetid in direct proportion to spirit's increasing vigor. *It is this endlessly dying nature to which spirit is bound*

in art by bonds of unconscious guilt. Art, thus, remains oriented by the dead nature that spirit judges disorienting.³⁷

As unconscious guilt, per the psychoanalytic connection between guilt and morality, art also becomes our conscience in the sense that it is made out of the nature, which resists easy organization into the modern stage and hence does not fit easily into the narrative of spirit's progress.

The key supposition of the negative dialectical reading is that, to refer back to Adorno's point, *in order* to claim that it has moved on to a different level of thought, philosophy must *deny* the adequacy of the previous stage. Hegel's dynamic transition from one form of Absolute Spirit has not occurred immanently, through the internal contradictions of the previous form, but has occurred by force. We might say that the historical decline of the self-evident relation between materiality and the idea in Greek art left its successor modes of Absolute Spirit with particulars that religion, science, and finally philosophy had to reconnect. The triumphalist narrative, which gave religion, science, and philosophy its authority, however, required that the connection among particulars be constituted as achieved even when it was not. Art's function is thus a double one: on the one hand, it insists on the need for a unification in the mode of a lost ideal (so far unachieved by religion, science, and philosophy) but, on the other hand, in its continued existence art remains as the witness that such a unification by religion, science, and philosophy has not yet been achieved. In this way, then, art sets itself in conflict with the model of truth as certainty adopted by the other moments of Absolute Spirit.³⁸

Film as Philosophy

The previous positions have each culminated in some question about the status of the sensible or skepticism about certainty as a way of arresting the particular. Only Greek art, it seems, has so far been able to find a place for it. The argument has even been that the subjective turn that occurred with religion has been exacerbated and reified by the scientific world view's reduction of truth to certainty. The notion of certainty has put a nondominating reconciliation between sensibility and concept out of reach because it insists that the sensible be comprehended in a way that also denies the subject's contribution to this comprehension. Let us also note again that the three twentieth-century figures who have been most associated with this critique—Wittgenstein, Heidegger, and Adorno—offer merely a diagnosis of the situation.

By contrast, while offering no "solution" either, Cavell has noticed a certain cooperation between objective spirit and Absolute Spirit that appears to be closely akin to what Hegel calls philosophy. Cavell's central thesis is that the experience of viewing a film *can* constitute an existential relief from, or alternative to, the demand that, if we wish to be taken seriously, we must be skeptical of reality. This relief, I shall argue in the following section, is what makes a sincere conversation about our social conditions possible. Our modern notion of reality, Cavell argues, has been formed by skepticism as the wish "for the connection between my claims of knowledge and the objects upon which the claims are to fall to occur without my intervention, apart from my agreements."[39] This wish, Cavell claims, is "unappeasable" in the sense that it is rooted in the desire to return to a period when the relation between the sensible and the concept was self-evident.[40] (In the context of this chapter, this relation occurs in the experience of beauty.) But while in the experience of beauty the subject is the recipient of pleasure, in the search for objectivity that takes over this very structure the self experiences not pleasure but the frantic compulsion to abstract from any remnants of itself.

In *The World Viewed*, Cavell writes: "Our condition has become one in which our natural mode of perception is to view, feeling unseen. We do not so much look at the world as look out at it, from behind the self."[41] The self, in effect, has become an obstacle for viewing or knowing the world. I take it that the position of viewing from behind the self's implication in what we see captures also the religious and scientific attitudes in which it is essential to abstract from nature in order to understand our relation to nature. But, Cavell goes on, for the scientific enterprise to succeed, the wish for "objectivity" must itself be denied because it is now the wish itself that has become the marker of our inability to achieve objectivity: it marks our *subjectivity*. Denying our wish for objectivity only highlights the fact that the wish "is our fantasies . . . which are unseen and must be kept unseen. . . . So we are less than ever in a position to marry them to the world."[42] To put it in Hegelian terms, since our ideals (*fantasies*) are precisely what need to be accommodated to objective spirit, the removal of these fantasies from Absolute Spirit serves us poorly. Repressing our fantasies cannot but impede social development, alienating us further from our communal spiritual project and individuating us. In film, Cavell finds a way we can become free from this enforced individuality and skepticism. I cannot give here more than the briefest of sketches of how film defeats skepticism, the claim that will have to be examined elsewhere, but several features pertaining to the Hegelian argument are crucial, centrally that the sensible becomes the object of reflection in film in such a way that, rather than dominating, the subject can be reconciled with it. Cavell points first to the fact that a photograph is cropped, that is, it is clearly a *partial* representation of the world. As such one would expect the photograph to be a cause of frustration for the subject. The fact that it *is not* is central to what film does: on the contrary, the cropping simply reveals that our status of being separated from the thing the film is representing is *ontological* (Cavell says it is "automatic"): "In viewing a movie my helplessness is mechanically assured: I am present not at something happening, which I must confirm, but at something that has happened, which I absorb (like a memory)."[43] At the movies, the fact of our exclusion from nature reveals itself as an essential fact about our way of being the world. This means that our doubts about our access to nature are confirmed. "Photography maintains the presentness of the world by accepting our absence from it."[44] Cavell's point, however, is that our doubts are confirmed in *so radical* a way that it now strikes us that perhaps there is no overcoming them.[45] And it is *this* insight, Cavell thinks, this acceptance of our limitation as subjects, that reveals to us that our subjectivity is a *necessary* element in how we see the world. Cavell writes:

> Movies seem more natural than reality. Not because they are escapes into fantasy, but because they are reliefs from private fantasy and its responsibilities; from the

fact that the world is *already* drawn by fantasy. And not because they are dreams, but because they permit the self to be wakened, so that we may stop withdrawing our longings further inside ourselves.[46]

Let me spell out a little more clearly why we should consider film philosophy in Hegel's sense. What film as a kind of thinking provides, according to Cavell, is not new insight into how the world is; it tells us nothing new about the world. Rather, the experience of film provides a way to unify the different perspectives we already have. We can say that film validates the inwardness of religion and the burden of scientific investigation of nature ("private fantasy and its responsibility") and locates this inwardness *within* the world of the sensible that we inhabit. In this way the thinking that film does permits a reconciliation between the concept and the sensible by revealing to us that the conceptual is already (ineluctably) involved, reflected, in our experience of sensibility. Like Cavell, Hegel thinks of this insight as intuitive awareness of something we essentially already have but were previously unable to recognize because our conceptual grasp was limited.[47] Now that we have it, however, this insight, the concept of philosophy, makes possible a new relation to objective spirit in which the possibility of greater freedom becomes available.

Film as Philosophy and the State

If film constitutes the achievement of philosophy as the reconciliation between the concept and the sensible, it must also be able to tell us something about the relation of the ideal to the actual existence of objective spirit, thereby moving us closer to the actualization of freedom. This reconciliation will involve recognizing what has previously been regarded as contingent nature as properly part of spiritual life or freedom. On Cavell's telling, film does just that:

> The genre [of comedies of remarriage] can be said to require the creation of a new woman, or the new creation of a woman, something I describe as a new creation of the human. . . . this phase of the history of cinema is bound up with a phase in the history of the consciousness of women. You might even say that these phases of these histories are part of the creation of one another.[48]

Cavell conceives of the sort of films he is interested in, the Hollywood comedies of the 1930s and 1940s, which he takes as exemplary, as having a central role in the communal project of the American nation, what Cavell tellingly calls "the inner agenda of a culture."[49] The clarification film makes possible concerns the "development in the consciousness women hold of themselves as this is developed in its relation to the consciousness men hold of them."[50] Film makes possible recognition, in the sense that men and women "*recognize* themselves as *mutually recognizing* one another."[51] The way this is to be understood as a mode of Absolute Spirit is that film's ability to reconcile us with nature freely opens the door for a discussion of the status of women, previously consigned to the sphere of nature, as free participants in the sphere of objective spirit.

But this is not all. For, as Cavell points out, a new form of *Sittlichkeit* is made possible by the insight that men and women must recognize each other as universal *in their particularities*. That is, the form of philosophy which film constitutes, in Cavell's telling, must deem it false to reconcile women and men to each other as universal beings—rational yet disembodied.

The achievement of this level of philosophical discourse, however, is not the reconciliation itself. It is rather the achievement of the proper dialectical relationship between objective spirit and Absolute Spirit in which the right sorts of questions can be posed *to* the structures of objective spirit, that is, those questions that might find an *answer* in objective spirit's own development can be posed.

Notes

1. Georg Wilhelm Friedrich Hegel, *Aesthetics: Lectures on Fine Art*, 2 vols. (Oxford: Clarendon Press, 1975), 11. Cavell's claim is made in all three of his film books, Stanley Cavell, *The World Viewed: Reflections on the Ontology of Film* (Cambridge, MA: Harvard University Press, 1979); *Pursuits of Happiness: The Hollywood Comedy of Remarriage* (Cambridge, MA: Harvard University Press, 1981); *Contesting Tears: The Hollywood Melodrama of the Unknown Woman* (Chicago: University of Chicago Press, 1996).
2. Cavell, *The World Viewed*, 14–15.
3. Georg Wilhelm Friedrich Hegel, *Philosophy of Mind*, trans. W. Wallace, A. V. Miller, and M. J. Inwood (Oxford: Oxford University Press, 2007), §§ 483–84. In the "Civil Society" section of the *Elements of the Philosophy of Right,* Hegel writes: "[Spirit's] end is . . . to work to eliminate *natural simplicity* . . . i.e. to eliminate the immediacy and individuality [*Einzelheit*] in which spirit is immersed, so that this externality may take on . . . the *form of universality*. . . . Only in this way is the spirit *at home* and with itself in this externality as such. Its freedom thus has an existence within the latter" (*Elements of the Philosophy of Right*, trans. Hugh Barr Nisbet [Cambridge: Cambridge University Press, 1991], §187R).
4. Hegel, *Philosophy of Mind*. §556; GW 20:543. See also *Lectures on the Philosophy of Art: The Hotho Transcript of the 1823 Berlin Lectures*, trans. Robert F. Brown (Oxford: Oxford University Press, 2014), 270; *Vorlesungen über die Philosophie der Kunst vol. 2, Vorlesungen: Ausgewahlte Nachschriften Und Manuskripte* (Frankfurt am Main: Meiner, 1982–), 105. The German edition of Hegel's 1823 *Lectures on the Philosophy of Art* will henceforth be abbreviated as V2: page number.
5. *Lectures on the Philosophy of Art*, 270; V2:105.
6. *The Science of Logic*, trans. George di Giovanni (Cambridge: Cambridge University Press, 2010), 735. *Wissenschaft der Logik II, Die Subjektive Logik (1816)*, vol. 12, *Gesammelte Werke* (Frankfurt am Main: Meiner, 1968), GW 12:236. Hegel says the same thing in the Encyclopedia: "Beautiful art, from its side, has thus performed the same service as philosophy: it has purified the spirit from its thraldom" (Hegel, *Philosophy of Mind*, §562; *Enzyklopädie der Philosophischen Wissenschaften Im Grundrisse (1830)*, vol. 20 *Gesammelte Werke* [Frankfurt am Main: Meiner, 1968–], GW 20:549). The German text of the *Encyclopedia* will henceforth be cited as GW 20: page number.

7 *Lectures on the Philosophy of Religion: Introduction and the Concept of Religion*, trans. Peter C. Hodgson and J. M. Stewart, III vols. (Berkeley: University of California Press, 1984), I:234. *Vorlesungen Über Die Philosophie der Religion*, vol. 3a, *Vorlesungen: Ausgewahlte Nachschriften und Manuskripte* (Frankfurt am Main: Meiner, 1982–), V3:143. Henceforth the Hegel's *Lectures on the Philosophy of Religion* will be cited as V3:page number.
8 Hegel, *Philosophy of Mind*, §553; GW 20:542; translation modified.
9 This thought is complicated by the fact that Hegel tells different stories about the different versions of Absolute Spirit. His philosophy of art, religion, and his history of philosophy all have different emphases, locating the apogee of each particular form in a different historical period. In each account, Hegel finds it difficult to condemn the Greek polis as something that has properly been sublated by subsequent developments. Modernity itself is, for Hegel, an ambiguous condition, which is seen to lack some of the advances made by ancient Greece.
10 "Appearing as a human being belongs to God as spirit, else God is not spirit. The anthropomorphic element is therefore something essential in the true concept of the divine nature." Hegel, *Lectures on the Philosophy of Art*, 315; V2:158.
11 *Lectures on the Philosophy of Religion: Introduction and the Concept of Religion*, I:180; V3:88.
12 Hegel, *Lectures on the Philosophy of Art*, 246; V2:78–79.
13 Ibid., 333; V2:179.
14 In the *Lectures on the Philosophy of Religion*, Hegel follows the Greek religion of beauty with the Jewish religion of the sublime and the Roman religion of purpose.
15 The depiction of Christian inwardness presents something of a problem for the artist as the artist may make Jesus neither ugly nor beautiful in the classical sense. Rather "human seriousness must express itself in Christ, as well as the love that finds the mean between the beauty of the ideal and the natural figure." Hegel, *Lectures on the Philosophy of Art*, 337; V2:186.
16 *Lectures on the Philosophy of Religion: Introduction and the Concept of Religion*, I:398; V3:293.
17 Ibid., I:400–01; V3:295–96.
18 Hegel, *Lectures on the Philosophy of Art*, 334–35; V2:182.
19 Dieter Henrich argues that in denying this freedom, Hegel turns away from his early ideal of modeling the modern state after the Greek conceptions of the beautiful ("Zur Aktualität Von Hegels Ästhetik," *Hegel Studien Beiheft* 11 [1970]). On this point, see also Georg W. Bertram, "Why Does the End of Art Matter for Art in General? Explaining the Modernity of Art with Hegel against Hegel," in *Morte dell'arte e rinascita dell'immagine*, ed. Alessandro Bertinetto and Gianluca Garelli (Canterona: Arcne editrice, 2017). Horowitz and Huhn also explore this question in their response to Danto's argument (see further). Arthur C. Danto, Gregg Horowitz, and Tom Huhn, *The Wake of Art: Essays: Criticism, Philosophy and the Ends of Taste* (Amsterdam: G+B Arts International, 1998), 26. For all these authors, the central question involves the status of the "after" of art, which lies outside this chapter's parameters.
20 The unhappy consciousness's attempt to end its suffering in the grave out of a conviction of its own radical subjectivity in the face of the divine seems to suggest the overcoming of subjectivity itself. See Georg Wilhelm Friedrich Hegel, *The Phenomenology of Spirit*, trans. Terry Pinkard (Cambridge: Cambridge University Press, 2018), §217; *Phänomenologie des Geistes*, vol. 9, *Gesammelte Werke* (Frankfurt am Main: Meiner, 1968), GW 9:126. Hegel's *Phenomenology* will henceforth be cited as GW 9: page number.

21 See the at times hilarious account of the enlightenment's struggle to overcome religion in *The Phenomenology of Spirit*, §§537–81.
22 "In utility, pure insight thus has as its object its own distinctive concept in its pure moments, and it is the consciousness of this metaphysics although not yet its comprehension." Hegel, *The Phenomenology of Spirit*, §580; GW 9:315.
23 *Philosophy of Mind*, §572; GW 20:554–55.
24 Karsten Harries, "Hegel on the Future of Art," *The Review of Metaphysics* 27, no. 4 (1974): 679.
25 As Hegel writes, "Art is also constrained as to its content; it has a sensuous material, and for that reason too only a certain stage of truth is capable of being the content of art. For there is a more profound existence of the idea, one that the sensuous is no longer capable of expressing, and this is the content of our religion, our culture" (*Lectures on the Philosophy of Art*, 185–86; V2:5).
26 Harries, "Hegel on the Future of Art," 695. See also Houlgate: "Art may no longer be the highest need of the modern spirit, but it is nevertheless still a need" ("Hegel and the 'End of Art,'" *The Owl of Minerva* 29, no. 1 (1997): 15.
27 Arthur C. Danto, "The End of Art," in *The Philosophical Disenfranchisement of Art* (New York: Columbia University Press, 1986), 114–15.
28 Ibid., 109.
29 Ibid., 111.
30 Ibid., 115.
31 Ibid., 113.
32 Ibid.
33 Theodor W. Adorno, *Aesthetic Theory*, trans. Robert Hullot-Kentor (Minneapolis: University of Minnesota Press, 1997), 51; *Ästhetische Theorie*, vol. 7, *Gesammelte Schriften* (Frankfurt am Main: Suhrkamp, 1970), 82.
34 On the question of the death of art from internal and external reasons, see Owen Houlat, "Hegel, Danto, Adorno, and the End and after of Art," *British Journal for the History of Philosophy* 24, no. 4 (2016): 742–63. Houlat argues that, while for Hegel and Danto art comes to an end naturally or of its own internal exhaustion, for Adorno the end of art is (might be) brought about by the increased pressures of capitalism.
35 T. J. Clark, *Farewell to an Idea: Episodes from a History of Modernism* (New Haven: Yale University Press, 1999), 2.
36 Ibid., 8.
37 Gregg Horowitz, *Sustaining Loss: Art and Mournful Life* (Stanford: Stanford University Press, 2001), 63.
38 It is worth noting that there is a third category of Hegel interpretation, which might be dubbed the accommodationist dialectical interpretation. This model, exemplified by both Robert Pippin and Dieter Henrich, holds, in Pippin's formulation, that, while it may be true that art has ended in its highest vocation, artworks did achieve a degree of the realization of freedom and can thus be used to understand objective spirit by, for instance, telling us about the inscrutability of the face in modern life (Robert B. Pippin, *After the Beautiful: Hegel and the Philosophy of Pictorial Modernism* [Chicago: The University of Chicago Press, 2014], Chapter 2, sections 5–6). Henrich and Georg Bertram argue that art is to be understood as a continuing practice within modernity but do not base this argument on the critical claims of the dialectical interpretation. See Dieter Henrich, *Versuch über Kunst und Leben: Subjektivität—Weltverstehen—Kunst* (München: Hanser, 2001); Georg W. Bertram, *Kunst als menschliche Praxis: eine Ästhetik* (Berlin: Suhrkamp, 2014). See also Bertram's contribution in this volume.

39 Stanley Cavell, *The Claim of Reason: Wittgenstein, Skepticism, Morality, and Tragedy* (Oxford: Oxford University Press, 1999), 351–52.
40 Ibid.
41 Cavell, *The World Viewed*, 102.
42 Ibid., 102.
43 Ibid., 26.
44 Ibid., 23.
45 Cavell also writes: "The camera has been praised for extending the senses; it may, as the world goes, deserve more praise for confining them, leaving room for thought" (Cavell, *The World Viewed*, 24).
46 Cavell, *The World Viewed*, 102.
47 "This movement, which philosophy is, finds itself already accomplished, when at the close it seizes its own notion—i.e. only *looks back* on its knowledge" (Hegel, *Philosophy of Mind*, §573; GW 20:555).
48 Cavell, *Pursuits of Happiness*, 16.
49 Ibid., 17.
50 Ibid.
51 Hegel, *The Phenomenology of Spirit*, §184; GW 9:110.

Bibliography

Adorno, Theodor W. *Aesthetic Theory*, translated by Robert Hullot-Kentor. Minneapolis: University of Minnesota Press, 1997.

Adorno, Theodor W. *Ästhetische Theorie*, edited by Gretel Adorno and Rolf Tiedemann, vol. 7, Gesammelte Schriften. Frankfurt am Main: Suhrkamp, 1970.

Bertram, Georg W. *Kunst als menschliche Praxis: eine Ästhetik*. Berlin: Suhrkamp, 2014.

Bertram, Georg W. "Why Does the End of Art Matter for Art in General? Explaining the Modernity of Art with Hegel against Hegel." In *Morte dell'arte e rinascita dell'immagine*, edited by Alessandro Bertinetto and Gianluca Garelli. Canterona: Arcne editrice, 2017.

Cavell, Stanley. *The Claim of Reason: Wittgenstein, Skepticism, Morality, and Tragedy*. Oxford: Oxford University Press, 1999.

Cavell, Stanley. *Contesting Tears: The Hollywood Melodrama of the Unknown Woman*. Chicago: University of Chicago Press, 1996.

Cavell, Stanley. *Pursuits of Happiness: The Hollywood Comedy of Remarriage*. Cambridge, MA: Harvard University Press, 1981.

Cavell, Stanley. *The World Viewed: Reflections on the Ontology of Film*. Cambridge, MA: Harvard University Press, 1979.

Clark, T. J. *Farewell to an Idea: Episodes from a History of Modernism*. New Haven: Yale University Press, 1999.

Danto, Arthur C. "The End of Art." In *The Philosophical Disenfranchisement of Art*. New York: Columbia University Press, 1986.

Danto, Arthur C., Gregg Horowitz, and Tom Huhn. *The Wake of Art: Essays: Criticism, Philosophy and the Ends of Taste*. Amsterdam: G+B Arts International, 1998.

Harries, Karsten. "Hegel on the Future of Art." *The Review of Metaphysics* 27, no. 4 (1974): 677–96.

Hegel, Georg Wilhelm Friedrich. *Aesthetics: Lectures on Fine Art*, 2 vols. Oxford: Clarendon Press, 1975.

Part III

Thinking beyond Hegel's Views on Art and Society

9

Greek Tragedy and Self-Authorship in Hegel's *Phenomenology of Spirit*

Eliza Starbuck Little

This chapter aims at laying the groundwork for a reconsideration of the role that tragedy plays in Hegel's *Phenomenology of Spirit*. My primary goal is to make perspicuous the way in which the discussions of tragedy in the Jena *Phenomenology* fit with an understanding of Hegel's philosophy as a systematic epistemology. Toward this end, I argue that, in the context of this particular Hegelian text, tragedy is best understood as a formal structure that characterizes a particular sort of coming to know. More specifically, tragedy describes the manner in which collective human mindedness— what Hegel calls *Geist*, and which I will translate here with the traditional "Spirit"— attains to self-knowledge. On my reading, this epistemic process is constituted by at least two distinct activities: self-recollection and self-recognition, both of which are centrally operative in the *Phenomenology*. I focus here on getting the latter of these two processes into view. I ground my reading in Christoph Menke's recent work on tragedy. In *Tragic Play*, Menke describes Sophocles's *Oedipus Tyrannus* as effecting a change of places between tragic author and tragic hero—at the end of the play, the author is reduced to the limited position of the character, while the hero attains to the unlimited authority of the tragedian. I argue that this claim offers insight into the structure of Hegel's conception of Spirit's self-recognition insofar as such recognition results from a structurally similar transposition between Spirit in its role as the author of its recollections and Spirit in its role as the protagonist of those same recollections.

My interest in rethinking the role of tragedy in the *Phenomenology* is informed by an understanding of Hegel's philosophical project as being a holistic system made up of mutually informing elements. As I read it, Hegel's system of science has four principal parts: the tripartite *Encyclopedia*, comprised of Logic, Nature, and Spirit, and the *Phenomenology of Spirit*, which serves as a propaedeutic to the *Encyclopedia* (more on this in a moment). The various lectures and notes that are compiled in supplementary texts, such as the *Lectures on Fine Art* and the *Lectures on the Philosophy of Religion*, can then all be contextualized within the *Encyclopedia*. They serve as expanded explorations of topics that have already been systematically described—that is, described as they arise dialectically within the architectonic of Hegel's system—in the *Encyclopedia*.

The systematic character of Hegel's philosophy poses a particular set of difficulties to an interpreter attempting to pick out some single element of Hegelian thought in the way that I am interested to do here with tragedy. Two challenges in particular arise. On the one hand, it is necessary to respect the holism of Hegel's philosophy insofar as it is specifically intended to present a unified system. This means that one ought not to take up a topic in one context (say, tragedy in the *Phenomenology*) and ignore its other iterations within the system without offering some sort of justification for doing so. On the other hand, the responsible interpreter must also acknowledge that Hegel's system is functionally articulated. By this I mean that different parts of the system fulfill different roles in the same way that the organs of a living being all ultimately contribute to the life of the individual, while performing different tasks. This, I want to claim, is how it is with the parts of Hegel's system in general, and, for my specific purpose here, with the respective discussions of tragic drama contained in the *Phenomenology* and the *Lectures on Fine Art* in particular.

Helpfully, the second challenge answers to the problem presented by the first challenge by providing the justification needed for considering the *Phenomenology*'s discussion of tragedy in distinction from treatments of tragedy elsewhere in the system. For, it is precisely in virtue of the fact that the Hegelian system is functionally articulated that certain topics can and must be treated distinctly depending on where in the system they come on the scene. Less felicitously, this solution leaves behind a potentially monumental third challenge: in order to correctly delineate any one topic of inquiry in Hegel's thought, it seems as if it might be necessary to understand the system as a whole. In the fullest sense, this might be true. For our limited purposes here, however, it will be sufficient to have some preliminary idea of how the *Phenomenology* differs from *Lectures on Fine Art*, which, as just noted, are an expansion of a section of the *Philosophy of Spirit*.

The general strategy that informs my reading of Hegel centers on the assumption that the *Phenomenology* and the Encyclopedic texts are functionally distinct from one another. This distinction hangs on the special status that the *Phenomenology* has with regard to the cognitive standpoint that Hegel takes to be a necessary achievement for the enactment of philosophical thinking, the standpoint that Hegel terms "Absolute Knowing" [*absolutes Wissen*]. Whereas the Encyclopedic texts operate from the perspective of Absolute Knowing, the *Phenomenology* describes the process by means of which Absolute Knowing is first attained. In Hegel's words, at the end of the *Phenomenology*, "Spirit has attained the concept . . . and it is science."[1] He goes on to characterize the relevant methodological difference between the *Phenomenology* and the subsequent scientific texts that rely on it as follows:

> If in the phenomenology of Spirit, each moment is both the distinction between knowledge [*Wissen*] and truth [*Wahrheit*] and the movement in which that distinction sublates itself [*sich aufhebt*], then, in contrast, science does not contain this distinction and its sublation. Rather, since the moment has the form of the concept, it unites the objective form of truth and that of the knowing self into an immediate unity.[2]

The crucial point here is that, until the very end of the *Phenomenology*, there is a philosophically significant discrepancy between the forms in which knowledge is made available and the truth that the knowledge in question is supposed to disclose. This discrepancy is the driving force of the dialectical progression of the text, the "movement in which that distinction sublates itself." The attainment of absolute knowledge at the end of the *Phenomenology* is nothing other than the arrival at a form of knowledge, the conceptual form, that is adequate to truth. Thus, the Encyclopedic texts, being systematically posterior to the *Phenomenology*, operate in the conceptual register and are no longer concerned with this formal discrepancy between knowledge and truth.

As I have laid them out here, these claims are merely programmatic. I mention them in this context because I take the adequacy of the form of knowledge to truth to be of crucial importance for understanding what Hegel is up to in his various treatments of tragedy. In the *Phenomenology*, tragedy comes on the scene as one among the series of inadequate forms of knowledge that precedes conceptual form—in fact, it is the very first inadequate form of knowledge that Spirit provides for itself. In the *Lectures on Fine Art*, the situation is otherwise because, there, tragedy is being treated from within the register of conceptual form. In the *Lectures*, Hegel's discussion of tragedy takes place in the context of an extended argument about the ways in which fine art itself *is* a form of Absolute Knowing. If this reading is correct, then the two accounts do not merely differ; rather, they stand in direct opposition with one another when viewed in terms of their systematic function. As I see it, this functional tension between the treatments of tragedy in these two distinct parts of Hegel's philosophical system burdens the interpreter with producing a story about the way in which the *Phenomenology*'s treatment of tragedy stands on its own, apart from the later Encyclopedic treatment. Making a beginning at such a self-standing account will be my aim in what follows.

I will start by describing and troubling two presuppositions that frequently arise in the literature on Hegel and tragedy in order to provide negative motivation for my own positive proposal. The first of these presuppositions has to do with the global coherence of a Hegelian theory of tragedy and the second has to do with the specific employment of tragedy in the *Phenomenology of Spirit*.

First, it is often assumed that there both should be and is strong continuity between the account of tragedy in the *Phenomenology* and the account of tragedy that is deployed at other points in Hegel's oeuvre, most extensively in the *Lectures on Fine Art*. Both presentations are highly complex, but the scholarly consensus favors the idea that these texts share in common a univocal theory of tragic collision wherein the clash between two opposing ethical principles plays out on the stage in the conflict between characters. A.C. Bradley gives an emblematic summary of this view when he writes that Hegelian tragedy in all cases figures "competing forces" that "are both in themselves rightful; but the right of each is pushed into the wrong because it ignores the right of the other."[3] Bradley was writing in 1909, but, as we will shortly see, the dominant interpretation has not changed all that much in the intervening century.

According to the collision of principles picture, the *Phenomenology* is to be read as employing this general tragic structure to depict the dialectical collapse of a specific shape of Spirit—namely that of Greek ethical life [*Sittlichkeit*]. Thus, Charles Taylor's seminal 1975 work on Hegel describes the *Phenomenology*'s discussion of tragedy as dealing with "the original unity of the Greek city-state and its breakdown" due to a dualistic conflict—that is to say, a collision of principles—between the divine and human laws.[4] Taylor writes, "The two laws take expression in two different kinds of people . . . each of whom is totally and uncritically identified with his or her part."[5] In a different philosophical context, Martha Nussbaum characterizes Hegel's aim in his reading of the *Antigone* as being to point "beyond [Antigone and Creon's] deficiencies to suggest the basis for a conflict-free synthesis of [their] opposing values."[6] And, more recently, Terry Pinkard has described the "Ethical Order" section that opens the fourth chapter of the *Phenomenology* as presenting a reading of Sophocles's *Antigone* that aims to "analyze the way in which this mode of self-understanding [i.e., Greek ethical life] must give rise to contradictions within itself."[7] On this reading, the section describes "a discord within Greek culture itself, between the two ethical powers that the Greek form of life recognizes as essential to itself: the divine law and the human law, embodied in the different individualities of men and women."[8]

The collision of principles reading is derived in large part from a narrow subset of explicit comments about tragedy that Hegel makes in his *Lectures on Fine Arts*. In that text he describes tragedy as one of three subgenres of dramatic poetry, a medium that he characterizes as "depend[ing] throughout on conditions of collision."[9] He proceeds to outline an extensive taxonomy of the possible types of collision, indicating which are best suited to artistic presentation and offering a rich variety of ancient and modern examples in all cases. According to Hegel, the collisions that occasion dramatic poetry arise from "violations of the world-condition."[10] As such, they are "change[s] in the previously existent state of harmony" which, moreover, are still "in process."[11] Thus, the collision is, first and foremost, a kind of opening up of a certain worldview or world-picture (say, that of Greek ethical life) to change. Hegel is quick to emphasize that this open-ended state of affairs is not in and of itself sufficient for dramatization; rather, the collision is merely a "stimulus to action."[12] And it is actions, specifically the sorts of human actions that arise in the field of uncertainty that is opened up by a collision, that are the real content of the best tragic dramas. This is only a brief sketch of one aspect of Hegel's highly complex treatment of tragic drama in the *Lectures on Fine Arts*, but I take a reduction of that account along these lines to lie in the background of the collision of principles reading of the *Phenomenology*.

Among recent commentators, Julia Peters has notably offered a more sensitive treatment that attempts to account for contextual differences between the *Phenomenology* and the *Lectures on Fine Arts* and, in so doing, gets beyond the collision of principles reading. Peters's aim, in her own words, is to show how "Hegel's theory of tragedy as it is presented in the Lectures on Aesthetics has its complement in a Hegelian theory of tragic experience, which can be derived from Hegel's discussion of tragic conflict in the *Phenomenology of Spirit*."[13] As Peters sees it, the *Phenomenology* account of tragedy is broadly congruent with the account given in the lectures, insofar as it relies on the same formal account of tragic conflict (what I have described above as the collision of principles reading). But, on her view, the *Phenomenology* also expands on and supplements the collision of principles view by providing a further investigation of the "value of a subject's tragic experience."[14] Peters argues that Hegelian tragic experience, as described in the *Phenomenology*, proceeds in two phases: first, it begins with a moment of alienation, and subsequently, it concludes with a moment of self-recognition wherein "what one previously considered alien or hostile is in reality one's own or part of one's own identity."[15] The process is driven forward by the tragic subject's suffering, a "subjective tragic experience" consisting in the self-inflicted psychic pain of reflection, and it culminates in the attainment of self-knowledge. On Peters's reading, however, the self-knowledge in question is always belated—because it is arrived at only in the aftermath of action, it "comes too late in order for the individual who achieves it to enter a state of genuine, livable reconciliation."[16] For this reason, tragic experience, at least in its specifically Attic Greek manifestation, is insufficient for the mature ethical life of Spirit and must ultimately be left behind.

There is much to praise in this reading. For one thing, it is responsive to Hegel's own claim in the *Lectures* that human actions (not collisions of principles) are the true content of tragedy, and it fruitfully investigates the subjective aspect of such tragic actions. Furthermore, Peters is rightly sensitive to the formal parallelism that exists between the experience of the tragic subject and the "experience of consciousness in general, as it is presented in the *Phenomenology*."[17] On this score, however, her reading does not go far enough: she is content to note the similarity without accounting for its particular importance within the argumentative structure of the *Phenomenology*. This leaves an open question about the precise identity of the tragic subject who undergoes the suffering in question: is it the tragic hero? The abstract figure of the Greek spectator? Or Spirit itself? As I will show, the application of Christoph Menke's reading of Oedipus to the *Phenomenology* provides a specific answer to this question that makes sense of the work that this parallelism between the experience of Spirit and the experience of the tragic hero does within the structure of Hegel's argument. Finally, Peters's reading is inflected by her reliance on the assumption, widespread in the literature, that the *Phenomenology* discussion of tragedy is concerned in a central way with the *Antigone*. This is precisely the second presupposition that I will call into question momentarily.

To sum up, it is undeniable that the respective accounts of tragedy given in the *Lectures* and the *Phenomenology* share things in common and can at times be fruitfully used to illuminate one another. But, on my view, there are limits to the utility of this intertextuality. Most problematically, an emphasis on the full applicability of the "collision of principles" model to the *Phenomenology* tends toward the exclusion of alternative or additional interpretive possibilities. Even if the reading is correct, it is not at all clear why Hegel is suddenly bringing to bear a piece of nascent aesthetic theory in a text that has, up to this point, been concerned with elaborating a series of evolving relationships between subjects and objects. The first three sections of the *Phenomenology* are many things, but one would be hard pressed to argue that they are centrally concerned with fine art.

And it is not clear, besides, that the reading *is* correct. The defects of the collision reading are made particularly manifest by the general lack of attention that is paid to the fact that there are two distinct discussions of tragedy that take place in the course of the *Phenomenology*, both equally substantive, but only the first of which describes a paradigmatic clash of ethical principles. The second discussion of tragedy occurs later, in the "Religion" chapter of the *Phenomenology* under the subheading "The Religion of Art." Here, Hegel is no longer concerned with collision, but rather with spectatorship—both with the tragic audience as spectators to the drama and with the chorus as spectators to the heroes. I will return to this passage in detail in a moment.

I want to stay with Greek ethical life for just a moment longer, though, in order to touch on a second presupposition about tragedy that derives from this section of the *Phenomenology*. Hegel's abiding interest in Sophocles's *Antigone* is well known (in the *Lectures on Fine Art*, he refers to the play as the "most magnificent and satisfying" tragedy), and the description of Greek ethical life in the *Phenomenology* is usually taken to be an unequivocal artifact of this interest. We saw this already in Nussbaum and Pinkard's glosses of the section. Peter Kalkavage puts the point even more bluntly in his *Logic of Desire*, where he writes, "The Antigone provides the paradigm and *Gestalt* for the fall of Greek harmony."[18] It is thus surprising to note that the word "Antigone" is used only twice in the entire course of the *Phenomenology of Spirit*, and just one of those instances occurs in the thirty paragraphs that comprise the section in question. I might be accused of being glib here: while it's true that Hegel does not frequently refer to the play or character by name, this is consistent with the stylistic conventions of the *Phenomenology* more generally, wherein specific texts are often referred to by means of metonymic descriptions of characters or plot points. And this is obviously what Hegel is up to with regard to the *Antigone* when he says things like, "the brother is the member of the family in whom its Spirit becomes an individuality . . . but the sister becomes . . . the guardian of the divine law"[19] or "ethical self-consciousness now learns from its deed the developed nature of what it actually did, as much when it obeyed the divine law as when it followed human law."[20] Yet, upon inspection, the majority of these descriptions are general enough that they remain thoroughly ambiguous. In Hegel's discussion of the relationship between brother and sister, he could just as well be describing Orestes and Electra in Aeschylus's *Oresteia*, and in his comment about self-consciousness learning from its deed, he could just as well be referring to Oedipus's murder of Laius (or, even less felicitously, Macbeth's murder of Duncan). And, in fact, Hegel also makes explicit reference to both the *Oresteia* and *Oedipus Tyrannus* in these paragraphs. None of which is to deny that Hegel has *Antigone* in mind here; he clearly does. I do not, however, see any textually compelling reason to think that he has it in mind exclusively, and I would like to propose that the horizons of our reading will be productively broadened by giving up an "*Antigone*-first" view of the *Phenomenology*. Before moving on, it is worth remarking explicitly that by broadening the scope of my reading beyond the limits of the *Antigone*, I do not intend to reject the possibility of advancing a relevant reading of this portion of the *Phenomenology* that does focus on the *Antigone*. As stated, it is clear that this tragedy is of particular interest to Hegel in both the *Phenomenology* and the *Lectures*, and it undeniably plays a crucial role in the Ethical Life section. The academic reception of Hegel's reading of *Antigone* in the *Phenomenology* has, moreover, had wide-ranging influence outside the narrow purview of Hegel interpretation. Hegel's take on the character of Antigone has been especially impactful for thinkers working in the critical theory tradition, due in large part to the feminist reading inaugurated by Luce Irigaray in her foundational 2002 book, *Speculum of the Other Woman*.

There is no room here to do justice to Antigone's various afterlives in the work of gender theorists, but I will mention one among these readings that I take to be of particular relevance to the epistemological take that I aim to offer here: specifically, the account put forth by Judith Butler in *Antigone's Claim*. Butler's book is not primarily intended to serve as a work of Hegel interpretation, but it does offer a nuanced engagement with the *Phenomenology*'s take on the *Antigone*. Butler summarizes her understanding of Hegel's text as follows:

> [Hegel] . . . has Antigone represent the laws of kinship, the household gods, a representation that leads to two strange consequences: one, that her insistence, according to him, on representing those laws is precisely what constitutes a crime in another more public order of law, and two, that she who stands for this feminine domain of the household becomes unnamable within the text, that the very representation she is said to enact requires an effacement of her name in the text of the *Phenomenology of Spirit*.[21]

I accept Butler's first claim and reject her second claim. Butler is precisely correct that Hegel's depiction of Antigone's crime inheres in her obedience to the wrong order of law. But, as I read Hegel, it is not at all the case that the feminine domain of the household comes under erasure for the subsequent duration of the text. Rather, Hegel's description of Spirit's inability to make sense of Antigone's deed is intended to pose a problem that must be solved in order for Absolute Knowing to be achieved; conceptual adequacy requires that there be no "remainder," feminine or otherwise. Thus, Butler's characterization of the problem that Antigone presents in Hegel's text is, up to a point, exactly right. She offers sensitive formulations such as: "For Hegel, the unconscious, or what he describes as 'nonexisting,' emerges in the claim of entitlement, the act that grounds itself in a law that counts as no law within the realm of law."[22] And she aptly poses the question regarding the realm of divine laws of which Antigone is the first finite agent: "Is this a law that defies conceptualization and that stands as an epistemic scandal within the realm of law, a law that cannot be translated, that marks the very limit of legal conceptualization, a breakage in law performed, as it were by a legality that remains uncontained by any and all positive and generalizable law?"[23] The answer to this question, simply put, is yes. But, on my reading, it is emphatically not the case that Hegel never offers a solution to this "epistemic scandal" in the course of the *Phenomenology*. Rather, overcoming this breakdown of finite legal conceptualization is Spirit's central task throughout the remainder of the text. In this way, the epistemic problematic that Antigone represents poses the question to which an adequate answer must be made in order for Spirit to attain to the standpoint of absolute knowledge.

* * *

So where does this leave us? If, as I am suggesting, tragedy's role in the *Phenomenology* is not fully comprehended by the *Antigone*-based clash of principles view, how should we seek to expand this account? The central demand we are presented with is to make sense of how the Ethical Order discussion of tragedy, which *does*, at least on the face of it, describe a clash of principles, fits with the subsequent Religion of Art discussion, which does not. Over and above this, we also face a background need to come to an understanding of how both of these episodes from the latter half of the *Phenomenology* fit with the arc of the text as a whole: if these two passages continue to present evolving relationships between subjects and objects, how do they do so? And, if they do not, what are they doing instead?

The subsequent discussion will be largely directed toward addressing the first question—that is, the internal relationship of the two discussions of tragedy—although I will come back to the larger question about textual unity at the end. With these desiderata in mind, I will turn to Menke's account of the relationship between tragic author and tragic character in his *Tragic Play*. My claim will be that Menke's description of this relationship and the way it unfolds in the staging of a tragic drama lends helpful insight into the connection between the "Spirit" and "Absolute Religion" sections of the *Phenomenology*: whereas "Spirit" portrays Spirit as a character acting, "Absolute Religion" portrays Spirit as the self-conscious author of its deed. The reconciliation of these two viewpoints constitutes what I will call Spirit's self-recognition, or, in properly Hegelian terms, the achievement of the standpoint of Absolute Knowing wherein the conceptual form adequate to truth becomes cognitively available to collective human mindedness.

In the service of such a reading, it will be helpful to reconsider the context in which tragedy is first introduced in the *Phenomenology*. As I have touched on already, Hegel's discussion of tragedy at the outset of the Spirit section of the *Phenomenology* is often discussed as if it presented a cut and dry argument about Ancient Greek Ethical Life that centers on a reading of Sophocles's *Antigone*. As anyone who has come to the text looking for something along those lines is aware, the actual situation is more complex. The text itself is fundamentally disorienting; on a first reading, it is not clear what argumentative strategy Hegel is employing, how he has arrived at his current topic, or what the topic in question properly even is. This is not due merely to Hegel's notoriously opaque style nor to a failure on the reader's part; rather, it is endemic to the project being undertaken by the text's author. This section of text is the first introduction of Hegel's conception of Spirit, which has a strong claim to being *the* single most important innovation introduced by Hegelian philosophy. What Hegel is up to here is intended to be philosophically novel and, as such, it is also unsurprisingly formally novel. This is not at all to say that the section cannot be read, understood, and analyzed; I simply want to emphasize the unique philosophical character of the section's form and content.

There is, of course, some continuity with the trio of chapters that has gone before, Consciousness, Self-Consciousness, and Observing Reason. These chapters have dealt with a series of evolving relationships between subjects and objects. More specifically, they have presented a dialectically driven progression of criteria for knowledge, beginning with the rudimentary case of sense-certainty and ending with a nascent form of Spirit that manifests its coming to awareness in the self-undermining exercise of its own practical capacity for reason. (Hegel terms this moment in the dialectic "Reason as testing laws," *gesetzprüfende Vernunft*.) Spirit proper comes on the scene when the distinction between an infallible eternal law and a fallible human law becomes explicit for a collective human mindedness that experiences itself as being conditioned by both sorts of law. In Hegel's own words at the outset of the Spirit section, "Spirit, which henceforth is divided in within itself, traces one of its worlds, the realm of culture, in the harsh reality of its objective element; over against this realm, it traces in the element of thought the world of belief or faith, the realm of essential being."[24] It is this dualism between the divine and the worldly sets of rules governing human actions that is the heir to the dichotomy of subject and object that drives the first three chapters of the *Phenomenology*.

The reconciliation of these two apparently opposed sources of law in a way that produces a "Spirit that is certain of itself" is the project of the Spirit and Absolute Religion sections of the *Phenomenology*.[25] The certainty in question will consist in the arrival at a form of self-knowledge that permits these two opposed aspects of Spirit to coexist. Hegel describes Spirit and Religion as being the two "worlds" of Spirit: "The ethical world, the world which is rent asunder into this world and a beyond, and the moral view of the world, are thus the spirits whose process and return into the simple self-consciousness of Spirit are now to be developed."[26] The conflict between these two worlds and their different laws arises for Spirit because of its character: Spirit is essentially active, it is a self that acts, an actor, and, as such, "*Action* divides it into substance and consciousness of the substance; and divides the substance as well as consciousness."[27] Here, it is important to attend to Hegel's emphasis of the fact that there are two divisions to be considered: on the one hand, the way individual human actors in the world have to contend with the double character of the law, and, on the other hand, the way a single transcendent actor (i.e., God) has to contend with the double character of the law. This, then, is the context in which Greek tragedy is first introduced in the *Phenomenology of Spirit*. It is the first moment, the objective, worldly side, of the dialectical reconciliation of the opposition between the apparently disjunctive ethical and moral worlds of Spirit.[28]

Before turning to the second discussion of tragedy that takes place in the Absolute Religion section, I will take up Menke's theoretical work on tragedy. Menke provides a structural account of tragedy that makes sense of the way in which the *Phenomenology*'s two treatments of the topic fit together. In *Tragic Play*, he takes Sophocles's *Oedipus Tyrannus* as the point of departure for a wide-ranging investigation of tragedy, both ancient and modern. According to Menke, *Oedipus* is not, as it is often construed, a tragedy of knowing, rather it is a tragedy of judging. More specifically, it is a tragedy that is brought about by the excess of judgment, namely, of Oedipus's self-judgment as it is enacted in the curse he pronounces against the murderer of his predecessor (and, unbeknownst to Oedipus, his father), King Laius. Thus, Oedipus:

> I charge you that unto that murderer, whosoever he be,
> No one of this land, of which I hold empire and throne,
> Shall give shelter or speak word;
> I forbid any to make him partner in prayer or sacrifice
> Or to serve him with purifying rites.
> I command that all ban him from their homes
> ... Upon the murderer I invoke this curse:
> Whether his hidden guilt is lonely or has partners,
> Evilly, as he is evil, may he wear out his unblessed life!

> And I pray: if, with my knowledge, he should dwell in my house
> That I myself may suffer my curse.[29]

This last couplet turns out to be prophetic since it is of course Oedipus himself who has murdered Laius. Thus, with his declamation, Oedipus judges himself, and in so doing condemns himself.

One aspect of the excessiveness of this judgment, on Menke's reading, consists in Oedipus's attempt to overreach the bounds of his own ontological position. Oedipus is a character in a play, a tragic hero, but the act of cursing is an inherently authorial action. This is so because the curse prescribes a fate for the person placed under it, in just the same way that a tragic author's script prescribes the fate of the characters whose actions it articulates. Menke draws attention to the way in which the emergence of tragedy as a form of art in ancient Greece represented an innovation in the nature of authorship. Unlike ritual and epic forms embedded in open-ended oral traditions, tragedy's conventions require the existence of a written text that is "recreated" in the play's performance. This, on Menke's view, brings about the genesis of two new forms of subjectivity: on one side, the tragic character who has been created by an author and, as such, exists "under a law of necessity, albeit a necessity executed by [himself] alone."[30] And, on the other side, the author, who has not only produced a text but also, in so doing, has "fix[ed] the existence of the characters."[31]

Oedipus Tyrannus, then, dramatizes the relationship between author and character insofar as that relation is composed of a fixer of fate and one who is fated. Menke, drawing on Friedrich Schlegel's work, calls this the "transcendental dramatic" or "self-reflective" character of tragedy: "it is a presentation of agents that is simultaneously a co-presentation of what is presenting them; the relations between the characters in the drama also present the relationships between character, text, and author."[32] According to this view, the tragic art form is in part constituted by the fact that it makes visible and thematizes itself as an art form. Further, on the Aristotelian view that both Menke and Hegel subscribe to, tragic drama also consists in the depiction of an action. In *Oedipus*, this action takes place in the register of the self-reflexivity just discussed: the play effects a "switch between [the positions of author and character], the *ascension* of the character to the position of the author and the *fall* of the author to the position of the character."[33]

Oedipus's ascension to authorship is the result of his curse. In cursing *himself*, he has literally become "the author of the judgment that then determines who he is . . . as a character."[34] Yet, this ascent to self-authorship, to becoming the fixer of his own fate, is emphatically not a liberation from being fated. In fact, precisely the opposite is true: Oedipus's curse consists in his prescription of a fate to himself, and he is thus simultaneously reduced to being a mere character in the very same act by which he attains to authorship. Consequently, Oedipus's authorial power, unlike the authorial power of Sophocles himself, "is not at his disposal, rather, on the contrary, he falls prey to it."[35]

Menke's reading of *Oedipus Tyrannus* draws on a more extensive theory of judgment, developed elsewhere, that lays emphasis on the special regulative role that aesthetic judgment—including critical judgments about aesthetic objects like tragic dramas—has the potential to take on in relation to judgment more generally. Menke writes,

> The aesthetic critique of judgment firstly refers to a specific kind of judging—the judgment in aesthetic matters. But since the judgment on something aesthetic has itself to be performed in an aesthetic way, the aesthetic critique of judgment means, secondly, a critique that is directed against judgment. Aesthetic critique is the aesthetic praxis of judgment that is simultaneously a questioning of judgment itself.[36]

Insofar as aesthetic judgment is self-reflexive, the very act of judging aesthetically calls the act of judging itself into question. In this way, the aesthetic judgment, like the tragic drama, thematizes its own form within its performance.

Menke draws attention to this relationship between Greek tragedy and aesthetic judgment elsewhere, arguing as follows:

> Tragedy does not dissolve the tragic quality of the action by its aesthetic self-reflection, but it discovers this tragic quality in the first place. Tragedy makes use of the new dramatic structure, to which it owes its existence and which determines its form, for a critical analysis of the new enlightened legal practice of judging that had only begun to take shape in its distinctly judicial form at this time.[37]

Accordingly, tragedy is defined as an art form by the way in which it mobilizes the critical potentiality of aesthetic judgment. Specifically, Greek tragic drama aesthetically stages and performs the act of judgment, thus demonstrating the possibilities and the limitations of the judicial structure belonging to Greek ethical life.

In the context of Hegel's *Phenomenology*, I take Menke's comment that tragedy "discovers" its own tragic quality to be of central relevance for understanding Hegel's interest in this particular aesthetic form. For, the discovery of a tension between the judicial system at work in political life (i.e., the ethical substance, Spirit's objective world) and a transcendent divine law that cannot be satisfied within the constraints of the former finite system of legality is precisely the point at issue when Spirit first comes on the scene. Thus, it is not simply the case that the discussion of tragedy presents a problem local to Greek ethical life that falls away both as an aesthetic medium and as a formal structure once Greek ethical life has been shown to contain a contradiction. Rather, tragedy lays out a problem that will be central for the remainder of Hegel's double exploration of the forms of Spirit in the Spirit and Absolute Religion chapters of the text. While, on the face of it, the binding, contradictory structure of judgment that Menke ascribes to *Oedipus Tyrannus* seems like it must be diametrically opposed to that of the *Phenomenology of Spirit*, which is everywhere and always concerned with Spirit's progress toward freedom and the reconciliation of contradiction, I will show in the next section that the circuit of self-authorship that Menke's *Oedipus* illustrates is, in fact, very similar to the relationship in which Spirit stands to itself in the Religion section of the *Phenomenology*. There, Spirit, like Oedipus, discovers itself to be the author of its actions, but simultaneously finds that it is bound by having performed these actions.

* * *

We are now in a position to return to Hegel in order to examine the second treatment of tragedy that takes place in the "Absolute Religion" section of the *Phenomenology*. This fifth chapter introduces Spirit at a new level of reflection, which Hegel describes as "absolute Being in and for itself, the self-consciousness of Spirit."[38] The *Phenomenology* is a text that, like a tragedy, is composed out of an intricate web of perspectives. Up to this point, the three primary ones have been those of the reader or phenomenological observer, an anonymous narrator (who, like the reader, occupies an observational position, but who serves additionally as a guide, along the lines of a museum docent or Dante's Virgil), and the text's main character, human knowing in all its iterations, which at this point in the text is Spirit. The transition from Spirit to Religion is best understood as the addition of a fourth such perspective, namely, the reflexively self-conscious viewpoint of Spirit, which has withdrawn into itself in order to escape from the conflict between the objective and the subjective laws that it has been wrangling with since it came on the scene in Greek Ethical Life. Put simply, in this section of the text, Spirit knows itself to be the author of the subjective law (at least in a preliminary way), whereas in the previous section it did not.

As in the previous section, the topic at issue remains how the two laws, objective and subjective, govern Spirit's actions. In Religion, however, a shift in the tense of the action under discussion from the present to the past has occurred: Spirit is no longer acting, but rather it has ceased to act. Now, Spirit faces the challenge of accounting for the compossibility of what it takes to be two distinct Spirits—the Spirit that acts and the Spirit that has acted—in order to unite its two worlds into one. This situation will be made clearer by examining a passage at the outset of the section on Absolute Knowing that concludes the book. Here, Hegel details the contrast between Spirit and Religion in a dense passage that is worth quoting in full:

> On the one hand, the concept [*der Begriff*] gave itself its fulfillment within the self-certain, *acting* Spirit and, on the other hand, in *religion*: In the latter it gained the absolute *content as content*, that is, in the form of *representational thought* [*Form der Vorstellung*], the form of otherness for consciousness. In contrast, in the former shape, the form is the self itself since it contains the self-certain *acting* Spirit, the self putting the life of absolute Spirit into practice. As we see, this shape is that former simple concept, but one which surrenders its eternal *essence* and is the concept which *exists there*, that is, which acts [*handelt*].[39]

For our purposes, the most important point Hegel is making here is that Spirit in its immediacy, that is, the Spirit who comes on the scene in Greek ethical life, is characterized by action [*Handlung*], while religion is characterized by *Vorstellung* or representation. The Spirit that acts is nothing more than its action: it is exhausted by acting—it "surrenders its eternal essence" and simply "exists there." In *Tragic Play*, Menke describes dramatic characters as "pure surface—nothing but the finite, surveyable series of acts they carry out in their present, in the time and space of the play and the stage; behind this and around this there is equally nothing."[40] This, as Hegel tells it here, is also how it is with Spirit in its immediacy.

Thus, the self-consciousness of Spirit that emerges in the Religion chapter has been dialectically won out of this lack of depth and duration, the literal superficiality, that Spirit suffers from as a mere actor when it first appears in Greek ethical life. Religion's definitive cognitive form, *Vorstellung*, is translated into English by A.V. Miller as "picture-thinking" and by Terry Pinkard as "representational thought." Both translators import the idea of thought into their translations of *Vorstellung*. The temptation is understandable, since thinking does seem to be the obvious contrast case with acting. But I think it is somewhat misleading to do so. I believe Hegel intends us to hear *Vorstellung* more literally, in the sense of setting something up in front of oneself in order to view it. In Religion, Spirit takes a step back from its actions; it relinquishes the role of actor, and takes on the twofold role of spectator and author (the latter in virtue of the fact that it knows what it is looking at to be *its own* action). Thus, Hegel employs *Vorstellung* not in its meaning as a narrowly cognitive technical term (as, for example, Kant does) but rather in its broader, more everyday, visual sense; it is an act of representation or picturing, period.[41]

The impact of this new capacity for representational self-reflexivity can be clearly seen when the depiction of tragedy in this section is juxtaposed with the depiction of tragedy from the previous section. Whereas in the Ethical Substance discussion of tragedy the distinctions between characters, actors, author, and spectators are generally left unacknowledged—a fact that can lead to confusion about precisely who or what the main subject of the section is—in the Religion treatment of tragedy, they are conscientiously picked apart. Hegel writes, for example, "the hero is himself the speaker, and the performance displays to the audience—who are also spectators—*self-conscious* human beings who know their rights and purposes . . . [and] these characters exists as actual human beings who impersonate the heroes."[42] Self-reflexivity enters in multiple registers here: the hero is displayed to an audience; that audience, in turn, is conscious of its spectatorial role; the characters themselves are also self-conscious, as demonstrated by their discursive descriptions of their actions; and, finally, the presence of the actor behind the mask of the character is brought to the fore. All of these pairs mirror the division of Spirit into actor and onlooker; into, on the one side, a self who is performing an action, and, on the other, a self who is looking on and being confronted by that same action.

At the same time as this newfound self-consciousness represents progress in Spirit's quest for self-knowledge, however, it is plagued by the fact of its internal division. Like Oedipus, Spirit finds that it cannot occupy the positions of author and character simultaneously. In Hegel's words, Spirit "is divided with respect to its *form* or to *knowing*. Spirit when *acting* appears *qua* consciousness over against the object to which its activity is directed and which, consequently, is determined as the negative of the knower."[43] Because Spirit acts first and then becomes a party to its own action in the backward-looking act of recollection, Spirit as knower is cut off from Spirit as actor as if behind a pane of glass. Hence, "the present reality is therefore one thing in itself and another thing for consciousness. . . . For this knowing is, in its principle, immediately a not-knowing, because *consciousness*, in its action, is in its own self this antithesis."[44] At this point in its trajectory, Spirit is ontologically separated from itself in precisely the same way that Oedipus as the author of his fate is separated from himself as the character doomed to enact that fate. Thus, in a sense, tragedy as I have glossed Menke's account of it here poses the question that the remainder of the *Phenomenology* must answer. Namely, how, if at all, is it possible for Spirit to reconcile being fated with being free?

Hegel's answer to this question is characteristically complex. The remainder of the dialectic of Religion and the breathless discussion of Absolute Knowing that round out the book offer the *Phenomenology*'s programmatically Hegelian conclusion: Absolute Knowing is the shape of Spirit in which "Spirit . . . knows itself in the shape of Spirit."[45] Hegel elaborates on this claim in terms familiar from the previous discussion, stating that "what in religion was content or a form for presenting an other, is here the self's own act."[46] Rephrased, Absolute Knowing consists precisely in the overcoming of the dualism of actor and act, of author and character, described earlier. There is no room here to attempt to parse the textually internal mechanics of this reconciliation, but I will outline a brief external overview. As I have gestured earlier, the *Phenomenology* describes a process of recollection, what, in the *Philosophy of Spirit*, Hegel calls "*Erinnerung*." But, for the purposes of Absolute Knowing, it is not enough to merely collect together all of these shapes of consciousness. Spirit must additionally recognize that these shapes are its own, that they are constitutive of what it is, rather than being merely contingent past accidents—for, if it does not, a dichotomy between Spirit as the omniscient spectator who looks on at these shapes and the Spirits that are made manifest in each of these finite instances will remain, preventing Spirit from knowing itself in a unified way. Thus, this recognition requires an account of how it is possible to breach the boundary between infinite knowing and finite acting. And, as I have argued, this is precisely the form that tragedy provides.[47]

* * *

To conclude, I have argued that Hegelian Spirit, like Menke's Oedipus, is fated to know itself as the author of its actions. And, in order to facilitate that self-knowledge, Spirit stages its past in a theater of recollected experience within which author, protagonist, and spectator must ultimately coincide. Hegel describes the challenge that this situation poses to Spirit in the following way in the Religion of Art section: "The self-consciousness of the hero must step forth from his mask and present itself as knowing itself to be the fate both of the gods of the chorus and of the absolute powers themselves, and as being no longer separated . . . from the universal consciousness."[48] On the reading I have presented, this situation is not merely a local one. Rather, the achievement of a mode of self-knowledge that reconciles Spirit in its objective, ethical manifestation and its subjective, divine manifestation is the central project of the final three chapters of the *Phenomenology*. Thus, tragedy describes a formal structure of presentation and spectatorship that is not merely one historic art form among many; rather, it is *the* aesthetic form, the form of recollection-based self-perception, which belongs to Spirit in its search for self-knowledge.

Notes

1 G. W. F. Hegel, *Phenomenology of Spirit*, trans. Terry Pinkard (Cambridge: Cambridge University Press, 2018), §807, 466.
2 Ibid.

3   A. C. Bradley, *Oxford Lectures on Poetry* (Oxford: Oxford University Press, 1909), 72.
4   Charles Taylor, *Hegel* (Cambridge: Cambridge University Press, 1975), 172.
5   Ibid., 175.
6   Martha Nussbaum, *The Fragility of Goodness* (Cambridge: Cambridge University Press, 2001), 52.
7   Terry Pinkard, *Hegel's Phenomenology: The Sociality of Reason* (Cambridge: Cambridge University Press, 1996), 144.
8   Ibid.
9   Ann Paolucci and Henry Paolucci, *Hegel on Tragedy* (New York: Harper Torchbooks, 1975), 52.
10 Ibid., 113.
11 Ibid.
12 Ibid.
13 Julia Peters, "A Theory of Tragic Experience According to Hegel," *European Journal of Philosophy* 19, no. 1 (March 1, 2011): 87.
14 Ibid.
15 Ibid.
16 Ibid., 101.
17 Ibid., 92.
18 Peter Kalkavage, *The Logic of Desire* (Philadelphia: Paul Dry Books, 2007), 247.
19 G. W. F. Hegel, *Phenomenology of Spirit*, trans. A. V. Miller (Oxford: Oxford University Press, 1977), §458–59, 275. Henceforth PhS. Unless otherwise indicated, I follow Miller throughout.
20 PhS §469, 283.
21 Judith Butler, *Antigone's Claim: Kinship between Life and Death* (New York: Columbia University Press, 2000), 29.
22 Ibid., 33.
23 Ibid.
24 PhS §442, 265.
25 Ibid.
26 Ibid.
27 PhS §444, 266.
28 The tragic problematic as I have outlined it here recurs most notably in the Encyclopedic texts in the *Philosophy of Right*. In that text, Hegel prefaces the third and final section of the text, the treatment of Ethical Life [*Sittlichkeit*] with the following remark on Antigone: "the law [of the inward life] is displayed as a law opposed to public law, to the law of the land. This is *the supreme opposition* in ethics and therefore in tragedy; and it is individualized in the same play in the opposing natures of man and woman." Hegel, *Elements of the Philosophy of Right*, trans. T. M. Knox (Oxford: Oxford University Press, 1967), §166, 169. My italics.
29 Sophocles, "Oedipus the King," in *The Tragedies of Sophocles*, trans. Sir Richard C. Jebb (Cambridge, 1917), 11 (lines 236–51). Translation modified.
30 Christoph Menke, *Tragic Play: Irony and Theater from Sophocles to Beckett*, trans. James Phillips (New York: Columbia University Press, 2009), 42.
31 Ibid., 44.
32 Ibid., 46.
33 Ibid.
34 Ibid., 47.
35 Ibid.

36 Christoph Menke, *The Power of Judgment: A Debate on Aesthetic Critique* (Frankfurt am Main: Sternbergpress, 2010), 17.
37 Christoph Menke, "The Aesthetics of Tragedy: Romantic Perspectives," in *Tragedy and the Idea of Modernity*, ed. Joshua Billings and Miriam Leonard (Oxford: Oxford University Press, 2015), 55.
38 PhS §672, 410.
39 PhS §798, 460. I follow Pinkard's translation and section numbering here.
40 Menke, *The Power of Judgment*, 38.
41 G. W. F. Hegel, *Philosophy of Mind*, translated from the 1830 Edition, together with the *Zusätze* by William Wallace and A. V. Miller, with Revisions and Commentary by M. J. Inwood (Oxford: Clarendon Press, 2007), §452, 203. The "Psychology" chapter of the *Philosophy of Spirit* robustly supports the gloss I offer here. There, Psychology is divided into three moments: Intuition [*Anschauung*], Representation [*Vorstellung*], and Thinking [*Denken*]. Thus, for Hegel, representation is specifically not thinking. But it also differs from intuition insofar as it is not immediate. Hegel writes that representation in its first moment is "recollected or inwardized [*erinnerte*] intuition" (PS §451, 201). The object of such recollection (what we might conceive of as the "unit of measure" for this modality of mind) is the image [*Bild*].
42 PhS §733, 444.
43 PhS §737, 446.
44 Ibid.
45 PhS §798, 485.
46 PhS §797, 485.
47 In a longer treatment, it would be of crucial importance to explore (1) the role that Christianity plays in the course of these three chapters and (2) the relationship between the passion narrative and the tragic structure I have elucidated here. Hegel's early writings, in particular the *The Spirit of Christianity and Its Fate* (1798) are of particular interest in this connection.
48 PhS §743, 450.

Bibliography

Bradley, A. C., *Oxford Lectures on Poetry*. Oxford: Oxford University Press, 1909.
Butler, Judith. *Antigone's Claim: Kinship between Life and Death*. New York: Columbia University Press, 2000.
Hegel, G. W. F. *Aesthetics: Lectures on Fine Art*, 2 vols., translated by T. M. Knox. Oxford: Oxford University Press, 1998.
Hegel, G. W. F. *Die Phänomenologie des Geistes*. Hamburg: Felix Meiner, 1999.
Hegel, G. W. F. *Early Theological Writings*, translated by T. M. Knox. Philadelphia: University of Pennsylvania Press, 1975.
Hegel, G. W. F. *Elements of the Philosophy of Right*, translated by T. M. Knox. Oxford: Oxford University Press, 1967. [PR]
Hegel, G. W. F. *Enzyklopädie der philosophischen Wissenschaften im Grundrisse* (1830), 3 vols. Frankfurt am Main: Suhrkamp, 1986.
Hegel, G. W. F. *Phenomenology of Spirit*, translated by A. V. Miller. Oxford: Oxford University Press, 1977. [PhS]
Hegel, G. W. F. *Phenomenology of Spirit*, translated by Terry Pinkard. Cambridge: Cambridge University Press, 2018. [PhS]

Hegel, G. W. F. *Philosophy of Mind*, translated from the 1830 Edition, together with the *Zusätze* by William Wallace and A. V. Miller, with Revisions and Commentary by M. J Inwood. Oxford: Clarendon Press, 2007. [PS]

Hegel, G. W. F. *Vorlesungen über die Aesthetik*, 3 vols. Frankfurt am Main: Suhrkamp, 1986.

Kalkavage, Peter. *The Logic of Desire*. Philadelphia: Paul Dry Books, 2007.

Menke, Christoph. "The Aesthetics of Tragedy: Romantic Perspectives." In *Tragedy and the Idea of Modernity*, edited by Joshua Billings and Miriam Leonard. Oxford: Oxford University Press, 2015.

Menke, Christoph. *The Power of Judgment: A Debate on Aesthetic Critique*. Frankfurt am Main: Sternberg Press, 2010.

Menke, Christoph. *Tragic Play: Irony and Theater from Sophocles to Beckett*, translated by James Phillips. Columbia University Press: New York, 2009.

Nussbaum, Martha. *The Fragility of Goodness*. Cambridge: Cambridge University Press, 2001.

Paolucci, Ann and Henry Paolucci. *Hegel on Tragedy*. Harper Torchbooks, 1975.

Peters, Julia. "A Theory of Tragic Experience According to Hegel." *European Journal of Philosophy* 19, no. 1 (March 1, 2011): 85–106.

Pinkard, Terry. *Hegel's Phenomenology: The Sociality of Reason*. Cambridge: Cambridge University Press, 1996.

Sophocles. "Oedipus the King." In *The Tragedies of Sophocles*, translated by Sir Richard C. Jebb. Cambridge: Cambridge University Press, 1917.

Taylor, Charles. *Hegel*. Cambridge: Cambridge University Press, 1975.

10

Rethinking Hegel's Modern Conception of Art

Georg W. Bertram

The end of art is its beginning. This seems to be a contradiction. And, even more, it seems to contradict the claims of the most prominent representative of the end-of-art thesis, Hegel. Hegel's conception of art, so it seems, tells us that art long passed its apex on the path to modernity. In his view, the end of art has to be understood as a symptom of the necessary decay of art, which is rooted in art's systematic relation to religion and philosophy. Put differently, Hegel seems to hold the view that art cannot be the most important form of self-expression for a modern society, which is to say, for a society characterized by individualism and plurality (to name only two important characteristics). In modernity, religion and philosophy, which is to say conceptual practices, are the most important means by which a society comes to understand itself. This, at least, is the impression given by traditional readings of Hegel. But a closer look makes it clear that Hegel's position is not so simple as one might think. There are at least three aspects of his aesthetics that resist the interpretation according to which it prioritizes a classical understanding of art. The first aspect is the dialectics of the symbolic, the classical, and the romantic forms of art.[1] If the three forms of art are understood as having a dialectical relation to one another, it is important to see the romantic form of art as providing something like a synthesis. Whatever the synthesis in question means, it certainly creates problems for interpretations of Hegel that give preference to a classical understanding of art. The second issue lies in Hegel's explanation of the system of the arts. If Hegel were the classicist one wants him to be, he should prefer the art that he sees as representative of the classical form of art, namely, sculpture. Without a doubt, Hegel takes sculpture to be one of the most important arts—but only one of them. According to Hegel, sculpture competes with dramatic poetry for the title of the most important type of art. As dramatic poetry belongs to the sphere of the romantic arts, Hegel's hierarchy of the arts also undermines the notion that he prefers classical art above all else. The third issue, finally, is the fact that Hegel has a high estimation of modern works of art. His judgments about Jan van Eyck, Shakespeare, Mozart, Goethe, and others clearly show that he does not subscribe to a narrative according to which the most important artworks were created in Antiquity. In his fight against what he sees as romantic misconceptions of art, Hegel proves to be interested in the criticism of works of art of his own time. An interest like this needs explanation, and it can be well explained if one attributes to Hegel the view that artworks that belong to the romantic form of art deserve to be understood as important realizations of what art is.

These are just a few of the difficulties facing those who claim that Hegel's aesthetics should be understood as prioritizing a classical conception of art. These points open room for a reassessment of Hegel's position and for an interpretation of his aesthetics that goes beyond the prejudices that bog down many readings of Hegel's philosophy in general and Hegel's aesthetics in particular. This chapter undertakes such a reassessment. My aim is to show that Hegel saw modern art as the paradigmatic mode of art[2] and that Hegel's aesthetics conceives of art as a particularly modern practice. Making this interpretation plausible necessitates showing that Hegel's critique of his romantic contemporaries is a critique of their misconception of what Hegel sees as the romantic constitution of art. In other words, it demands seeing that Hegel offers a conception of romantic art that differs from that which he attributes to his romantic contemporaries.

I will develop my reading of Hegel in four steps and will structure my argument with ten claims. In a first step, I offer a reinterpretation of Hegel's conception of the three forms of art by making the case that the romantic form of art sublates the symbolic and the classical. This provides the foundation for the second step, in which I offer a systematic reading of Hegel's end-of-art thesis. The third step describes the meaning of the claim that art is a plural practice, a practice in which works of art present different perspectives and struggle with one another over how everyday practices should be developed within specific historical-cultural contexts. The final step analyzes the arts' constitutive relation to conceptual practices. For a modern conception of art, art is constitutively bound up with interpretation and art criticism, and thus with conceptual activity (and is thus dependent on philosophy, taken in a broad sense). I will argue that these points are cornerstones both of Hegel's conception of art and, more generally, of any treatment of art as a constitutively modern practice.

The Romantic Form of Art as Sublating Symbolic and Classical Art

One of the most important elements of Hegel's aesthetics is his conception of the three forms of art. As mentioned earlier, this confronts Hegel's readers with a puzzle: On the one hand, it seems that Hegel prioritizes the classical form of art, an impression bolstered by his claim that classical art realizes art's "highest vocation."[3] On the other hand, the structure of the three forms of art seems to be dialectical in nature, from which it would follow that the romantic form of art has to be understood as providing what one might call a completion of art's movement and thus as constituting the highest form of art. How to reconcile these two tendencies? In my view, an essential part of interpreting Hegel's process of thought lies in seeing the dialectics of the three forms of art as *leading up to* the romantic form of art. Thus, my reflections begin as follows.

First Claim
With his distinction between the symbolic, the classical, and the romantic forms of art, Hegel has to be understood as making a dialectical argument. Thus, it is important to read the romantic form of art as being, for Hegel, the realization of the apex of art.

If one takes the classical form of art as being sublated by the romantic form of art, one has to ask about what makes this sublation necessary. In which sense does the classical form of art fail to fulfill its own standards? In which sense does the classical form of art suffer from an essential shortcoming? Hegel gives an important hint as to why he thinks that the classical form of art has to be overcome when he says: "The supreme works of beautiful sculpture are sightless, and their inner being does not look out of them as self-knowing inwardness in this spiritual concentration which the eye discloses."[4] At first sight, one might think that Hegel is just articulating what he takes to be a fact about classical sculptures: that they don't have eyes (which is in fact a historical error on Hegel's part). But this is not enough. Clearly, Hegel has something else in mind. His claim states that classical sculptures do not represent individuality. Rather, they represent a specific cultural understanding of what the human being is. But the understanding of what human beings are that is represented by classical sculptures does not differentiate between different individuals who live within the cultural context in which the sculptures were produced. Rather, they equally represent them all, and it is in this sense that sculptures have no gaze.

Another way of articulating sculptures' shortcomings is to say that they lack the perspective of a subject. In explaining the characteristics of sculpture in the same context as the last quote, Hegel writes: "The mutability and contingency of empirical individuality is indeed expunged in those lofty figures of the gods, but what they lack is the actuality of self-aware subjectivity in the knowing and willing of itself."[5] In other words, that which the sculpture expresses holds true for all subjects of the specific form of life of that culture. It transcends individual subjects. In Hegel's view, this is why the sculpture is not able to realize art in the full sense. This, however, gives rise to the justified question as to whether this does not contradict Hegel's claim that the classical form of art realizes art's "highest vocation." At this point, I think it is too early to answer this question, so we should just keep it in mind for the time being. Before continuing, it seems helpful to sum up what the classical form of art lacks.

Second Claim
The shortcoming of the classical form of art lies in the fact that artworks that belong to it lack individuality and thus do not articulate the perspectives of subjects.

Why does Hegel think this is a shortcoming? Why should art represent individuality? Does Hegel's diagnosis rely on some conception of art that implicitly functions as a standard measure? In my view, it is not possible to make sense of what Hegel means by just looking at art as such. A full understanding of Hegel's position demands taking into account the social structures that underlie the three different forms of art. For Hegel, art makes an impact on us because it informs how people understand social structures. In other words, one can, according to Hegel, only make sense of art if one considers it in its social context. For the classical form of art, this means that classical sculptures give expression to a homogeneous community. In such a community, no subject or individual has a position that would distinguish him or her from any other. Basically, classical sculpture reflects a social homogeneity that does not allow for differences between individuals. At first sight, it might again seem as if Hegel were just stating some fact about the social context in which classical art was produced, which is to say the social structure of *polis* communities in ancient Greece. But Hegel is interested in something quite different, namely in the question of whether particular forms of art correspond with a social structure capable of maintaining its own stability. This guiding question leads him to draw the conclusion that the classical form of art reflects social homogeneity. For him, the classical form of art reflects the fact that the social structure underlying it left no room for individuality. Going on his statement about art reaching its "highest vocation" in the classical era, one might be tempted to think that Hegel is in favor of social homogeneity. But as his comments on the shortcomings of the classical form of art clearly show, this is not the case.

Hegel's reflections on social homogeneity from the beginning of the "spirit" chapter of the *Phenomenology of Spirit* help underscore this point. There, Hegel explains why it is necessary that social structures in which the individual does not have a place be overcome—or, in Hegel's words, why it is necessary to "leave this happy fortune" of a homogenized society "behind."[6] Hegel's argument essentially revolves around the problem of freedom. The argument claims that a primary characteristic of homogenized societies is that they force their members to rigidly adhere to the community's rules. The key implication is that those people are not permitted to take a position on the rules in question because they simply have to blindly follow them.[7] An important consequence is that members of such societies cannot deal with normative structures that differ from their own. They lack the capacity to understand that which deviates from the norms that they themselves blindly follow. In such situations, the appearance of different normative structures can only give rise to collisions that ultimately lead to the breakdown of the homogeneous society, a necessity that Hegel thinks is pointedly expressed in Sophocles's tragedy *Antigone*.[8]

Hegel thus believes that it is important that individuals be free to take a stance on the norms they are confronted with, because only if they are free can they deal with divergences between normative structures and thus elide the occurrence of mere collisions (as opposed to a conflictual mediation of the two structures). The simple point that Hegel makes is that homogenized societies necessarily lack stability. Only a society whose members can deal with conflicts can ever be really stable.

Interestingly, this position is reflected in Hegel's conception of the dialectics between the three forms of art. The dialectics of the three forms of art basically articulates the different ways in which art holds relevance for the formation of community. Because Hegel thinks that art is a practice through which people come to form an understanding of themselves, he concludes that works of art do more than just express convictions that are essential for the society in which the works of art are created. More importantly, art has the function of both developing and stabilizing social structures.[9] Thus, the dialectics of the three forms of art can basically be understood as a series of different ways that art forms and reflects social structures, a point that might be summed up as follows.

Third Claim
The dialectic of the three forms of art (the symbolic, the classical, and the romantic forms of art) is rooted in the social structures that are specific to each of the three forms of art. At the heart of these dialectics stands the question of how social structures are stabilized.

The End of Art as Its Beginning

Inquiring into art's function in a homogeneous society might help make clear how the foregoing reflections bring us closer to understanding Hegel's end-of-art thesis. Simply put, in a homogeneous society, works of art function in a self-evident way. Since all members of the society in question adhere to the same rules and since works of art express orientations foundational for these rules, the members of these societies who engage with these works of art understand them at once. Simply put, there is no distance between the members of the society and its artworks. In this sense, we can say that works of art produced in homogenized societies have *self-evident foundations*. This gives us what we need to explain what we wanted to explain earlier: how Hegel conceives of art's "highest vocation." The highest vocation of art is for art to be taken for granted. No member of a homogeneous society has doubts as to whether a concrete work of art expresses her understanding of herself, because she can tell right away. The self-evident foundations of art in its classical form are reflected in art's relation to other forms of reflective practice, namely to religion and philosophy. If art's foundations are self-evident, it has no need of religion and philosophy to achieve what it aims to achieve. Thus, another way to explain what Hegel means when he talks about art's "highest vocation" is to say that it is art's highest vocation to stand on its own.

This explanation of the particular mode of efficacy of art in its classical form gives us a clue for how to understand Hegel's end-of-art thesis. The end-of-art thesis states that art has lost its self-evident foundations. After the end of art, art is no longer taken for granted. Rather, it is constantly being placed into question. A basic aspect of what this means can be grasped by saying that, in this state, every work of art is confronted with the question as to whether it succeeds according to the standards it sets for itself. This can help us understand a second aspect of what the end-of-art thesis implies: after the end of art, art is inextricably bound up with conceptual activity. In interacting with an object that purports to be a work of art, one has to engage in conceptual activity if one is to make a judgment about whether it succeeds in achieving what it aims to achieve. If we understand conceptual activity as being philosophical in nature, we can say that, in its romantic form, art needs to be supplemented by philosophical reflection in order to achieve what it aims to achieve. In other words, it no longer stands on its own. The understanding of the end-of-art thesis developed thus far might be condensed in the following claim.

Fourth Claim
Hegel's thesis that art has come to an end has to be understood as saying that art has lost its self-evident foundations and, therefore, no longer stands on its own.[10]

But, do not the explanations given thus far clearly show that the classical form of art is—as the form of art that realizes art's "highest vocation"—art's apex? Doesn't it seem obvious that the highest thing art could possibly achieve would be to stand on its own? Why should art's having self-evident foundations be considered a shortcoming? Answering these questions demands that we ask what Hegel thinks art is supposed to accomplish. Hegel explains that art's basic aim is to demonstrate that there is no difference between spirit and nature.[11] In simple terms, art does this by presenting a concept in the form of a real, sensuous object.[12] The aforementioned sketch of the dialectic of the forms of art should make clear that Hegel does not simply pose this question in the abstract, because every form of art—and thus every way of negating the difference between spirit and nature—is embedded in and informed by a particular social structure.

When art has self-evident foundations, it has the appearance of being natural. The social reality it presents is the only reality there is for that society's members. Here, even the mere notion that there might be a difference between spirit and nature does not come into play. But this very fact means that art with self-evident foundations cannot fulfill what it, in Hegel's mind, seeks to accomplish. The issue is that the realization of art's aim implicitly requires that recipients be capable of thinking the difference between nature and spirit. But the members of a homogeneous society do not conceptualize nature, as they unreflectively accept things as they are as natural. In such a society, nature is simply what one is accustomed to. Of course, there are differences between the habituated, quasi-natural tradition and other normative practices that might confront the members of this society. However, in a homogeneous society, certain structures make it such that these differences are not productive and that they can only lead to destruction. We have already seen how these differences can be made productive: they have to have the chance to play out in the form of a conflict (in contrast to a mere collision). For a conflict to take place within a society, conflicting parties have to have a mutual understanding of the differences at play. In a conflict, the object of struggle are not norms of different societies but rather competing norms within a single society.[13]

This gives us a better understanding of the sense in which art is kept from fulfilling its aims in a homogeneous society. In short, such societies do not enable their members to experience and cope with differences that art might put on display. In order to achieve what it aims to achieve, art has to deal with differences. It has to show that differences do not divide, for example, spirit and nature, society and individual, and it does this by showing that both sides can coexist. In this sense, art cannot realize what it aims to accomplish if it has self-evident foundations: it has to have roots in a context in which it can unfold its reconciliatory force, which means that recipients have to be able to grapple with differences in the first place. The issue with art having self-evident foundations can be put as follows.

Fifth Claim
Art with a self-evident foundation is always bound up with a social structure that does not allow its members to experience essential differences. Because of this, art's "highest vocation" is inextricably connected to a naturalization of both art and society. Such naturalization has the consequence that art is not fully able to realize its aim of showing that we can deal with essential differences and that these differences, thus, do not have the last word.

This claim gives us a clue as to why the end of art is an essential part of what art aims to achieve. But in which sense does the end of art belong to what art is? It might be easier to grasp Hegel's position if we first elaborate on what it would mean for art to *not* have self-evident foundations. In the romantic form of art, every single work of art has to develop on its own terms how it is going to achieve what art aims to achieve. Let's call this art's *essential modernity*.[14] It consists in the uncertainty of whether a work of art will achieve what it aims to achieve. This uncertainty should not to be understood as a failure or shortcoming, but rather as an achievement in itself. According to Hegel, the romantic form of art represents a fundamental shift in the relation between society and art, because in it, art's effectiveness and contribution to society are always in question and can take a number of different shapes. In this sense, the end of art is inscribed into every work of art as the possibility of its failure. Every work of art has to find a way to grapple with its constitutive lack of self-evident foundations, which means nothing less than that every work of art has to reinvent what art is and what art should be.

That every work of art bears the burden of having to reinvent what art is is the most important consequence of art's loss of self-evident foundations. Since there is no stable ground upon which individual works might rely, every work of art has to put art as such into question and thus posit anew what art is supposed to achieve. Individual works of art develop their own terms for what art aims to achieve by working within an established art form, such as the string quartet. In composing his first string quartet, someone like Johannes Brahms struggles with how the form of the string quartet has been developed by, say, Robert Schumann and Franz Schubert. He seeks to find a new interpretation of the very form in question. In doing so, the form of the string quartet is, in a sense, reinvented. But the necessity of reinventing art bears with it the possibility that artworks might fail in this their very task. There is nothing that could guarantee that Brahms will succeed in reinventing the idea of art by composing his first string quartet.

Now, one may wonder how such failure is possible given the fact that in modernity art has no stable foundations. Why doesn't the loss of self-evident foundations simply imply that, in modern art, anything goes? It is precisely such conclusions that provoked Hegel to criticize some of his contemporaries and their conceptions of romantic art.[15] He criticizes the subjectivist realization of art that makes it seem as if modern art is defined by arbitrariness.[16] Hegel thinks this view is erroneous for the simple reason that one of art's key aims is to contribute to the objective world of a society. Art's loss of self-evident foundations does not entail a loss of value or significance. Quite the opposite: as we have seen, the loss of self-evident foundations is the condition of the realization of art's aims.

Thus, one misunderstands Hegel's criticism of some of his romantic contemporaries if one reads it as a general criticism of the romantic form of art. Rather, his critique simply points out a possibility that is, in the end, inescapable, namely, the possibility that a work of art fails to have an impact on society. The aim of art (to show that essential differences do not have the last word) can only be realized if art can always fail in this sense. An artwork can only fail on its own standards. The possibility of failure inherent in every work of art is an index of the end of art. In this sense, every artwork refers to the end of art. If each work of art aims at reinventing what art is, then each work has to address the possibility of its own failure.

What bearing does all this have on how we should understand the end of art? The end of art is art's own self-awareness of not being secured by a stable grounding. Thus, the end of art must be understood as something that is productive for art as such;

that is, the very lack of self-evident foundations discloses artistic possibilities. We misunderstand the notion of the end of art if we take it to imply that art has lost its ability to make important contributions to society. It is the other way around: with the awareness of the possibility of its failure, art gains the potential to give new impulses to the development of society. This is not to say that in modernity every artwork is successful and productive. But in containing the end of art in itself, each artwork is compelled to grapple with the possibility of its own failure and thus to develop new forms and rules in an attempt to preserve its own efficacy and successfully carry out its goal of reinventing art as such. In this way, the end of art matters for art in general:

Sixth Claim
Art that no longer has self-evident foundations realizes an essential aspect of art in general: its being fundamentally unstable. In this sense, art's end is its beginning.

The Essential Plurality of Art

Hegel's aesthetics makes it clear that the end of art has important consequences for how we define what art is. First, it means that art is essentially plural. Hegel's most famous way of expressing art's plurality is in what is usually called Hegel's system of the arts. However, the common expression obscures the core of Hegel's explanation of the arts, which states that art in general is realized by different arts and that it thus cannot be reduced to one art alone. The differences between the arts are irreducible and those that are insurmountable.

At first glance, it seems as if Hegel's system of the arts has no relation to his end-of-art thesis, but some key connections to it can be found in the relation between the three forms of art and the system of the arts. According to Hegel, the different arts can be divided up according to their relations to the differences between the three forms of art. In other words, the relations between architecture, sculpture, painting, music, and poetry are relations structured by the dialectics of the symbolic, the classical, and the romantic forms of art. It is evident that Hegel argues that the relations are structured in this way, but it is far from evident what this means. How should we understand the systematic insight about art Hegel wants to express here? What kind of systematic relevance might Hegel's explanations have for a conception of art that can be grasped independently of Hegel's dialectical construction?

I think that Hegel's end-of-art thesis can help us explain why he connects both the three forms of art and the system of the arts. To recapitulate, the end-of-art thesis has to be understood as stating that art has no self-evident foundations. The unstable situation of art has the effect that artworks struggle with each other. They struggle to achieve what art aims at achieving. Because of this, they are inevitably confronted with the possibility of failure, a possibility that, according to Hegel, is inscribed in every single work of art. My claim is that we can understand this basic dimension of the end of art as the key mediating concept that allows Hegel to connect the three forms of art with the system of the arts. The point is that Hegel is basically interested in art as a plural practice.

If no work of art can guarantee that it will succeed according to the standards it sets for itself, then every work of art struggles with its own end as art. As discussed earlier, in Hegel's view, works of art aim at overcoming differences between nature and spirit, and they do so in a concrete way. Think of a piece of music. It aims at articulating affective structures in such a way that they disclose what one is confronted with in the objective world (e.g., relations between individual subjects). But different pieces of music realize this aim in different ways. Thus, a work of art's struggle to succeed according to the aims it sets for itself is related to other works of art and the ways in which they do or do not succeed according to their aims. Works of art compete with one another to realize what they seek to achieve. Even though every work of art stands on its own in determining what it seeks to achieve, it struggles to achieve this aim not only with itself but with other artworks as well. Thus, it is a constitutive aspect of artworks that they stand in relation to other artworks. Other artworks with related aims can always do better. In Hegel's view, it is important for us to understand the competition in question as something productive. Ultimately, it enlivens the practice of art.[17]

In this sense, each work of art's constitutive relation to its own end has the consequence that works of art are essentially plural. They depend on each other. They can only determine what they aim to achieve through their relations to other works of art. In his criticism of romantic works of art, Hegel clearly underlines an important consequence of the interrelatedness of works of art: every work of art only presents a particular perspective. No artwork is capable of providing a comprehensive, total perspective on a cultural-historical form of life. It seems as if Hegel is criticizing the particularity of the plurality of perspectives given in romantic works of art.[18] But he wants to make it clear that these works are particular in what they present. They have to be understood as being essentially dependent on the relations in which they stand to other works of art.

Hegel explains the particularity of each artwork's perspective by drawing on the example of Dutch genre painting, which often thematizes various aspects of everyday life. Hegel's claim that romantic art "makes *Humanus* its new holy of holies" is telling.[19] At first glance, it might again seem as if Hegel were criticizing this feature of romantic art, but in fact, he is very explicit in affirming it: "What is an ingredient in any work of art is one in painting too: the vision of what man is as man, what the human spirit and character is, what man and *this* man is."[20] This is to say that everything that concerns human beings within their cultural surroundings is a suitable subject for an artwork. But this does not only hold for romantic art as a historical period of art's development. According to Hegel, it holds for art in general. Art in general is a thematization of what concerns human beings within their forms of life.

The essentially modern condition of art places different works of art in the position of having to struggle with one another to present something that is relevant to human beings in their historical-cultural circumstances. As Hegel clearly states, it is a misunderstanding of the romantic constitution of art to think that "anything goes" in art. Even though every artwork is free to shed light on particular (and potentially irrelevant) aspects of a human culture, it has to defend what it chooses to portray within what one might call the contention among artworks. However particular (and potentially irrelevant) the subject matter of an artwork seems to be, the artwork has to prove that it is important for how we as human beings understand ourselves. Another way of putting this is to say that the particularity of artworks' perspectives is misunderstood if artworks are taken as objects that simply archive culture. They do not just record aspects of a human form of life, but rather present these things as being relevant for the form of life in question. This characteristically modern constitution is, according to Hegel, essential for art in general—from Antiquity on. It can be summed up in the following claim.

Seventh Claim
Since works of art always have to face the possibility of their own failure, they necessarily maintain relations to a plurality of works of art and can thus do nothing other than present a particular perspective.

Up to this point, I have only discussed the romantic (i.e., modern) constitution of art. But what consequences does this have for Hegel's conception of the system of the arts? In which way is the system of the arts, in Hegel's perspective, to be understood as an outcome of the fact that art is essentially romantic? At this point, it is important to explain a little further what it means that artworks reflect "*Humanus*" as the "holy of holies." Thus far, I have interpreted this as saying that works of art present particular aspects of a human form of life. But it is important to note that these aspects are bound up with different forms of practice and sensuous engagement with the world. The different bodily senses are related to different aspects of what is relevant to human beings. Thus, the particularity of an artwork's perspectives is realized in different arts.

Hegel's presentation of the system of the arts is telling in this regard. Hegel discusses whether the differences between the arts could be explained in relation to the different bodily senses. Even though he does not mention Herder, he makes implicit reference to Herder's explanation of the differences between the arts in his fourth *Critical Forest*.[21] Hegel is skeptical about Herder's claims because, as he argues, the mere differences between bodily senses have nothing to do with what art aims to achieve. Why are the differences between the bodily senses of human beings nevertheless relevant for how art is constituted? Hegel's answer to this question invokes what he before said was the aim of art, namely, to overcome the difference between spirit and nature. Artworks do more than simply present some aspects of a human form of life in some sensuous form. Rather, they portray something that is relevant and thus valuable for human beings in the context of a form of life. Because of this, Hegel thinks that the differences between the arts have to be understood as being rooted in artworks' aims to present relevant aspects of a human form of life.

Hegel explains: "Art has no other mission but to bring before sensuous contemplation the truth as it is in the spirit, reconciled in its totality with objectivity and the sphere of sense. Now since this is to come about at this stage in the medium of the external reality of artistic productions, the totality which is the Absolute in its truth falls apart here in its different moments."[22] The "different moments" that "fall apart" within the system of the arts are the different arts, and since they have to be understood as belonging to what Hegel calls "the totality," the arts' differences have to be understood as being essential for the realization of art's general aim. This claim might be easier to understand if we say that what is essential for human beings is differentiated in different sensuous forms and practices. Thus, art needs different arts to realize what it aims at achieving.

This gives us some material for answering the question as to why the system of the arts has to be understood as an outcome of art's characteristically romantic, that is, modern constitution. The struggle among works of art to thematize something particular that is relevant within a form of life necessarily implies that works of art are developed in relation to different senses and different types of practice. Some works of art deal with how we see the world—others with how we move within it. Art's struggle to capture what is relevant to human beings has to take all aspects of what concerns individuals within historical-cultural contexts into account. This is why art's lack of self-evident foundations, or, in short, its romantic constitution, has to be understood as the basis of the system of the arts as it is presented by Hegel:

Eighth Claim
The struggle of works of art to thematize relevant aspects of a human form of life can only be realized within a plurality of arts because only a plurality of arts can address all aspects of what matters to human beings within human practices.

Art, Interpretation, and Art Criticism

Now I would like to come to the most important aspect of Hegel's conception of the romantic form of art, namely, its relation to conceptual practices. Hegel characterizes the development from the classical form of art to the romantic form of art as a sublation of art's material-bodily externality. Inwardness is the central characteristic of the romantic form of art. This means first and foremost that romantic art is always connected with conceptual practices. Here, art is spiritualized in the sense that it simply does not and cannot work without conceptual practices.[23] As the theories and works of Hegel's romantic contemporaries make clear, the conceptual practices in question are twofold: they encompass, on the one hand, interpretation and, on the other hand, art criticism.

I think it is important to take Hegel's claim about art's relation to conceptual practices as a key to understanding how he views the end of art as being essential for what art is. Thus, the final part of my chapter is dedicated to explaining how Hegel thinks that art is inextricably bound up with practices of interpretation and art criticism. Understanding the significance of these practices can best be approached by further analyzing the particularity of works of art. As discussed earlier, Hegel thinks that works of art are misunderstood if they are taken as mere cultural archives. Art is not cultural memory. Rather, it is, within the human form of life in general, a practice of self-understanding. Artworks present what they thematize as being relevant for those who engage with them. But how do those who engage with a specific work of art know that what is presented is relevant to them? The answer can only be found by interpreting the work of art.

Here, interpretation is to be understood in a literal sense. It signifies linguistic practices by which producers and recipients of artworks say something about what they think a specific work of art is about and why what it is about is relevant to human beings within a specific form of life. We are familiar with interpretation in this sense from various practices: discussions with a friend while reading a novel, discussions after a film, art criticism, and so on. In different practices, we try to make sense of an artwork and discern why what we can make sense of is relevant to us.

According to Hegel, it is a key characteristic of art without self-evident foundations that it has to be interpreted in this sense. If the meaning of works of art were self-evident (as Hegel suggests was the case for the classical form of art), there would be no need for interpretation, and their relevance for a specific form of life would be immediately obvious. But the romantic form of art lacks self-evident foundations that would guarantee that everyone understands an artwork's meaning and relevance. Out of this stems the necessity for interpretation. Simply put, the romantic constitution of works of art means that they can only fulfill their aims if they are interpreted:

Ninth Claim
The struggle of works of art with one another to thematize relevant aspects of a human form of life necessitates that works of art are interpreted and thus bound up with conceptual practices.

As mentioned earlier, the romantic understanding of art, in the narrow sense of Hegel's contemporaries, accentuates art criticism as an integral part of artistic practice. So, my reactualization of Hegel's modern conception of art still has one more step, namely, to argue that art criticism plays a crucial role in constituting what art is. Doing so is not difficult, and the argument draws on a point I have stressed multiple times in this chapter. For Hegel, a key aspect of works of art is that they realize something that is valuable for those who engage with them. Put in abstract terms, the value in question lies in art's ability to show that the human situation is not dominated by a difference between nature and spirit. As already explained, artworks do this in concrete ways; for instance, by showing how a specific way of seeing discloses the (natural) world and thus brings us into contact with it.

The concept of value helps us understand the relevance of art criticism for art in its essentially romantic constitution. After all, if something aims at realizing a value, we have to take a critical perspective in order to ask whether it effectively realizes that value. A critical perspective is always a key part of evaluating whether something actualizes a particular value, a fact that holds true far beyond art. In the case of art, those who grapple with works of art have to critically reflect on and evaluate what the artworks confront them with. They do so in the form of conceptual linguistic activities. They make judgments of taste, engage in critical reasoning, and articulate their perspectives in discussions with others.[24]

Once again, it might seem surprising to claim that Hegel makes an apology for art criticism. Is there not widespread textual evidence that he takes art criticism as estranging us from art and that he blames the romantics for this regrettable state of alienation? I think that Hegel's position is more nuanced. On the one hand, he offers an argument for art criticism as belonging to what art is. On the other, he is critical of forms of art criticism that undermine the realization of what art aims at achieving. Hegel criticizes the conception of art criticism championed by his romantic contemporaries as being of the latter sort. For Hegel, the Romantics with a capital "R" take art criticism as a practice that denies that art could realize substantial goals—as a practice that thoroughly relativizes art. Whether this assessment of the Romantics is correct or not, Hegel has to be understood as advocating for a practice of art criticism that seeks to ensure that art makes a substantial contribution to what human beings are in their cultural environments.

In this sense, Hegel's own practice in his lectures on aesthetics is telling, because Hegel again and again acts as an art critic. For instance, he praises Sophocles's *Antigone* as being one of the greatest works of art ever created. As just mentioned, he criticizes some parts of the art of his romantic contemporaries. And he is explicit in his praise of Goethe's work. In his value judgments about specific artworks and specific artists, Hegel seeks to discern in which sense art in its concrete realizations is relevant for specific human forms of life. All this bears definitive witness to the fact that Hegel does not reject art criticism in general. He is best understood as differentiating between, on the one hand, forms of art criticism that further the realization of art's substantive aims and, on the other hand, forms of art criticism that have a relativizing effect.

Thus, for Hegel, the importance of art criticism for art in general has to be understood against the background of art's lacking self-evident foundations. Since the relevance of works of art for a specific form of life cannot be taken for granted, those who engage with works of art have to evaluate whether and how works of art are relevant to them. This is done by way of art criticism. If art is—as Hegel thinks—a constitutively unstable practice, it is in need of critical reflection. Thus, the last part of Hegel's modern conception of art could be explained as follows.

Tenth Claim
Since works of art have to determine on their own how to contribute to the form of life they aim at contributing to, they need art criticism as a practice that critically reflects on whether and how the works of art in question succeed or fail in achieving what they aim to achieve.

Notes

1 For another rejection of readings of Hegel as championing classic art cf. Martin Donougho, "Art and History: Hegel on the End, the Beginning, and the Future of Art," in *Hegel and the Arts*, ed. Stephen Houlgate (Evanston: Northwestern University Press, 2007), 179–215.
2 For a similar argument cf. Benjamin Rutter, *Hegel on the Modern Arts* (Cambridge: Cambridge University Press, 2010).
3 G. W. F. Hegel, *Aesthetics: Lectures on Fine Art*, trans. T. M. Knox (Oxford: Clarendon, 1975), 1:11.
4 Ibid., I:521.
5 Ibid., I:520.
6 G. W. F. Hegel, *Phenomenology of Spirit*, trans. Terry Pinkard (Cambridge: Cambridge University Press, 2018), 206.

7 For an explanation of the shortcomings of the classical form of art that goes in the same direction cf. Terry Pinkard, "Symbolic, Classical, and Romantic Art," in *Hegel and the Arts*, ed. Stephen Houlgate (Evanston: Northwestern University Press, 2007), 3–28, here: 17. Surprisingly, Pinkard does not infer from this diagnosis that the sublation of the shortcoming in question implies that the romantic form of art has to be the highest form.
8 Cf. Hegel, *Phenomenology of Spirit*, 267ff. Hegel interprets Sophocles's tragedy as illustrating the structural problems of a homogenous society, cf. Georg W. Bertram, *Hegels "Phänomenologie des Geistes." Ein systematischer Kommentar* (Stuttgart: Reclam, 2017), 176ff.
9 I have argued elsewhere that Hegel conceives of practices of self-understanding as practical forms of self-reference that have the potential to be transformative. Cf. Georg W. Bertram, *Art as Human Practice: An Aesthetics* (London: Bloomsbury, 2019), ch. 2.
10 For this interpretation cf. Georg W. Bertram, "Why Does the End of Art Matter for Art in General? Explaining the Modernity of Art with Hegel against Hegel," in *Morte dell'arte e rinascita dell'immagine*, ed. Alessandro Bertinetto and Gianluca Garelli (Rome: Aracne editrice, 2017), 19–29.
11 Hegel is very explicit about this: "Against this [one-sided conceptions of art's aims—gwb] we must maintain that art's vocation is to unveil the truth in the form of sensuous artistic configuration, to set forth the reconciled opposition just mentioned [the opposition "between the will in its spiritual universality and the will in its sensuous natural particularity"—gwb], and so to have its end and aim in itself, in this very setting forth and unveiling." Cf. Hegel, *Aesthetics*, I:55, 53.
12 Cf. Hegel, *Aesthetics*, I:106ff.
13 Robert Pippin claims that Hegel gives us a conception of modern art according to which modern art reflects the essentially "amphibious" nature of subjects within modern societies (cf. Robert Pippin, *After the Beautiful: Hegel and the Philosophy of Pictorial Modernism* [Chicago: University of Chicago Press, 2014]). In my view, Pippin is mistaken in implying that Hegel believed that the differences within a modern society could not be reconciled. Hegel takes art to be one important means for demonstrating that the reconciliation is in fact always already realized. In this context, art's aim can be understood as consisting in prompting a transformation of one-sided self-understandings. If one thinks, as Pippin does, that Hegel views modern art as simply reflecting irreconcilable differences, one misses a key aspect of Hegel's conception of art, namely art's transformative potential.
14 I thus reject those readings of Hegel's end-of-art thesis that claim that it predicted developments of modern art that ultimately led to a crisis of the arts; for an interpretation on these lines cf. Karsten Harries, "Hegel on the Future of Art," *The Review of Metaphysics* 27, no. 4 (1974): 677–96.
15 Hegel characterizes this development as a "culmination [*Endpunkt*]" of the romantic form of art. Cf. the famous passage from Hegel's introduction to the romantic form of art: "Therefore we acquire as the culmination of the romantic in general the contingency of both outer and inner, and the separation of these two sides" (Hegel, *Aesthetics*, I:529).
16 Hegel finds an example of such arbitrariness in the works of Jean Paul, which he characterizes as presenting "often scarcely guessable combinations which have casually floated before the poet's mind" (Hegel, *Aesthetics*, I:601).
17 For an explanation of the enlivening dimension of the romantic plurality of artworks' perspectives cf. Rutter, *Hegel on the Modern Arts*.

18 In this sense, Dieter Henrich argues that Hegel thinks romantic art has a "partial character" (Dieter Henrich, "Kunst und Kunstphilosophie der Gegenwart," in *Fixpunkte. Abhandlungen und Essays zur Theorie der Kunst* [Frankfurt/Main: Suhrkamp, 2003], 126–55, here: 131). Henrich takes the partiality of modern art as being symptomatic of art's decay. But Hegel thinks it has to be understood as a specific accomplishment of modern art: Only if artworks present particular perspectives can they realize a struggle with other artworks and, thereby, enliven human practices.
19 Hegel, *Aesthetics*, I:607.
20 Ibid., II:887.
21 Cf. Johann Gottfried Herder, "Critical Forests: Fourth Grove. On Riedel's Theory of the Beaux Arts," in *Selected Writings on Aesthetics*, trans. and ed. Gregory Moore (Princeton: Princeton University Press, 2006), 177–290.
22 Hegel, *Aesthetics*, II:623.
23 In an important passage on the romantic form of art, Hegel gives the following characterization of it: "The simple solid totality of the Ideal is dissolved and it falls apart into the double totality of (a) subjective being in itself and (b) the external appearance, in order to enable the spirit to reach through this cleavage a deeper reconciliation in its own element of inwardness" (Hegel, *Aesthetics*, I:518). Spirit's "own element of inwardness" is realized through conceptual practices, which are thus an important element of the realization of art in its modern form.
24 For a more detailed presentation of this line of reasoning cf. Bertram, *Art as Human Practice*, ch. 4, parts 4 and 5.

Bibliography

Bertram, Georg W. *Art as Human Practice: An Aesthetics*. London: Bloomsbury, 2019.

Bertram, Georg W. *Hegels "Phänomenologie des Geistes." Ein systematischer Kommentar*. Stuttgart: Reclam, 2017.

Bertram, Georg W. "Why Does the End of Art Matter for Art in General? Explaining the Modernity of Art with Hegel against Hegel." In *Morte dell'arte e rinascita dell'immagine*, edited by Alessandro Bertinetto and Gianluca Garelli, 19–29. Rome: Aracne editrice, 2017.

Donougho, Martin. "Art and History: Hegel on the End, the Beginning, and the Future of Art." In *Hegel and the Arts*, edited by Stephen Houlgate, 179–215. Evanston: Northwestern University Press, 2007.

Harries, Karsten. "Hegel on the Future of Art." *The Review of Metaphysics* 27, no. 4 (1974): 677–96.

Hegel, Georg Wilhelm Friedrich. *Aesthetics: Lectures on Fine Art*, translated by T. M. Knox. Oxford: Clarendon, 1975.

Hegel, Georg Wilhelm Friedrich. *Phenomenology of Spirit*, translated and edited by Terry Pinkard. Cambridge: Cambridge University Press, 2018.

Henrich, Dieter. "Kunst und Kunstphilosophie der Gegenwart." In *Fixpunkte. Abhandlungen und Essays zur Theorie der Kunst*, 126–55. Frankfurt am Main: Suhrkamp, 2003.

Herder, Johann Gottfried. "Critical Forests: Fourth Grove. On Riedel's Theory of the Beaux Arts." In *Selected Writings on Aesthetics*, translated and edited by Gregory Moore, 177–290. Princeton: Princeton University Press, 2006.

Pinkard, Terry. "Symbolic, Classical, and Romantic Art." In *Hegel and the Arts*, edited by Stephen Houlgate, 3–28. Evanston: Northwestern University Press, 2007.

Pippin, Robert. *After the Beautiful: Hegel and the Philosophy of Pictorial Modernism*. Chicago: University of Chicago Press, 2014.

Rutter, Benjamin. *Hegel on the Modern Arts*. Cambridge: Cambridge University Press, 2010.

11

Hegel contra Moralism

Hegel's Aesthetics as an Argument against the Moralist Approach to Art

Vladimir Marchenkov

Introduction

In this chapter, I examine Hegel's philosophy of art for its potential to serve as an antidote against the prevailing mood in contemporary debates about art in aesthetics, art criticism, and popular culture, namely, against pervasive moralism. While he unequivocally proclaims his commitment to an anti-moralist position, Hegel is not an unproblematic ally in opposing this trend, and I delve into what seems to be the most troubling area in his philosophy in this regard: the distinction between art and religion. This distinction is not sufficiently consistent, and my contention is that the source of inconsistency is Hegel's failure to appreciate the ludic nature of art. By incorporating a philosophical account of art's ludic nature, I argue, Hegel's own philosophy of Absolute Spirit can be made more Hegelian, that is to say, more dialectically coherent than the picture bequeathed to us in his lectures.

Moralism has triumphed in today's discourse on art, while its traditional foe, aesthetic formalism, has withdrawn into shadows. A quarter of a century ago, Mary Devereaux perhaps still had cause to speak of aestheticians having to face "a theoretical assault on the division between art and politics," but the situation has since changed.[1] Advocates for art as a human pursuit with its own intrinsic goals are no longer to be found among scholars, critics, or museum curators. Art's existence and value are everywhere justified by an appeal to moral grounds. The most animated debates and responses are provoked precisely by open attempts to use art as a vehicle for ideological and political messages. In this sense, Jacques Derrida and Jessie Helms are birds of a feather. Differing on all else, the Stalinist party bureaucrat Andrei Zhdanov and the contemporary American musicologist Susan McClary entirely agree as far as their attitude to music as a vehicle for ideology is concerned. The hegemony of moralism is especially evident in critical theory, beginning with its founders Theodor Adorno and Walther Benjamin. Although both possessed a fine aesthetic sensibility that has since been largely lost by their followers and heirs, they clearly belonged to that variety of commentators on art for whom the moral criterion was unassailably superior to the aesthetic one. But even in such an ostensibly nonideological account as Arthur Danto's, the story of art from impressionism to Marcel Duchamp to Andy Warhol is vaguely parallel to the story of political emancipation during the same period (and is inspired, one suspects, by similar ideals).[2]

In philosophical terms, art's relation to morality falls under the dialectic of will and reason. Practical reason is the realm that is dominated by will; here reason appears in the form of the instrumental intellect and its work consists not in setting and pursuing its own goals, but in providing support for fulfilling the purposes that are imposed on it by will. Will, in turn, appears in the modern world as the will to power, elevated to the top of the hierarchy of human faculties. The dominion of ideological moralism both over art and over the theories that animate the art world rests on the hegemony of the will to power that aspires to subjugate rational thought and to keep it in bondage, strictly within the confines of practical reason. And, finally, the ethic-aesthetic dilemma of modern art needs also to be seen as the force that drives the two extremes to morph into each other until all distinction between them is lost. The moralistic stance masks a thoroughly aestheticized underlying sense of reality, while the aesthete claims the role of humanity's quasi-moral savior. The underpinnings of progressivist social criticism are rooted in the modern mythology of infinitely pliable nature and society in the hands of man-the-technologist, which surfaces, among other places, in Karl Marx' notion of shaping history by revolutionary action, Foucault's proposal for aesthetic construction of human life, or Hayden White's doctrine of history as literary fiction. Such are the vagaries of the moralist-aestheticist dichotomy, forced upon us by the abstract intellect of the modern subject.

The Anti-moralism of Hegel's Aesthetics

Hegel's *Aesthetics* rests on a different foundation. It makes a decisive stride toward transcending the abstractions of the instrumental intellect. According to him, the rational order of society is where the state in particular and the entire moral domain in general are *in the service* of culture. This view is the direct opposite of what both pre- and post-Hegelian philosophy propagated, with a handful of exceptions making the rule only more obvious. Hegel's own thought has been and continues to be routinely slandered as the handmaiden of the Prussian state in one of the most pervasive and persistent, if utterly baseless, Hegel myths.[3] To liberate art and the discourse about it from the despotic reign of moralism is the most urgent task in today's philosophy of art. In philosophical terms, it translates into the task of formulating such a theory that would commit neither the error of subordinating art to morality nor that of dissolving morality in aesthetic games. However, I should forthwith qualify this by stating that I see no evidence of such games at present. Contemporary art practice and discourse about art seem to have become moralistic through and through. But in order to lay the foundations of a balanced theory that would help us overcome this near-universal bias, one needs clearly to grasp the specificity of art. In Hegel's system, the boundaries among various components are also moments of transition from one to the other, and thus the question of what art is becomes the question of how it relates to morality, religion, and philosophy, that is, how the transitions from one to the other are understood.

Art is the lower tier, as it were, in Hegel's triad of Absolute Spirit, below religion and philosophy. As such it is raised above, however, the domain of objective spirit and, in particular, practical reason.[4] The opposite opinion, according to which art's vocation is to provide moral instruction and generally "to serve as a means to moral purposes" is false, Hegel resolutely declares, and even "perverse." He addresses this universally revered view in the Introduction to his *Lectures*, as he deals with prior schools of thought and insists in no uncertain terms that art must not be made to serve purposes other than its own, that the purpose of art is valid in its own right, and that it consists in "unveiling the truth" in its own specific manner.[5] By taking this stance, Hegel radically parted ways with the typical modern philosophical approach to art. For the modern intellect, the highest authority and ultimate reality are not represented, as they were for Hegel, by anything even remotely resembling his vision of Absolute Spirit. Instinctual aversion to all and any absolutes apart from the will of the immanent human subject stems from the deepest mythical strata of the modern *Weltanschauung*. As I have pointed out earlier, this worldview upholds precisely the moral humanity, that is to say, human society understood in terms of practical reason, as its highest authority and ultimate reality. By contrast, Hegel insists that, as long as the human mind remains in the moral domain (which comprises ideology, politics, and the law as narrower categories), it remains finite and seeks, therefore, to transcend itself, to rise to a resolution of its dilemmas at a higher level.[6]

This higher truth, according to Hegel, is revealed, first and foremost, in religion.[7] Art, says Hegel, shares its content with religion, in which finite being transcends itself and becomes infinite while still remaining immediate and sensible. The Absolute presents itself as one with this finite, sensuous being.[8] Hegel leaves no doubt regarding the anti-moralist thrust of such a view: like religion, art serves the Absolute in its own way that cannot be subsumed under interests other than its own.[9] But already these initial reflections give cause for concern. The higher truth makes its first appearance in religion, according to Hegel, yet the agency that gives it its original shape is art. Art's problem is that it is based on finite, sensuous intuition yet religious cult, which is just as sensuous, is where the finite is reconciled with the infinite and, once again, this cult is, in the final analysis, nothing other than art. And yet at the end of art's both historical and conceptual trajectories, it is supposed to yield the pride of place to religion as a more adequate mode of articulating the highest truth, before religion, in turn, yields this role to philosophy. And, finally, to make matters even worse, when religion steps forth to replace art, it turns out to be filled with moral content—even though we were told by Hegel that art has already transcended this plane in the life of spirit and one would assume that religion marks an even further elevation of spirit above practical reason.

The Inconsistencies of Hegel's View: Art and Religion

Hegel's anti-moralism is thus inconsistent, and the inconsistency has to do with his treatment of the relation between art and religion. In order to understand its precise meaning, though, one must carefully disentangle Hegel's attempts to formulate this relation. It is no easy matter, for in these attempts one can find both strikingly compelling insights and striking errors of judgment. But first it would be useful to situate Hegel's reflections in the broader history of aesthetic ideas that I briefly outlined earlier. The Middle Ages perceived Greco-Roman religion precisely as religion, albeit a false one. The perception of it as art began to take shape at the end of the medieval period and became widespread during the Renaissance. By the end of the Enlightenment, that is, the time when Hegel's philosophical biography begins, this attitude had become the norm and it was understandable that Hegel should have followed it. In the era of romanticism, which encompasses much of Hegel's philosophical maturity, the same aestheticization was applied in turn to medieval religious culture.[10] (The term "Romanticism" itself, as is well known, owes its origins to medieval romance.) But romanticism simultaneously raised art to the rank of religion, which only exacerbated the problem of comprehending the two as mutually distinct endeavors, each with its own intrinsic goal. Hegel's conception of art is lodged in this phase of the process; his grappling with the relation between art and religion is vivid testimony of the unfinished nature of his aesthetics. Annemarie Gethmann-Siefert insists that Hegel's lectures on the philosophy of art should not be viewed as a completed system, contrary to Hotho's approach in his rendition of them; Hegel's ideas, according to her, were still in flux at the time of his sudden death.[11] The problem of jumbled relations between art and religion in Hegel's aesthetics certainly lends credibility to such a view. Let us take a closer look.

Hegel was doubtlessly right to regard art, religion, and philosophy in close trilateral interactions with one another, but precisely for this reason it is so important to understand *what* interacts with *what* and *how* these types of activity, these symbolic forms, to use Ernst Cassirer's expression, relate to one another. Hegel was deeply concerned with these questions and repeatedly returned to them, but art in his aesthetics is only partially comprehended as an independent form of Absolute Spirit; it does not quite attain a sufficiently distinct silhouette of its own and remains in the shadow of religion. And precisely for this reason religion suffers a similar fate: it, too, falls short of its own unique definition, in part because Hegel brings it too close to philosophy and in part because he fails to comprehend some essential aspects that distinguish it from art. Hegel struggled with this problem from the early stages of his philosophical development. According to Walter Jaeschke, he viewed art and religion as most intimately connected already in his Jena period.[12] Both art and religion are, for Hegel, intuitions of the speculative idea, with religion complementing art and science; "the cultus," says Hegel, "raises subjectivity and freedom to their highest enjoyment."[13] Notably, Hegel emphasizes that religion is distinct from art and science by virtue of being "objective," or by "being tied to the life of a people, and its reconciliation of individuality and universality by the destruction of a part of individuality in sacrifice."[14] Hegel's ambition even then, Jaeschke observes, is to avoid reducing religion to either art or morality (while recognizing its ties to the *ethical life* of a people). Jaeschke's account brings out the fact that religion is a form of *practice* for Hegel with the *cultus* at its center.[15] At the same time, Hegel's tendency to merge philosophy of religion and philosophy of art clearly betrays Schelling's influence. In particular, Schelling's conception of modernity as coextensive with Christianity, which, as Jaeschke observes, he adopted in response to the debate about ancient and modern art that had gone on since the Renaissance and was rekindled by Winkelmann's writings, seems to have cast its shadow over Hegel's notion of romantic art in his own subsequent periodization.[16] As Hegel gradually extricates himself from Schelling's terminology and apparatus, he begins to understand the reconciliation of the modern "disruption" as an act of *thinking* rather than that of artistic or religious intuition and comes to doubt the possibility of a Schellingian "new myth."[17] Modernity becomes for Hegel the era when all mythology ends and the reconciliation afforded by religion must be understood *philosophically*.[18] And yet Hegel continues to share the romantic belief that "a compelling art needs a compelling mythology"—even as he develops the view that neither art nor myth can serve any longer as the true arena for restoring the unity of the ideal and the real, violated by modernity. As Jaeschke sums up this point, "Faced with the loss of the beautiful world of the gods, the artist can, to be sure, conjure up his dream of a world, but this is then only a dream world, not the actual one."[19] Let us note that the unreality of the world created by modern art is perceived here as a defect.

In the *Phenomenology*, Hegel speaks of the "consummation of the ethical sphere" as simultaneously marking "the passing of the ethical order" into the new moment in which "self-consciousness grasps itself as essence."[20] "This is Spirit," Hegel writes, "inwardly sure of itself, which mourns over the loss of its world, and now out of the purity of self creates its own essence which is raised above the real world. In such an epoch, absolute art makes its appearance."[21] Then, a few lines later, follows the description of art's own passing: "Spirit transcends art in order to gain a higher representation of itself."[22] Art is transformed into religion, more specifically, revealed religion, where "the pure Notion into which Spirit has fled from its body [i.e., the human shape of the ancient gods] is an individual which Spirit selects to be the vessel of its sorrow [i.e., the Christ]."[23] Ambivalence hovers over these pages, for, when he describes, for example, the transformation of ancient mythology and ritual into (modern) art, Hegel speaks of it as the *loss* of ethical substance. The "works of the Muses," he says, "have become what they are for us now—beautiful fruit already picked from the tree," they are detached from "the spring and summer of the *ethical life* in which they blossomed and ripened."[24] But didn't "absolute art" *arise* as a result of the "passing of the ethical order"? Now it turns out that it *thrived* on the substance and actuality of ethical life, which means that it was not a purely formal activity of spirit, but a substantive one.

Hegel's philosophy of art emerged gradually from its Siamese-twin-like association with philosophy of religion. Gethmann-Siefert points out that his first course on aesthetics, read at Heidelberg in 1818, was still based on the idea of the unity of aesthetics and philosophy of religion, "true to the proto-image of the chapter on religion in the *Phenomenology of Spirit*."[25] Hegel planned to use the same approach for his Berlin lectures of 1820–21, but at that time his aesthetics finally separated itself from philosophy of religion.[26] In Hotho's version of Hegel's *Lectures on Fine Art*, the distinction between art and religion is described as a process in which art is absorbed into religion as one of the latter's aspects.[27] In this process, Hegel puts the emphasis on worship—which he understands in terms of the believer's subjective attitude rather than external cultic action and expression—as the distinguishing feature of religion and interprets the eucharist as the vanishing of the objective element, which becomes irrelevant or, perhaps, negatively relevant precisely as vanishing. In his interpretation of religious ritual, the blood and body of Christ consumed by the worshipper in the communion are significant only insofar as they stir the worshipper's inner devotion. They are, in other words, stimulating allegorical reminders but to believe that they *are* the mystically transformed Savior is sheer idolatry. How religious *cult* differs from *artistic* expression thus becomes the focal point of the distinction between art and religion.

In the 1826 lectures, Hegel stresses art's inability to represent the truly spiritual content. "In Romantic art," he says, "the Idea as spirit confronts the immediate: spirit does not lend itself to manifestation in sensuous form."[28] Romantic art, according to Hegel, once again breaks the unity of content and form that was achieved in classical art, but this time, in contrast to symbolic art, their misalignment points to the limitation not of the religious content, but of art itself. The unity that held classical art together was *substance*; in romantic art it is *subjectivity* whose infinite inwardness cannot be adequately represented in a sensuous medium.[29] This account is parallel to the transition from art to religion as it is described in the *Encyclopaedia of Philosophical Sciences*, where Hegel states that "*fine* art (schöne *Kunst*) can belong only to those religions whose principle is the *concrete* internally liberated *spirituality*, but not yet the absolute one."[30] It is significant for my argument that, as he describes the effect of art upon religion in the classical phase, Hegel puts the emphasis on the *freedom* of spirit, that is, on a concept from the lexicon of practical reason. Fine art is predicated on the self-awareness of free spirit, he points out, and it exposes the dependent and limited nature of the purely sensuous and natural existence that it turns into "the inner form, which expresses only itself."[31] The advent of art, says Hegel, spells the decline of that religion which is still chained to sensuous externality. Art arrives at the intuition and awareness of free spirit and accomplishes in its own way the same purification as philosophy, purification from unfreedom. In the next phase, the classical "religion of art" becomes the revealed, the true, and the absolute religion, Christianity. Art recedes from its center-stage position in cultural history, yielding to this new religion in which all externality is supposed to be merely marginal and spirit reveals its infinite innermost subjectivity. But let us note the extraordinary role that Hegel assigns to art in these transformations: he views art as the power that creates—or at the very least prepares the rise of—absolute (revealed) religion from the religion of art. Art is, in other words, one of the decisive factors in the history of religion. Also noteworthy is that it has this power by virtue of what in post-Hegelian aesthetics came to be known as "formalism," that is, by being "the inner form, which expresses only itself."

In the *Lectures on the Philosophy of Religion*, Hegel speaks of "the cultus" as part of the idea of God, alongside with "the determinacy and knowledge" of God.[32] Further, while explaining the significance of subjectivity in religion, Hegel understands the cultus as the locus of the subject's unity with God: "This unity, this reconciliation, this restoration of oneself, giving oneself, from out of previous cleavage, the positive feeling of sharing, of participating in this oneness, partaking in one's positive character, <fulfilling oneself, [achieving] divine knowledge>—this is a form of doing or acting that can at once be more external or more internal in character; in general it is the cultus."[33] In the 1840 edition of the lectures, the idea of the human person's oneness with the Absolute in religious cult is expressed with especial clarity: "The subject knows the absolute substance into which it has to sublate itself to be at the same time *its* essence, *its* substance, in which, therefore, self-consciousness is implicitly conserved."[34] Cult is thus an indispensable element in the concept of religion.[35] Religious cult *actualizes*, says Hegel, this unity of the subject and divine substance. And yet, insofar as in Christianity "the previously hidden and concealed divine essence, content, and determination" have been revealed, the cultus now manifests its own purely subjective, man-made nature, and "no faith and conviction can get a foothold on the basis of these specific [ritual] actions and of such self-generated assurance since the objectively binding moment is lacking in them."[36] And once again the 1840 edition puts it vividly, not to say bluntly: "The cultus now becomes something barren and empty, its activity a movement that makes no advance, its orientation toward God a relation to a nullity, *a shooting into the blue*."[37] The only thing that is left of the cult is pure "subjective sensibility."[38] "Giving religion a purely subjective direction," Hegel sums up, "—my heart is everything—has destroyed the cultus."[39] This analysis is the path by which Hegel leads his audience to the idea that *knowledge* is what remains when the rituals are exposed as "barren and empty." This begs the question: Did the essence of religion consist in cultic action and its setting (the cultus), or in knowledge?[40] And, all of a sudden, the theme of morality re-emerges: Hegel virtually reduces the expiring cultus to the moral component of religion. The consummate religion, that is, religious cult that has attained its highest and truest form, is said to have an irrepressible need to reach beyond its own domain and to expand into secular life. As Hegel puts it, "This going out into the actual world is essential to religion, and by means of this transition into the world, religion appears as morality in relation to the state and the entire life of the state."[41] Spirit seems to have traveled a full circle, first rising above its own subjective phase in art, then leaving its sensuous forms behind as art evolves into religion, and, finally, returning from religion back to humanity's moral life.

But something is amiss in this process. As we saw, for Hegel, it is art, rather than religion, that serves as the region where subjective spirit rises above itself and becomes absolute. But then, Absolute Spirit's *return* to the domain of morality, politics, and law bypasses art, for Hegel speaks of religion, rather than art, as the power that "appears as morality" in "the actual world." (Let us also recall that the absolute truth reveals itself *first* in religion, according to Hegel.) Should we understand this in the sense that religion at the end of its evolution as cultic practice *returns* to the condition of art, from whence it then "appears as morality"? However, if that is the case, what happens to the argument that art is perverted when it is made to serve moral instruction? The "tangle" here, contrary to what may seem, is due not to too much dialectics but, quite the opposite, to the fact that the dialectic of these relations and transitions is thwarted and deformed. T. M. Knox eloquently summarized this confusion when he described Hegel's response to the criticism that his philosophy seems to make modern art redundant: "The religious material, [Hegel] says, which is the content of romantic art, needs art because in Christianity the divine coalesces with an individual actually perceived and therefore entwined with the finitude of nature. The events in the life of Jesus Christ have passed away; his sufferings, death, resurrection, and ascension belong to history, but all these events are repeated and perpetually renewed in art alone." Knox then adds: "This must be one of the weakest arguments Hegel ever used, if only because it seems to contradict his view of art as something not useful but valuable in itself."[42]

It would be more consistent with Hegel's own tenets to regard religion instead of art as the domain of spiritual life that is adjacent to the practical concerns of society, that is, where Absolute Spirit begins to transcend the sphere of morality and practical reason and, conversely, where it passes into this sphere on its way back from the philosophical peak of its journey. It is more consistent to regard art as a more advanced form of spirit than religion, to view it as more philosophical than religious faith and devotion, and such a modification of Hegel's hopelessly confused scheme would in fact make it elegantly Hegelian. But if one takes this path, one must explain the distinction between religion and art with greater clarity than Hegel's own account offers. The sensuous element in art and the subjective element in religion are unsuitable criteria for drawing the main contrast between them. Art's truly substantive distinction from religion consists in the *ludic* character of the one and the *serious* character of the other. Religion is serious, art plays; religion is life, art is an activity detached from reality. Hegel ignored this element, although it was available to him in the form of Schiller's doctrine. He did recognize play as an important concept, but only in reference to divinity: God plays, Love disports with itself, as he wrote in the *Phenomenology* (only to deflate this image by stating the necessity of suffering and of the negative labor of spirit).[43] And yet his philosophy of Absolute Spirit at once suffers from the absence of this concept and invites it; that is to say, in order to solve the problem of the relation between religion and art, one needs a Hegelian theory of play.

The Ludic Nature of Art

We have no such theory at the moment. Despite the surge of interest in the subject of play that Eugen Fink noted in his essay "Oasis of Happiness," and despite the fact that the phenomenon of play has been analyzed in many important ways, a truly dialectical theory of play that would rise to meeting the challenge posed by this concept has not yet been offered.[44] The classic accounts by Johan Huizinga, Hans-Georg Gadamer, and Fink, to mention only a few, provide detailed and insightful views of play, but they tend to conflate it with religious cult and, more generally, with social rituals, as well as vice versa. Their common shortcoming is similar to the blending of the enlightened reduction of religion with the romantic pseudo-exaltation of art that we found in Hegel's aesthetics. Huizinga wrote in *Homo ludens*, for example, "In all the wild imaginings of mythology a fanciful spirit is playing on the border-line between jest and earnest. Primitive society performs its sacred rites, its sacrifices, consecrations and mysteries, all of which serve to guarantee the well-being of the world, in a spirit of *pure play truly understood.*"[45] Gadamer in *Truth and Method* echoes the sentiment: "The presentation of a god in a religious rite, the presentation of a myth in a play, are play."[46] At the same time, he understands art as the true and pure manifestation of the play impulse in which the latter "reaches ideality" and becomes a "structure."[47] "The transformation into structure," he continues, "is a transformation into *the true*. It is not enchantment in the sense of bewitchment that waits for the relieving word that will transport things back to what they were; rather it is itself redemption and transformation back into *true being*."[48] "Structure" here evokes, among other things, Hegel's "inner form," and like Hegel, Gadamer believes that "a superior truth speaks through it." Nonetheless, he is quite mistaken to claim that the play of art rises "above all comparisons" and especially that it "no longer permits of any comparison with reality as the secret measure of all verisimilitude." The romantic fallacy here is the belief that "in being presented in play, what is emerges" and that in this "what is" the drama of life is indistinguishable from the drama on the stage.[49] Against this one should remark that the play of art is not yet "the raising up (*Aufhebung*) of reality into its truth," as Gadamer claims, but merely a *suspension* of it in the state of uncertainty. The play of art does indeed subject reality to a great and irrevocable transformation, but it does not say the last word in the story of this transformation and, left to its own devices, it stops at producing only the state of profound ambivalence. It is the hallmark of the romantic attitude to celebrate this result as insight into the ultimate mystery of things. I shall return to this point presently.

Seeing past these reductions, we should recognize a completely different set of relations in the play of art. The frank "illusion" of the tragic stage—that which Schiller said "the candid artist" should create—invites us to new insights concerning our real lives, and it is impossible to comprehend this effect without bearing in mind the distinction between the so-called "illusion" of art and the reality of life.[50] (The language of "illusion" has produced so much muddle that philosophy of art would be better off without it or at least with a suitable replacement, such as "artistic image," which has little if anything to do with illusions proper.) However, the peculiarity of so much modern grappling with art consists in erasing this distinction in favor of now the one, now the other side of the relation, now illusion (the aesthetic reduction of reality), now reality (the moralistic reduction of art).

One of the chief trajectories along which the confusion between religion and art unfolds in modernity is the reduction of myth to poetry, a pervasive problem in Hegel's aesthetics and philosophy of religion. His famous passages about poetry, which "in its original and substantive form" is "the most universal and widespread teacher of the human race";[51] about Greek poets as creators of the gods;[52] about the premodern artist who finds the content for his work immediately present in his own consciousness (in contrast to the modern artist who has no such content and whose work is therefore purely formal);[53] and many others, too numerous to mention, describe *myth* rather than poetry. The young girl who brings us the fruit in the *Phenomenology* is the symbol of the power that changes the one into the other. The fruits on the tree are myths that she turns, by "the gleam of her self-conscious eye" and by "the gesture with which she offers them," into works of art.[54] Characteristically, Hegel comes close to speaking of the ludic nature of art when he describes the gods of ancient Greek poetry: they represent the Ideal that is "self-enclosed, free, self-reliant," "enjoying and delighting in its own self" (notably, without seriousness).[55] It is no accident that he recalls Schiller at this point, who said, he quotes, "Life is serious, art cheerful."[56] The *ideality* of art, in the contrast Hegel draws between it and ordinary life, clearly has as its background Kant's "free play of the imagination and understanding."[57] As Hegel puts it, "The imagination, out of which art creates, is a pliant, simple element which easily and flexibly draws from its inner being everything on which nature, and man in his natural existence, have to work hard."[58] But the concept of play in these allusions remains implicit and never rises to the surface of Hegel's aesthetics. By contrast, the conflation of poetry with myth, which is a conflation of ludic with serious speech, of mediated with immediate expression, is rampant in it.

Premodern consciousness is openly mythical (as opposed to modern consciousness that is crypto-mythical). Myth, further, is realist, immediate, and practical and as such it is sharply distinct from poetry, which is a vivid manifestation of the play principle in the arts. The mythical subject *lives* in its world, while the poet plays with many possible worlds, some of which may even be probable, as Aristotle thought.[59] (Aristotle, let us note in passing, was only partially correct in making this observation, for poets are often interested least in verisimilitude and probability and most in the fantastical and the unlikely.) Myth *articulates* the living reality of a human person; it contains only an implicit possibility of reflection on this reality but is not such a reflection explicitly. Poetry does not create myth, as Hegel claims, but, quite the opposite, originates *from* it as a result of the evolution of mythical consciousness that occurs along lines similar to the evolution of reason in Hegel's philosophy. Art in general and poetry in particular express in the forms of external existence a specific phase of this process. The play principle finds in them its most vivid embodiment, but this process spans several consecutive stages that can be understood both conceptually and historically.[60]

The first mode of thinking and speech to emerge from myth in which the latter is implicitly undermined and begins to disintegrate is that of the trickster. This is a familiar figure from mythology itself: Hermes, Loge, Krishna, and the coyote all belong to this type. The trickster knows how to use the forms of myth to create the *illusion* that helps him or her achieve his or her goals. These goals, however, remain fully immersed in the mythical world itself and the trickster, while objectively working to bring about its collapse, does not separate himself or herself from this world. The first separation of thinking and speech from mythical consciousness is accomplished by the next figure, the epic poet who perceives himself as at once a faithful observer of that world and far removed from it. Myth becomes for him, in Schelling's phrase, "the absolute past." But this mythical past is still treated in epic speech as a reality and the epic eye contemplates this lost world with nostalgia from a present in which there are neither heroes like Achilles and Arjuna nor miraculous divine interventions any longer. It is out of this loving contemplation suffused with the sense of loss and longing that the next figure emerges: the dramatic poet who *recreates* the lost world of myth and epos *in the here and now*. But the price for this transfer of the absolute past into the contingent present is that the mythical world loses its reality and becomes *candid illusion*. The trickster used his or her powers of illusion for *practical* purposes, while the dramatic artist, having learned these powers from the trickster, uses them for the pure pleasures of *contemplation*.

The next type of consciousness, with its own unique attitude toward speech, is embodied in the *sophist* who is the recurrence of the trickster in a world that has been demythologized by art but not yet brought out of the state of artistic play to a new encounter with reality. The sophist is the first panludist, for he regards the world around him as mere play, all opinions as infinitely pliable constructs and instruments of manipulation. Yet he is not an artist who plays for the sake of playing; he *uses* play for extrinsic ends, falling into a basic contradiction with his own overt claims (and thus making himself vulnerable to Socrates's mockery). When the sophist finally becomes aware that the concepts he plays with are not mere means to his particular and proximate ends, but, on the contrary, constitute the basis of both natural and social reality and that only for this reason is he capable of using them as his tools, in that moment he turns into a lover of wisdom. Thus, the philosopher is born in the theater of public discourse, from the sophist, whose quasi-play with concepts he or she likewise turns into the *comprehension of reality*. Philosophy is a return of thought to the real world originally articulated by myth, except now this world has been "processed," as it were, by the trickster, the epic poet, the dramatic artist, and the sophist and has gone through pragmatic manipulation, detached contemplation, ludic re-creation, and conceptual manipulation, respectively. Philosophy contains in itself, in sublated form, all the preceding phases of the evolution of these modes of speech and thinking, from myth to sophism, but for the actual life of a culture their sublated form is not sufficient. Cultural life demands that they also be directly present in their immediate form, they must continue to participate in a dialogue with all the other forms; philosophy is culture folded into concepts and culture is philosophy unfolded into external forms. Their unity is reflected in the Hegelian principle, according to which the inner content and the outer form share an unbreakable dialectical bond. "The power of Spirit," he wrote in the Preface to *Phenomenology*, "is only as great as its expression, its depth only as great as it dares to spread out and lose itself in its exposition."[61] Such is Hegel's Idea, as well as his Spirit, as well as his Concept. To detach their inner intelligible content from their external existence or to reduce one side to the other is to violate this dialectical principle.

And, in a similar manner, art contains in itself all the prior stages from which it arises: myth, the trickster's half-witting subversion of it, and the epic nostalgia for the lost enchantment of reality. The play of art is all these things, in sublated form. Art truly fulfills its unique function in this great unfolding when it is being *ludic*, and the proper role of its *ludus* consists in suspending the reality articulated by myth precisely *qua* reality. In other words, art does not suspend the materiality of the mythical world; the world of art's play remains just as immersed in material reality as the world of ordinary human activity and the world of religious cult. But the world of play offers a vision of an *alternative* to the mythical world, potentially an infinite number of alternatives. We can call this the *polycosmic* effect of art; it takes away from the mythical world its claim of exclusive singularity. Fink comes close to describing this effect, when he writes, "For the first time ever, the concept of actuality thus attains a deep dimensionality with many levels."[62] One could recall here Kant's notion of art as "the second nature."[63] In art reality is not rejected and forgotten, but sublated; it is not negated by art, but transfigured. And, most important, art sublates not reality itself, but only certain aspects of it, namely, from the only possible state of affairs reality in art becomes merely a probable one. From an immutable state of affairs that is objectively imposed on the human being the world becomes the human being's own creation; in the play of art the human being ceases to be an object determined by external powers and becomes a subject who determines these powers themselves. The polycosmic effect of art's play is the opposite of what Gadamer and others see as its most valuable accomplishment: it *distances* us from the mythical world rather than reuniting us with it. The open, unconcealed, and, in fact, ostentatious unreality of the world created by art is not a defect, but its greatest philosophical accomplishment. Art should be praised rather than condemned for it.

The language of proximity and distance is somewhat misleading here. "Face-to-face a face cannot be seen," a Russian poet once observed, "Great things are only seen at distance."[64] He captured the limitations of the metaphor of proximity, in a metaphor of his own. To abide in identity with something in the cognitive sense equals being at the farthest remove from it, for this something does not present itself to consciousness at all. Consciousness must separate itself from its object in order to enter into relations with it. It is precisely this step that is accomplished by art's play with regard to reality—not the reality of one thing or another, but reality as such, the reality of all things and of all existence. Gadamer's and Fink's neo-romanticism, by contrast, is the quest for some primordial identity that permeates all the multiplicity and diversity of the world's life. Unlike the medieval transcendent God, however, this principle is understood in immanentist terms, and the organ by which it is comprehended is considered "meta-philosophical." Philosophy, from the neo-romantic point of view, is "finite reason"; the dialectical method remains here in its Kantian rather than Hegelian version.[65] The "meta-philosophical" organ is understood by neo-romantics mostly as poetic intuition. Elements of medieval mysticism are preserved here, but they are woven into an immanentist outlook, devoid of any transcendent dimension.[66]

Incidentally, neo-romanticism misunderstands the so-called "mystical" nature of art. "The play of human beings," writes Fink, for example, "with which we all are intimately acquainted as an often already actualized possibility of our existence, is a phenomenon of existence of an entirely enigmatic sort. It escapes from the intrusiveness of the rational concept into the polysemy of its masks."[67] Art does indeed share with mystical forms of expression the moment of immediacy, and the immediate manner in which it synthesizes the diverse elements that it brings together in a work does indeed bear a certain resemblance to the mysticism of a religious cult. Namely, in both cases these immediate syntheses are carefully built up toward in order to make the moment of the final revelation as impressive as possible. Such is Diotima's description of the lover's ascent along the cosmic scale of beauty in Plato's *Symposium*, such is also Dante's grand design in *Divine Comedy*. Both are products of careful reflection and design whose aim is to frame the final flash of mystical illumination and elevate it to supreme significance. But neither Plato nor Dante would ever dream of a world in which their poetic-philosophic exercises, no matter how profound, have *replaced* those human activities that are performed in full earnest. The rituals of the society that Plato describes in the *Laws* aim at reshaping its *real* existence. That is to say, they both belonged to cultural contexts whose foundations were formed by *mythical* thinking that nourished, as Hegel correctly said, the artistic and philosophical work of spirit. And, as he reduced the cultus to art, Hegel also pointed to the distinction between them that needs to be brought out against the neo-romantic reduction of art to ritual: In art, there *is* no mystery, *everything* is created by the artist, *all* thoughts and their embodiment pass through the artist's mind and hands as the material that he or she freely sculpts into the work. The ludic chronotope of art strips this material of all objective independence;

the light of art's play renders it fully transparent and dissolves all obscurities in it. What mystery there is in art belongs exclusively to the artist, who is now in full command of it and *uses* it, just as he or she uses all other elements of the work. The flash of the artist's genius manifests itself in the perfect spontaneity with which the diverse elements of the work come together and form a free, unforced unity. And yet this free, unforced spontaneity is brought about by none other than the artist herself: this is the manner in which the artist remains the trickster. The mystery of religious cult is objective; that of art, as Hegel correctly pointed out, subjective but the latter cannot replace the former nor can one fully subsume the other. From a consistently dialectical point of view, once they emerge, they must remain simultaneously mutually distinct and mutually connected.

No other human activity opens the possibility of changing the existing order of things at will, except for art and philosophy, but philosophy can neither come into being nor bring its content to realization without art. However, art, too, relies for its existence on all the forms of thought and expression that precede it, and these forms likewise require one another in order for each to attain their full individuality and to work their irreplaceable effects upon the others. In this lies the great truth of neo-romanticism, which refuses to accept the enlightened idea of the death of myth and to make peace with a thoroughly demythologized existence. The old chestnut of Hegel's "end of art" thesis has given rise to so many misconceptions in large part because it is not about art, but mythology. Hegel was lamenting the decline of the mythical power of poetic speech, that is, he saw mythopoeia rather than poetry proper receding into the past. He need not have worried. Mythopoeia is alive and, in fact, on the loose in the modern world—precisely because this world is so certain of its own myth-free nature. That is to say, Schelling's conviction that myth is as relevant in modern times as it has always been seems wiser and more prophetic than Hegel's over-enlightened faith in a progress that leaves its older forms behind like empty husks. Cultural history, including post-Hegelian history, down to the current moment shows that older forms do not fall away but continue to coexist with newer ones, interacting with them and giving rise to new hybrid phenomena. It is important correctly to understand the nature of their relations to one another. The moralistic focus on *hierarchy* is profoundly misleading; these relations rise above the voluntaristic notion of hegemony and subjugation. Nietzsche was quite deluded by his own metaphysics of power and his contemporary poststructuralist admirers are likewise in error regarding the essence of these relations. Instead of dominance and subordination, the idea of the rational multilateral relatedness of myth, art, and philosophy should be the guiding principle in comprehending the whole of cultural life that they constitute.[68] At the moment, however, just to recognize the dialectic of subjective and Absolute Spirit, of will and reason, to which the issue of art and morality belongs, would be revolutionary enough. And Hegel's philosophical method helps us discern and correct particular biases in his own views.

While appreciating the profound and indispensable part that art plays in the unfolding of symbolic forms and especially in the rise of philosophy, one should clearly see the limited nature of artistic play, its insufficiency in the comprehensive picture of the work done by what Hegel called "spirit." The transformations that art accomplishes are possible only within strictly defined limits; art can realize its own unique essence only within its own specially designed ludic chronotope and within a special ontological realm, the ludic form of being. Ludic being, further, needs to be seen in a dialectical relation with its non-ludic counterpart, and we need to recognize the serious and the ludic as mutually necessary categories.[69] Panludism, a close cousin of aestheticism, is just as abstract as the moralism that appears to be its opposite.[70] At the same time it is critical to understand that, while belonging to the essence of art, the play principle simultaneously constitutes its inner limit, and the need to overcome this limit is an essential feature of art's play itself. Technology cannot count as such an overcoming; it is rather a step backward into ordinary practice. Religious ritual is likewise a step backward into more immediate forms of consciousness, crossing in turn into practical activity. And thus the only path forward is the *sublation* of the ludic principle in philosophy. Like "a certain prophet" in Plato's *Republic*, art lays out before the human soul the endless variety of human lots but in order to choose her true path this soul must exercise wisdom.[71] By contrast, those who accept the existing mores, unable either to imagine others or to see them in the light of truth, are doomed endlessly to repeat the same histories.

Concluding Remarks

As long as there is a sufficiently broadly shared cultural intuition of the integrity of the world's edifice, such as the intuition of the cosmos in Antiquity and the intuition of Divine Creation in the Middle Ages, the culture in question preserves its fertile soil for mythopoeia, that is, for the continuation of existing and creation of new myths. Hegel's lament about poetry losing its mythological character is often linked in his writings precisely to the fragmentation of human experience, to the loss of the intuition of a holistic world order and of an integral context for human thought and action. Hegel's thought constantly seeks to restore this integrity, along with the clear understanding that the old means of doing so, that is, cosmologism and transcendental theocentrism, are no longer up to this task. The Enlightenment had fatally undermined their validity. The greatness of the Enlightenment consists in establishing Reason as the supreme principle of human thought and action, but it perceived reason then and continues to perceive it to this day as the abstract understanding. Romanticism responded to this by isolating poetic intuition within reason as its synthesizing nucleus, and Hegel developed romantic thought further by unfolding this poetic intuition into his dialectical-speculative method. It is precisely this method that he laid as the foundation of his system, developing its parts in accordance with this new—and simultaneously traditional—understanding of the nature of rational thinking. His lecture courses were the laboratories where he carried on this work, the fact that was keenly registered by Gethmann-Siefert. The nucleus of the system, the *Science of Logic*, was being unfolded here into the philosophical doctrines of art, religion, history, and morality. Hegel did not finish this work and this explains the transitional nature of his philosophy of art, where, nonetheless, one can find almost all the resources for the clarification of the concept of art that I have proposed earlier, but the conclusions that follow from these insights were not yet fully drawn. This chapter can be viewed as an attempt to continue Hegel's work where he left it, in the light of post-Hegelian philosophy of culture.

It would be an error to think that the clarification of the dialectic of religion and art is an isolated moment not touching on the broader horizons of Hegel's thought. However, to show how a consistently dialectical approach would lead to a revision of widespread modern notions about the nature of historical progress would greatly exceed the limits of the current discussion. Still the germ of this further critique is already contained in the idea of the mutual necessity of all three domains within Hegel's Absolute Spirit (which he himself called simply culture), including the idea of the mutual dialectical necessity of religion and art that presupposes their essential difference from each other as well.

Hegel drew a sufficiently clear line between the domain of practical reason and that of art, having acknowledged the latter as more advanced and more philosophical, but he then made the error of setting religion over and above art, attempting to present it as more philosophical. Yet he also understood very well that the essence of religion rested in "the cultus," that is, real, practical life of the human community, including its moral life, organized in accordance with the community's highest values. Simultaneously he declined to see art's most basic quality, that is, the fact that it is *play* in the purest sense of the word. He failed to comprehend the true philosophical meaning of play or, to put it more accurately, he was prepared to acknowledge play as one of the activities of the Absolute, but did not follow this idea through to its logical conclusion: Art is, after all, a part of Absolute Spirit! In the meantime, the mode of Hegel's philosophizing leads up precisely to such an understanding of play and art. Neither the neo-romanticism of phenomenologists and hermeneuticians nor the helpless empiricism of Wittgenstein's pseudo-games, nor the open pragmatism of game theory, nor the deceptive panludism of poststructuralism is capable of providing an adequate account of the relations between the earnest *care* of real life and the *care-free* play of art. Such understanding, as I have tried to show, opens up to us within that horizon of thought which was sketched by Hegel, but it requires further comprehension, a comprehension that expands this horizon. With such an approach, open to both continuity and innovation, Hegel's aesthetics points toward a healthy alternative to moralism.

Abbreviations

A   Hegel, *Aesthetics*, followed by a Roman numeral volume number and Arabic numeral page number.

PS   Hegel, *Phenomenology of Spirit*.

Notes

1 Mary Devereaux, "Protected Space: Politics, Censorship, and the Arts," in *Ethics and the Arts*, ed. David E. W. Fenner (New York and London: Garland Publishing, Inc., 1995), 41.

2 Arthur Danto, *Beyond the Brillo Box: The Visual Arts in Post-Historical Perspective* (New York: Farrar, Straus, Giroux, 1992). William Maker correctly points out that, from the postmodern point of view, reason itself is an instrument of "domination and terror" (William Maker, *Hegel and Aesthetics* (Albany: State University of New York Press, 2000), xv.).
3 The collection *The Hegel Myths and Legends*, ed. Jon Stewart (Evanston: Northwestern University Press, 1996), contains a part on "The Myth of Hegel as Totalitarian Theorist or Prussian Apologist" that explodes this piece of calumny (pp. 53–128).
4 Cf. Knox, "The Puzzle of Hegel's Aesthetics," in *Selected Essays on G. W. F. Hegel*, ed. Lawrence S. Stepelevich (New Jersey: Humanities Press, 1993), 3.
5 A I:55.
6 A I:99.
7 Ibid.
8 Ibid., 101.
9 Ibid., 102.
10 Cf. Knox, "The Puzzle of Hegel's Aesthetics," 4.
11 See her introduction "Die systematische Bestimmung der Kunst und die Geschichtlichkeit der Künste Hegels Vorlesung über 'Aestheticen sive philosophiam artis' von 1826," in Hegel, *Phillosophie der Kunst. Vorlesung von 1826*, 18. I leave aside Gethmann-Siefert's broader argument that Hegel did not *pursue* a systematic comprehension of art, let alone her puzzling animosity toward the dialectical nature of Hegel's aesthetics, which she calls "*dialektische Verwicklung* [dialectical tangle]" (29).
12 Walter Jaeschke, *Reason in Religion: The Foundations of Hegel's Philosophy of Religion*, trans. J. Michael Stewart and Peter Hodgson (Berkeley and London: University of California Press, 1990 [German 1986]), 146–47. The section that deals with this theme in Jaeschke's book is titled, tellingly, "Philosophy of Religion as Aesthetics" (145–168).
13 Ibid., 147. Jaeschke quotes Karl Rosenkrantz's lecture notes published in his *Hegel's Leben* (1844) (English translation from *System of Ethical Life*, 178–180).
14 Ibid.; Jaeschke's paraphrase.
15 Ibid., 148.
16 Ibid., 152.
17 Ibid., 161.
18 Ibid., 165.
19 Ibid., 166.
20 *PS* 425–426.
21 *PS* 426.
22 Ibid.
23 *PS* 426–427.
24 *PS* 455.
25 G. W. F. Hegel, *Philosophie der Kunst. Vorlesung von 1826*, ed. Annemarie Gethmann-Siefert, Jeong-Im Kwon, and Karsten Berr (Frankfurt am Main: Suhrkamp, 2005), 10; my translation. Knox remarks that there is no special section on art in the *Phenomenology*, where it is subsumed under the "Religion of Art" ("The Puzzle of Hegel's Aesthetics," 2).
26 Ibid., 11.
27 A I:103–4.
28 Hegel, *Philosophie der Kunst*, 68; my translation.
29 Ibid.

30 *Enzyklopädie der philosophischen Wissenschaften im Grundrisse (1830)*, ed. Friedhelm Nicoln and Otto Pöggeler (Hamburg: Felix Meiner Verlag, 1991), 444 (§562); my translation.
31 Ibid., 445.
32 Hegel, *Lectures on the Philosophy of Religion. Vol I. Introduction and the Concept of Religion*, ed. Peter C. Hodgson, trans. R. F. Brown, P. C. Hodgson, and J. M. Stewart (Berkeley, Los Angeles and London: University of California Press, 1984), 187.
33 Ibid.
34 Ibid., 189n13–190n13.
35 Ibid., 190.
36 Ibid., 192.
37 Ibid., 192n20; emphasis added.
38 Ibid.
39 Ibid., 193.
40 That Hegel conceived of the knowledge afforded by religion as philosophy rather than theology is clear from his remarks in the *Lectures on the Philosophy of Religion* (see ibid., 155n13 and 158–159).
41 Ibid., 193n25.
42 Knox, "The Puzzle of Hegel's Aesthetics," 5–6.
43 *PS* 10. In his "Oasis of Happiness," Eugen Fink paraphrases a statement allegedly made by Hegel: "In its indifference and great levity, play is the loftiest and only true seriousness." Fink, *Play as Symbol of the World and Other Writings*, trans. Alexander Moore and Christopher Turner (Bloomington and Indianapolis: Indiana University Press, 2016), 26. I have not been able to locate Fink's source.
44 Fink, *Play as Symbol of the World*, 14.
45 Johan Huizinga, *Homo Ludens: A Study of the Play-Element in Culture* (Brooklyn: Angelico Press, 2016), 4–5; emphasis added.
46 Hans-Georg Gadamer, *Truth and Method*, Second Revised Edition, translation revised by Joel Weinsheimer and Donald G. Marshall (New York: Continuum, 1998), 109.
47 Ibid., 110.
48 Ibid., 112; emphasis added.
49 Ibid., 112–13. I examined a similar conflation or poetry and myth in Giorgio Agamben's book *The Man without Content* (see my paper "Poiesis, Praxis, and the Romantic Fallacy of Modern Aesthetics," *Phenomenological Inquiry* 28 (2004): 36–51). Another example is Clifford Geertz' equivocation between ritual and theater in his *Negara: The Theatre State in Nineteenth-Century Bali* (see my analysis in "The Continuing Relevance of Symbolist Thought: The Case of Clifford Geertz and Aleksei Losev," *Slavic and East European Journal* 62, no. 1 (2018): 77–92.
50 Cf. Schiller: "Only insofar as he is *candid* (expressly renouncing all claim to reality), and only insofar as it is *self-dependent* (dispensing with all assistance from reality), is appearance aesthetic. As soon as it is deceitful and simulates reality, as soon as it is impure and requires reality for its operation, it is nothing but a base tool for material ends and can prove nothing for the freedom of the spirit." *On the Aesthetic Education of Man in a Series of Letters*, trans. Reginald Snell (New York: Frederick Ungar Publishing Co., 1965), 128.
51 *A* II:972–73.
52 *A* I:102.
53 *A* I:603.
54 *PS* 456.

55 A I:157.
56 Ibid. Knox notes that these words are a quotation from Schiller's preface to *Wallenstein* (1799) (*A* I:157n2).
57 Kant, *Critique of the Power of Judgment*, ed. Paul Guyer and trans. Paul Guyer and Eric Matthews (Cambridge: Cambridge University Press, 2000), 103, §9.
58 Ibid., 163. Cf. play vs. work in Fink's *Play as Symbol of the World*, 204–5.
59 *Poetics* IX 1451b. Aristotle, *The Basic Works of Aristotle*, ed. Richard McKeon (New York: Random House, 1941), 1463–1464.
60 The explanation of the sequence of symbolic forms that follows is a brief sketch of a longer and more detailed analysis in my essay "The Chronotope in Myth, Epic, and Novel," 631–35. See also my essay "The Narrative Dialectic of the *Bhagavad Gita*," *The Sri Lanka Journal of the Humanities* 41, no. 1 (2017): 5–7, where this sequence is used to analyze a particular religious text.
61 *PS* 6.
62 Fink, *Play as Symbol of the World*, 162. Fink evokes this effect in his discussion of cultic, that is, religious play but this is the result of the Heideggerian neo-romantic bias that he shares with Gadamer. This effect properly belongs to art rather than religious ritual, which is the enactment of a myth, as Fink correctly points out—failing, however, to distinguish myth from poetry.
63 Kant, *Critique of the Power of Judgment*, 192, §49.
64 Sergei Esenin, "*Pis'mo k zhenshchine* (A Letter to a Woman)," *Sobranie sochinenii v trekh tomakh* (Collected Works in Three Volumes), (Moscow: Pravda, 1970), II:110, my translation.
65 Cf. Fink, *Play as Symbol of the World*, 19. Fink goes so far as to say bluntly: "The truth of religion remains inaccessible to philosophy" (ibid., 146).
66 Meyer Howard Abrams borrowed Thomas Carlyle's phrase "natural supernaturalism" to capture romanticism's "general tendency," as he put it, "in diverse degrees and ways, to naturalize the supernatural and to humanize the divine" (*Natural Supernaturalism: Tradition and Revolution in Romantic Literature* [New York: W. W. Norton & Company, Inc., 1971], 67–68).
67 Fink, *Play as Symbol of the World*, 21–22.
68 For Nietzsche's reduction of philosophy to instrumental voluntaristic moralizing, see *Beyond Good and Evil: Prelude to a Philosophy of the Future*, trans. Walter Kaufmann (New York: Vintage Books, 1966), 13–14 (§6) and 16 (§9); his voluntaristic vitalism, 21 (§13); further immanentist reductions, 29 (§21).
69 See Marchenkov, "The Dialectic of the Ludic and the Serious" (*Analecta Husserliana: The Yearbook of Phenomenological Research*, Vol. XCVII: *Beauty's Appeal: Measure and Excess*, ed. Anna-Teresa Tymieniecka [Dordrecht: Springer Netherlands, 2008], 173–80). Fink's odd outburst against such an idea in his famous "Oasis of Happiness" is quite out of place, especially because his own book is filled with illuminating contrasts between play and work, as well as with excellent examples of their mutual necessity (Fink, *Play as Symbol of the World*, 21).
70 See Kostas Axelos for one of the most unabashed panludist statements: "The great powers which comprehend thought—while thought, for its part, tries to comprehend them—as well as the fundamental forces which unveil themselves in saying and doing, are developed as *play*" ("Planetary Interlude," in *Game, Play, Literature*, ed. Jacques Ehrmann [Boston: Beacon Press, 1968], 6). Fink slips into a similar mode when he says such things as, "We play seriousness, play genuineness, play actuality, we play work and struggle, play love and death. And we even play play" (Fink, *Play as Symbol of the World*, 21).

71 Plato, *Republic*, X:617d–620d (*The Collected Dialogues of Plato Including the Letters*, ed. Edith Hamilton and Huntington Cairns [New York: Bollingen Foundation, 1963], 841–44).

Bibliography

Abrams, Meyer Howard. *Natural Supernaturalism: Tradition and Revolution in Romantic Literature*. New York: W. W. Norton & Company, Inc., 1971.

Aristotle. *The Basic Works of Aristotle*, edited by Richard McKeon. New York: Random House, 1941.

Danto, Arthur. *Beyond the Brillo Box: The Visual Arts in Post-Historical Perspective*. New York: Farrar, Straus, Giroux, 1992.

Devereaux, Mary. "Protected Space: Politics, Censorship, and the Arts." In *Ethics and the Arts*, edited by David, E. W. Fenner, 41–58. New York and London: Garland Publishing, Inc., 1995.

Diderot, Denis. *Rameau's Nephew and D'Alembert's Dream*, edited and translated by Leonard Tancock. London: Penguin Books, 1966.

Ehrmann, Jacques, ed. *Game, Play, Literature*. Boston: Beacon Press, 1968.

Esenin, Sergei. *Sobranie sochinenii v trekh tomakh* (Collected Works in Three Volumes), vol. 2. Moscow: Pravda, 1970.

Fink, Eugen. *Play as Symbol of the World and Other Writings*, translated by Ian Alexander Moore and Christopher Turner. Bloomington and Indianapolis: Indiana University Press, 2016 [German 2010].

Gadamer, Hans-Georg. *Truth and Method*, Second Revised Edition, translation revised by Joel Weinsheimer and Donald G. Marshall. New York: Continuum, 1998 [German 1960].

Hegel, G. W. F. *Aesthetics: Lectures on Fine Art*, in 2 vols, translated by T. M. Knox. Oxford: Clarendon Press, 1975.

Hegel, G. W. F. *The Encyclopaedia Logic (with the Zusätze)*, translated by T. F. Gaerets, W. A. Suchting, and H. S. Harris. Indianapolis/Cambridge: Hackett Publishing Company, Inc., 1991.

Hegel, G. W. F. *Enzyklopädie der philosophischen Wissenschaften im Grundrisse (1830)*, edited by Friedhelm Nicoln and Otto Pöggeler. Hamburg: Felix Meiner Verlag, 1991.

Hegel, G. W. F. *Lectures on the Philosophy of Religion. Vol I. Introduction and the Concept of Religion*, edited by Peter C. Hodgson and translated by R. F. Brown, P. C. Hodgson, and J. M. Stewart. Berkeley, Los Angeles and London: University of California Press, 1984.

Hegel, G. W. F. *Phenomenology of Spirit*, translated by A. V. Miller. Oxford: Oxford University Press, 1977.

Hegel, G. W. F. *Philosophie der Kunst. Vorlesung von 1826*, edited by Annemarie Gethmann-Siefert, Jeong-Im Kwon, and Karsten Berr. Frankfurt am Main: Suhrkamp, 2005.

Hegel, G. W. F. *System of Ethical Life (1802/3) and First Philosophy of Spirit (Part III of the System of Speculative Philosophy 1803/4)*, edited and translated by H. S. Harris and T. M. Knox. Albany: State University of New York Press, 1979.

Huizinga, Johan. *Homo Ludens: A Study of the Play-Element in Culture*. Brooklyn: Angelico Press, 2016.

Jaeschke, Walter. *Reason in Religion: The Foundations of Hegel's Philosophy of Religion*, translated by J. Michael Stewart and Peter Hodgson. Berkeley and London: University of California Press, 1990 [German 1986].
Kant, Immanuel. *Critique of the Power of Judgment*, edited by Paul Guyer and translated by Paul Guyer and Eric Matthews. Cambridge: Cambridge University Press, 2000.
Knox, T. M. "The Puzzle of Hegel's Aesthetics." In *Selected Essays on G. W. F. Hegel*, edited by Lawrence S. Stepelevich, 2–10. New Jersey: Humanities Press, 1993.
Losev, Aleksei. *The Dialectics of Myth*, translated by Vladimir Marchenkov. London and New York: Routledge, 2003.
Maker, William, ed. *Hegel and Aesthetics*. Albany: State University of New York Press, 2000.
Marchenkov, Vladimir. "The Chronotope in Myth, Epic, and the Novel." In *Proceedings of the European Society for Aesthetics*, vol. 7, edited by F. Dorsch and D.-E. Ratiu (European Society for Aesthetics, 2015), 594–638. Available online: http://www.eurosa.org/volume-7/.
Marchenkov, Vladimir. "The Continuing Relevance of Symbolist Thought: The Case of Clifford Geertz and Aleksei Losev." *Slavic and East European Journal* 62, no. 1 (2018): 77–92.
Marchenkov, Vladimir. "The Dialectic of the Serious and the Ludic." In *Analecta Husserliana: The Yearbook of Phenomenological Research*, vol. XCVII: Beauty's Appeal: Measure and Excess, edited by Anna-Teresa Tymieniecka, 173–80. Dordrecht: Springer Netherlands, 2008.
Marchenkov, Vladimir. "Poiesis, Praxis, and the Romantic Fallacy of Modern Aesthetics." *Phenomenological Inquiry* 28 (2004): 36–51.
Marchenkov, Vladimir. "Teleology in Nature and Life-Transforming Art." In *Phenomenology of Space and Time: Book 1. The Forces of the Cosmos and the Ontopoietic Genesis of Life, Analecta Husserliana 116*, edited by Anna-Theresa Tymieniecka, 227–36. Switzerland: Springer International Publishing, 2014.
Nietzsche, Friedrich. *Beyond Good and Evil: Prelude to a Philosophy of the Future*, translated by Walter Kaufmann. New York: Vintage Books, 1966.
Plato, *The Collected Dialogues of Plato Including the Letters*, edited by Edith Hamilton and Huntington Cairns. New York: Bollingen Foundation, 1963.
Schiller, Friedrich. *On the Aesthetic Education of Man in a Series of Letters*, translated by Reginald Snell. New York: Frederick Ungar Publishing Co., 1965.
Stewart, Jon, ed. *The Hegel Myths and Legends*. Evanston: Northwestern University Press, 1996.

Index

Abrams, Meyer Howard   11–12, 26, 29, 229, 230
Absolute   5, 17, 76, 96–105, 107–8, 111, 114, 115 n.11, 116 n.22, 123–4, 126, 131–2, 137 n.41, 144, 164, 205, 214, 218
absolute knowledge (also Knowing)   7, 180–1, 185–6, 190, 192
Adorno, Theodor   6, 14, 26 n.4, 26 n.13, 158–9, 163, 168–9, 174 nn.33–4, 212
Aeschylus   184
Agamben, Giorgio   228 n.49
Alberti, Leon Battista   108, 117 n.39
Antigone   4, 39–40, 50 n.37, 127, 136 n.32, 182, 184–5, 193 n.28, 199, 208
Antigone   39–40, 116 n.22, 182–6
The Archaic Torso of Apollo   102
Ares   101, 136 n.33
Ariosto, Lodovico   54–5
Aristophanes   85
Aristotle   22, 28 n.48, 144, 154 n.25, 221, 229 n.59
art
  Christian   23, 128, 141
  classical   7, 19, 23, 28 n.37, 99–106, 110–11, 115 n.17, 116 n.19, 126–8, 130, 135 n.24, 140–2, 196–8, 217
  death/end of   6–7, 12–13, 20, 48 n.7, 83, 88 n.2, 138 n.46, 158–9, 162, 166–8, 173 n.19, 174 n.26, 174 n.34, 196–7, 200–3, 206, 209 n.9, 209 n.14, 224
  and philosophy   5, 96, 98–9, 164, 224
  and religion   73, 87, 96, 98, 103, 111, 113, 127, 160, 164, 212, 214–17
  religion of   31, 183, 185, 192, 217, 227 n.25
  romantic   5, 7, 19, 24, 28 n.46, 31, 48 n.5, 48 n.8, 54–6, 79, 81–5, 95–6, 99, 102–6, 111–14, 114 n.2, 116 n.26, 116 n.31, 119–20, 123–4, 126–8, 131–3, 135 n.24, 136 nn.35–6, 137 n.38, 137 n.41, 138 n.42, 138 n.44, 142, 160, 162–3, 165, 196–7, 202, 204, 206, 209 n.7, 210 n.18, 216–18
  symbolic   6, 19, 23, 74, 99–105, 115 n.17, 116 n.19, 126, 135 n.24, 140–2, 147, 217
Augustin, St.   152
Axelos, Kostas   229 n.70

Bakhtin, Mikhail Mikhailovich   59, 62–3, 66, 69 n.25, 69 n.38, 117 n.41
beauty   31–5, 38–41, 46–7, 48 n.4, 48 n.8, 48 n.14, 49 n.28, 50 n.35, 50 n.44, 173 n.15, 223
  ideal of   4, 50 n.35, 75–6, 100–3, 110, 122, 137 n.41, 141, 161–3, 165, 168, 170
  religion of   74–5, 173 n.14
Benjamin, Walther   212
Bernstein, Jay   14, 16, 26 n.13, 26 n.16
Beuys, Joseph   114
Bildung   4, 52–3, 57, 60–3, 65–6, 69 n.29, 138 n.46, 166–7
Bildungsroman   62, 68 n.6, 86
The Birth of Tragedy   28 n.34, 91 n.91, 88, see also Nietzsche
The Body of the Dead Christ in the Tomb   127, see also Holbein
Brahms, Johannes   202
Bruegel, Pieter (the Elder)   109–10
Buonarroti, Michelangelo   108
Butler, Judith   185
Bychkov, Oleg   144, 154 n.28

Cavell, Stanley   6–7, 158–9, 168–72, 172 n.1, 175 n.45
Cervantes Saavedra, Miguel de   4, 54–5

Christ 24, 48 n.7, 79, 82–4, 90 nn.65–6, 105, 108–10, 127, 136 n.35, 136–7 n.37, 145, 163, 173 n.15, 216–18, *see also* Jesus
Christianity 31–2, 48 n.7, 76, 83, 87, 102–3, 107, 111, 113, 116 n.25, 127–8, 136 n.35, 137 n.41, 138 n.46, 142, 145, 162–4, 194 n.47, 216–18
Clark, T. J. 6, 158–9, 168
Coleridge, Samuel Taylor 11
consciousness 2, 13, 18, 23, 27 n.18, 32, 43, 56, 62–3, 75–7, 79–80, 104, 150, 160, 163–4, 171, 183, 186–7, 190–2, 220–1, 223, 225
  unhappy 115 n.9, 115 n.11, 119, 122, 124, 127, 134 n.9, 141, 149, 163–4, 173 n.20
Correggio, Antonio da 82
Creon 39–40, 182
The Crucifixion 105

Dante, Alighieri 90 n.56, 190, 223
Danto, Arthur 6, 107, 116 n.33, 158–9, 166–7, 173 n.19, 174 n.34, 213
De Man, Paul 26 n.2, 142–3
Derrida, Jacques 98, 134 n.8, 135 n.13, 212
Devereaux, Mary 212
Diderot, Denis 1–2, 8 n.2, 53, 163
Diotima 223
The Dissolute Household 110, *see also* Steen
Divine Comedy 223, *see also* Dante
Don Quixote 54, 58, 60, *see also* Cervantes
Duchamp, Marcel 213
Duncan 184, *see also* Macbeth
Dürer, Albrecht 108

Eldridge, Richard 5, 88
Electra 184
Eliot, T. S. 102
Enlightenment, the 1–2, 8 n.3, 112, 163–4, 174 n.21, 215, 225
Eyck, Jan van 108, 196

Fielding, Henry 57–8

Fink, Eugen 219, 222–3, 228 n.43, 229 n.57, 229 n.62, 229 n.65, 229 nn.69–70
Fluxus 114
Frank, Manfred 12, 26 n.3

Gadamer, Hans-Georg 219–20, 223, 229 n.62
Geertz, Clifford 228 n.49
Gethmann-Siefert, Annemarie 53, 63, 66, 67–8 n.1, 68 n.7, 70 n.53, 72, 153 n.1, 215–16, 225
Geuss, Raymond 3, 13–14, 26 n.8
Goethe, Johann Wolfgang von 4, 8 n.2, 53, 55, 62, 66, 85, 152, 196, 208

Habermas, Jürgen 4, 65, 70 nn.52–3, 165
Hafiz 85
Hals, Frans 109–10
Harries, Karsten 159, 166–7, 209 n.14
Harris, Errol 73, 88 n.6
The Harvesters 109–10, *see also* Bruegel
Heidegger, Martin 135 nn.12–13, 153 n.3, 158, 168–9, 229 n.62
Hephaistos 101
Hera 101
Hercules 151
Hermes 101, 221
Hesiod 150–2
Hinduism 126
Holbein, Hans (the Younger) 108
Hölderlin, Friedrich 11
Horkheimer, Max 163
Horowitz, Gregg 6, 14, 26 n.13, 158–9, 168, 173 n.19
Hotho, Heinrich Gustav 53, 57–8, 66, 68 n.7, 72, 78, 88 n.2, 90 n.56, 153 n.1, 215–16
Houlgate, Stephen 48 n.7, 91 n.73, 117 n.47, 136 n.35, 137 n.41, 174 n.26
Huizinga, Johan 219

ideal, the 20, 78, 84, 136 n.24, 141, 159, 161, 166, 171, 173 n.15, 210 n.23, 220
  of beauty 4, 50 n.35, 76
Irigaray, Luce 184

Jaeschke, Walter   215–16, 227 n.12
Jesus   107, 111, 137 n.37, 173 n.15, 218,
    see also Christ
John, St.   105

Kalkavage, Peter   184
Kant, Immanuel (also Kantian)   1, 8,
    15–16, 39, 87, 97, 111, 115 n.4,
    115 n.8, 123, 135 n.13, 145, 191,
    220, 222–3
Keen, Sam   145, 154 n.30
Knox, T. M.   153 n.1, 218–19, 227 n.25,
    229 n.56

Laius   184, 187–8
La Mettrie, Julien Offray de   163
Losev, Aleksei   6, 141, 143–4, 146–53,
    153 n.3, 154 n.28, 155 n.50,
    228 n.49
The Love Song of J. Alfred Prufrock   102,
    see also Eliot
Lukács, Georg   57–8, 66, 68 n.1, 68 n.17,
    70 n.54

Macbeth   184
McClary, Susan   212
Marx, Karl   165
Mary Magdalene   105
The Massacre of the Innocents, see Rubens
Medici, Cosimo de' and Giovanni di Bicci
    de'   108
Las Meniñas   108
Menke, Christoph   7, 14, 26 n.13, 179,
    183, 186–92
Merrymakers at Shrovetide   109, see also
    Hals
Miller, A. V.   191
Moses   100
Mozart, Wolfgang Amadeus   196
Muses, the   216

Neoplatonists   152
Nietzsche, Friedrich   5, 20, 25, 28 n.34,
    88, 111, 163, 224, 229 n.68
Novalis   11
Nussbaum, Martha   182, 184

Oedipus   183, 187–9, 191–2

Oedipus Tyrannus   7, 179, 184, 187–9
Oresteia   184
Orestes   184
Osiris   75

Paper Piece   114, *see also* Patterson
Patterson, Benjamin   114
Peters, Julia   28 n.37, 50 n.44, 182–3
Pinkard, Terry   136 n.36, 138 n.44, 182,
    184, 191, 209 n.7
Pippin, Robert   3, 14, 26 n.15, 133 n.3,
    138 n.46, 174 n.38, 209 n.13
Polyneices   40
Praxiteles   101
Promethée, The Poem of Fire   152, *see also*
    Skryabin
Prometheus   6, 116 n.22, 140, 146,
    150–2, 156 n.58
Protagoras   150–2

Raphael   82, 90 n.56
Rauch, Leo   90
reason   8, 12, 41–2, 49 n.23, 63, 79, 87,
    112, 117 n.45, 123, 125, 132,
    186, 213, 221, 224–4, 227 n.2
  finite   223
  observing   186
  practical   1, 8, 213–14, 217, 219, 226
reformation   5, 48 n.4, 83–4
religion   2–6, 8, 12, 25, 48 n.15, 63, 72–6,
    80, 83, 87, 90 n.56, 95–6, 98–
    100, 103, 111–14, 115 nn.11–12,
    116 n.22, 122, 124, 127, 134 n.9,
    137 n.41, 143, 158–65, 169, 171,
    173 n.9, 173 n.14, 174 n.21, 174
    n.25, 189–90, 196, 200, 212,
    214–20, 225–6, 228 n.40, 229
    n.65
  absolute   186–7, 189–90, 217
  of Art   31, 183, 185, 192, 217, 227
    n.25
  Christian   104, 107, 112
  Greek   127–8, 136 n.35, 173 n.14, 215
  revealed   48 n.4, 103–4, 111, 114, 116
    n.25, 216–17
Renaissance   1, 81–2, 108, 110, 138 n.46,
    152, 215–16
Rilke, Rainer Maria   102

romanticism 2, 26 n.2, 215, 225, 229 n.66
Rubens, Paul 102

Satie, Eric 102
Schelling, Friedrich Wilhelm Joseph von 11–12, 103, 144, 149, 154 n.28, 215–16, 221, 224
Schiller, Friedrich 11, 27 n.18, 219–20, 228 n.50, 229 n.56
Schlegel
  the brothers 11, 152
  Friedrich Wilhelm 60–1, 188
Scholiast, the 150–2
Schubert, Franz 202
Schumann, Robert 202
science 72, 108, 111, 145, 152, 154 n.25, 155 n.33, 163–5, 169, 179–80, 215
self-consciousness (also capitalized) 32, 74, 77–80, 135 n.13, 184, 186–7, 190–2, 216, 218
Shakespeare, William 196
Shelley, Percy Bysshe 11
Sittlichkeit 158
Skryabin, Alexander 152
Socrates 95, 101, 104, 111, 135 n.13, 222
Solger, Karl 11
Sophocles 7, 39, 116 n.22, 179, 182, 184, 186–8, 199, 208, 209 n.8
Sphinx 126
spirit 4, 12–13, 15–22, 24, 27 n.19, 28 n.34, 31–2, 34, 38–9, 41, 46, 48 n.5, 48 n.15, 50 n.44, 53, 69 n.29, 69 n.33, 69 n.44, 73–82, 86–7, 109, 115 n.11, 116 n.31, 119–20, 123–4, 128, 134 n.9, 137 nn.37–8, 145, 162–3, 167–8, 172 n.3, 172 n.6, 173 n.10, 174 n.26, 179–81, 183–7, 189–92, 204–5, 210 n.23, 214, 216–19, 222–4, 228 n.50
  absolute 5–6, 8, 23, 50 n.44, 73–4, 76, 80, 120, 123–5, 131–3, 134 n.5, 158–66, 168–72, 173 n.9, 190, 212, 214–15, 218–19, 224, 226
  finite 17, 22, 79
  nature and 16–20, 23, 26 n.4, 76, 78, 136 n.24, 136 n.33, 144, 161, 163, 179, 200–1, 204–5, 207
  objective 5, 7–8, 87, 121–2, 131, 158–60, 162–3, 165–6, 168–72, 174 n.38, 214
  subjective 218
  world-historical 53, 67 n.1
Steen, Jan 110
The Sufferings of Young Wether 86
Szondi, Péter 143

Taylor, Charles 182
Tieck, Ludwig 11
Titian 108
Total Art Matchbox 114, *see also* Vautier
Trois Gymnopédies 102

Vautier, Ben 114
Velazquez, Diego 108
Verona, Stefano da 105
A View from an Apartment 130–1, 133, *see also* Wall
Vinci, Leonardo da 108
Virgil 190
Virgin Mary 105, 136 n.35

Wall, Jeff 129, 131, 133
Warhol, Andy 213
Weber, Max 163, 165
West-Östlicher Divan 85
Wilhelm Meisters Lehrjahre 53, 59–62
Williams, Robert 89 n.36, 90 n.46, 91 n.87
Wilson, Fred 113
Wittgenstein, Ludwig 6, 145–6, 168–9, 226
Wordsworth, William 11

Zeus 101, 136 n.33, 151–2
Zhdanov, Andrei 212
Zoroastrianism 99, 126

www.ingramcontent.com/pod-product-compliance
Lightning Source LLC
Chambersburg PA
CBHW050327020526
44117CB00031B/1833